1995 Supplement to LOCAL GOVERNMENT LAW

CASES AND MATERIALS

Fourth Edition

By

William D. Valente
Professor of Law, Emeritus
Villanova University School of Law

David J. McCarthy, Jr.
Professor of Law
Georgetown University Law Center

AMERICAN CASEBOOK SERIES®

WEST PUBLISHING CO.
ST. PAUL, MINN., 1995

610 Opperman Drive
P.O. Box 64526
St. Paul, MN 55164–0526
1–800–328–9352

Printed in the United States of America

ISBN 0–314–06407–9

TEXT IS PRINTED ON 10% POST CONSUMER RECYCLED PAPER

PRINTED WITH SOY INK™

Preface

This Supplement covers developments in Local Government Law from the end of 1991 when the main volume (Fourth Edition) went to press and early 1995. It tracks the chapter and section sequence of the main volume.

The period covered by this Supplement has been one of great activity in courts and legislatures affecting almost every area of the course. This activity includes: the 1991 Civil Rights Act; Supreme Court decisions involving federalism, first-amendment issues, elections and redistricting, regulatory takings, state and local taxation, and 42 U.S.C.A. § 1983; and state activity in a host of areas such as special tax districts. We have tried to keep the supplementary material from unduly extending the course readings both in our selectivity in adding reported opinions and in the extensive use of expanded notes. Our rule of thumb has been to include what we would deem necessary to add to our students' casebook-aided knowledge of Local Government Law. Some of what we have included will substitute for items in the main volume.

There is no "best" time to publish a supplement. Judicial and legislative activity in this field seems to have no "slack time." We have chosen this time because we believe that the main volume will benefit from these additions and ought not wait for them. Nevertheless, we are aware that every state legislature but Kentucky will meet this year and that the U.S. Supreme Court's interest in issues pertinent to this course is extensive. As we go to press, the Court has pending matters that we have mentioned in this Supplement such as: redistricting minority-representational efforts as racial gerrymandering; the constitutionality under the Eleventh Amendment of the provision of the Indian Gaming Regulatory Act permitting tribes to sue states; the conflict, if any, between a state public-accommodations law's applicability and First Amendment rights when parade organizers deny participation to a gay, lesbian, and bisexual group covered by the law; the continued viability of the distinction between Congress' national responsibilities and those of states and localities in responding to disadvantaged business enterprises; continued conflicts involving the Kansas City School District, the State of Missouri, and the federal court's expensive magnet-school remedy for de jure segregation; and the role of state courts asked to decide challenges to state tax systems under 42 U.S.C.A. § 1983.

We are very grateful to Kathryn E. Kovacs, JD 1995, Georgetown, for her help in preparing these materials.

William D. Valente
Villanova, Pa.

David J. McCarthy, Jr.
Washington, D.C.

*

Table of Contents

*

Table of Cases

The principal cases are in bold type. Cases cited or discussed in the text are roman type. References are to pages. Cases cited in principal cases and within other quoted materials are not included.

*

1995 Supplement to

LOCAL GOVERNMENT LAW

CASES AND MATERIALS

Fourth Edition

*

Chapter I

INTRODUCTION

B. FORMS AND FUNCTIONS OF LOCAL GOVERNMENT UNITS

1. HISTORICAL DEVELOPMENT

p. 4: Add to "see generally" at end of (5)

Hendrik Hartog, Public Property and Private Power: The Corporation of the City of New York in American Law (1983); Gerald E. Frug, *The City As A Legal Concept,* 93 Harv.L.Rev. 1059 (1980); Joan C. Williams, *The Invention of the Municipal Corporation: A Case Study In Legal Change,* 34 American U.L.Rev. 369 (1985); Joan C. Williams, *The Constitutional Vulnerability of American Local Government: The Politics of City Status In American Law,* 83 Wisconsin L.Rev. 83 (1986).

2. LEGAL CLASSIFICATIONS OF LOCAL GOVERNMENTS

b. Classification According to Structure

pp. 5–12:

The following data and report are drawn from the 1992 Census of Governments, U.S. Bureau of the Census, pp. v through ix, and may be used to substitute for or supplement the text at pp. 5 through 12.

1992 CENSUS OF GOVERNMENTS

GOVERNMENTAL UNITS

There were 85,006 governmental units in the United States as of January 1992. In addition to the Federal Government and the 50 State governments, there were 84,955 units of local government. Of these, 38,978 are general purpose local governments—3,043 county governments, and 35,935 subcounty general purpose governments (including 19,279 municipal governments and 16,656 town or township governments). The remainder, more than half the total number, are special-purpose local governments, including 14,422 school district governments and 31,555 special district governments. The total of 84,955 local governments in 1992 was 1,769 more than that reported for the 1987 census, an overall increase of 2.1 percent. Virtually all of the increase is in special district governments, which increased 6.9 percent over the 5–year period.

The following paragraphs summarize the characteristics for each of the five major types of local governments. See "Criteria for Classifying Governments," on page IX, for a statement of the criteria used for the classification of governments in census statistics on governments. See appendix A for an application of these criteria to the local governmental structure in each State.

County Governments

Organized county governments are found throughout the Nation except in Connecticut, Rhode Island, the District of Columbia, and limited portions of other States where certain county areas lack a distinct county government (see appendix C for a listing of county-type areas without county government). In Louisiana, the county governments are officially designated as "parish" governments, and the "borough" governments in Alaska resemble county governments in other States. Both are classified as county governments for census statistics on governments.

The increase in the number of county governments from 3,042 in 1987 to 3,043 in 1992 reflects the creation of three new borough governments in Alaska which were partially offset by the elimination of two county governments that were consolidated with municipal governments (one in Georgia and one in Tennessee).

Not all geographic areas known as counties have county governments. Where municipal and county governments have been consolidated, or substantially merged, the composite units are counted as municipal governments in census statistics on governments. Moreover, the cities of Baltimore and St. Louis are outside the areas of adjacent counties, and a similar situation exists among 41 independent cities in Virginia. Since these exceptional areas also include New York City, Philadelphia, and several other of the most populous cities (or composite city-counties) in the Nation, almost 10 percent of the total United States population is not served by a county government.

The number of county governments per State ranges widely, from the Texas total of 254 down to fewer than 20 in several States.

There are 174 county governments, located in 38 States, that serve populations of at least 250,000. These 174 county governments, account for 53.6 percent of the population served by all county governments in the Nation. The overwhelming majority of county governments (74 percent) each serve fewer than 50,000 persons, and the 728 counties that serve fewer than 10,000 inhabitants each serve altogether only 4 million persons. The number of county governments in each State, by population size group, appears in table 6.

The average population served by a county government is about 74,000, but Loving County, Texas, had only 107 inhabitants in 1990, while Los Angeles County, California, had more than 8 million.

MUNICIPAL AND TOWNSHIP GOVERNMENTS

The 35,935 subcounty general-purpose governments enumerated in 1992 include 19,279 municipal governments and 16,656 town or township governments. A breakdown by State between municipal and township governments appears in table 3. These two types of governments are distinguished primarily by the historical circumstances surrounding their incorporation. In many States, most notably in the Northeast, municipal and township governments have similar powers and perform similar functions. The scope of governmental services provided by these two types of governments varies widely from one State to another, and even within the same State.

As defined for census statistics on governments, the term "municipal governments" refers to political subdivisions within which a municipal corporation has been established to provide general local government for a specific population concentration in a defined area, and includes all active government units officially designated as cities, boroughs (except in Alaska), towns (except in the six New England States, and in Minnesota, New York, and Wisconsin), and villages. This concept corresponds generally to the "incorporated places" that are recognized in Census Bureau reporting of population and housing statistics, subject to an important qualification—the count of municipal governments in this report excludes places that are currently governmentally inactive.

The number of municipal governments per State varies widely. Illinois, Pennsylvania, and Texas each has more than 1,000, while at the other extreme, there are seven States with fewer than 50 municipal governments each—Connecticut, Hawaii, Maine, Massachusetts, Nevada, New Hampshire, and Rhode Island. Five of these seven States are in New England, where a town government often provides urban services provided by municipal governments in other States.

In the United States, nearly 154 million people live in areas with municipal governments, and about 64 million of these municipal residents live in cities of at least 100,000 population. Slightly more than one-half of all municipalities have fewer than 1,000 inhabitants. However, these small municipalities account for only 2.5 percent of the total population served by municipal governments. The number of municipal governments in each State, by population size group, appears in table 7.

The 19,279 municipal governments reported in 1992 reflect an increase of 79 since 1987. Changes by State ranged from a decrease of 5 in Vermont to a gain of 21 in North Carolina. Two thirds of the total gain of 79 occurred in 3 States: California, North Carolina, and Texas. Most of the increase is the result of new incorporations.

The term "town or township governments" is applied here to 16,656 organized governments located in the following 20 States in the Northeast and the Midwest:

Connecticut	Massachusetts	New Hampshire	Pennsylvania
Illinois	Michigan	New Jersey	Rhode Island
Indiana	Minnesota	New York	South Dakota
Kansas	Missouri	North Dakota	Vermont
Maine	Nebraska	Ohio	Wisconsin

This category includes governmental units officially designated as "towns" in the six New England States, New York, and Wisconsin and some "plantations" in Maine and "locations" in New Hampshire, as well as townships in other areas. In Minnesota, the terms "town" and "township" are used interchangeably with regard to township governments. Although towns in the six New England States and New York, and townships in New Jersey and Pennsylvania, are legally termed "municipal corporations," perform municipal-type functions, and frequently serve densely populated urban areas, they have no necessary relation to concentration of population, and are thus counted for census purposes as town or township governments.

Excluded from this count of town or township governments are unorganized township areas, townships coextensive with cities where the city governments have absorbed the township functions, and townships known to have ceased to perform governmental functions. Also excluded are the townships in Iowa, which are not counted as separate governments, but are classified as subordinate agencies of county governments.

Of the 16,656 town or township governments in the United States, only 1,087 (6.5 percent) had as many as 10,000 inhabitants in 1990 and 55 percent of all towns or townships had fewer than 1,000 inhabitants. The number of town or township governments in each State, by population size group, appears in table 7.

Consistent with past intercensal periods, there was a small decrease in the number of town or township governments—from 16,691 in 1987 to 16,656 in 1992. Nearly all of the decline in numbers of town or township governments since 1987 occurred in the Midwest.

Only one State, Indiana, has township governments covering all its area and population. In six States (Massachusetts, New Hampshire, New Jersey, Pennsylvania, Rhode Island, and Wisconsin), operating towns or townships comprise all territory other than that served by municipalities. The same is true for Maine, except for "unorganized territory" that lacks any local government. Of the remaining 12 town or township States, there are 10 where this type of government occurs only in certain county or county-type geographic areas as of early 1992: Illinois, in 85 of the 102 county-type areas; Kansas, in 97 of 105; Minnesota, in 85 of 87; Missouri, in 23 of 115; Nebraska, in 28 of 93; North Dakota, in 48 of 53; Pennsylvania, in 66 of 67; South Dakota, in

52 of 66; and Wisconsin, in 71 of 72. In New York, town governments exist in each county outside New York City.

The area served by municipal and town or township governments may overlap in 11 States. All municipal governments in Indiana, and some but not all municipalities in 10 other town or township States (Connecticut, Illinois, Kansas, Michigan, Minnesota, Missouri, Nebraska, New York, Ohio, and Vermont) operate within territory that is served also by town or township governments. In the remaining 9 of the 20 town or township States (Maine, Massachusetts, New Hampshire, New Jersey, North Dakota, Pennsylvania, Rhode Island, South Dakota, and Wisconsin), there is no geographic overlapping of these two kinds of units.

Special District Governments

Special district governments are independent, special-purpose governmental units (other than school district governments) that exist as separate entities with substantial administrative and fiscal independence from general-purpose local governments. As defined for census purposes, the term "special district governments" excludes school district governments.

Special district governments provide specific services that are not being supplied by existing general purpose governments. Most perform a single function, but, in some instances, their enabling legislation allows them to provide several, usually related, types of services. The services provided by these districts range from such basic social needs as hospitals and fire protection to the less conspicuous tasks of mosquito abatement and upkeep of cemeteries. The number of special district governments in each State, by function performed, appears in table 15.

The Census Bureau classification of special district governments covers a wide variety of entities, most of which are officially called districts or authorities. Not all public agencies so termed, however, represent separate governments. Many entities that carry the designation "district" or "authority" are, by law, so closely related to county, municipal, town or township, or State governments that they are classified as subordinate agencies of those governments in census statistics on governments, and are not counted as separate special district governments.

In order to be counted as a special district government, rather than be classified as a subordinate agency, an entity must possess three attributes—existence as an organized entity, governmental character, and substantial autonomy. See "Criteria for Classifying Governments," on page IX, for an explanation of the criteria for determining whether an entity is counted as a separate government. Appendix A of this report explains how these criteria were applied, including a summary description in each State of legally authorized special district governments. That appendix also lists in each State various statutory authorities, commissions, corporations, and other forms of organizations that have certain governmental characteristics, but are subject by law to administrative or fiscal control by the State or by independent local governments, and are, therefore, classified as subordinate agencies of those governments.

As a group, special district governments are by far the most rapidly growing type of government, rising to a total of 31,555, an increase of about 2,023, or 6.9 percent, since the 1987 Census of Governments. This growth over the past 5 years—on top of a 5 percent rise between 1982 and 1987, and an 8 percent rise between 1977 and 1982—reflects the increased public demand for the provision of specialized services either not offered or not performed by existing governments. Since most special districts perform only one function, or a very limited number of functions, their establishment allows a greater degree of concentrated effort in providing services. As shown in table 5, the number of special district governments reported in 1992 is more than 2.5 times the number of special district governments reported in 1952.

The increasing number of special districts often reflects financial considerations. As new programs are initiated, or new services required, the establishment of special districts may reduce the need to increase the burden on general purpose governments which may be unable to meet the fiscal requirements necessary to implement these new programs. Debt and tax limitations are further stimulants for creating special districts for raising both capital construction and operating expenditure funds.

The number of special district governments varies considerably among the States, and has only a weak relationship to population size. The following nine States, each having at least 1,000 special district governments, account for more than half of all such local governments:

California	2,797
Colorado	1,252
Illinois	2,920
Kansas	1,482
Missouri	1,386
Nebraska	1,047
Pennsylvania	2,006
Texas	2,266
Washington	1,157

Four State areas contained fewer than 50 special district governments each: Alaska (14), District of Columbia (1), Hawaii (16), and Louisiana (30).

Of the 31,555 special district governments reported in 1992, over 92 percent performed a single function. Close to 20 percent of all special district governments perform functions related to natural resources—drainage and flood control, irrigation, and soil and water conservation. The next most frequent function performed by such units is fire protection followed by housing and community development, and water supply. A variety of functions account for the remaining number of special district governments. Most of the units recognized as multiple-function in nature involve some combination of water supply with other services, most commonly sewerage services. A total of more than 4,777 special district governments (15 percent) provide water supply either as the sole function or as one of a combination of functions.

Information in table 17 of this report indicates that about one-third of all special district governments serve an area with the same boundaries as those of some other local government—county, municipal, or town or township government. The number of these special districts with boundaries coterminous with a single municipal, town, or township government comprised more than one half of all coterminous special districts. Although the vast majority of special district governments are located entirely within a single county or county-type geographic area, about 11 percent have territory extending into two or more county-type areas. Governments serving two or more county-type areas are discussed more fully under "Intercounty Local Governments" on page XII.

The operations of special district governments vary greatly, as shown in table 18. Approximately 46 percent—less than half—of special district governments reported providing a program or service directly with their own employees. Another 23 percent reported providing a program or service indirectly under contractual provisions. An additional 23 percent reported financing public facilities or services by issuing public debt. The remainder reported constructing public facilities. It should be noted that some special district governments may have more than one type of operation. Thus, some districts may provide a program or service with its own employees and, in addition, construct facilities or finance facilities or services by issuing public debt.

School District Governments and Public School Systems

Of the 15,834 public school systems in the United States in 1992, only the 14,422 that are independent school districts are included in the count of governments. The other 1,412 "dependent" public school systems are classified as agencies of other governments—State, county, municipal, or town or township—and are not counted as separate governments. The number of public school systems in each State, by type of organization, appears in table 20.

Because of the variety of State legislative provisions for the administration and operation of public schools, marked diversity is found in school organization throughout the United States. The number of States providing for public schools solely through independent school districts numbered 33 in 1992. This independent district arrangement, which prevails in most parts of the country, is practically universal in the West.

A "mixed" situation is found in 12 States, with the public schools that provide elementary and secondary education operated in some areas by independent school districts and elsewhere by a county, municipal, town or township, or State government. In the District of Columbia and in five States (Alaska, Hawaii, Maryland, North Carolina, and Virginia), there are no independent school districts; all public schools in those jurisdictions are administered by systems that are agencies of the county, municipal, or State government.

Alaska, Hawaii, Maine, and New Jersey have State-dependent public school systems. The 21 State-dependent public school systems in Alaska serve sparsely-populated areas not served by borough or city school systems. All public schools in Hawaii are administered directly as part of the State government, but, in Maine, this arrangement applies only to four sparsely populated areas. In New Jersey, two public school systems that are undergoing reorganization are State-operated.

Public school systems operating as dependent agencies of county governments appear mostly in North Carolina, Tennessee, and Virginia, which contain nearly two-thirds of all county-dependent systems. However, California has 54 county-dependent systems and New Jersey 47. Other States with public school systems operating as dependent agencies of county governments are Alaska (11), Arizona (12), Maryland (39), Massachusetts (3), Mississippi (4), New York (27), and Wisconsin (6). Systems dependent on town or township governments are found only in Connecticut, Maine, Massachusetts, New Jersey, and Rhode Island. There are public school systems operated by municipal governments in each of 11 States and the District of Columbia, but in most of these States, some other pattern predominates, and only in the District of Columbia are all public schools operated by a municipally dependent system.

The decrease in the number of school district governments reported since 1987 reflects a continued decline over the past 50 years, primarily as a result of school district consolidation and reorganization. Most of this decrease occurred among single-school and nonoperating school districts. As shown in table 5, the number of school district governments in 1992 is approximately one fourth of the total in 1952. The rate of decrease in school district governments was 2 percent from 1987 to 1992, compared with 1 percent from 1982 to 1987, 2 percent from 1977 to 1982, and 4 percent from 1972 to 1977.

Nebraska, declining by 155, accounted for 52 percent of the intercensal decrease in school districts. An additional 20 States had decreases ranging from 1 to 44. There was either no change or an increase in the total number of school districts in 29 States.

California and Texas—each of which had more than 1,000 school district governments—accounted for 15 percent of all school district governments in the Nation. The number of States having at least 1,000 school district governments decreased from 25 in 1942 to 20 in 1952, 15 in 1962, 4 in 1972 and 1982, and 3 in 1987.

The total of public school systems includes some systems that do not provide elementary-secondary education services. There are 247 public school systems, located in 20 separate States, that do not operate schools. Instead, these "nonoperating" systems are responsible for providing transportation and paying tuition or reimbursement to other school systems for public school students who live in their respective areas, or for providing special services to those systems that operate schools. In addition, there are 686 public school systems, found in 30 separate States, that provide for vocational, special, or college-grade education only. The number of public school systems in each State, by grade coverage, appears in table 23.

There are 516 public school systems that provide college-level instruction. Of these, 389 are independent school districts and 127 are dependent systems associated with county or municipal governments. Most of these 516 systems provide advanced education only at the junior college level. In the school year 1991–92, only four of them operated institutions recognized by the U.S. Department of Education as degree-granting colleges or universities. In addition, every State has one or more State-operated institution of higher education, although State-operated institutions of higher education are not included in the tables of this report.

(6) Newly Evolving Government Structures

p. 13: Add as Note 1

1. Enforcement of private entity rules and covenants. A condominium use restriction prohibiting most pets was upheld under a California law that made such restrictions "enforceable equitable servitudes, unless unreasonable." The court found that the restriction was not arbitrary and did not violate fundamental public policy, and that the burden on the use of property did not outweigh its benefits. Nahrstedt v. Lakeside Village Condominium Association, 8 Cal.4th 361, 33 Cal.Rptr.2d 63, 878 P.2d 1275 (1994).

Add new heading to existing note

2. Relationships between "private governments" and the public government.

p. 14: Add to note

The Montgomery County ordinance imposed registration fees on common ownership communities to fund dispute resolution and technical-assistance activities. The Maryland Court of Appeals held that the fees did not violate state laws barring the imposition of burdens on condominiums that are not imposed on other properties of similar character, although similar fees were not imposed on apartment complexes. Dumont Oaks Community Association, Inc. v. Montgomery County, 333 Md. 202, 634 A.2d 459 (1993).

The interaction of voter-accountable government with the private-covenant-created "private governments," however, is not confined to services such as dispute resolution and technical assistance and protection against unmet community needs. State laws on special tax districts may permit local governments to impose taxes supporting activities of the homeowners' association that fulfill public purposes, upon petition of a majority of covenanted residents. See Williams v. Anne Arundel County, 334 Md. 109, 638 A.2d 74 (1994), reported at p. 179 of this supplement. Such cases effectively conjoin the government functions of a special tax district with the management functions of the private organization. Private government thus moves beyond the model of a distinct "company town" stage to one of empowerment at an existing level of existing government. A cognate concept, the business improvement district, has expanded rapidly in major metropolitan areas. Taxpayers volunteer for government imposition of benefit taxes to fund increase police, sanitation, and other services. See Thomas J. Lueck, "Business Districts Grow At Price of Accountability," The New York Times, Nov. 20, 1994, at p. 1.

The Florida Legislature accelerated this evolution by approval of special-district status and powers for Disney World, and, even more dramatically, for Wayne Huizenga's multi-county Blockbuster sports complex. See Geoffrey Tomb, "Outside Disney's World, A Rising Resentment, Report On A Florida Empire," The Philadelphia Inquirer, May 29, 1988, at 2A; William Booth, "Republic of Huizenga Carved Out of Florida for Games," The Washington Post, August 21, 1994, at A3. Note that plans for the Blockbuster sports complex have been canceled as no longer fitting the company's strategies. See Digest, The Washington Post, December 10, 1994, at F1.

C. LOCAL GOVERNMENTS IN METROPOLITAN AREAS

4. POLITICAL CONSIDERATIONS

p. 18: Add at end

Additional examples of the rich literature on this subject include such books as David Osborne and Ted Gaebler, Reinventing Government: How the Entrepreneurial Spirit Is Transforming the Public Sector (1989); Neil R. Pierce, Citistates: How Urban America Can Prosper In A Competitive World (1993); and David Rusk, Cities Without Suburbs (1993).

Chapter III

ADJUSTING STATE–LOCAL RELATIONS: LEGISLATIVE AND CONSTITUTIONAL SOURCES OF CONTROL

A. STATE LEGISLATIVE SUPREMACY

p. 46: add to introduction after *Missouri v. Jenkins*

Board of Education of Kiryas Joel Village School District v. Grumet, ___ U.S. ___, 114 S.Ct. 2481, 129 L.Ed.2d 546 (1994) (statute creating special school district to serve religious enclave, which was incorporated community under state law, violated the federal constitution's Establishment of Religion Clause).

1. CREATION, DESTRUCTION AND CONTROL OF LOCAL GOVERNMENT ENTITIES

p. 48: Add to Note 3

For further illustration of state intervention to control local functions in extreme local crises, see Fox Butterfield, "Insolvent Boston Suburb Faces Threat of Takeover," The New York Times, September 8, 1991, at 18; William Claiborne, "Bringing a Battered City Back From the Brink: Consensus–Building Process Inspires Citizen Involvement and a New Charter in Chelsea, Mass.," The Washington Post, September 7, 1994, at A3.

B. STATE CONSTITUTIONAL LIMITS ON LEGISLATIVE SUPREMACY

p. 76: Add after the end of the Comment: State Constitutions—Obstacles to Reform

See also, U.S. Advisory Commission on Intergovernmental Relations, "Local Government Autonomy: Needs For State Constitutional, Statutory, and Judicial Clarification," A–127 (October 1993), excerpted below. Not all state constitutional provisions obstruct local autonomy. As will be seen later, state constitutions often protect local autonomy, contain many provisions not reflected at all in provisions of the federal constitution, and effectively restrict state controls by individual-rights provisions that go beyond federal counterparts. See generally, Mark Glasser and John Kincaid, *Selected Rights Enumerated in State Constitutions,* Intergovernmental Perspective 35 (Fall 1991); Barry Latzer, *Four Half–Truths About State Constitutional Law,* 65 Temple L.Rev. 1123 (1992).

1. SPECIAL LEGISLATION

pp. 82–83: Add to Note 6

In Wilkinsburg Police Officers Association v. Commonwealth, 535 Pa. 425, 636 A.2d 134 (1993), the court rejected a special legislation claim that the challenged statute improperly created separate classifications for municipalities in poor financial condition and between labor and non-labor contracts in providing for state coordination of relief for financially distressed municipalities.

2. GENERAL LIMITS ON LEGISLATIVE DELEGATION

p. 95: Add to Note

For further examination of the delegation and separation of powers concepts, see Communication Workers v. Florio, 130 N.J. 439, 617 A.2d 223 (1992) (legislative attempt to restrict Governor's reduction of state employee corps in light of reduced legislative appropriations unconstitutionally interfered with authority of executive branch); Judy v. Schaefer, 331 Md. 239, 627 A.2d 1039 (1993) (legislative delegation of authority to Governor to reduce appropriations did not violate separation of powers); Richard Briffault, *The Item Veto In State Courts,* 66 Temple L.Rev. 1171 (1993).

p. 98: Add to Note 3

See also Christ v. Maryland Department of Natural Resources, 335 Md. 427, 644 A.2d 34 (1994) (upholding administrative regulations prohibiting powerboating by minors under broad delegation to regulate power boats).

4. OTHER STATE CONSTITUTIONAL LIMITATIONS

p. 109: Add after *Flynn* citation in fifth full paragraph

See also Opinion of the Justices (Materials in Solid Waste Stream), 135 N.H. 543, 608 A.2d 870 (1992) (statute was a prohibition of certain waste disposal not a direct requirement of municipal expenditure and hence did not violate constitutional provision). As of 1994, twenty-five states limit unfunded mandates. Of those, fifteen prohibit unfunded mandates in their state constitutions and an overlapping fourteen limit such mandates by statute. Zimmerman, *State Mandate Relief: A Quick Look,* 20 Intergovernmental Perspective 28 (Spring 1994). See also Junge, *Free To Be Better,* State Government News, May 1994, at 17.

C. HOME RULE

p. 110: Add to first paragraph

According to a study of the U.S. Advisory Commission On Intergovernmental Relations, 48 states grant some form of home rule to municipalities. Thirty-seven states do so for counties. The grants range from Illinois where local governments can generally select their own taxes and spending, to Alabama where property taxes may not be increased by a vote of the people without a special act of the State Legislature. Hovey, "State Policy and Local Governments," State Policy Reports, Volume 12, Issue 1, January 1994, at 15.

1. FORMS OF HOME RULE

The reference to the California provision in the opening paragraph should cite pages 126–27 of the principal text.

p. 115: Add the following after comment and before subsection a

LOCAL GOVERNMENT AUTONOMY

Needs for State Constitutional, Statutory, and Judicial Clarification.
U.S. Advisory Commission on Intergovernmental Relations A–127 October 1993.
[Printed abstract appended].

EXECUTIVE SUMMARY

Local government in the United States has a rich history. Cities, counties, towns, townships, boroughs, villages, school districts, and a host of special purpose districts, authorities, and commissions make up the 86,743 units of local government counted in the 1992 Census of Governments. These local governments have many different forms and organizational structures. Variations in the numbers and forms of local government arise from each state's unique political culture.

Local self-government has been institutionalized in thousands of compacts, charters, special acts, statutes, constitutional provisions, resolutions, ordinances, administrative rulings, and court decisions. Among these enactments, state constitutional provisions are singled out for special attention in this report.

State constitutional provisions that speak directly to the allocation of authority between state and local government embody a judgment about the preferred allocation of power within the state. These provisions have been created, revised, and refined over time as a popular political response to empirical conditions. As such, they are the cornerstones on which any sound theory of local government autonomy can be built.

The Commission's findings on the relationship of the states and local government autonomy are as follows:

Home rule for municipal and county governments is now available in most states. By state constitutional and/or general law provisions, 48 states grant home rule authority to municipalities and 37 states grant such powers to counties.

Two legal concepts of local government have contended for ascendancy in the American federal system: home rule and creatures of the state. The home rule concept of granting greater discretionary authority to local governments has been gaining ground on the creatures-of-the-state concept of strict limits on local discretionary authority. Most states have adopted a system of devolved powers for local governments within which they can act freely.

Local government autonomy consists of degrees of discretionary authority separately established for cities and counties in four basic areas: (1) structure—determining their form of government and internal organization; (2) function—choosing the functions they perform; (3) fiscal—raising revenue, borrowing, and spending; and (4) personnel—fixing the numbers, types, and employment conditions of their employees.

The most common form of home rule grants initiative to local governments. Local governments, however, are not immune from constitutional and/or statutory limits on these grants of initiative. State restrictions do not present local government immunity in strongly positive terms, allowing the courts to rule in favor of the state more often than not.

Home rule is jeopardized if the state legislature is free to impose unfunded mandates on local governments. Sometimes, these state mandates are the result of federal mandates. States have not always relaxed the restrictions on the fiscal autonomy of local governments or provided them with additional resources to cope with mandates. This double burden places financial pressures on local governments and reduces their ability to make choices about local priorities—effectively reducing local autonomy.

As home rule has become a common feature of state constitutions and general state law, the relationship between the states and their local governments has become more complicated. Increasingly, state courts are serving as arbiters of state-local relations. Courts have begun to recognize local governments as "juridical persons" able to sue their parent state government. In addition, courts have played a major role in defining the constitutional framework of interlocal cooperation.

There is no single best model of constitutional language that states can apply to clarify the extent and limits of local government autonomy. Different state courts can, and often do, interpret identical constitutional language differently. A state's civic culture, legislative traditions, and judicial temperament all affect such interpretations. Local governments in some states prefer a statutory rather than constitutional approach to the definition of local government autonomy.

Based on these findings, the Commission recommends the following:

(1) *That the states increase and clarify local home rule by adopting constitutional and/or statutory provisions granting broad powers of structural, functional, fiscal, and personnel authority to local governments and authorizing joint exercise of authority.*

(2) *That the states review their constitutional provisions and/or statutes governing the powers of local governments and consider amending them as appropriate to clarify the extent of local power, the degree of immunity from state statutes, liberal rules of construction to be followed by the courts in interpreting constitutional or statutory provisions in favor of local governments, the status of local governments as juridical persons, and the extent to which autonomy and discretion are to be accorded to different types of local governments.*

(3) *That the statewide local government organizations and their national counterparts cooperate to provide legal support to advocating local assertion of initiative powers and immunity from the reach of state government.*

(4) *That state and federal courts reconsider local government as entailing citizen rights of local self-government, not merely as creatures of the states.*

FINDINGS AND RECOMMENDATIONS

Findings

The States and Local Government Autonomy

1. *Home rule for municipal and county governments is now available in most states.*

Forty-eight states grant home rule authority to municipalities and 37 states grant such powers to counties. These grants of authority are provided by the state constitutions and/or by general law.

For municipalities, 37 states grant home rule by constitutional provision and 34 by general law (24 states have both types of provisions, 13 use the constitution only, and 10 use general law only).

For counties, 23 states grant home rule authority by constitutional provision and 25 by general law (12 states have both types of provisions, 11 use the constitution only, and 13 use general law only).

Between 1978 and 1992, five states granted home rule authority to municipalities. On the county side, nine more states provide home rule authority now than in 1978.

2. *Two legal concepts of local government have contended for ascendancy in the American federal system: home rule and creatures of the state. The home rule concept (granting greater discretionary authority to local governments) has been gaining ground on the creatures-of-the-state concept of strict limits on local discretionary authority.*

The idea of local governments as creatures of the state is embodied in Dillon's Rule, which holds that the political subdivisions of a state owe their existence to grants of power from the state. Therefore, local governments possess no inherent sovereignty. Their powers are construed strictly to be no more than what is expressly permitted by state statute. No room can be made for discretionary authority or even incidental powers.

The home rule concept was initially articulated in the Cooley doctrine, holding that local government is a matter of absolute right, which cannot be taken away by the state. Few states have followed this rule, however. Instead, most states adopted what became known as the Fordham Rule, which sets out an area of devolved powers for local governments within which they can act freely. This approach provides home rule localities with a liberal construction of their powers, limiting state court imposition of a doctrine of implied preemption.

3. Local government autonomy consists of degrees of discretionary authority separately established for cities and counties in four basic areas: (1) structure—determining their form of government and internal organization; (2) function—choosing the functions they perform; (3) fiscal—raising revenue, borrowing, and spending; and (4) personnel—fixing the numbers, types, and employment conditions of their employees.

In most states, the amount of discretionary authority differs for cities and counties and for the four different types of power. Grants of structural and functional authority frequently exceed grants of financial and personnel powers. These imbalances can create difficulties for local governments.

4. Home rule can (1) empower local governments to take initiative, (2) confer immunity on local governments from the reach of state legislation, and (3) instruct the state courts to interpret grants of local authority liberally in favor of local discretion. States have focused most of their authorizations on initiative; few state grants of home rule authority include or adequately address immunity and liberal construction.

The most common form of home rule grants initiative to local governments, subject to constitutional and/or statutory limits. Such limitations are frequently substantial. Immunity from such limitations often are weak or absent. Also, instructions to the courts to interpret liberally in favor of local governments are frequently absent. Without these provisions, the courts generally rule in favor of the state.

5. Home rule is jeopardized if the state legislature is free to impose unfunded mandates on local governments.

State legislatures have imposed an increasing number of mandates and regulatory restrictions on local governments as the result of statewide policies. Sometimes, these state mandates are the result of federal mandates. At the same time, states have not always relaxed the restrictions on the fiscal autonomy of local governments or provided them with additional resources to cope with mandates. This double burden places severe financial pressures on local governments and reduces their ability to make choices about local priorities—effectively reducing local autonomy.

6. As home rule has become a common feature of state constitutions and general state law, the relationship between the states and their local governments has become more complicated. Increasingly, therefore, state courts are serving as arbiters of state-local relations.

During the colonial era, the royal executive granted local government charters, following the English tradition. After the Revolution, state legislatures ordinarily exercised this responsibility by special acts that provided local governments with individualized powers—always subject to legislative revision. By the 1870s, however, misuse of the legislative power to create local governments led to reform movements seeking general laws for local government authority and constitutional recognition of home rule outside the scope of state legislative discretion.

As a result, state-local relations have become more complex. Today, in any one state, the scope of home rule or local autonomy is often difficult to discern. Moreover, constitutional and statutory protections of local autonomy do not eliminate legislative authority. State courts, therefore, have taken on a key role in interpreting the limits of the exercise of local powers and state legislative powers.

In several states, the courts have begun to recognize local governments as "juridical persons" able to sue their parent state government, thus conferring (or at least asserting) state constitutional claims against the state sovereign. Also, some state courts have scrutinized more closely legislation intended to affect specific local governments and have heard challenges to these acts as special or local laws. In addition, courts have played a major role in defining the constitutional framework of interlocal cooperation. In each area of local discretionary authority—structural, functional, fiscal, and personnel—state courts have made major contributions to the definition of state-local relations.

Nevertheless, state courts across the nation take very different approaches to home rule. Even the same state court may issue confusing dicta on the subject of state-local relations. Thus, although there is a discernible trend toward a greater recognition for local government autonomy, the guidance for local governments is far from clear.

7. There is no single best model of constitutional language that states can apply to clarify the extent and limits of local government autonomy.

Different state courts can, and often do, interpret identical constitutional language differently. A state's civic culture, legislative traditions, and judicial temperament all affect interpretations of constitutional language. Thus, constitutional language with respect to local government must be adapted to the civic culture and traditions of each state. Indeed, because of prevailing traditions, local governments in some states prefer a statutory rather than constitutional approach to the definition of local government autonomy.

RECOMMENDATIONS

Recommendation 1
Reaffirming the Need for Local Discretionary Authority While Preserving State Responsibilities

The Commission finds that its previous recommendations encouraging states to formalize a thriving system of local self-government are as important as ever. To be effective and accountable, local governments need the flexibility and autonomy to undertake the responsibilities allocated to them and the responsibilities chosen for them by their citizens.

The Commission reaffirms, therefore, its previous recommendations to the states to increase and clarify local home rule by adopting constitutional and/or statutory provisions granting broad powers of structural, functional, fiscal, and personnel authority to local governments and to authorize them to exercise their authority jointly with other governments as they deem best.

Recommendation 2
Strengthening Local Immunity from State Preemptions and Mandates

The Commission finds that the provisions for local home rule and discretionary authority in many states are being eroded by increases in regulatory and statutory control of local government functioning through enactment of federal and state mandates and preemption of local decisionmaking. The state courts have increasingly asserted their power to adjudicate state-local relations, supplying their own solutions in the absence of clear constitutional and/or statutory direction. Thus, ambiguity in state-local relations places substantial political decisionmaking authority in the hands of the judiciary.

The Commission recommends, therefore, that the states review the local government articles in their constitutions and/or statutes governing the powers of local governments, and consider amending them as appropriate to clarify:

(a) The extent of local power intended to initiate structural, functional, fiscal, and personnel matters without prior permission of the state, and to ensure a proper balance among these powers;

(b) The degree of immunity from the reach of state statutes intended, including limitations on the right of the state to preempt local authority and to mandate functions without giving local governments the fiscal resources to carry out required functions;

(c) Liberal rules of construction to be followed by the courts in interpreting these constitutional or statutory provisions in favor of local governments;

(d) The status of local governments as juridical persons having the same capacity and rights to assert legal claims against the state as natural persons and private corporations; and

(e) *The extent to which autonomy and discretion are to be accorded to different types of local governments, including counties, municipalities, townships, school districts, and special districts.*

Recommendation 3
Enhancing the Ability of Local Governments to Challenge State Governments in Suits over Powers

The Commission finds that, in virtually all states, local government interests are represented in the state capital by local government associations or leagues. Their effectiveness in challenging state legislation that affects local governments adversely varies across states. Some statewide local government associations possess strong in-house counsel that monitors state legislative activities actively and represents local interests quickly and thoroughly in court. Others, however, rely on private ad hoc expert counsel, leaving the results very much to chance. Moreover, individual local governments rarely have the time and resources to match the state's legal resources in specific cases. Such an inconsistent arrangement for professional counsel is not conducive to sustained local government advocacy.

The Commission recommends, therefore, that the state-wide local government organizations and their national counterparts cooperate to provide continuous, well-financed, and well-staffed legal support devoted to advocating the local government assertion of local initiative powers and local immunity from the reach of state government.

Recommendation 4
Recognizing an Alternative Theory of Local Government Autonomy

Although the United States Supreme Court has sanctioned the view that local governments are essentially the legal creatures of the states, the Commission finds that there is another, equally persuasive, theory of local government status in America. Best articulated by Judge Thomas Cooley of Michigan in the late nineteenth century, this theory holds that American local government has an inherent right to self-rule, that is, a sovereignty of its own. This concept was embodied in some early state constitutions, such as Massachusetts, that gave local governments representation in the state legislature.

Nevertheless, such a view has not been favored by the federal courts and many state courts. Given the historical strength of this alternative view of American local government, the Commission finds that the courts are distorting a vibrant chapter in the American history of local government.

The Commission recommends that the courts begin to look more seriously again at an alternative view of local government in America, which stresses the primacy of local government sovereignty. Such a view should be evaluated as the basis for making decisions about the powers of local governments, thus challenging the authority of the creatures-of-the-state theory confirmed by the U.S. Supreme Court.

a. State Laws Bearing Directly on Local Governments

p. 125: Add to Note

As the principal case and *Talbot County* on page 151 of the principal text make clear, close attention must be given to the specific language of each home rule provision. The source and scope classifications mentioned earlier must be coupled with the precise language in predicting what the courts may do when local autonomy is asserted. Compare, e.g., City of New Orleans v. Board of Commissioners of Orleans Levee Dist., 640 So.2d 237 (La.1994); Fraternal Order of Police v. City of Pittsburgh, 644 A.2d 246 (Pa.Cmwlth. 1994); City of Claremont v. Craigue, 135 N.H. 528, 608 A.2d 866 (1992); Opinion of the Justices (Weirs Beach), 134 N.H. 711, 598 A.2d 864 (1991).

b. State Laws Affecting Local Government's Regulatory or Fiscal Powers

p. 141: Add

3. **Conflict With State and Federal Law.** The Supreme Court of Iowa struck down a Des Moines ordinance which established a minimum wage for public improvement contracts. The court held that the ordinance exceeded the city's home rule power because it was inconsistent with a state public improvement statute. The court also found that the ordinance was preempted by the federal ERISA law. City of Des Moines v. Master Builders of Iowa, 498 N.W.2d 702 (Iowa 1993).

2. INTERPLAY OF HOME RULE AND OTHER CLAUSES

p. 153: Add

Note

The Maryland court had occasion to apply the *Talbot County* rationale to a later tax reform effort, there invalidating both a local initiative provision and a roll back of previously enacted taxes, while upholding a cap on future taxes. Board of Supervisors of Elections of Anne Arundel County v. Smallwood, 327 Md. 220, 608 A.2d 1222 (1992).

Chapter IV

ADJUSTING INTERLOCAL GOVERNMENT RELATIONS

A. TERRITORIAL AND BOUNDARY CHANGES

pp. 193–94: Add to introductory note

Laurie Reynolds, *Rethinking Municipal Annexation Powers,* 24 The Urban Lawyer 247 (1992).

1. FEDERAL LAW RESTRICTIONS ON LOCAL REORGANIZATION

p. 194:

The page reference in the principal text for discussion of the Voting Rights Act is 376.

Add to the text

For example, the U.S. Supreme Court struck down a New York statute that carved out of an existing public school district a new district conforming to the boundaries of an incorporated village exclusively populated by members of a strict, Jewish, religious sect, as a violation of the Establishment Clause made applicable to the states by the fourteenth amendment. The new school district concentrated its efforts on education of the sect's children who were handicapped; non-handicapped children continued to attend private schools. Board of Education of Kiryas Joel Village School District v. Grumet, ___ U.S. ___, 114 S.Ct. 2481, 129 L.Ed.2d 546 (1994). Compare Zobrest v. Catalina Foothills School District, ___ U.S. ___, 113 S.Ct. 2462, 125 L.Ed.2d 1 (1993) (government provision of a signer for deaf parochial school student did not run afoul of the Establishment Clause).

2. ANNEXATION—CONSOLIDATION

p. 195: Add to the text at the end of the first full paragraph

It appears that according annexation only historical significance would indeed be premature. See, e.g., David Rusk, Cities Without Suburbs

(1993); Laurie Reynolds, *Rethinking Municipal Annexation Powers,* 24 The Urban Lawyer 247 (1992).

p. 195: Add to the note on "Methods of Annexation"

In the article *Rethinking Municipal Annexation Powers,* Professor Reynolds reviewed the several methods of annexation and their particular idiosyncrasies. She proposed: to free the annexation decision from the need for consent in the territory to be annexed; to encourage negotiated resolution of competitive annexation disputes by requiring neighboring municipalities to establish extraterritorial spheres of influence that would determine each entity's future growth; and to ameliorate the harshness of unconsented annexation by imposing objective prerequisites to an annexation and enforceable post-annexation duties upon the annexing entity.

c. *Popular Determination*

p. 200: Add to Note 2, Federal-law Implications

Cf. Board of Supervisors of Sacramento County v. Sacramento Local Agency Formation Commission, 3 Cal.4th 903, 13 Cal.Rptr. 245, 838 P.2d 1198 (1992), cert. denied, ___ U.S. ___, 113 S.Ct. 1588, 123 L.Ed.2d 154 (1993) (Act under which only voters residing in the area to be incorporated may vote to confirm the incorporation not a violation of equal protection; matter involves, not fundamental right to vote, but state's plenary power to set conditions for creation of its political subdivisions).

p. 207: Add to Note

Supplemented discussion of the important relationships among states, local governments, and the Indian Tribes will appear in conjunction with the principal text's reporting of the *Duro v. Reina* (p. 318—tribal sovereignty) and *Oklahoma Tax Commission v. Citizen Band Potawatomi Indian Tribe of Oklahoma* (p. 738—tribal collection of state sales taxes in sales to non-Indians) cases. Among other matters there noted are Congress' efforts to deal with state and Indian sovereignty and the gambling issue in the Indian Gaming Regulatory Act, 25 U.S.C. §§ 2701–2721, which was enacted in response to the principal case. The enthusiasm with which the Tribes have pursued their rights under the act has produced strong political reaction and litigation which have yet to run their full course.

d. *Impartial Tribunals*

p. 217: Add to Note 1

No boards, of course, are "apolitical." It might be desirable, however, to involve political considerations more directly. Often, such methods as requiring approval by elected county boards, or by an electorate that includes voters in the surrounding counties, serve to bring extended political, social, and economic influences to bear on the decision. Is there an analogy to the political considerations that the U.S. Supreme Court's reading of the Interstate Compact Clause assigns to Congress? See *United States Steel*

Corp. v. Multistate Tax Commission, reported at page 261 of the principal text. An effort to mandate inclusion of fringe-citizen voters in incorporation referenda, in the name of equal protection, was doomed in *Board of Supervisors of Sacramento County v. Sacramento Local Agency Formation Commission,* noted at p. 22, supra, of this supplement. There the California court decided that legislative voting restrictions that precluded county residents from voting on the formation of new municipalities unless they lived in the area to be incorporated did not involve fundamental voting-rights classifications, but only an exercise of the state's plenary authority over the formation of its political subdivisions.

4. CITY–COUNTY CONSOLIDATION

p. 225–26: Add to first full paragraph on 226

County Governments In an Era of Change, (David R. Berman, ed. 1993).

p. 233: Add after *Lennox v. Clark*

Note

The issue of the Register of Wills addressed in the principal case was revisited in Walsh v. Tate, 444 Pa. 229, 282 A.2d 284 (1971). Subsequent constitutional amendments in 1968 that virtually restated the 1951 amendments at issue in *Lennox* did not include the Register of Wills. The *Lennox* formula might have suggested the office's subordination, therefore, to the city's home-rule charter. But as the *Walsh* court noted, the 1968 amendments directed instead that the powers and functions, so closely connected to the judiciary, continue until the voters elect by referendum or initiative to cover the office under the charter.

p. 235: Add to Note 1

Begun successfully in 1805, there exist twenty-eight city-county consolidations in the United States, with concentrations in such states as Virginia, Louisiana, and Montana. Many more efforts have been rejected by the voters. See generally Report, "Consolidated City–County Governments in the United States," The National Association of Counties, Research Department (March 1994).

B. INTEGRATING PARTICULAR FUNCTIONS

1. FEDERATION OF LOCAL UNITS

p. 241: Add to Notes 1(c)

Decentralization efforts begun in London under the administration of Prime Minister Margaret Thatcher and recently reported strains leading to decentralization talk in Toronto combined with the effort of Staten Island (Richmond County) to secede from New York City may suggest that, with regard to federation as a metropolitan solution, the "bloom is off the rose," that, for the time being at least, it is an idea whose time has passed.

C. INTERSTATE COMPACTS—INTERSTATE DISTRICTS

p. 249: Substitute for final paragraph of introductory text, before *Younger* opinion

HESS v. PORT AUTHORITY TRANS–HUDSON CORP.

Supreme Court of the United States, 1994.
___ U.S. ___, 115 S.Ct. 394, 130 L.Ed.2d 245.

JUSTICE GINSBURG delivered the opinion of the Court.

These paired cases arise out of work-related accidents in which a locomotive engineer and a train conductor, employees of a bistate railway authorized by interstate compact, sustained personal injuries. The courts below—the United States District Court for the District of New Jersey, and the United States Court of Appeals for the Third Circuit—rejected both complaints on the ground that the Eleventh Amendment sheltered the respondent railway from suit in federal court. We granted certiorari to resolve an intercircuit conflict on this issue. 510 U.S. ___, 114 S.Ct. 1292, 127 L.Ed.2d 646 (1994). Concluding that the respondent bistate railway, the Port Authority Trans–Hudson Corporation (PATH), is not cloaked with the Eleventh Amendment immunity that a State enjoys, we reverse the judgment of the Third Circuit.

* * *

B

The Port Authority, whose Eleventh Amendment immunity is at issue in these cases, was created in 1921, when Congress, pursuant to the Constitution's Interstate Compact Clause, consented to a compact between the Authority's parent States. 42 Stat. 174. Through the bistate compact, New York and New Jersey sought to achieve "a better co-ordination of the terminal, transportation and other facilities of commerce in, about and through the port of New York." N.J.Stat.Ann. § 32:1–1 (West 1990); N.Y.Unconsol.Laws § 6401 (McKinney 1979). The compact grants the Port Authority power to

> "purchase, construct, lease and/or operate any terminal or transportation facility within [the Port of New York D]istrict; and to make charges for the use thereof; and for any of such purposes to own, hold, lease and/or operate real or personal property, to borrow money and secure the same by bonds or by mortgages upon any property held or to be held by it." N.J.Stat.Ann. § 32:1–7 (West 1990); accord, N.Y.Unconsol.Laws § 6407 (McKinney 1979).

The Port Authority's domain, the Port of New York District, is a defined geographic area that embraces New York Harbor, including parts of New York and New Jersey. See N.J.Stat.Ann. § 32:1–3 (West 1990); N.Y.Unconsol.Laws § 6403 (McKinney 1979).

"The Port Authority was conceived as a financially independent entity, with funds primarily derived from private investors." *United States Trust Co. of N.Y. v. New Jersey,* 431 U.S. 1, 4, 97 S.Ct. 1505, 1509, 52 L.Ed.2d 92 (1977). Tolls, fees, and investment income account for the Authority's secure financial position. See App. to Pet. for Cert. 60a–61a.

* * *

C

The Third Circuit's assessment of PATH's qualification for Eleventh Amendment immunity conflicts with the judgment of the Court of Appeals for the Second Circuit on the same matter. See *Feeney v. Port Authority Trans–Hudson Corporation,* 873 F.2d 628, 631 (1989), aff'd on other grounds, 495 U.S. 299, 110 S.Ct. 1868, 109 L.Ed.2d 264 (1990). The Second Circuit concluded:

> "No provision [of the compact or of state legislation pursuant to the compact] commits the treasuries of the two states to satisfy judgments against the Port Authority * * *. We believe that this insulation of state treasuries from the liabilities of the Port Authority outweighs both the methods of appointment and gubernatorial veto so far as the Eleventh Amendment immunity is concerned." 873 F.2d at 631.

We affirmed the Second Circuit's judgment in *Feeney,* but we bypassed the question whether PATH enjoyed the States' Eleventh Amendment immunity. See *Port Authority Trans–Hudson Corporation v. Feeney,* 495 U.S. 299, 110 S.Ct. 1868, 109 L.Ed.2d 264 (1990). Assuming, *arguendo,* that the suit in *Feeney* was tantamount to a claim against the States, we ruled that New York and New Jersey had effectively consented to the litigation. See *id.,* at 306–309, 110 S.Ct., at 1873–1875 (relying on N.J.Stat.Ann. §§ 32:1–157, 32:1–162 (West 1963); N.Y.Unconsol.Laws §§ 7101, 7106 (McKinney 1979)). Consent is not arguable here, because Hess and Walsh commenced suit too late to meet the 1–year prescription specified by the States. See *supra,* at 397. Accordingly, we confront directly the sole question petitioners Hess and Walsh present, and we hold that PATH is not entitled to Eleventh Amendment immunity from suit in federal court.

II

The Eleventh Amendment largely shields States from suit in federal court without their consent, leaving parties with claims against a State to present them, if the State permits, in the State's own tribunals. Adoption of the Amendment responded most immediately to the States' fears that "federal courts would force them to pay their Revolutionary War debts, leading to their financial ruin." * * * More pervasively, current Eleventh Amendment jurisprudence emphasizes the integrity retained by each State in our federal system:

> "The Amendment is rooted in a recognition that the States, although a union, maintain certain attributes of sovereignty, including

sovereign immunity. See *Hans v. Louisiana,* 134 U.S. 1, 13, 10 S.Ct. 504, 506, 33 L.Ed. 842 (1890). It thus accords the States the respect owed them as members of the federation." *Puerto Rico Aqueduct and Sewer Authority v. Metcalf & Eddy, Inc.,* 506 U.S. ___, ___, 113 S.Ct. 684, 689, 121 L.Ed.2d 605 (1993).

Bistate entities occupy a significantly different position in our federal system than do the States themselves. The States, as separate sovereigns, are the constituent elements of the Union. Bistate entities, in contrast, typically are creations of three discrete sovereigns: two States and the federal government. Their mission is to address " 'interests and problems that do not coincide nicely either with the national boundaries or with State lines' "—interests that " 'may be badly served or not served at all by the ordinary channels of National or State political action.' " * * *

A compact accorded congressional consent "is more than a supple device for dealing with interests confined within a region * * *. [I]t is also a means of safeguarding the national interest * * *." *West Virginia ex rel. Dyer v. Sims,* 341 U.S. 22, 27, 71 S.Ct. 557, 560, 95 L.Ed. 713 (1951). The Port Authority of New York and New Jersey exemplifies both the need for, and the utility of, Compact Clause entities:

* * *

Suit in federal court is not an affront to the dignity of a Compact Clause entity, for the federal court, in relation to such an enterprise, is hardly the instrument of a distant, disconnected sovereign; rather, the federal court is ordained by one of the entity's founders. Nor is the integrity of the compacting States compromised when the Compact Clause entity is sued in federal court. As part of the federal plan prescribed by the Constitution, the States agreed to the power sharing, coordination, and unified action that typify Compact Clause creations. Again, the federal tribunal cannot be regarded as alien in this cooperative, trigovernmental arrangement. This is all the more apparent here, where the very claims in suit—the FELA claims of Hess and Walsh—arise under federal law. See *supra,* at 398.

Because Compact Clause entities owe their existence to state and federal sovereigns acting cooperatively, and not to any "one of the United States," see *supra,* at 397, n. 2, their political accountability is diffuse; they lack the tight tie to the people of one State that an instrument of a single State has: * * *

In sum, within any single State in our representative democracy, voters may exercise their political will to direct state policy; bistate entities created by compact, however, are not subject to the unilateral control of any one of the States that compose the federal system.

Accordingly, there is good reason not to amalgamate Compact Clause entities with agencies of "one of the United States" for Eleventh Amendment purposes. This Court so recognized in *Lake Country Estates, Inc. v. Tahoe Regional Planning Agency,* 440 U.S. 391, 99 S.Ct.

1171, 59 L.Ed.2d 401 (1979), the only case, prior to this one, in which we decided whether a bistate entity qualified for Eleventh Amendment immunity.

Lake Country rejected a plea that the Tahoe Regional Planning Agency (TRPA), an agency created by compact to which California and Nevada were parties, acquired the immunity which the Eleventh Amendment accords to each one of TRPA's parent States. TRPA had argued that if the Amendment shields each State, then surely it must shield an entity "so important that it could not be created by [two] States without a special Act of Congress." *Id.,* at 400, 99 S.Ct., at 1177. That "expansive reading," we said, was not warranted, for the Amendment specifies "the State" as the entity protected:

> "By its terms, the protection afforded by [the Eleventh] Amendment is only available to 'one of the United States.' It is true, of course, that some agencies exercising state power have been permitted to invoke the Amendment in order to protect the state treasury from liability that would have had essentially the same practical consequences as a judgment against the State itself. But the Court has consistently refused to construe the Amendment to afford protection to political subdivisions such as counties and municipalities, even though such entities exercise a 'slice of state power.' " *Id.,* at 400–401, 99 S.Ct., at 1177 (footnotes omitted).

We then set out a general approach: we would presume the Compact Clause agency does not qualify for Eleventh Amendment immunity "[u]nless there is good reason to believe that the States structured the new agency to enable it to enjoy the special constitutional protection of the States themselves, and that Congress concurred in that purpose." *Id.,* at 401, 99 S.Ct., at 1177.

* * *

This case is more complex. Indicators of immunity or the absence thereof do not, as they did in *Lake Country,* all point the same way. While 8 of the Port Authority's 12 commissioners must be resident voters of either New York City or other parts of the Port of New York District, this indicator of local governance is surely offset by the States' controls. All commissioners are state appointees. Acting alone, each State through its governor may block Port Authority measures; and acting together, both States, through their legislatures, may enlarge the Port Authority's powers and add to its responsibilities.

The compact and its implementing legislation do not type the Authority as a state agency; instead they use various terms: "joint or common agency"; "body corporate and politic"; "municipal corporate instrumentality of the two states for the purpose of developing the port and effectuating the pledge of the states in the * * * compact." State courts, however, repeatedly have typed the Port Authority an agency of the States rather than a municipal unit or local district. See, *e.g., Whalen v. Wagner,* 4 N.Y.2d 575, 581–583, 176 N.Y.S.2d 616, 617–621,

152 N.E.2d 54, 56–57 (1958) (legislation authorizing specific Port Authority projects does not pertain to the "property, affairs or government" of a city because "the matters over which the Port Authority has jurisdiction are of State concern").

Port Authority functions are not readily classified as typically state or unquestionably local. States and municipalities alike own and operate bridges, tunnels, ferries, marine terminals, airports, bus terminals, industrial parks, also commuter railroads. This consideration, therefore, does not advance our Eleventh Amendment inquiry.

Pointing away from Eleventh Amendment immunity, the States lack financial responsibility for the Port Authority. Conceived as a fiscally independent entity financed predominantly by private funds, see *United States Trust Co. v. New Jersey,* 431 U.S. 1, 4, 97 S.Ct. 1505, 1508–1509, 52 L.Ed.2d 92 (1977), the Authority generates its own revenues, and for decades has received no money from the States. * * *

The States, as earlier observed, bear no legal liability for Port Authority debts; they are not responsible for the payment of judgments against the Port Authority or PATH. The Third Circuit, in *Port Authority PBA,* assumed that, "if the Authority is ever in need," the States would pay. 819 F.2d, at 416. But nothing in the compact or the laws of either State supports that assumption. See *supra,* at 399. * * *

III

When indicators of immunity point in different directions, the Eleventh Amendment's twin reasons for being remain our prime guide. See *supra,* at 400. We have already pointed out that federal courts are not alien to a bistate entity Congress participated in creating. Nor is it disrespectful to one State to call upon the Compact Clause entity to answer complaints in federal court. See *supra,* at 11. Seeing no genuine threat to the dignity of New York or New Jersey in allowing Hess and Walsh to pursue FELA claims against PATH in federal court, we ask, as *Lake Country* instructed, whether there is here "good reason to believe" the States and Congress designed the Port Authority to enjoy Eleventh Amendment immunity. 440 U.S., at 401, 99 S.Ct., at 1177.

PATH urges that we find good reason to classify the Port Authority as a state agency for Eleventh Amendment purposes based on the control New York and New Jersey wield over the Authority. The States appoint and can remove the commissioners, the governors can veto Port Authority actions, and the States' legislatures can determine the projects the Port Authority undertakes. See *supra,* at 398–399. But ultimate control of every state-created entity resides with the State, for the State may destroy or reshape any unit it creates. * * * Moreover, no one State alone can control the course of a Compact Clause entity. See *supra,* at 401–402 and n. 11. Gauging actual control, particularly when an entity has multiple creator-controllers, can be a "perilous inquiry," "an uncertain and unreliable exercise." * * *

Moreover, rendering control dispositive does not home in on the impetus for the Eleventh Amendment: the prevention of federal court judgments that must be paid out of a State's treasury. * * * Accordingly, Courts of Appeals have recognized the vulnerability of the State's purse as the most salient factor in Eleventh Amendment determinations. * * * In sum, as New York and New Jersey concede, the "vast majority of Circuits * * * have concluded that the state treasury factor is the most important factor to be considered * * * and, in practice, have generally accorded this factor dispositive weight." Brief for States of New Jersey, New York et al. as *Amici Curiae* 18–19.

The Port Authority's anticipated and actual financial independence—its long history of paying its own way, see *supra,* at 399, and n. 7, 403—contrasts with the situation of transit facilities that place heavy fiscal tolls on their founding States. In *Alaska Cargo Transport, Inc. v. Alaska R. Corp.,* 5 F.3d 378 (CA9 1993), for example, Eleventh Amendment immunity was accorded a thinly capitalized railroad that depends for its existence on a state-provided "financial safety net of broad dimension." *Id.,* at 381. And in *Morris v. Washington Metropolitan Area Transit Authority,* 781 F.2d 218 (CADC 1986), Eleventh Amendment immunity was accorded an interstate transit system whose revenue shortfall Congress and the cooperating States anticipated from the start, an enterprise constantly dependent on funds from the participating governments to meet its sizable operating deficits. See *id.,* at 225–227. As the *Morris* court concluded: "[W]here an agency is so structured that, as a practical matter, if the agency is to survive, a judgment must expend itself against state treasuries, common sense and the rationale of the eleventh amendment require that sovereign immunity attach to the agency." *Id.,* at 227. There is no such requirement where the agency is structured, as the Port Authority is, to be self-sustaining. * * *

This reasoning misses the mark. A charitable organization may undertake rescue or other good work which, in its absence, we would expect the State to shoulder. But none would conclude, for example, that in times of flood or famine the American Red Cross, to the extent it works for the public, acquires the States' Eleventh Amendment immunity. The proper focus is not on the use of profits or surplus, but rather is on losses and debts. If the expenditures of the enterprise exceed receipts, is the State in fact obligated to bear and pay the resulting indebtedness of the enterprise? When the answer is "No"—both legally and practically—then the Eleventh Amendment's core concern is not implicated.

* * *

A discrete entity created by constitutional compact among three sovereigns, the Port Authority is financially self-sufficient; it generates its own revenues, and it pays its own debts. Requiring the Port Authority to answer in federal court to injured railroad workers who assert a federal statutory right, under the FELA, to recover damages does not touch the concerns—the States' solvency and dignity—that underpin the Eleventh Amendment. The judgment of the Court of Appeals is accordingly reversed, and the *Hess* and *Walsh* cases are remanded for further proceedings consistent with this opinion.

It is so ordered.

p. 268: Add after the *Multistate Tax Commission* case

Note

Students may wish to read Barclays Bank PLC v. Franchise Tax Board of California, ___ U.S. ___, 114 S.Ct. 2268, 129 L.Ed.2d 244 (1994), and the cases cited therein, all of which grapple with the implications of the U.S. Constitution's Foreign Commerce Clause for state and local taxation of multinational corporations, as they decide whether the majority or the dissent have the stronger arguments about the federal and state political implications of the compact in the principal case.

D. ADJUSTMENTS—CONSOLIDATING PARTICULAR FUNCTIONS

4. INTERLOCAL CONTRACTS

p. 298: Add to Note 1

The U.S. Supreme Court's later decision in the national savings and loan crisis, that the federal securities act's § 10(b) did not, without fraud, make secondary actors in the securities market liable, might have been relevant to the settlement recoveries from lawyers, accountants, and others. See Central Bank of Denver v. First Interstate Bank of Denver, ___ U.S. ___, 114 S.Ct. 1439, 128 L.Ed.2d 119 (1994).

The Vermont Supreme Court ruled that the state legislature could enact subsequent curative legislation validating what had been held to be unauthorized delegation by municipalities of legislative spending power in electric-power efforts. Massachusetts Municipal Wholesale Electric Co. v. State of Vermont, ___ Vt. ___, 639 A.2d 995 (1994).

Chapter V

ADJUSTING FEDERAL–STATE–LOCAL RELATIONS

B. THE IMPACT OF SOVEREIGNTY CONCEPTS UPON LOCAL GOVERNMENT

1. THE NATURE AND LIMITS OF SOVEREIGN POWERS IN AMERICA

p. 318: Add new Note 1

1. Larry Gene Heath was executed by the State of Alabama on March 20, 1992.

Add to "State and Local Prosecutions"

In United States v. Dixon, ___ U.S. ___, 113 S.Ct. 2849, 125 L.Ed.2d 556 (1993), the Court partially modified its ruling in *Grady* and withdrew the latter's "same conduct" test for double jeopardy. See also, Department of Revenue of Montana v. Kurth Ranch, ___ U.S. ___, 114 S.Ct. 1937, 128 L.Ed.2d 767 (1994) (state's tax on illegal drugs is motivated by punishment, not revenue purposes and, hence, attempt to collect tax following guilty pleas to drug charges involved double jeopardy; the tax violates the constitutional prohibition against successive punishments for the same crime).

Add new Note 3

3. As boundary-dispute, water-rights, and other cases attest, the U.S. Supreme Court must resolve disputes between state sovereigns. See, e.g., Wyoming v. Oklahoma, 502 U.S. 437, 112 S.Ct. 789, 117 L.Ed.2d 1 (1992) (Wyoming had standing to sue Oklahoma because the latter's legislation concerning coal use lowered the former's revenues from severance taxes).

p. 324: After *Duro,* add a new Note 1

1. As the principal case suggests, the relationships among Indian Tribes and the federal, state and local governments have necessarily responded to the operative premises: conquered sovereignty or assimilation. The presently operative premise is that of conquered sovereignty. The federal government, by virtue of the Indian Commerce Clause, is the

predominant sovereign. Its laws and the treaties with the Tribes have the backing of the Supremacy Clause. Exercise of powers by state and local governments, therefore, whether regulation or taxation, raises questions of federal permission and preemption like those considered at pages 352, et seq. of the principal text, matters of treaty interpretation, and jurisdictional questions like the meaning and extent of congressionally denominated "Indian Country." See, e.g., Hagen v. State of Utah, ___ U.S. ___, 114 S.Ct. 958, 127 L.Ed.2d 252 (1994); Oklahoma Tax Commission v. Sac and Fox Nation, ___ U.S. ___, 113 S.Ct. 1985, 124 L.Ed.2d 30 (1993); Negonsott v. Samuels, ___ U.S. ___, 113 S.Ct. 1119, 122 L.Ed.2d 457 (1993); Cotton Petroleum Corp. v. New Mexico, 490 U.S. 163, 109 S.Ct. 1698, 104 L.Ed.2d 209 (1989); "The Long Road From Federal Domination To Self-Determination," State Legislatures, March 1992, at 15.

p. 325: After the *Blatchford* note, now Note 2, add a new Note 3

3. **Gambling On Indian Lands.** As noted earlier in this supplement, Congress has attempted to balance Indian economic and state sovereignty interests. Under the Indian Gaming Regulatory Act, 25 U.S.C.A. § 2701 et seq. (1988), if a state allows any type of gambling, it must permit its Indian Tribes to have gambling on Indian land. Courts interpreted that law to permit Tribes to operate gambling casinos even if a state permitted gaming ("Las Vegas Nights") only for charitable organizations. Upon a Tribe's application, the state is required to negotiate an agreement in good faith, or face federal administrative and cabinet-level proceedings and orders. Sycuan Band of Mission Indians v. Roache, 38 F.3d 402 (9th Cir.1994); Mashantucket Pequot Tribe v. Connecticut, 913 F.2d 1024 (2d Cir.1990), cert. denied, 499 U.S. 975, 111 S.Ct. 1620, 113 L.Ed.2d 717 (1991).

As has been widely reported, Indian gaming is big business and currently generates annual revenues of six billion dollars, some substantial portion of which may be shared with the pertinent states. See, e.g., Pauline Yoshihashi, "As Indian Casinos Spread, Politicians and Rivals Maneuver to Fight the Trend," Wall Street Journal, May 4, 1993, at B-1; Harry C. Cashen and John C. Dill, "The Real Truth About Indian Gaming and the States," State Legislatures, March 1992, at 23.

Here too, as in *Blatchford,* there lurk eleventh-amendment questions (see principal text, pp. 1072, and this supplement in connection therewith). In Seminole Tribe of Florida v. State of Florida, 11 F.3d 1016 (11th Cir.1994), the court upheld the state's challenge to a suit by the tribe. It found that Congress had been sufficiently clear in its abrogation of state sovereign immunity in the Indian Gaming Regulatory Act, but that Congress lacked the power to abrogate. The organized-crime connection, if any, was not the motivating purpose of the act; hence, the interstate commerce considerations were not paramount. The Commerce Clause contains interstate, foreign, and Indian commerce provisions. The U.S. Supreme Court has held that Congress possessed power to abrogate state eleventh-amendment immunity only under the *Interstate* Commerce Clause. The Indian Commerce Clause serves different purposes and no power to abrogate may be inferred there, said the Eleventh Circuit.

Certiorari has been granted in the case, 1994 WL 372198, after the Court had invited the Solicitor General to file briefs expressing the views of the United States, 63 U.S.L.W. 3257. The seeming disarray among the lower courts addressing the Act argues for clarification. Compare the *Seminole* case with Cheyenne River Sioux Tribe v. South Dakota, 3 F.3d 273 (8th Cir.1993); Spokane Tribe of Indians v. Washington, 28 F.3d 991 (9th Cir.1994); Ponca Tribe of Oklahoma v. Oklahoma, 37 F.3d 1422 (10th Cir.1994) (also adding that Congress' directing the states to consider gaming compacts with tribes does not constitute compelling entry into them and thus commandeer state legislative processes in violation of the tenth amendment). These disputes may also implicate the U.S. Constitution's Appointments Clause and separation of powers principles. See, e.g., Confederated Tribes of Siletz Indians of Oregon v. United States, 841 F.Supp. 1479 (D.Or.1994).

2. FEDERAL REGULATIONS TOUCHING STATE AND LOCAL GOVERNMENT ACTIVITIES

a. Federal–State Conflicts

p. 335: Add to *Notes,* third full paragraph

A fire-service fee imposed upon commercial and residential property owners in the city, including federal agencies, was held to be not a user fee which federal agencies had to pay, but a local tax from which the federal government and its agencies were immune. United States v. City of Huntington, 999 F.2d 71 (4th Cir.1993), cert. denied, ___ U.S. ___, 114 S.Ct. 1048, 127 L.Ed.2d 371 (1994). Compare United States v. Hynes, 20 F.3d 1437 (7th Cir.1994) (upholding state statute that exempted from taxation property that is being purchased by a governmental entity under an installment contract, unless the purchasing government permits such property to be taxed).

p. 336: Add after *Davis* citation in second full paragraph

Davis and other cases involving state taxation caused a litigative furor over these decisions' retroactive application. See Harper v. Virginia, ___ U.S. ___, 113 S.Ct. 2510, 125 L.Ed.2d 74 (1993), and *Reich v. Collins,* reported infra. See generally, Note, *Retroactivity and the Remains of* Chevron Oil *After* Harper v. Virginia Department of Taxation, 47 Tax Lawyer 455 (1994).

p. 337: Add to "Other Federal Interests"

The 1982 Debt Collection Act exempted states from the *statutory* liability for minimum pre-judgment interest on their debts to the U.S., but it left in place state obligation to pay such interest under the common law. Texas thus owed pre-judgment interest on its debt for lost or stolen federal food stamps which it chose to transmit by mail. United States v. Texas, ___ U.S. ___, 113 S.Ct. 1631, 123 L.Ed.2d 245 (1993).

p. 337: Add at end of text

REICH v. COLLINS

Supreme Court of the United States, 1994.
___ U.S. ___, 115 S.Ct. 547, 130 L.Ed.2d 454.

JUSTICE O'CONNOR delivered the opinion of the Court.

In a long line of cases, this Court has established that due process requires a "clear and certain" remedy for taxes collected in violation of federal law. *Atchison, T. & S.F.R. Co. v. O'Connor,* 223 U.S. 280, 285 (1912) (Holmes, J.). A State has the flexibility to provide that remedy before the disputed taxes are paid (predeprivation), after they are paid (postdeprivation), or both. But what it may not do, and what Georgia did here, is hold out what plainly appears to be a "clear and certain" postdeprivation remedy and then declare, only after the disputed taxes have been paid, that no such remedy exists.

I

For many years, numerous States, including Georgia, exempted from state personal income tax retirement benefits paid by the State, but not retirement benefits paid by the Federal Government (or any other employer). In March 1989, this Court held that such a tax scheme violates the constitutional intergovernmental tax immunity doctrine, which dates back to *McCulloch v. Maryland,* 4 Wheat. 316, 4 L.Ed. 579 (1819), and has been generally codified at 4 U.S.C. § 111. See *Davis v. Michigan Dept. of Treasury,* 489 U.S. 803, 109 S.Ct. 1500, 103 L.Ed.2d 891 (1989).

In the aftermath of *Davis,* most of these States, Georgia included, repealed their special tax exemptions for state retirees, but few offered federal retirees any refunds for the unconstitutional taxes they had paid in the years before *Davis* was decided. Not surprisingly, a great deal of litigation ensued in an effort to force States to provide refunds. The instant suit is part of that litigation.

In April 1990, Reich, a retired federal military officer, sued Georgia in Georgia state court, seeking a refund for the tax years 1980 and after. The principal legal basis for Reich's lawsuit was Georgia's tax refund statute, which provides: "A taxpayer shall be refunded any and all taxes or fees which are determined to have been erroneously or illegally assessed and collected from him under the laws of this state, whether paid voluntarily or involuntarily * * *." Ga.Code Ann. § 48–2–35(a) (Supp.1994).

* * *

Reich's petition for reconsideration in light of *McKesson* was denied. He then petitioned for certiorari. While the petition was pending, we decided *Harper v. Virginia Dept. of Taxation,* 509 U.S. ___, 113 S.Ct. 2510, 125 L.Ed.2d 74 (1993), which relied on *McKesson* in circumstances similar to this case. Accordingly, we remanded Reich's case to the

Georgia Supreme Court for further consideration in light of *Harper*. See *Reich v. Collins,* 509 U.S. ___, 113 S.Ct. 3028, 125 L.Ed.2d 717 (1993).

On remand, the Georgia Supreme Court focused on the portion of *Harper* explaining that, under *McKesson,* a State is free to provide its "clear and certain" remedy in an exclusively predeprivation manner. "[A] meaningful opportunity for taxpayers to withhold contested tax assessments and to challenge their validity in a predeprivation hearing," we said, is " 'a procedural safeguard [against unlawful deprivations] sufficient by itself to satisfy the Due Process Clause.' " See *Harper,* 509 U.S., ___, 113 S.Ct. at 2519, quoting *McKesson,* 496 U.S., at 38, n. 21. The court then reviewed Georgia's predeprivation procedures, found them "ample," and denied Reich's refund claim. *Reich v. Collins,* 263 Ga. 602, 604, 437 S.E.2d 320, 322 (1993) *(Reich II).*

Reich again petitioned for certiorari, and we granted the writ, 510 U.S. ___, 114 S.Ct. 1048, 127 L.Ed.2d 370 (1994), to consider whether it was proper for the Georgia Supreme Court to deny Reich relief on the basis of Georgia's predeprivation remedies.

II

The Georgia Supreme Court is no doubt right that, under *McKesson,* Georgia has the flexibility to maintain an exclusively predeprivation remedial scheme, so long as that scheme is "clear and certain." Due process, we should add, also allows the State to maintain an exclusively postdeprivation regime, see, *e.g., Bob Jones Univ. v. Simon,* 416 U.S. 725, 746–748, 94 S.Ct. 2038, 2050–2052, 40 L.Ed.2d 496 (1974), or a hybrid regime. A State is free as well to reconfigure its remedial scheme over time, to fit its changing needs. Such choices are generally a matter only of state law.

But what a State may *not* do, and what Georgia did here, is to reconfigure its scheme, unfairly, in *mid-course*—to "bait and switch," as some have described it. Specifically, in the mid–1980's, Georgia held out what plainly appeared to be a "clear and certain" postdeprivation remedy, in the form of its tax refund statute, and then declared, only after Reich and others had paid the disputed taxes, that no such remedy exists. In this regard, the Georgia Supreme Court's reliance on Georgia's predeprivation procedures was entirely beside the point (and thus error), because even assuming the constitutional adequacy of these procedures—an issue on which we express no view—no reasonable taxpayer would have thought that they represented, in light of the apparent applicability of the refund statute, the *exclusive* remedy for unlawful taxes. See generally Rakowski, *Harper* and Its Aftermath, 1 Fla.Tax Rev. 445, 474 (1993).

Nor can there be any question that, during the 1980's, prior to *Reich I,* Georgia did appear to hold out a "clear and certain" postdeprivation remedy. To recall, the Georgia refund statute says that the State "*shall* " refund "*any and all* taxes or fees which are determined to have been erroneously or *illegally assessed* and collected from [a taxpayer] under the laws of this state, whether paid voluntarily or involuntarily

* * *." Ga.Code Ann. § 48–2–35(a) (Supp.1994) (emphasis added). In our view, the average taxpayer reading this language would think it obvious that state taxes assessed in violation of federal law are "illegally assessed" taxes. Certainly the United States Court of Appeals for the Eleventh Circuit thought this conclusion was obvious when, in a 1986 case, it denied federal court relief to taxpayers raising claims similar to Reich's, in part because it thought Georgia's refund statute applied to the claims. See *Waldron v. Collins,* 788 F.2d 736, 738, cert. denied, 479 U.S. 884, 107 S.Ct. 274, 93 L.Ed.2d 250 (1986).

Respondents, moreover, do not point to any Georgia Supreme Court cases prior to *Reich I* that put any limiting construction on the statute's sweeping language; indeed, the cases we have found are all entirely consistent with that language's apparent breadth. * * * Even apart from the statute and the cases, we find it significant that, for obvious reasons, States ordinarily *prefer* that taxpayers pursue only postdeprivation remedies, *i.e.,* that taxpayers "pay first, litigate later." This preference is significant in that it would seem especially unfair to penalize taxpayers who may have ignored the possibility of pursuing predeprivation remedies out of respect for that preference.

* * *

Finally, Georgia contends that Reich had no idea (before *Davis*) that the taxes he was paying throughout the 1980's might be unconstitutional. Even assuming Reich had no idea, however, we are not sure we understand the argument. If the argument is that Reich would not have taken advantage of the State's predeprivation remedies no matter how adequate they were (and thus has no standing to complain of those remedies), the argument is beside the point for the same reason that we said that the Georgia Supreme Court's reliance on those remedies was beside the point: Reich was entitled to pursue what appeared to be a "clear and certain" postdeprivation remedy, regardless of the State's predeprivation remedies. Alternatively, if the argument is that Reich needed to have known of the unconstitutionality of his taxes in order to pursue the State's postdeprivation remedy, the argument is wrong. It is wrong because Georgia's refund statute has a relatively lengthy statute of limitations period, and, at least until this case, see *Reich I,* 262 Ga., at 629, 422 S.E.2d, at 849, contained no contemporaneous protest requirement. Under such a regime, taxpayers need not have taken any steps to learn of the possible unconstitutionality of their taxes at the time they paid them. Accordingly, they may not now be put in any worse position for having failed to take such steps.

For the reasons stated, the judgment is reversed and the case remanded for the provision of " 'meaningful backward-looking relief,' " *Harper,* 509 U.S., at ___, 113 S.Ct. 2519, quoting *McKesson,* 496 U.S., at 31, 110 S.Ct., at 2247, consistent with due process and our *McKesson* line of cases. See, *e.g., Carpenter v. Shaw,* 280 U.S. 363, 50 S.Ct. 121, 74 L.Ed. 478 (1930).

It is so ordered.

b. Federal–Local Conflicts

p. 347: Add to Note following *Garcia*

Judicial Response. As the dissenting opinions in *South Carolina* and *Garcia* suggest, the matter of reconciling federal power and state sovereignty has not been laid to rest. The following case illustrates.

NEW YORK v. UNITED STATES

Supreme Court of the United States, 1992.
___ U.S. ___, 112 S.Ct. 2408, 120 L.Ed.2d 120.

JUSTICE O'CONNOR delivered the opinion of the Court.

This case implicates one of our Nation's newest problems of public policy and perhaps our oldest question of constitutional law. The public policy issue involves the disposal of radioactive waste: In this case, we address the constitutionality of three provisions of the Low–Level Radioactive Waste Policy Amendments Act of 1985, Pub.L. 99–240, 99 Stat. 1842, 42 U.S.C. § 2021b *et seq.* The constitutional question is as old as the Constitution: It consists of discerning the proper division of authority between the Federal Government and the States. We conclude that while Congress has substantial power under the Constitution to encourage the States to provide for the disposal of the radioactive waste generated within their borders, the Constitution does not confer upon Congress the ability simply to compel the States to do so. We therefore find that only two of the Act's three provisions at issue are consistent with the Constitution's allocation of power to the Federal Government.

I

We live in a world full of low level radioactive waste. Radioactive material is present in luminous watch dials, smoke alarms, measurement devices, medical fluids, research materials, and the protective gear and construction materials used by workers at nuclear power plants. Low level radioactive waste is generated by the Government, by hospitals, by research institutions, and by various industries. The waste must be isolated from humans for long periods of time, often for hundreds of years. Millions of cubic feet of low level radioactive waste must be disposed of each year. See App. 110a–111a; Berkovitz, Waste Wars: Did Congress "Nuke" State Sovereignty in the Low–Level Radioactive Waste Policy Amendments Act of 1985?, 11 Harv.Envtl.L.Rev. 437, 439–440 (1987).

Our Nation's first site for the land disposal of commercial low level radioactive waste opened in 1962 in Beatty, Nevada. Five more sites opened in the following decade: Maxey Flats, Kentucky (1963), West Valley, New York (1963), Hanford, Washington (1965), Sheffield, Illinois (1967), and Barnwell, South Carolina (1971). Between 1975 and 1978, the Illinois site closed because it was full, and water management problems caused the closure of the sites in Kentucky and New York. As a result, since 1979 only three disposal sites—those in Nevada, Washington, and South Carolina—have been in operation. Waste generated in the rest of the country must be shipped to one of these three sites for disposal. See Low–Level Radioactive Waste Regulation 39–40 (M. Burns ed. 1988).

In 1979, both the Washington and Nevada sites were forced to shut down temporarily, leaving South Carolina to shoulder the responsibility of storing low level radioactive waste produced in every part of the country. The Governor of South Carolina, understandably perturbed, ordered a 50% reduction in the quantity of waste accepted at the Barnwell site. The Governors of Washington and Nevada announced plans to shut their sites permanently. App. 142a, 152a.

Faced with the possibility that the Nation would be left with no disposal sites for low level radioactive waste, Congress responded by enacting the Low–Level Radioactive Waste Policy Act, Pub.L. 96–573, 94 Stat. 3347. Relying largely on a report submitted by the National Governors' Association, see App. 105a–141a, Congress declared a federal policy of holding each State "responsible for providing for the availability of capacity either within or outside the State for the disposal of low-level radioactive waste generated within its borders," and found that such waste could be disposed of "most safely and efficiently * * * on a regional basis." § 4(a)(1), 94 Stat. 3348. The 1980 Act authorized States to enter into regional compacts that, once ratified by Congress, would have the authority beginning in 1986 to restrict the use of their disposal facilities to waste generated within member States. § 4(a)(2)(B), 94 Stat. 3348. The 1980 Act included no penalties for States that failed to participate in this plan.

By 1985, only three approved regional compacts had operational disposal facilities; not surprisingly, these were the compacts formed around South Carolina, Nevada, and Washington, the three sited States. The following year, the 1980 Act would have given these three compacts the ability to exclude waste from nonmembers, and the remaining 31 States would have had no assured outlet for their low level radioactive waste. With this prospect looming, Congress once again took up the issue of waste disposal. The result was the legislation challenged here, the Low–Level Radioactive Waste Policy Amendments Act of 1985.

The 1985 Act was again based largely on a proposal submitted by the National Governors' Association. In broad outline, the Act embodies a compromise among the sited and unsited States. The sited States agreed to extend for seven years the period in which they would accept low level radioactive waste from other States. In exchange, the unsited States agreed to end their reliance on the sited States by 1992.

The mechanics of this compromise are intricate. The Act directs: "Each State shall be responsible for providing, either by itself or in cooperation with other States, for the disposal of * * * low-level radioactive waste generated within the State," 42 U.S.C. § 2021c(a)(1)(A), with the exception of certain waste generated by the Federal Government, §§ 2021c(a)(1)(B), 2021c(b). The Act authorizes States to "enter into such [interstate] compacts as may be necessary to provide for the establishment and operation of regional disposal facilities for low-level radioactive waste." § 2021d(a)(2). For an additional seven years beyond the period contemplated by the 1980 Act, from the beginning of 1986 through the end of 1992, the three existing disposal sites "shall make disposal capacity available for low-level radioactive waste generated by any source," with certain exceptions not relevant here. § 2021e(a)(2). But the three States in which the disposal sites are located are permitted to exact a graduated surcharge for waste arriving from outside the regional compact—in 1986–1987, $10 per cubic foot; in 1988–1989, $20 per cubic foot; and in 1990–1992, $40 per cubic foot. § 2021e(d)(1). After the seven-year transition period expires, approved regional compacts may exclude radioactive waste generated outside the region. § 2021d(c).

The Act provides three types of incentives to encourage the States to comply with their statutory obligation to provide for the disposal of waste generated within their borders.

1. *Monetary incentives.* One quarter of the surcharges collected by the sited States must be transferred to an escrow account held by the Secretary of Energy. § 2021e(d)(2)(A). The Secretary then makes payments from this account to each State that has complied with a series of deadlines. By July 1, 1986, each State was to have ratified legislation either joining a regional compact or indicating an intent to develop a disposal facility within the State. §§ 2021e(e)(1)(A), 2021e(d)(2)(B)(i). By January 1, 1988, each unsited compact was to have identified the State in which its facility would be located, and each compact or standalone State was to have developed a siting plan and taken other identified steps. §§ 2021e(e)(1)(B), 2021e(d)(2)(B)(ii). By January 1, 1990, each State or compact was to have filed a complete application for a license to operate a disposal facility, or the Governor of any State that had not filed an application was to have certified that the State would be capable of disposing of all waste generated in the State after 1992. §§ 2021e(e)(1)(C), 2021e(d)(2)(B)(iii). The rest of the account is to be paid out to those States or compacts able to dispose of all low level radioactive waste generated within their borders by January 1, 1993. § 2021e(d)(2)(B)(iv). Each State that has not met the 1993 deadline must either take title to the waste generated within its borders or forfeit to the waste generators the incentive payments it has received. § 2021e(d)(2)(C).

2. *Access incentives.* The second type of incentive involves the denial of access to disposal sites. States that fail to meet the July 1986 deadline may be charged twice the ordinary surcharge for the remainder of 1986 and may be denied access to disposal facilities thereafter. § 2021e(e)(2)(A). States that fail to meet the 1988 deadline may be charged double surcharges for the first half of 1988 and quadruple surcharges for the second half of 1988, and may be denied access thereafter. § 2021e(e)(2)(B). States that fail to meet the 1990 deadline may be denied access. § 2021e(e)(2)(C). Finally, States that have not filed complete applications by January 1, 1992, for a license to operate a

disposal facility, or States belonging to compacts that have not filed such applications, may be charged triple surcharges. §§ 2021e(e)(1)(D), 2021e(e)(2)(D).

3. *The take title provision.* The third type of incentive is the most severe. The Act provides:

> "If a State (or, where applicable, a compact region) in which low-level radioactive waste is generated is unable to provide for the disposal of all such waste generated within such State or compact region by January 1, 1996, each State in which such waste is generated, upon the request of the generator or owner of the waste, shall take title to the waste, be obligated to take possession of the waste, and shall be liable for all damages directly or indirectly incurred by such generator or owner as a consequence of the failure of the State to take possession of the waste as soon after January 1, 1996, as the generator or owner notifies the State that the waste is available for shipment." § 2021e(d)(2)(C).

These three incentives are the focus of petitioners' constitutional challenge.

In the seven years since the Act took effect, Congress has approved nine regional compacts, encompassing 42 of the States. All six unsited compacts and four of the unaffiliated States have met the first three statutory milestones. Brief for United States 10, n. 19; *id.,* at 13, n. 25.

New York, a State whose residents generate a relatively large share of the Nation's low level radioactive waste, did not join a regional compact. Instead, the State complied with the Act's requirements by enacting legislation providing for the siting and financing of a disposal facility in New York. The State has identified five potential sites, three in Allegany County and two in Cortland County. Residents of the two counties oppose the State's choice of location. App. 29a–30a, 66a–68a.

Petitioners—the State of New York and the two counties—filed this suit against the United States in 1990. They sought a declaratory judgment that the Act is inconsistent with the Tenth and Eleventh Amendments to the Constitution, with the Due Process Clause of the Fifth Amendment, and with the Guarantee Clause of Article IV of the Constitution. The States of Washington, Nevada, and South Carolina intervened as defendants. The District Court dismissed the complaint. 757 F.Supp. 10 (NDNY1990). The Court of Appeals affirmed. 942 F.2d 114 (CA2 1991). Petitioners have abandoned their Due Process and Eleventh Amendment claims on their way up the appellate ladder; as the case stands before us, petitioners claim only that the Act is inconsistent with the Tenth Amendment and the Guarantee Clause.

II

A

In 1788, in the course of explaining to the citizens of New York why the recently drafted Constitution provided for federal courts, Alexander Hamilton observed: "The erection of a new government, whatever care or wisdom may distinguish the work, cannot fail to originate questions of intricacy and nicety; and these may, in a particular manner, be expected to flow from the establishment of a constitution founded upon the total or partial incorporation of a number of distinct sovereignties." The Federalist No. 82, p. 491 (C. Rossiter ed. 1961). Hamilton's prediction has proved quite accurate. While no one disputes the proposition that "[t]he Constitution created a Federal Government of limited powers," *Gregory v. Ashcroft,* 501 U.S. ___, ___, 111 S.Ct. 2395, 2399, 115 L.Ed.2d 410 (1991); and while the Tenth Amendment makes explicit that "[t]he powers not delegated to the United States by the Constitution, nor prohibited by it to the States, are reserved to the States respectively, or to the people"; the task of ascertaining the constitutional line between federal and state power has given rise to many of the Court's most difficult and celebrated cases. At least as far back as *Martin v. Hunter's Lessee,* 1 Wheat. 304, 324, 4 L.Ed. 97 (1816), the Court has resolved questions "of great importance and delicacy" in determining whether particular sovereign powers have been granted by the Constitution to the Federal Government or have been retained by the States.

These questions can be viewed in either of two ways. In some cases the Court has inquired whether an Act of Congress is authorized by one of the powers delegated to Congress in Article I of the Constitution. See, *e.g., Perez v. United States,* 402 U.S. 146, 91 S.Ct. 1357, 28 L.Ed.2d 686 (1971); *McCulloch v. Maryland,* 4 Wheat. 316, 4 L.Ed. 579 (1819). In other cases the Court has sought to determine whether an Act of Congress invades the province of state sovereignty reserved by the Tenth Amendment. See, *e.g., Garcia v. San Antonio Metropolitan Transit Authority,* 469 U.S. 528, 105 S.Ct. 1005, 83 L.Ed.2d 1016 (1985); *Lane County v. Oregon,* 7 Wall. 71, 19 L.Ed. 101 (1869). In a case like this one, involving the division of authority between federal and state governments, the two inquiries are mirror images of each other. If a power is delegated to Congress in the Constitution, the Tenth Amendment expressly disclaims any reservation of that power to the States; if a power is an attribute of state sovereignty reserved by the Tenth Amendment, it is necessarily a power the Constitution has not conferred on Congress. * * *

It is in this sense that the Tenth Amendment "states but a truism that all is retained which has not been surrendered." *United States v. Darby,* 312 U.S. 100, 124, 61 S.Ct. 451, 462, 85 L.Ed. 609 (1941). As Justice Story put it, "[t]his amendment is a mere affirmation of what, upon any just reasoning, is a necessary rule of interpreting the constitution. Being an instrument of limited and enumerated powers, it follows irresistibly, that what is not conferred, is withheld, and belongs to the state authorities." 3 J. Story, Commentaries on the Constitution of the United States 752 (1833). This has been the Court's consistent understanding: "The States unquestionably do retai[n] a significant measure of sovereign authority * * * to the extent that the Constitution has not divested them of their original powers and transferred those powers to the Federal Government." *Garcia v. San Antonio Metropolitan Transit*

Authority, supra, 469 U.S., at 549, 105 S.Ct., at 1017 (internal quotation marks omitted).

Congress exercises its conferred powers subject to the limitations contained in the Constitution. Thus, for example, under the Commerce Clause Congress may regulate publishers engaged in interstate commerce, but Congress is constrained in the exercise of that power by the First Amendment. The Tenth Amendment likewise restrains the power of Congress, but this limit is not derived from the text of the Tenth Amendment itself, which, as we have discussed, is essentially a tautology. Instead, the Tenth Amendment confirms that the power of the Federal Government is subject to limits that may, in a given instance, reserve power to the States. The Tenth Amendment thus directs us to determine, as in this case, whether an incident of state sovereignty is protected by a limitation on an Article I power.

The benefits of this federal structure have been extensively catalogued elsewhere, see, *e.g., Gregory v. Ashcroft, supra,* 501 U.S. at ___, ___, 111 S.Ct., at ___, ___, 115 L.Ed.2d 410; Merritt, The Guarantee Clause and State Autonomy: Federalism for a Third Century, 88 Colum.L.Rev. 1, 3–10 (1988); McConnell, Federalism: Evaluating the Founders' Design, 54 U.Chi.L.Rev. 1484, 1491–1511 (1987), but they need not concern us here. Our task would be the same even if one could prove that federalism secured no advantages to anyone. It consists not of devising our preferred system of government, but of understanding and applying the framework set forth in the Constitution. "The question is not what power the Federal Government ought to have but what powers in fact have been given by the people." *United States v. Butler,* 297 U.S. 1, 63, 56 S.Ct. 312, 318, 80 L.Ed. 477 (1936).

This framework has been sufficiently flexible over the past two centuries to allow for enormous changes in the nature of government. The Federal Government undertakes activities today that would have been unimaginable to the Framers in two senses; first, because the Framers would not have conceived that *any* government would conduct such activities; and second, because the Framers would not have believed that the *Federal* Government, rather than the States, would assume such responsibilities. Yet the powers conferred upon the Federal Government by the Constitution were phrased in language broad enough to allow for the expansion of the Federal Government's role. Among the provisions of the Constitution that have been particularly important in this regard, three concern us here.

First, the Constitution allocates to Congress the power "[t]o regulate Commerce * * * among the several States." Art. I, § 8, cl. 3. Interstate commerce was an established feature of life in the late 18th century. See, *e.g.,* The Federalist No. 42, p. 267 (C. Rossiter ed. 1961) ("The defect of power in the existing Confederacy to regulate the commerce between its several members [has] been clearly pointed out by experience"). The volume of interstate commerce and the range of commonly accepted objects of government regulation have, however, expanded considerably in the last 200 years, and the regulatory authority of Congress has expanded along with them. As interstate commerce has become ubiquitous, activities once considered purely local have come to have effects on the national economy, and have accordingly come within the scope of Congress' commerce power. See, *e.g., Katzenbach v. McClung,* 379 U.S. 294, 85 S.Ct. 377, 13 L.Ed.2d 290 (1964); *Wickard v. Filburn,* 317 U.S. 111, 63 S.Ct. 82, 87 L.Ed. 122 (1942).

Second, the Constitution authorizes Congress "to pay the Debts and provide for the * * * general Welfare of the United States." Art. I, § 8, cl. 1. As conventional notions of the proper objects of government spending have changed over the years, so has the ability of Congress to "fix the terms on which it shall disburse federal money to the States." *Pennhurst State School and Hospital v. Halderman,* 451 U.S. 1, 17, 101 S.Ct. 1531, 1539, 67 L.Ed.2d 694 (1981). Compare, *e.g., United States v. Butler, supra,* 297 U.S., at 72–75, 56 S.Ct., at 322–323 (spending power does not authorize Congress to subsidize farmers), with *South Dakota v. Dole,* 483 U.S. 203, 107 S.Ct. 2793, 97 L.Ed.2d 171 (1987) (spending power permits Congress to condition highway funds on States' adoption of minimum drinking age). While the spending power is "subject to several general restrictions articulated in our cases," *id.,* at 207, 107 S.Ct., at 2796, these restrictions have not been so severe as to prevent the regulatory authority of Congress from generally keeping up with the growth of the federal budget.

The Court's broad construction of Congress' power under the Commerce and Spending Clauses has of course been guided, as it has with respect to Congress' power generally, by the Constitution's Necessary and Proper Clause, which authorizes Congress "[t]o make all Laws which shall be necessary and proper for carrying into Execution the foregoing Powers." U.S. Const., Art. I, § 8, cl. 18. See, *e.g., Legal Tender Case (Juilliard v. Greenman),* 110 U.S. 421, 449–450, 4 S.Ct. 122, 131, 28 L.Ed. 204 (1884); *McCulloch v. Maryland,* 4 Wheat., at 411–421.

Finally, the Constitution provides that "the Laws of the United States * * * shall be the supreme Law of the Land * * * any Thing in the Constitution or Laws of any State to the Contrary notwithstanding." U.S. Const., Art. VI, cl. 2. As the Federal Government's willingness to exercise power within the confines of the Constitution has grown, the authority of the States has correspondingly diminished to the extent that federal and state policies have conflicted. See, *e.g., Shaw v. Delta Air Lines, Inc.,* 463 U.S. 85, 103 S.Ct. 2890, 77 L.Ed.2d 490 (1983). We have observed that the Supremacy Clause gives the Federal Government "a decided advantage in th[e] delicate balance" the Constitution strikes between State and Federal power. *Gregory v. Ashcroft,* 501 U.S., at ___, 111 S.Ct., at 2400.

The actual scope of the Federal Government's authority with respect to the States has changed over the years, therefore, but the constitutional structure underlying and limiting that authority has not. In the end, just as a cup may be half empty or half full, it makes no difference whether one views the question at issue in this case as one of ascertaining the limits of the power delegated to the Federal Government under the affirmative provisions of the Constitution or one of discerning the core of sovereignty retained by the States under the Tenth Amendment. Either way, we must determine whether any of the three challenged provisions of the Low–Level Radioactive Waste Policy Amendments Act of 1985 oversteps the boundary between federal and state authority.

B

Petitioners do not contend that Congress lacks the power to regulate the disposal of low level radioactive waste. Space in radioactive waste disposal sites is frequently sold by residents of one State to residents of another. Regulation of the resulting interstate market in waste disposal is therefore well within Congress' authority under the Commerce Clause. Cf. *Philadelphia v. New Jersey,* 437 U.S. 617, 621–623, 98 S.Ct. 2531, 2534–2535, 57 L.Ed.2d 475 (1978); *Fort Gratiot Sanitary Landfill, Inc. v. Michigan Dept. of Natural Resources,* 504 U.S. ___, ___, 112 S.Ct. 2019, 2023, 119 L.Ed.2d 139 (1992). Petitioners likewise do not dispute that under the Supremacy Clause Congress could, if it wished, pre-empt state radioactive waste regulation. Petitioners contend only that the Tenth Amendment limits the power of Congress to regulate in the way it has chosen. Rather than addressing the problem of waste disposal by directly regulating the generators and disposers of waste, petitioners argue, Congress has impermissibly directed the States to regulate in this field.

Most of our recent cases interpreting the Tenth Amendment have concerned the authority of Congress to subject state governments to generally applicable laws. The Court's jurisprudence in this area has traveled an unsteady path. See *Maryland v. Wirtz,* 392 U.S. 183, 88 S.Ct. 2017, 20 L.Ed.2d 1020 (1968) (state schools and hospitals are subject to Fair Labor Standards Act); *National League of Cities v. Usery,* 426 U.S. 833, 96 S.Ct. 2465, 49 L.Ed.2d 245 (1976) (overruling *Wirtz*) (state employers are *not* subject to Fair Labor Standards Act); *Garcia v. San Antonio Metropolitan Transit Authority,* 469 U.S. 528, 105 S.Ct. 1005, 83 L.Ed.2d 1016 (1985) (overruling *National League of Cities*) (state employers are once again subject to Fair Labor Standards Act). See also *New York v. United States,* 326 U.S. 572, 66 S.Ct. 310, 90 L.Ed. 326 (1946); *Fry v. United States,* 421 U.S. 542, 95 S.Ct. 1792, 44 L.Ed.2d 363 (1975); *Transportation Union v. Long Island R. Co.,* 455 U.S. 678, 102 S.Ct. 1349, 71 L.Ed.2d 547 (1982); *EEOC v. Wyoming,* 460 U.S. 226, 103 S.Ct. 1054, 75 L.Ed.2d 18 (1983); *South Carolina v. Baker,* 485 U.S. 505, 108 S.Ct. 1355, 99 L.Ed.2d 592 (1988); *Gregory v. Ashcroft,* 501 U.S. ___, 111 S.Ct. 2395, 115 L.Ed.2d 410 (1991). This case presents no occasion to apply or revisit the holdings of any of these cases, as this is not a case in which Congress has subjected a State to the same legislation applicable to private parties. Cf. *FERC v. Mississippi,* 456 U.S. 742, 758–759, 102 S.Ct. 2126, 2137, 72 L.Ed.2d 532 (1982).

This case instead concerns the circumstances under which Congress may use the States as implements of regulation; that is, whether Congress may direct or otherwise motivate the States to regulate in a particular field or a particular way. Our cases have established a few principles that guide our resolution of the issue.

1

As an initial matter, Congress may not simply "commandee[r] the legislative processes of the States by directly compelling them to enact and enforce a federal regulatory program." *Hodel v. Virginia Surface Mining & Reclamation Assn., Inc.,* 452 U.S. 264, 288, 101 S.Ct. 2352, 2366, 69 L.Ed.2d 1 (1981). In *Hodel,* the Court upheld the Surface Mining Control and Reclamation Act of 1977 precisely because it did *not* "commandeer" the States into regulating mining. The Court found that "the States are not compelled to enforce the steep-slope standards, to expend any state funds, or to participate in the federal regulatory program in any manner whatsoever. If a State does not wish to submit a proposed permanent program that complies with the Act and implementing regulations, the full regulatory burden will be borne by the Federal Government." *Ibid.*

The Court reached the same conclusion the following year in *FERC v. Mississippi, supra.* At issue in *FERC* was the Public Utility Regulatory Policies Act of 1978, a federal statute encouraging the States in various ways to develop programs to combat the Nation's energy crisis. We observed that "this Court never has sanctioned explicitly a federal command to the States to promulgate and enforce laws and regulations." *Id.,* 456 U.S., at 761–762, 102 S.Ct., at 2139. As in *Hodel,* the Court upheld the statute at issue because it did not view the statute as such a command. The Court emphasized: "Titles I and III of [the Public Utility Regulatory Policies Act of 1978 (PURPA)] require *only consideration* of federal standards. And if a State has no utilities commission, or simply stops regulating in the field, it need not even entertain the federal proposals." 456 U.S., at 764, 102 S.Ct., 2140 (emphasis in original). Because "[t]here [wa]s nothing in PURPA 'directly compelling' the States to enact a legislative program," the statute was not inconsistent with the Constitution's division of authority between the Federal Government and the States. *Id.,* 456 U.S., at 765, 102 S.Ct., at 2141 (quoting *Hodel v. Virginia Surface Mining & Reclamation Assn., Inc., supra,* 452 U.S., at 288, 101 S.Ct., at 2366). See also *South Carolina v. Baker, supra,* 485 U.S., at 513, 108 S.Ct., at 1361 (noting "the possibility that the Tenth Amendment might set some limits on Congress' power to compel States to regulate on behalf of federal interests"); *Garcia v. San Antonio Metropolitan Transit Authority, supra,* 469 U.S., at 556, 105 S.Ct., at 1020 (same).

These statements in *FERC* and *Hodel* were not innovations. While Congress has substantial powers to govern the Nation directly, including in areas of intimate concern to the States, the Constitution has never been understood to confer upon Congress the ability to require the

States to govern according to Congress' instructions. See *Coyle v. Oklahoma,* 221 U.S. 559, 565, 31 S.Ct. 688, 689, 55 L.Ed. 853 (1911). The Court has been explicit about this distinction. "Both the States and the United States existed before the Constitution. The people, through that instrument, established a more perfect union by substituting a national government, acting, with ample power, *directly upon the citizens,* instead of the Confederate government, which acted with powers, greatly restricted, only upon the States." *Lane County v. Oregon,* 7 Wall., at 76 (emphasis added). The Court has made the same point with more rhetorical flourish, although perhaps with less precision, on a number of occasions. In Chief Justice Chase's much-quoted words, "the preservation of the States, and the maintenance of their governments, are as much within the design and care of the Constitution as the preservation of the Union and the maintenance of the National government. The Constitution, in all its provisions, looks to an indestructible Union, composed of indestructible States." *Texas v. White,* 7 Wall. 700, 725, 19 L.Ed. 227 (1869). See also *Metcalf & Eddy v. Mitchell,* 269 U.S. 514, 523, 46 S.Ct. 172, 174, 70 L.Ed. 384 (1926) ("neither government may destroy the other nor curtail in any substantial manner the exercise of its powers"); *Tafflin v. Levitt,* 493 U.S. 455, 458, 110 S.Ct. 792, 795, 107 L.Ed.2d 887 (1990) ("under our federal system, the States possess sovereignty concurrent with that of the Federal Government"); *Gregory v. Ashcroft,* 501 U.S., at ___, 111 S.Ct., at 2401 ("the States retain substantial sovereign powers under our constitutional scheme, powers with which Congress does not readily interfere").

Indeed, the question whether the Constitution should permit Congress to employ state governments as regulatory agencies was a topic of lively debate among the Framers. Under the Articles of Confederation, Congress lacked the authority in most respects to govern the people directly. In practice, Congress "could not directly tax or legislate upon individuals; it had no explicit 'legislative' or 'governmental' power to make binding 'law' enforceable as such." Amar, Of Sovereignty and Federalism, 96 Yale L.J. 1425, 1447 (1987).

The inadequacy of this governmental structure was responsible in part for the Constitutional Convention. Alexander Hamilton observed: "The great and radical vice in the construction of the existing Confederation is in the principle of LEGISLATION for STATES or GOVERNMENTS, in their CORPORATE or COLLECTIVE CAPACITIES, and as contra-distinguished from the INDIVIDUALS of whom they consist." The Federalist No. 15, p. 108 (C. Rossiter ed. 1961). As Hamilton saw it, "we must resolve to incorporate into our plan those ingredients which may be considered as forming the characteristic difference between a league and a government; we must extend the authority of the Union to the persons of the citizens—the only proper objects of government." *Id.,* at 109. The new National Government "must carry its agency to the persons of the citizens. It must stand in need of no intermediate legislations * * *. The government of the Union, like that of each State, must be able to address itself immediately to the hopes and fears of individuals." *Id.*, No. 16, p. 116.

The Convention generated a great number of proposals for the structure of the new Government, but two quickly took center stage. Under the Virginia Plan, as first introduced by Edmund Randolph, Congress would exercise legislative authority directly upon individuals, without employing the States as intermediaries. 1 Records of the Federal Convention of 1787, p. 21 (M. Farrand ed. 1911). Under the New Jersey Plan, as first introduced by William Paterson, Congress would continue to require the approval of the States before legislating, as it has under the Articles of Confederation. 1 *id.*, 243–244. These two plans underwent various revisions as the Convention progressed, but they remained the two primary options discussed by the delegates. One frequently expressed objection to the New Jersey Plan was that it might require the Federal Government to coerce the States into implementing legislation. As Randolph explained the distinction, "[t]he true question is whether we shall adhere to the federal plan [*i.e.*, the New Jersey Plan], or introduce the national plan. The insufficiency of the former has been fully displayed * * *. There are but two modes, by which the end of a Gen[eral] Gov[ernment] can be attained: the 1st is by coercion as proposed by Mr. P[aterson's] plan[, the 2nd] by real legislation as prop[osed] by the other plan. Coercion [is] *impracticable, expensive, cruel to individuals* * * *. We must resort therefore to a national *Legislation over individuals.*" 1 *id.*, at 255–256 (emphasis in original). Madison echoed this view: "The practicability of making laws, with coercive sanctions, for the States as political bodies, had been exploded on all hands." 2 *id.*, at 9.

Under one preliminary draft of what would become the New Jersey Plan, state governments would occupy a position relative to Congress similar to that contemplated by the Act at issue in this case: "[T]he laws of the United States ought, as far as may be consistent with the common interests of the Union, to be carried into execution by the judiciary and executive officers of the respective states, wherein the execution thereof is required." 3 *id.*, at 616. This idea apparently never even progressed so far as to be debated by the delegates, as contemporary accounts of the Convention do not mention any such discussion. The delegates' many descriptions of the Virginia and New Jersey Plans speak only in general terms about whether Congress was to derive its authority from the people or from the States, and whether it was to issue directives to individuals or to States. See 1 *id.*, at 260–280.

In the end, the Convention opted for a Constitution in which Congress would exercise its legislative authority directly over individuals rather than over States; for a variety of reasons, it rejected the New Jersey Plan in favor of the Virginia Plan. 1 *id.*, at 313. This choice was made clear to the subsequent state ratifying conventions. Oliver Ellsworth, a member of the Connecticut delegation in Philadelphia, explained the distinction to his State's convention: "This Constitution does not attempt to coerce sovereign bodies, states, in their political capacity * * *. But this legal coercion singles out the * * * individual." 2 J. Elliot, Debates on the Federal Constitution 197 (2d ed. 1863). Charles Pinckney, another delegate at the Constitutional Convention, emphasized to the South Carolina House of Representatives that in Philadelphia "the necessity of having a government which should at once operate upon the people, and not upon the states, was conceived to be indispensable by every delegation present." 4 *id.,* at 256. Rufus King, one of Massachusetts' delegates, returned home to support ratification by recalling the Commonwealth's unhappy experience under the Articles of Confederation and arguing: "Laws, to be effective, therefore, must not be laid on states, but upon individuals." 2 *id.,* at 56. At New York's convention, Hamilton (another delegate in Philadelphia) exclaimed: "But can we believe that one state will ever suffer itself to be used as an instrument of coercion? The thing is a dream; it is impossible. Then we are brought to this dilemma—either a federal standing army is to enforce the requisitions, or the federal treasury is left without supplies, and the government without support. What, sir, is the cure for this great evil? Nothing, but to enable the national laws to operate on individuals, in the same manner as those of the states do." 2 *id.,* at 233. At North Carolina's convention, Samuel Spencer recognized that "all the laws of the Confederation were binding on the states in their political capacities, * * *, but now the thing is entirely different. The laws of Congress will be binding on individuals." 4 *id.,* at 153.

In providing for a stronger central government, therefore, the Framers explicitly chose a Constitution that confers upon Congress the power to regulate individuals, not States. As we have seen, the Court has consistently respected this choice. We have always understood that even where Congress has the authority under the Constitution to pass laws requiring or prohibiting certain acts, it lacks the power directly to compel the States to require or prohibit those acts. *E.g., FERC v. Mississippi,* 456 U.S., at 762–766, 102 S.Ct., at 2138–2141; *Hodel v. Virginia Surface Mining & Reclamation Assn., Inc.,* 452 U.S., at 288–289, 101 S.Ct., at 2366; *Lane County v. Oregon,* 7 Wall., at 76. The allocation of power contained in the Commerce Clause, for example, authorizes Congress to regulate interstate commerce directly; it does not authorize Congress to regulate state governments' regulation of interstate commerce.

2

This is not to say that Congress lacks the ability to encourage a State to regulate in a particular way, or that Congress may not hold out incentives to the States as a method of influencing a State's policy choices. Our cases have identified a variety of methods, short of outright coercion, by which Congress may urge a State to adopt a legislative program consistent with federal interests. Two of these methods are of particular relevance here.

First, under Congress' spending power, "Congress may attach conditions on the receipt of federal funds." *South Dakota v. Dole,* 483 U.S., at 206, 107 S.Ct., at 2795. Such conditions must (among other requirements) bear some relationship to the purpose of the federal spending, *id.,* at 207–208, and n. 3, 107 S.Ct., at 2796, and n. 3; otherwise, of course, the spending power could render academic the Constitution's other grants and limits of federal authority. Where the recipient of federal funds is a State, as is not unusual today, the conditions attached to the funds by Congress may influence a State's legislative choices. See Kaden, Politics, Money, and State Sovereignty: The Judicial Role, 79 Colum.L.Rev. 847, 874–881 (1979). *Dole* was one such case: The Court found no constitutional flaw in a federal statute directing the Secretary of Transportation to withhold federal highway funds from States failing to adopt Congress' choice of a minimum drinking age. Similar examples abound. * * *

Second, where Congress has the authority to regulate private activity under the Commerce Clause, we have recognized Congress' power to offer States the choice of regulating that activity according to federal standards or having state law pre-empted by federal regulation. *Hodel v. Virginia Surface Mining & Reclamation Assn., Inc., supra,* 452 U.S., at 288, 101 S.Ct., at 2366. See also *FERC v. Mississippi, supra,* 456 U.S., at 764–765, 102 S.Ct., at 2140. This arrangement, which has been termed "a program of cooperative federalism," *Hodel, supra,* 452 U.S., at 289, 101 S.Ct., at 2366, is replicated in numerous federal statutory schemes. These include the Clean Water Act, 86 Stat. 816, as amended, 33 U.S.C. § 1251 *et seq.,* see *Arkansas v. Oklahoma,* 503 U.S. ___, ___, 112 S.Ct. 1046, 1054, 117 L.Ed.2d 239 (1992) (Clean Water Act "anticipates a partnership between the States and the Federal Government, animated by a shared objective"); the Occupational Safety and Health Act of 1970, 84 Stat. 1590, 29 U.S.C. § 651 *et seq.,* see *Gade v. National Solid Wastes Management Assn.,* ___ U.S. ___, ___ 112 S.Ct. 2374, ___, ___ L.Ed.2d ___ (1992); the Resource Conservation and Recovery Act of 1976, 90 Stat. 2796, as amended, 42 U.S.C. § 6901 *et seq.,* see *United States Dept. of Energy v. Ohio,* 503 U.S. ___, ___, 112 S.Ct. 1627, 1632, 118 L.Ed.2d 255 (1992); and the Alaska National Interest Lands Conservation Act, 94 Stat. 2374, 16 U.S.C. § 3101 *et seq.,* see *Kenaitze Indian Tribe v. Alaska,* 860 F.2d 312, 314 (CA9 1988), cert. denied, 491 U.S. 905, 109 S.Ct. 3187, 105 L.Ed.2d 695 (1989).

By either of these two methods, as by any other permissible method of encouraging a State to conform to federal policy choices, the residents of the State retain the ultimate decision as to whether or not the State will comply. If a State's citizens view federal policy as sufficiently contrary to local interests, they may elect to decline a federal grant. If state residents would prefer their government to devote its attention and resources to problems other than those deemed important by Congress, they may choose to have the Federal Government rather than the State bear the expense of a federally mandated regulatory program, and they may continue to supplement that program to the extent state law is not preempted. Where Congress encourages state regulation rather than compelling it, state governments remain responsive to the local electorate's preferences; state officials remain accountable to the people.

By contrast, where the Federal Government compels States to regulate, the accountability of both state and federal officials is diminished. If the citizens of New York, for example, do not consider that making provision for the disposal of radioactive waste is in their best interest, they may elect state officials who share their view. That view can always be preempted under the Supremacy Clause if it is contrary to the national view, but in such a case it is the Federal Government that makes the decision in full view of the public, and it will be federal officials that suffer the consequences if the decision turns out to be detrimental or unpopular. But where the Federal Government directs the States to regulate, it may be state officials who will bear the brunt of public disapproval, while the federal officials who devised the regulatory program may remain insulated from the electoral ramifications of their decision. Accountability is thus diminished when, due to federal coercion, elected state officials cannot regulate in accordance with the views of the local electorate in matters not pre-empted by federal regulation. See Merritt, 88 Colum.L.Rev., at 61–62; La Pierre, Political Accountability in the National Political Process—The Alternative to Judicial Review of Federalism Issues, 80 Nw.U.L.Rev. 577, 639–665 (1985).

With these principles in mind, we turn to the three challenged provisions of the Low–Level Radioactive Waste Policy Amendments Act of 1985.

III

* * *

We therefore decline petitioners' invitation to construe § 2021c(a)(1)(A), alone and in isolation, as a command to the States independent of the remainder of the Act. Construed as a whole, the Act comprises three sets of "incentives" for the States to provide for the disposal of low level radioactive waste generated within their borders. We consider each in turn.

A

The first set of incentives works in three steps. First, Congress has authorized States with disposal sites to impose a surcharge on radioactive waste received from other States. Second, the Secretary of Energy collects a portion of this surcharge and places the money in an escrow account. Third, States achieving a series of milestones receive portions of this fund.

The first of these steps is an unexceptionable exercise of Congress' power to authorize the States to burden interstate commerce. While the Commerce Clause has long been understood to limit the States' ability to discriminate against interstate commerce, see, *e.g., Wyoming v. Oklahoma,* 502 U.S. ___, ___, 112 S.Ct. 789, 800, 117 L.Ed.2d 1 (1992); *Cooley v. Board of Wardens of Port of Philadelphia,* 12 How. 299, 13 L.Ed. 996 (1851), that limit may be lifted, as it has been here, by an expression of the "unambiguous intent" of Congress. *Wyoming, supra,* 502 U.S., at ___, 112 S.Ct., at 802; *Prudential Ins. Co. v. Benjamin,* 328 U.S. 408, 427–431, 66 S.Ct. 1142, 1153–1156, 90 L.Ed. 1342 (1946). Whether or not the States would be permitted to burden the interstate transport of low level radioactive waste in the absence of Congress' approval, the States can clearly do so *with* Congress' approval, which is what the Act gives them.

The second step, the Secretary's collection of a percentage of the surcharge, is no more than a federal tax on interstate commerce, which petitioners do not claim to be an invalid exercise of either Congress' commerce or taxing power. Cf. *United States v. Sanchez,* 340 U.S. 42, 44–45, 71 S.Ct. 108, 110, 95 L.Ed. 47 (1950); *Steward Machine Co. v. Davis,* 301 U.S. 548, 581–583, 57 S.Ct. 883, 888–889, 81 L.Ed. 1279 (1937).

The third step is a conditional exercise of Congress' authority under the Spending Clause: Congress has placed conditions—the achievement of the milestones—on the receipt of federal funds. Petitioners do not contend that Congress has exceeded its authority in any of the four respects our cases have identified. See generally *South Dakota v. Dole,* 483 U.S., at 207–208, 107 S.Ct., at 2796. The expenditure is for the general welfare, *Helvering v. Davis,* 301 U.S. 619, 640–641, 57 S.Ct. 904, 908, 81 L.Ed. 1307 (1937); the States are required to use the money they receive for the purpose of assuring the safe disposal of radioactive waste. 42 U.S.C. § 2021e(d)(2)(E). The conditions imposed are unambiguous, *Pennhurst State School and Hospital v. Halderman,* 451 U.S., at 17, 101 S.Ct., at 1540; the Act informs the States exactly what they must do and by when they must do it in order to obtain a share of the escrow account. The conditions imposed are reasonably related to the purpose of the expenditure, *Massachusetts v. United States,* 435 U.S., at 461, 98 S.Ct., at 1164; both the conditions and the payments embody Congress' efforts to address the pressing problem of radioactive waste disposal. Finally, petitioners do not claim that the conditions imposed by the Act violate any independent constitutional prohibition. *Lawrence County v. Lead–Deadwood School Dist.,* 469 U.S. 256, 269–270, 105 S.Ct. 695, 702–703, 83 L.Ed.2d 635 (1985).

* * *

The Act's first set of incentives, in which Congress has conditioned grants to the States upon the States' attainment of a series of milestones, is thus well within the authority of Congress under the Commerce and Spending Clauses. Because the first set of incentives is supported by affirmative constitutional grants of power to Congress, it is not inconsistent with the Tenth Amendment.

B

In the second set of incentives, Congress has authorized States and regional compacts with disposal sites gradually to increase the cost of access to the sites, and then to deny access altogether, to radioactive waste generated in States that do not meet federal deadlines. As a simple regulation, this provision would be within the power of Congress to authorize the States to discriminate against interstate commerce. See *Northeast Bancorp, Inc. v. Board of Governors, Fed. Reserve System,* 472 U.S. 159, 174–175, 105 S.Ct. 2545, 2554, 86 L.Ed.2d 112 (1985). Where federal regulation of private activity is within the scope of the Commerce Clause, we have recognized the ability of Congress to offer states the choice of regulating that activity according to federal standards or having state law pre-empted by federal regulation. See *Hodel v. Virginia Surface Mining & Reclamation Association,* 452 U.S., at 288, 101 S.Ct., at 2366; *FERC v. Mississippi,* 456 U.S., at 764–765, 102 S.Ct., at 2140.

This is the choice presented to nonsited States by the Act's second set of incentives: States may either regulate the disposal of radioactive waste according to federal standards by attaining local or regional self-sufficiency, or their residents who produce radioactive waste will be subject to federal regulation authorizing sited States and regions to deny access to their disposal sites. The affected States are not compelled by Congress to regulate, because any burden caused by a State's refusal to regulate will fall on those who generate waste and find no outlet for its disposal, rather than on the State as a sovereign. A State whose citizens do not wish it to attain the Act's milestones may devote its attention and its resources to issues its citizens deem more worthy; the choice remains at all times with the residents of the State, not with Congress. The State need not expend any funds, or participate in any federal program, if local residents do not view such expenditures or participation as worthwhile. Cf. *Hodel, supra,* 452 U.S., at 288, 101 S.Ct., at 2366. Nor must the State abandon the field if it does not accede to federal direction; the State may continue to regulate the generation and disposal of radioactive waste in any manner its citizens see fit.

The Act's second set of incentives thus represents a conditional exercise of Congress' commerce power, along the lines of those we have held to be within Congress' authority. As a result, the second set of incentives does not intrude on the sovereignty reserved to the States by the Tenth Amendment.

C

The take title provision is of a different character. This third so-called "incentive" offers States, as an alternative to regulating pursuant to Congress' direction, the option of taking title to and possession of the low level radioactive waste generated within their borders and becoming liable for all damages waste generators suffer as a result of the States' failure to do so promptly. In this provision, Congress has crossed the line distinguishing encouragement from coercion.

* * *

The take title provision offers state governments a "choice" of either accepting ownership of waste or regulating according to the instructions of Congress. Respondents do not claim that the Constitution would authorize Congress to impose either option as a freestanding requirement. On one hand, the Constitution would not permit Congress simply to transfer radioactive waste from generators to state governments. Such a forced transfer, standing alone, would in principle be no different than a congressionally compelled subsidy from state governments to radioactive waste producers. The same is true of the provision requiring the States to become liable for the generators' damages. Standing alone, this provision would be indistinguishable from an Act of Congress directing the States to assume the liabilities of certain state residents. Either type of federal action would "commandeer" state governments into the service of federal regulatory purposes, and would for this reason be inconsistent with the Constitution's division of authority between federal and state governments. On the other hand, the second alternative held out to state governments—regulating pursuant to Congress' direction—would, standing alone, present a simple command to state governments to implement legislation enacted by Congress. As we have seen, the Constitution does not empower Congress to subject state governments to this type of instruction.

Because an instruction to state governments to take title to waste, standing alone, would be beyond the authority of Congress, and because a direct order to regulate, standing alone, would also be beyond the authority of Congress, it follows that Congress lacks the power to offer the States a choice between the two. Unlike the first two sets of incentives, the take title incentive does not represent the conditional exercise of any congressional power enumerated in the Constitution. In this provision, Congress has not held out the threat of exercising its spending power or its commerce power; it has instead held out the threat, should the States not regulate according to one federal instruction, of simply forcing the States to submit to another federal instruction. A choice between two unconstitutionally coercive regulatory techniques is no choice at all. Either way, "the Act commandeers the legislative processes of the States by directly compelling them to enact and enforce a federal regulatory program," *Hodel v. Virginia Surface Mining & Reclamation Assn., Inc., supra,* 452 U.S., at 288, 101 S.Ct., at 2366, an outcome that has never been understood to lie within the authority conferred upon Congress by the Constitution.

Respondents emphasize the latitude given to the States to implement Congress' plan. The Act enables the States to regulate pursuant to Congress' instructions in any number of different ways. States may avoid taking title by contracting with sited regional compacts, by building a disposal site alone or as part of a compact, or by permitting private parties to build a disposal site. States that host sites may employ a wide range of designs and disposal methods, subject only to broad federal regulatory limits. This line of reasoning, however, only underscores the critical alternative a State lacks: A State may not decline to administer the federal program. No matter which path the State chooses, it must follow the direction of Congress.

The take title provision appears to be unique. No other federal statute has been cited which offers a state government no option other than that of implementing legislation enacted by Congress. Whether one views the take title provision as lying outside Congress' enumerated powers, or as infringing upon the core of state sovereignty reserved by the Tenth Amendment, the provision is inconsistent with the federal structure of our Government established by the Constitution.

IV

Respondents raise a number of objections to this understanding of the limits of Congress' power.

A

The United States proposes three alternative views of the constitutional line separating state and federal authority. While each view concedes that Congress *generally* may not compel state governments to regulate pursuant to federal direction, each purports to find a limited domain in which such coercion is permitted by the Constitution.

First, the United States argues that the Constitution's prohibition of congressional directives to state governments can be overcome where the federal interest is sufficiently important to justify state submission. This argument contains a kernel of truth: In determining whether the Tenth Amendment limits the ability of Congress to subject state governments to generally applicable laws, the Court *has* in some cases stated that it will evaluate the strength of federal interests in light of the degree to which such laws would prevent the State from functioning as a sovereign; that is, the extent to which such generally applicable laws would impede a state government's responsibility to represent and be accountable to the citizens of the State. * * * But whether or not a particularly strong federal interest enables Congress to bring state governments within the orbit of generally applicable *federal* regulation, no Member of the Court has ever suggested that such a federal interest would enable Congress to command a state government to enact *state* regulation. No matter how powerful the federal interest involved, the Constitution simply does not give Congress the authority to require the States to regulate. The Constitution instead gives Congress the authority to regulate matters directly and to pre-empt contrary state regulation. Where a federal interest is sufficiently strong to cause Congress to legislate, it must do so directly; it may not conscript state governments as its agents.

Second, the United States argues that the Constitution does, in some circumstances, permit federal directives to state governments. Various cases are cited for this proposition, but none support it. Some of these cases discuss the well established power of Congress to pass laws enforceable in state courts. * * * These cases involve no more than an application of the Supremacy Clause's provision that federal law "shall be the supreme Law of the Land," enforceable in every State. More to the point, all involve congressional regulation of individuals, not congressional requirements that States regulate. Federal statutes enforceable in state courts do, in a sense, direct state judges to enforce them, but this sort of federal "direction" of state judges is mandated by the text of the Supremacy Clause. No comparable constitutional provision authorizes Congress to command state legislatures to legislate.

Additional cases cited by the United States discuss the power of federal *courts* to order state officials to comply with federal law. * * * Again, however, the text of the Constitution plainly confers this authority on the federal courts, the "judicial Power" of which "shall extend to all Cases, in Law and Equity, arising under this Constitution, [and] the Laws of the United States * * *; [and] to Controversies between two or more States; [and] between a State and Citizens of another State." U.S. Const., Art. III, § 2. The Constitution contains no analogous grant of authority to Congress. Moreover, the Supremacy Clause makes federal law paramount over the contrary positions of state officials; the power of federal courts to enforce federal law thus presupposes some authority to order state officials to comply. * * *

In sum, the cases relied upon by the United States hold only that federal law is enforceable in state courts and that federal courts may in proper circumstances order state officials to comply with federal law, propositions that by no means imply any authority on the part of Congress to mandate state regulation.

Third, the United States, supported by the three sited regional compacts as *amici,* argues that the Constitution envisions a role for Congress as an arbiter of interstate disputes. The United States observes that federal courts, and this Court in particular, have frequently resolved conflicts among States. See, *e.g., Arkansas v. Oklahoma,* 503 U.S. ___, 112 S.Ct. 1046, 117 L.Ed.2d 239 (1992); *Wyoming v. Oklahoma,* 502 U.S. ___, 112 S.Ct. 789, 117 L.Ed.2d 1 (1992). Many of these disputes have involved the allocation of shared resources among the States, a category perhaps broad enough to encompass the allocation of scarce disposal space for radioactive waste. See, *e.g., Colorado v. New Mexico,* 459 U.S. 176, 103 S.Ct. 539, 74 L.Ed.2d 348 (1982); *Arizona v. California,* 373 U.S. 546, 83 S.Ct. 1468, 10 L.Ed.2d 542 (1963). The United States suggests that if the Court may resolve such interstate disputes, Congress can surely do the same under the Commerce Clause. * * *

While the Framers no doubt endowed Congress with the power to regulate interstate commerce in order to avoid further instances of the interstate trade disputes that were common under the Articles of Confederation, the Framers did *not* intend that Congress should exercise that power through the mechanism of mandating state regulation. The Constitution established Congress as "a superintending authority over the reciprocal trade" among the States, The Federalist No. 42, p. 268 (C. Rossiter ed. 1961), by empowering Congress to regulate that trade directly, not by authorizing Congress to issue trade-related orders to state governments. As Madison and Hamilton explained, "a sovereignty over sovereigns, a government over governments, a legislation for communities, as contradistinguished from individuals, as it is a solecism in theory, so in practice it is subversive of the order and ends of civil polity." *Id.,* No. 20, p. 138.

B

* * * Respondents then pose what appears at first to be a troubling question: How can a federal statute be found an unconstitutional infringement of State sovereignty when state officials consented to the statute's enactment?

The answer follows from an understanding of the fundamental purpose served by our Government's federal structure. The Constitution does not protect the sovereignty of States for the benefit of the States or state governments as abstract political entities, or even for the benefit of the public officials governing the States. To the contrary, the Constitution divides authority between federal and state governments for the protection of individuals. State sovereignty is not just an end in itself: "Rather, federalism secures to citizens the liberties that derive from the diffusion of sovereign power." *Coleman v. Thompson,* 501 U.S. ___, ___, 111 S.Ct. 2546, 2570, 115 L.Ed.2d 640 (1991) (BLACKMUN, J., dissenting). "Just as the separation and independence of the coordinate Branches of the Federal Government serves to prevent the accumulation of excessive power in any one Branch, a healthy balance of power between the States and the Federal Government will reduce the risk of tyranny and abuse from either front." *Gregory v. Ashcroft,* 501 U.S., at ___, 111 S.Ct., at 2400 (1991). See The Federalist No. 51, p. 323.

Where Congress exceeds its authority relative to the States, therefore, the departure from the constitutional plan cannot be ratified by the "consent" of state officials. An analogy to the separation of powers among the Branches of the Federal Government clarifies this point. The Constitution's division of power among the three Branches is violated where one Branch invades the territory of another, whether or not the encroached-upon Branch approves the encroachment. In *Buckley v. Valeo,* 424 U.S. 1, 118–137, 96 S.Ct. 612, 682–691, 46 L.Ed.2d 659 (1976), for instance, the Court held that the Congress had infringed the President's appointment power, despite the fact that the President himself had manifested his consent to the statute that caused the infringement by signing it into law. See *National League of Cities v. Usery,* 426 U.S., at 842, n. 12, 96 S.Ct., at 2469 n. 12. In *INS v. Chadha,* 462 U.S. 919, 944–959, 103 S.Ct. 2764, 2780–2788, 77 L.Ed.2d 317 (1983), we held that the legislative veto violated the constitutional requirement that legislation be presented to the President, despite Presidents' approval of hundreds of statutes containing a legislative veto provision. See *id.,* at 944–945, 103 S.Ct., at 2781. The constitutional authority of Congress cannot be expanded by the "consent" of the governmental unit whose domain is thereby narrowed, whether that unit is the Executive Branch or the States.

State officials thus cannot consent to the enlargement of the powers of Congress beyond those enumerated in the Constitution. Indeed, the facts of this case raise the possibility that powerful incentives might lead both federal and state officials to view departures from the federal structure to be in their personal interests. Most citizens recognize the need for radioactive waste disposal sites, but few want sites near their homes. As a result, while it would be well within the authority of either federal or state officials to choose where the disposal sites will be, it is likely to be in the political interest of each individual official to avoid being held accountable to the voters for the choice of location. If a federal official is faced with the alternatives of choosing a location or directing the States to do it, the official may well prefer the latter, as a means of shifting responsibility for the eventual decision. If a state official is faced with the same set of alternatives—choosing a location or having Congress direct the choice of a location—the state official may also prefer the latter, as it may permit the avoidance of personal responsibility. The interests of public officials thus may not coincide with the Constitution's intergovernmental allocation of authority. Where state officials purport to submit to the direction of Congress in this manner, federalism is hardly being advanced.

Nor does the State's prior support for the Act estop it from asserting the Act's unconstitutionality. While New York has received the benefit of the Act in the form of a few more years of access to disposal sites in other States, New York has never joined a regional radioactive waste compact. Any estoppel implications that might flow from membership in a compact, see *West Virginia ex rel. Dyer v. Sims,* 341 U.S. 22, 35–36, 71 S.Ct. 557, 564, 95 L.Ed. 713 (1951) (Jackson, J., concurring), thus do not concern us here. The fact that the Act, like much federal legislation, embodies a compromise among the States does not elevate the Act (or the antecedent discussions among representatives of the States) to the status of an interstate agreement requiring Congress' approval under the Compact Clause. Cf. *Holmes v. Jennison,* 14 Pet. 540, 572, 10 L.Ed. 579 (1840) (plurality opinion). That a party collaborated with others in seeking legislation has never been understood to estop the party from challenging that legislation in subsequent litigation.

V

Petitioners also contend that the Act is inconsistent with the Constitution's Guarantee Clause, which directs the United States to "guarantee to every State in this Union a Republican Form of Government." U.S. Const., Art. IV, § 4. Because we have found the take title provision of the Act irreconcilable with the powers delegated to Congress by the Constitution and hence with the Tenth Amendment's reservation to the States of those powers not delegated to the Federal Government, we need only address the applicability of the Guarantee Clause to the Act's other two challenged provisions.

We approach the issue with some trepidation, because the Guarantee Clause has been an infrequent basis for litigation throughout our history. In most of the cases in which the Court has been asked to apply the Clause, the Court has found the claims presented to be nonjusticiable under the "political question" doctrine. * * *

More recently, the Court has suggested that perhaps not all claims under the Guarantee Clause present nonjusticiable political questions. * * *

We need not resolve this difficult question today. Even if we assume that petitioners' claim is justiciable, neither the monetary incentives provided by the Act nor the possibility that a State's waste producers may find themselves excluded from the disposal sites of another State can reasonably be said to deny any State a republican form of government. As we have seen, these two incentives represent permissible conditional exercises of Congress' authority under the Spending and Commerce Clauses respectively, in forms that have now grown commonplace. Under each, Congress offers the States a legitimate choice rather than issuing an unavoidable command. The States thereby retain the ability to set their legislative agendas; state government officials remain accountable to the local electorate. The twin threats imposed by the first two challenged provisions of the Act—that New York may miss out on a share of federal spending or that those generating radioactive waste within New York may lose out-of-state disposal outlets—do not pose any realistic risk of altering the form or the method of functioning of New York's government. Thus even indulging the assumption that the Guarantee Clause provides a basis upon which a State or its subdivisions may sue to enjoin the enforcement of a federal statute, petitioners have not made out such a claim in this case.

VI

* * *

It is apparent in light of these principles that the take title provision may be severed without doing violence to the rest of the Act. The Act is still operative and it still serves Congress' objective of encouraging the States to attain local or regional self-sufficiency in the disposal of low level radioactive waste. It still includes two incentives that coax the States along this road. A State whose radioactive waste generators are unable to gain access to disposal sites in other States may encounter considerable internal pressure to provide for the disposal of waste, even without the prospect of taking title. The sited regional compacts need not accept New York's waste after the seven-year transition period expires, so any burden caused by New York's failure to secure a disposal site will not be borne by the residents of other States. The purpose of the Act is not defeated by the invalidation of the take title provision, so we may leave the remainder of the Act in force.

VII

Some truths are so basic that, like the air around us, they are easily overlooked. Much of the Constitution is concerned with setting forth the form of our government, and the courts have traditionally invalidated measures deviating from that form. The result may appear "formalistic" in a given case to partisans of the measure at issue, because such measures are typically the product of the era's perceived necessity. But the Constitution protects us from our own best intentions: It divides power among sovereigns and among branches of government precisely so that we may resist the temptation to concentrate power in one location as an expedient solution to the crisis of the day. The shortage of disposal sites for radioactive waste is a pressing national problem, but a judiciary that licensed extra-constitutional government with each issue of comparable gravity would, in the long run, be far worse.

States are not mere political subdivisions of the United States. State governments are neither regional offices nor administrative agencies of the Federal Government. The positions occupied by state officials appear nowhere on the Federal Government's most detailed organizational chart. The Constitution instead "leaves to the several States a residuary and inviolable sovereignty," The Federalist No. 39, p. 245 (C. Rossiter ed. 1961), reserved explicitly to the States by the Tenth Amendment.

Whatever the outer limits of that sovereignty may be, one thing is clear: The Federal Government may not compel the States to enact or administer a federal regulatory program. The Constitution permits both the Federal Government and the States to enact legislation regarding the disposal of low level radioactive waste. The Constitution enables the Federal Government to pre-empt state regulation contrary to federal interests, and it permits the Federal Government to hold out incentives to the States as a means of encouraging them to adopt suggested regulatory schemes. It does not, however, authorize Congress simply to direct the States to provide for the disposal of the radioactive waste generated within their borders. While there may be many constitutional methods of achieving regional self-sufficiency in radioactive waste disposal, the method Congress has chosen is not one of them. The judgment of the Court of Appeals is accordingly

Affirmed in part and reversed in part.

JUSTICE WHITE, with whom JUSTICE BLACKMUN and JUSTICE STEVENS join, concurring in part and dissenting in part.

* * *

Note

See generally, *Symposium, Federalism's Future,* 47 Vand.L.Rev. 1205 (1994).

C. FEDERALLY DERIVED LOCAL GOVERNMENT JURISDICTION—INSULATED FROM STATE CONTROL

p. 352: Add to Note 4, after "Accord" and before "Scenic Hudson"

PUD No. 1 of Jefferson County v. Washington Department of Ecology, ___ U.S. ___, 114 S.Ct. 1900, 128 L.Ed.2d 716 (1994) (state environmental agency properly conditioned permit for hydroelectric project on maintenance of minimum stream flows to protect salmon and steelhead runs).

D. FEDERAL INDUCEMENTS TO STATE AND LOCAL GOVERNMENT ACTS OR FORBEARANCE

p. 352: Add to the first paragraph

See also the Violent Crime Control and Law Enforcement Act of 1994, P.L. 103–322, §§ 30201 et seq., providing for federal payments to local governments for their use in carrying out specified purposes.

E. FEDERAL PREEMPTION OF LOCAL GOVERNMENT ACTS AND AUTHORITY

p. 356: Add to Note 1

After the principal case, Congress expressly provided that the proprietary rights and powers of municipal airport owners were not preempted by federal law. 49 U.S.C.A. § 1305(b)(1). This action, in turn, was repealed on July 5, 1994. PL 103–272, § 7(b). See 49 U.S.C.A. § 40101 et seq.

p. 357: Add to the third paragraph of Note 3

See also Coparr, Ltd. v. City of Boulder, 942 F.2d 724 (10th Cir.1991) (FIFRA did not preempt city's pesticide ordinance requiring notice of commercial applicators). [The *Mortier* citation should read 501 U.S. 597, 111 S.Ct. 2476, 115 L.Ed.2d 532 (1991).]

p. 358: Add to Note 4

Cf. Morales v. Trans World Airlines, Inc., 504 U.S. 374, 112 S.Ct. 2031, 119 L.Ed.2d 157 (1992) (application of state consumer protection statutes to prohibit deceptive airline fare advertising held preempted by 1978 federal Airline Deregulation Act).

p. 358: Add new Note 6

6. **Preemption and Treaties.** Both the North American Free Trade Agreement and the General Agreement On Tariffs and Trade (ending the Uruguay Round of negotiations) raise the possibility that, whether the issue be the environment or taxation, international implications of state and local action will cause other parties to invoke dispute provisions. The disputes may be resolved adversely to the United States, which, in order to avoid agreement sanctions, may invoke its constitutional powers to limit state or local government actions that are deemed inconsistent with U.S. international obligations, with a consequent loss of state sovereignty or local autonomy. See, e.g., Dan R. Bucks, "Trade Trouble Ahead," State Government News, May 1994, at 6; Robert Stumberg, "NAFTA Rewrites Status of States," State Government News, May 1994, at 10; Kathleen Tammaro, "Why the

States Should Worry About GATT," in Policy Alternatives on the Environment 7 (Center For Policy Alternatives 1992).

F. FEDERAL REGULATION OF AND LIMITATIONS ON LOCAL GOVERNMENT ACTIVITY

p. 364: Add after the first paragraph in Note 1

When prices or rates are initially set by the private parties, the necessary steps to show actual government involvement require government's active supervision of the private actors. Federal Trade Commission v. Ticor Title Insurance Co., ___ U.S. ___, 112 S.Ct. 2169, 119 L.Ed.2d 410 (1992).

p. 365: Add to Note 1

The federal antitrust laws have left insurance regulation to the states, except in specified conspiracy circumstances. Efforts to change this are intensifying. In the meantime, several states have responded to the steep increase in government insurance costs and occasional unavailability of government insurance by investigating and alleging conspiracy in violation of the federal antitrust laws. While the theories of the suits survived Supreme Court review, the Court held that domestic insurers did not lose their McCarran–Ferguson Act immunity to federal antitrust regulation simply because they agreed or acted with foreign reinsurers allegedly not regulated by state laws. Hartford Fire Insurance Co. v. California, ___ U.S. ___, 113 S.Ct. 2891, 125 L.Ed.2d 612 (1993). The parties settled the case upon defendants' payment of $36 million. See The Washington Post, October 7, 1994, at A4.

State and local governments have actively litigated in a number of areas attempting to lower costs of their operations imposed by private markets. For example, shortly after the settlement of the insurance cases, governments reached agreement with air lines that will help to reduce near-term costs of official travel.

p. 365: The principal case was affirmed by the Second Circuit. Replace the lower court opinion with the following

B.F. GOODRICH COMPANY v. MURTHA

United States Court of Appeals, Second Circuit, 1992.
958 F.2d 1192.

CARDAMONE, CIRCUIT JUDGE:

This appeal deals with the disposal of municipal solid waste that contains hazardous substances and as such is one piece of the national environmental problem. The problem is precipitated by the presence of over 200 municipal landfills, comprising about 20 percent of the more than 1,000 sites, that pose sufficient environmental concerns to warrant priority in federal cleanup efforts. *See generally* Interim Municipal Settlement Policy, 54 Fed.Reg. 51,071 (1989). Whether, when, and at what cost this environmental muddle will be resolved is unknown; but to maintain Congress' comprehensive statutory chain of responsibility it is essential that one step at a time be taken.

To take that step on this appeal we must carefully analyze the Comprehensive Environmental Response, Compensation, and Liability Act of 1980 (CERCLA or Act), 42 U.S.C. § 9601, *et seq.,* as amended by the Superfund Amendments and Reauthorization Act of 1986 (Superfund Amendments), Pub.L. No. 99–499, 100 Stat. 1613 *et seq.,* and while remaining aware of the interaction of CERCLA with other federal environmental statutes—in this case primarily the Resource Conservation and Recovery Act (Resource and Recovery Act or RCRA), 42 U.S.C. § 6901, *et seq.*—determine what CERCLA defines as hazardous substances, and whether CERCLA imposes liability on a municipality which arranges for the disposal or treatment of municipal solid waste that contains primarily household waste.

BACKGROUND

At the center of this litigation lie the Beacon Heights and Laurel Park landfills, both located in Connecticut, designated as Superfund sites on a National Priority List by the Environmental Protection Agency (EPA). Four actions, now consolidated, were commenced separately in 1987 by the EPA, the State of Connecticut Department of Environmental Protection, Uniroyal Chemical Company, Inc., and a coalition of corporations led by B.F. Goodrich Company (collectively, plaintiffs). Plaintiffs sought reimbursement for past and future cleanup costs from the owners or operators of the landfills, including Terrence and Harold Murtha and their several corporations (collectively, Murtha).

In turn, Murtha commenced third-party actions seeking contribution or indemnification and other statutory and common law relief against approximately 200 third-party defendants. Among the third-party defendants are the Connecticut municipal appellants. They include the cities and/or towns of Ansonia, Beacon Falls, Bethany, Hamden, Killingworth, Middlebury, Milford, New Haven, Orange, Plymouth, Seymour, Shelton, Stamford, Stratford, Thomaston, Waterbury, Watertown, Westport, Woodbury, the borough of Naugatuck, the Housing Authorities of New Haven and Watertown, and the Connecticut Resources Recovery Authority.

In 1988 the district court permitted plaintiffs to amend their complaints and add the third-party defendants as defendants in the original action. Fundamental to both the original and the third-party actions are the allegations that the municipal defendants arranged for the disposal and/or treatment of hazardous substances at the two landfills and are therefore subject to liability under § 9607 of CERCLA for a share of past and future cleanup costs, now estimated to exceed $47.9 million.

After serving answers denying liability, the municipal defendants as a group moved for summary judgment arguing that, as a matter of law, their generation and collection of municipal solid waste did not subject them to liability under CERCLA. The United States District Court for the District of Connecticut (Dorsey, J.) denied this motion in a judgment dated January 8, 1991. *B.F. Goodrich Co. v. Murtha,* 754 F.Supp. 960 (D.Conn.1991). It held that CERCLA does not contain any exemption for municipal waste, and that the exclusion for household solid waste found in the Resource and Recovery Act is not incorporated into the CERCLA definition of hazardous substances. It held further that a municipality disposing of hazardous substances at a site where there is a release or threatened release of such substances may be liable under § 9607 and that plaintiffs had raised genuine issues of material fact as to whether the municipal defendants' waste contained hazardous substances covered by CERCLA. The municipalities appeal from the judgment denying them summary judgment. We affirm.

DISCUSSION

The focus of our inquiry is the question of municipal liability under CERCLA for arranging for the disposal or treatment of municipal solid waste. Procedurally, we review a denial of appellants' motion for summary judgment; summary judgment may appropriately be granted only if the record demonstrates that there is no genuine issue as to any material fact and that the movant is entitled to a judgment as a matter of law. Fed.R.Civ.P.Rule 56(c); *Celotex Corp. v. Catrett,* 477 U.S. 317, 330, 106 S.Ct. 2548, 2556, 91 L.Ed.2d 265 (1986) (Brennan, J., dissenting). Appellants do not seriously dispute the district court's finding that genuine issues of material fact exist, *i.e.,* that plaintiffs raised a genuine issue, unrefuted by the municipalities, as to the existence of CERCLA-defined hazardous substances in the municipalities' solid waste. *See* 754 F.Supp. at 968–72. Rather the municipal defendants argue that CERCLA provides plaintiffs no grounds for relief and, as a result, the municipalities are entitled to judgment as a matter of law.

At the center of our discussion is the subject of municipal solid waste which, while possibly containing material from commercial and industrial sources, is primarily composed of household waste. *See* 54 Fed.Reg. at 51,075. Despite the tremendous volume of household waste, surveys generally reveal that it contains very low concentrations—less than 1 percent by weight—of substances the EPA considers hazardous to the environment or to public health. *See* Ferrey, *The Toxic Time Bomb: Municipal Liability for the Cleanup of Hazardous Waste,* 57 Geo.Wash. L.Rev. 197, 200–10 (1988). Yet, even though household waste has a low concentration of hazardous substances, when the EPA determines that a cleanup under CERCLA is warranted the costs of cleanup at municipal landfills may be greater than at similar industrial or commercial toxic waste sites due to household waste's greater volume and reduced toxicity. With this in mind, we turn to the statutory framework.

I Statutory Framework Under CERCLA

In CERCLA Congress enacted a broad remedial statute designed to enhance the authority of the EPA to respond effectively and promptly to toxic pollutant spills that threatened the environment and human health. The EPA is authorized to commence "response actions" to abate any actual or threatened releases of hazardous substances, § 9604(a)(1), and a federal Superfund exists to pay for mandated clean-ups. Response actions include remedial efforts to prevent or minimize releases as well as attempts to remove hazardous substances entirely. The Act also authorizes the EPA to recover its costs from responsible parties as a means to replenish and maintain the Superfund. *See* § 9607(a)(4)(A). Alternatively, the EPA may seek to compel potentially responsible parties to commence private response actions if there is an "imminent and substantial endangerment to the public health." § 9606(a). Such parties may recover a portion of their response costs from other potentially responsible parties. § 9613(f).

CERCLA imposes strict liability. *See Tanglewood East Homeowners v. Charles–Thomas, Inc.,* 849 F.2d 1568, 1572 (5th Cir.1988); *State of New York v. Shore Realty Corp.,* 759 F.2d 1032, 1042 (2d Cir.1985). Where the environmental harm is indivisible liability is joint and several. *See O'Neil v. Picillo,* 883 F.2d 176, 178–79 (1st Cir.1989), *cert. denied sub nom. American Cyanamid Co. v. O'Neil,* 493 U.S. 1071, 110 S.Ct. 1115, 107 L.Ed.2d 1022 (1990); *United States v. R.W. Meyer, Inc.,* 889 F.2d 1497, 1506–08 (6th Cir.1989), *cert. denied,* 494 U.S. 1057, 110 S.Ct. 1527, 108 L.Ed.2d 767 (1990). CERCLA establishes four classes of responsible parties liable for the costs of responding to releases or threatened releases of hazardous substances. These include past and present owners or operators of facilities, transporters of hazardous substances, and those, such as appellants, who generate or arrange for the disposal or treatment of hazardous substances. § 9607(a). The Act's broad reach extends liability to all those contributing to—from generation through disposal—the problems caused by hazardous substances.

Because it is a remedial statute, CERCLA must be construed liberally to effectuate its two primary goals: (1) enabling the EPA to respond efficiently and expeditiously to toxic spills, and (2) holding those parties responsible for the releases liable for the costs of the cleanup. In that way Congress envisioned the EPA's costs would be recouped, the Superfund preserved, and the taxpayers not required to shoulder the financial burden of a nationwide cleanup. *See United States v. Aceto Agric. Chems. Corp.,* 872 F.2d 1373, 1377, 1380 (8th Cir.1989) (quoting *Dedham Water Co. v. Cumberland Farms Dairy, Inc.,* 805 F.2d 1074, 1081 (1st Cir.1986)); *City of New York v. Exxon Corp.,* 744 F.Supp. 474, 485 (S.D.N.Y.1990). Potential affirmative defenses are limited to those listed in § 9607(b). *See Shore Realty,* 759 F.2d at 1048–49; *United States v. Hooker Chems. & Plastics Corp.,* 680 F.Supp. 546, 557–58 (W.D.N.Y.1988). Hence, liability under § 9607(a) is precluded only by a defense that the release or threatened release was caused solely by an act of God, an act of war, or certain acts or omissions of third parties other than those with whom a defendant has a contractual relationship. *See* § 9607(b). Undeterred by the inapplicability of any of these affirmative defenses to the present case, appellants insist that a municipality may not be held liable under CERCLA, § 9607(a)(3), for arranging for the disposal or treatment of municipal solid waste because that waste is not defined as a hazardous substance under the Act.

A *prima facie* cause of action under CERCLA requires a plaintiff to establish: (1) defendant fits one of the four classes of responsible parties outlined in § 9607(a); (2) the site is a facility; (3) there is a release or threatened release of hazardous substances at the facility; (4) the plaintiff incurred costs responding to the release or threatened release; and (5) the costs and response actions conform to the National Contingency Plan set up under the Act and administered by the EPA in order to prioritize hazardous substance release sites throughout the nation. *See Shore Realty,* 759 F.2d at 1043. The municipalities' summary judgment motion turns on whether their arranging for the disposal of municipal solid waste satisfies the first and third elements.

II Responsible Party

As to the first element, it is clear that a municipality may be liable as a potentially responsible party if it arranges for the disposal of hazardous substances. CERCLA expressly includes municipalities, states, and other political subdivisions within its definition of persons who can incur such liability under § 9607. § 9601(21). The Supreme Court has held that the "cascade of plain language" clearly demonstrates Congress aimed to abrogate sovereign immunity for the states. *Pennsylvania v. Union Gas Co.,* 491 U.S. 1, 7–13, 109 S.Ct. 2273, 2277–80, 105 L.Ed.2d 1 (1989). As further evidence of Congress' plan that municipalities be held as responsible parties, CERCLA includes limited exceptions to potential municipal liability. Where, as an "owner or operator," a municipality acquires ownership or control of a facility involuntarily as a result of its sovereign function, § 9601(20)(D), or where a municipality acts in response to an emergency caused by the release of hazardous substances from a facility owned by another party and does not act with gross negligence or willful misconduct, § 9607(d)(2), no liability attaches. These express exceptions to liability are strong evidence that municipalities are otherwise subject to CERCLA liability.

* * *

* * * To construe CERCLA as providing an exemption for municipalities arranging for the disposal of municipal solid waste that contains hazardous substances simply because the municipality undertakes such action in furtherance of its sovereign status would create an unwarranted break in the statutory chain of responsibility.

III Hazardous Substance

A. CERCLA Definition

Since release or threatened release is not here at issue, discussion of the third element—which is the principal subject of this opinion—turns to whether municipal solid waste falls within CERCLA's definition of hazardous substance. * * *

The Act's silence on the subject of municipal solid waste is not evidence that such should be excluded from the definition of hazardous substances. To the contrary, § 9601(14)'s comprehensive definition of hazardous substances, coupled with the specific exclusions of oil and natural gas, leads to the opposite conclusion. Municipal waste need not be listed by name—instead of its constituent components—to fall within the Act. For us to consider the whole separate from its hazardous constituent parts would be to engage in semantic sophistry. When a mixture or waste solution contains hazardous substances, that mixture is itself hazardous for purposes of determining CERCLA liability. *See, e.g., Eagle–Picher,* 759 F.2d at 930–31; *Exxon Corp.,* 744 F.Supp. at 483–84; *Carolawn,* 21 E.R.C. at 2126. Liability under CERCLA depends only on the presence in any form of listed hazardous substances. Hence, if a municipality arranges for the disposal or treatment of waste containing substances listed as hazardous in any of the four identified environmental statutes or in Table 302.4, it may be held liable for contribution or response costs under the Act if a subsequent release or threatened release requires cleanup efforts.

B. Resource and Recovery Act Exemption for Household Waste

The municipalities strenuously insist further that the exemption for household hazardous waste—promulgated by EPA and subsequently confirmed in part by Congress—from certain regulatory requirements under the Resource and Recovery Act extends, through incorporation by reference, to the definition of hazardous substance under CERCLA. This latter argument, as the former, is not persuasive. The Resource and Recovery Act is designed primarily to regulate on-going treatment, storage, and disposal of solid and hazardous wastes. *See Aceto Agric. Chems.,* 872 F.2d at 1376–77. Pursuant to RCRA, EPA promulgated two distinct regulatory systems for the transportation of wastes and the operation of waste storage and disposal facilities: one for *solid* wastes (under Subpart D of RCRA, §§ 6941–49a); and the other for *hazardous* wastes (under Subpart C of RCRA, §§ 6921–39b). *Hazardous wastes,* identified in 40 C.F.R. §§ 261.30–33, are subject to more stringent standards than are solid wastes.

"In regulations identifying and listing hazardous wastes subject to the RCRA Subtitle C regulations, EPA excluded for regulatory purposes certain solid wastes from the definition of hazardous wastes, *even though these wastes might otherwise be considered hazardous wastes.*" Notification of Treatment, Storage and Disposal Facilities, 46 Fed.Reg. 22,144, 22,145 (1981) (emphasis added). The EPA included household wastes, under 40 C.F.R. § 261.4(b)(1), pursuant to Congressional plan, among those wastes excluded from the Resource and Recovery Act's Subpart C hazardous waste regulations. Subsequently, Congress "clarified" the household waste exclusion with respect to resource recovery facility regulations under that Act for the recovery of energy through the mass burning of municipal waste by adding § 3001(i). That section provides that such facilities are not deemed to be handling hazardous wastes if they receive only household waste and other solid waste not containing hazardous waste. § 6921(i). From this statutory exclusion, appellants assert that municipal solid waste cannot be a hazardous waste under CERCLA.

The household waste exclusion was promulgated pursuant to a Congressional scheme that such waste not be subjected to the same stringent standards during the day-to-day management of transportation, storage and disposal. The legislative history relied on by the EPA in promulgating the household waste exclusion follows Congress' narrow aim to exclude specific waste streams from Resource and Recovery Act coverage. * * * To construe this exemption to apply also to CERCLA would frustrate that Act's broad remedial purposes as well as unjustifiably expand the scope of the Resource and Recovery Act's regulations.

Congress and the EPA have carefully distinguished between *wastes,* to which the Resource and Recovery Act applies, and *substances,* to which CERCLA applies. * * * This statutory and regulatory distinction is a substantial one and should be preserved, absent a clear legislative intent to the contrary.

In addition, application of the Resource and Recovery Act's regulations turns in part upon threshold quantity or concentration requirements—considerations which are irrelevant in defining hazardous substances under CERCLA. * * *

Nor does including wastes that are not subject to the stringent Subpart C regulations under the Resource and Recovery Act within the definition of hazardous substances under CERCLA create a conflict between the two statutes. Subpart C imposes tough standards for operating *active* toxic waste sites, but does not cover sites operated *prior* to its enactment, *nor* sites where the owner is unknown or bankrupt, *nor* does it address spills, illegal dumping or releases generally. RCRA is preventative; CERCLA is curative. It does not follow that because the environmental risk posed by household waste is deemed insufficient to justify the most stringent regulations governing its day-to-day handling that the environmental harm caused when that risk is realized is insufficient to require holding liable those responsible for that harm. In fact, the EPA expressly recommended that household waste, though exempt from subtitle C regulations, should be managed as a hazardous waste. EPA Directive 9574.00–1 at p. 2. The agency has also noted that the additional safeguards of management under Subpart C regulations merely *reduce* the likelihood of liability arising under CERCLA. *See id. See also* Solid Waste Disposal Facility Criteria, 56 Fed.Reg. 50,978 (1991) (to be codified at 40 C.F.R. pts. 257, 258) (final rule creating new criteria, more stringent than Subpart D but less stringent than Subpart C, for municipal solid waste landfills). Even total compliance with Subpart C regulations will not prevent releases or avoid CERCLA liability. Similarly, the increased likelihood of a release occurring pursuant to Subpart D regulations does not necessarily suggest a proportional increased likelihood that a response will be warranted under CERCLA, because of the small concentrations of hazardous substances found in wastes regulated under that Subpart.

Other courts have concluded that exemptions from Resource and Recovery Act coverage do not extend so far as to exclude those materials from the definition of hazardous substances under CERCLA. *See, e.g., Eagle–Picher,* 759 F.2d at 927 (exclusion in § 9601(14)(C) for material suspended from RCRA regulation by Congress restricted in application to that subsection). We agree that had Congress aimed to exempt such materials from § 9601(14) it could have placed the exemption explicitly in the section exactly as it did with petroleum and natural gas. *See id.; see also State of Idaho v. Hanna Mining Co.,* 699 F.Supp. 827, 833 (D.Idaho 1987), *aff'd,* 882 F.2d 392 (9th Cir.1989); *Metate Asbestos Corp.,* 584 F.Supp. at 1147 (asbestos mill and mine wastes statutorily exempt from RCRA are hazardous substances under CERCLA, §§ 9601(14)(D), (E)); *Transportation Leasing Co. v. California,* 32 E.R.C. 1499, 1501, 1990 WL 300777 (C.D.Cal.1990) (RCRA exemption for household waste does not extend to the CERCLA definition for hazardous substances). Where a substance is not exempted from the definition of hazardous substance set forth in CERCLA, but merely is exempted from regulation under a separate statute, we decline to incorporate the exemption into § 9601(14). A regulatory exemption cannot take precedence over Congress' concerns spelled out in § 9601(14) of the Act.

* * *

Contrary to the municipalities' argument, the EPA's exemption of household wastes from *notification* requirements under CERCLA does not suggest that disparate treatment of municipal solid waste under the Act's *liability* provisions is appropriate.

* * *

Examination of the legislative history reveals no further discussion relating to whether municipal solid waste could trigger liability under CERCLA. Rather, most of the debate upon which the municipalities would have us rely focused on Congress' scheme to hold the parties responsible for releases liable for the ensuing cleanup costs, and not taxpayers generally. * * *

* * * To impose CERCLA liability on these local governments results, appellants continue, in taxpayers within their jurisdictions shouldering the costs of cleanup. We agree that this will inevitably be the result, but are unable to agree that it is adverse to Congress' aim. To the contrary, a narrow interpretation of CERCLA that exempts municipalities arranging for the disposal of municipal solid waste from liability increases the probability that cleanup costs will never be recovered, and will be paid instead from the Superfund funded in part by the taxpayers at large. To accept the municipalities' argument that the municipal waste exemption in the Resource and Recovery Act should apply to CERCLA would free a potentially responsible party from liability, in blatant contravention of the statute's goals.

Although municipalities do not benefit in a proprietary sense from arranging for the disposal of municipal solid waste, their taxpayers do obtain a benefit—given the necessity of disposal of such waste. Thus, our refusal to exempt such waste from the definition of hazardous substance under CERCLA cannot be said to create an irrational and clearly unintended result. *See United States v. Rutherford,* 442 U.S. 544, 555, 99 S.Ct. 2470, 2477, 61 L.Ed.2d 68 (1979). On this question, review of the legislative history reveals a picture more confusing than pellucid, and a Congressional purpose not so discernible that it should cause us to depart from the plain meaning of § 9601(14).

* * *

Other EPA pronouncements point out its unambiguous position and provide strong support for the argument that it does not believe Congress planned for municipal waste to be exempt from CERCLA. * * * We conclude consequently that the EPA emphatically construes CERCLA to impose liability on municipalities disposing of household waste that contains hazardous substances.

Conclusion

Plaintiffs have sufficiently established a *prima facie* cause of action under CERCLA, including the first and third elements challenged by the appellants on this appeal. We are aware that holding the municipal defendants as responsible parties and including municipal solid waste within the definition of hazardous substances will have far reaching implications for municipalities and their taxpayers. But burdensome consequences are not sufficient grounds to judicially graft an exemption onto a statute, a graft that would thwart the language, purpose, and agency interpretation of the statute.

Appellant municipalities are not without recourse to avoid inequitable and disproportionate burdens that may arise from their liability as third-party contributors. Courts have the authority to "allocate response costs among liable parties using such equitable factors as the court determines are appropriate." § 9613(f)(1). An array of equitable factors may be considered in this allocation process, including the relative volume and toxicity of the substances for disposal of which the municipalities arranged, the relative cleanup costs incurred as a result of these wastes, the degree of care exercised by each party with respect to the hazardous substances, and the financial resources of the parties involved. Consequently, the amount of liability imposed will not necessarily be a function solely of the total volume of municipal waste disposed of in the landfills, but rather will be a function of the extent to which municipal dumping of hazardous substances both engendered the necessity, and contributed to the costs, of cleanup.

In sum, the plain meaning of CERCLA, its stated purposes, the absence of a clearly expressed Congressional aim to the contrary, and unequivocal agency policy support the view that the municipal defendants are responsible parties under the Act and that the definition of hazardous substance under CERCLA includes municipal solid waste if that waste contains a hazardous substance, found in any amount, that is listed in any of the subsections of § 9601(14). The municipal defendants are not entitled to summary judgment as a matter of law declaring otherwise.

The judgment is affirmed.

p. 376: Add to Note 2

The Court has also held that ash generated by incineration of municipal solid waste was subject to the regulatory scheme governing hazardous waste. City of Chicago v. Environmental Defense Fund, ___ U.S. ___, 114 S.Ct. 1588, 128 L.Ed.2d 302 (1994).

Congressional proposals to relieve municipalities and local taxpayers of liability for clean-up costs of hazardous waste sites (see, e.g., S.343/H.R. 870, H.R. 2767; 103d Cong., 139 Cong.Rec. § 1385–02, § 1455, 1993 WL 27083, pp. 521 et seq.) died as the session ended. Federal imposition of local government liability for clean-up costs exemplifies the challenges that unfunded federal mandates present to the federal-state-local relationship. Consider the impact on state and local governments of the self-evaluation, transition, and accessibility requirements of the Americans With Disabilities Act. See, e.g., Tyler v. City of Manhattan, 157 F.R.D. 508 (D.Kan.1994) (handicapped-accessible parking); Kinney v. Yerusalim, 812 F.Supp. 547 (E.D.Pa.1993) affirmed 9 F.3d 1067 (3d Cir.1993), cert. denied, ___ U.S. ___, 114 S.Ct. 1545, 128 L.Ed.2d 196 (1994) (resurfacing city street is "alteration" obliging city to install curb ramps and slopes under ADA regulations). Like the states, the federal government is now attempting to address the cost implications of federal requirements upon state and local governments. See Unfunded Mandate Reform Act of 1995, PL 104–4 (HR 5, 5.1 signed 3/22/95, 141 Cong.Rec.D. 407). The latter are far from satisfied that the problem has been resolved. See generally, Symposium, Regulatory Federalism, 18 Intergovernmental Perspective 7 (A.C.I.R.1992).

p. 376: Add to Note 3

The Supreme Court continues to apply the dormant Commerce Clause to state and local efforts to deal with pressing waste problems. See, e.g., Chemical Waste Management, Inc. v. Hunt, 504 U.S. 334, 112 S.Ct. 2009, 119 L.Ed.2d 12 (1992) (higher fee for disposal in Alabama of hazardous out-of-state waste discriminates against interstate commerce); Fort Gratiot Sanitary Landfill, Inc. v. Michigan Department of Natural Resources, 504 U.S. 353, 112 S.Ct. 2019, 119 L.Ed.2d 139 (1992) (law prohibiting private landfill operators from accepting solid waste generated in another county, state, or country unless explicitly authorized by receiving county discriminates against interstate commerce); Oregon Waste Systems v. Department of Environmental Quality, ___ U.S. ___, 114 S.Ct. 1345, 128 L.Ed.2d 13 (1994) (higher surcharge on in-state disposal of out-of-state solid waste is facially discriminatory and is not saved by assertion that it is a compensatory tax reflective of additional general taxes paid by in-state firms); C & A Carbone, Inc. v. Town of Clarkstown, N.Y., ___ U.S. ___, 114 S.Ct. 1677, 128 L.Ed.2d 399 (1994) (Court held ordinance that reflected town's effort to guarantee a minimum waste flow to private company that built a transfer station in the town, by requiring all non-hazardous solid waste to be deposited there, discriminated against interstate commerce).

As suggested by the Michigan statute invalidated above, the waste problem is one of international dimensions. See Vicki Arroyo Cochran, Note: Waste Wars: The Fight Over Hazardous Waste Importation, 6 Geo. Int'l.Env'l L.Rev. 191, 203 (1993).

Michigan exporters of radioactive waste could not get a Michigan federal court to order out-of-state dump sites to accept their waste, because long-arm jurisdiction did not reach the dump-site officials of other states. Michigan Coalition of Radioactive Material Users v. Griepentrog, 954 F.2d 1174 (6th Cir.1992). "Market participant" cities may burden their own markets but may not impose burdens on other markets. Thus, a city's effort to prevent trash hauler from disposing of solid waste at a facility other than that designated in the municipal ordinance may raise interstate-commerce issues. City of Auburn v. Tri–State Rubbish, Inc., 630 A.2d 227 (Me.1993).

p. 381: Add to Note 1

Redistricting following the decennial census inevitably raises a number of distinct constitutional and statutory questions. To prove a violation of the Voting Rights Act, challengers must meet the conditions set forth in Thornburg v. Gingles, 478 U.S. 30, 106 S.Ct. 2752, 92 L.Ed.2d 25 (1986). In Johnson v. De Grandy, ___ U.S. ___, 114 S.Ct. 2647, 129 L.Ed.2d 775 (1994), a state-court-approved redistricting was challenged in the federal courts. The Supreme Court held that proof of the *Gingles* factors, while necessary to support an alleged violation of Section 2 of the Voting Rights Act, may not alone always be sufficient, and that vote dilution cannot be inferred from the mere failure to guaranty minority (there Hispanics) voters *maximum* political influence.

In Voinovich v. Quilter, ___ U.S. ___, 113 S.Ct. 1149, 122 L.Ed.2d 500 (1993), newly redrawn voting districts were challenged on the theory that packing minorities into a few districts diminished the influence they would have if they were placed as a significant voting block in white majority districts. The Court held that the Voting Rights Act does not prohibit the creation of legislative districts that are dominated by a minority group. The plaintiffs here failed to prove that there was white-majority bloc voting sufficient to frustrate the election of the minority group's choice. Earlier, the Court had held that such challenges also had to show the political cohesiveness of the minority group. Growe v. Emison, ___ U.S. ___, 113 S.Ct. 1075, 122 L.Ed.2d 388 (1993).

In Presley v. Etowah County Commission, 502 U.S. 491, 112 S.Ct. 820, 117 L.Ed.2d 51 (1992), African–American county commissioners, newly elected from districts established by consent decrees, asserted that their respective counties had failed to obtain required preclearance under Section 5 of the Voting Rights Act when, shortly after their elections but before they took office, the counties reduced each commissioner's discretionary authority over how to spend funds allocated to that commissioner's road district. The Supreme Court held that Section 5 does not cover changes other than those affecting rules governing voting and that the changes in question did not affect voting rules.

In other recent rulings, the Court held that Section 2 of the Voting Rights Act does not *ipso facto* require a county to have other than a single-commissioner form of government and that vote dilution challenges based on the size of governmental authority are not actionable under Section 2. Holder v. Hall, ___ U.S. ___, 114 S.Ct. 2581, 129 L.Ed.2d 687 (1994). Justice Thomas' controversial and heavily criticized concurring opinion asserted that the Court had for years extended the reach of the Act beyond its legislative purposes, and ought more rigorously to adhere to those purposes. Id. at ___, 114 S.Ct. at 2591.

With regard to complaints of Equal Protection discrimination, *Voinovich,* supra, reasserted the principle that, though deviations in district size of over ten percent establish a prima facie case of discrimination in violation of the Equal Protection Clause, a state may successfully rebut the charge by showing that the deviation was necessary to preserve the integrity of political subdivisions (there county boundaries).

Since racial classifications are presumptively invalid, white voters could challenge under the Equal Protection Clause newly created congressional districts designed to concentrate minority voters, where those districts gave evidence of being arbitrarily race-based. Shaw v. Reno, ___ U.S. ___, 113 S.Ct. 2816, 125 L.Ed.2d 511 (1993). On remand, the North Carolina district was upheld by the lower court. Shaw v. Hunt, 861 F.Supp. 408 (E.D.N.C. 1994). Other lower courts, however, have upheld challenges to congressional districts in Louisiana, Texas, and even in Georgia where earlier efforts had failed to receive the required Justice Department approval under Section 5 of the Voting Rights Act. Hays v. State, 862 F.Supp. 119 (W.D.La.1994); Vera v. Richards, 861 F.Supp. 1304 (S.D.Tex.1994); Johnson v. Miller, 864 F.Supp. 1354 (S.D.Ga.1994). Supreme Court review has been granted or probable jurisdiction has been noted in the Louisiana and Georgia cases, ___ U.S. ___, 115 S.Ct. 687, 130 L.Ed.2d 597 (1994); ___ U.S. ___, 115 S.Ct. 713, 130 L.Ed.2d 620 (1995), and has been sought in the North Carolina (63 U.S.L.W. 3439 (1995)) and Texas (63 U.S.L.W. 3388 (1995)) cases.

The complicated tasks involved in redistricting and drawing proportional districts, including maps and charts, are illustrated in Mellow v. Mitchell, 530 Pa. 44, 607 A.2d 204 (1992), cert. denied, ___ U.S. ___, 113 S.Ct. 88, 121 L.Ed.2d 50 (1992).

G. FEDERAL INVALIDATION OF LOCAL GOVERNMENT ACTIONS

1. OVERVIEW

p. 386: Add to the final paragraph after *Cleburne*

Evans v. Romer, 854 P.2d 1270 (Colo.1993), cert. denied, ___ U.S. ___, 114 S.Ct. 419, 126 L.Ed.2d 365, affirmed 882 P.2d 1335 (Colo.1994), cert. granted, ___ U.S. ___, 115 S.Ct. 1092, 130 L.Ed.2d 1061 (1995) (voter-approved amendment to state constitution prohibiting protection against discrimination on the basis of sexual preference voided as infringing without compelling justification on the federal constitutionally protected fundamental right to participate equally in the political process and as not narrowly tailored to serve asserted state interest in preserving religious, familial, and personal privacy, or the state's fiscal resources devoted to enforcement of other civil-rights laws).

p. 386: Add to the final paragraph after *Waller*

See also Brown v. Mahaffey, 35 F.3d 846 (3d Cir.1994) (assertion that municipal activities *intentionally* impeded access to religious meetings on private property states actionable claim regardless of whether conduct amounted to "substantial burden"); Harris v. Zion, Ill., 927 F.2d 1401 (7th Cir.1991), cert. denied, ___ U.S. ___, 112 S.Ct. 3025, 120 L.Ed.2d 897 (1992); Friedman v. Board of County Commissioners of Bernalillo, 781 F.2d 777 (10th Cir.1985), cert. denied, 476 U.S. 1169, 106 S.Ct. 2890, 90 L.Ed.2d 978 (1986) (Establishment Clause violated by use of municipal insignias with religious symbols). Compare Murray v. Austin, Texas, 947 F.2d 147 (5th Cir.1991), cert. denied, ___ U.S. ___, 112 S.Ct. 3028, 120 L.Ed.2d 899 (1992) (municipal insignias with religious symbols held not to have the primary effect of advancing religion).

3. LOCAL ELECTIONS

pp. 395–96: Add to the first paragraph in Note 1

Cf. Cane v. Worcester County, Md., 35 F.3d 921 (4th Cir.1994) (district court erred in adopting cumulative voting scheme as remedy for violation of Section 2 of the Voting Rights Act and in failing to defer appropriately to county's expressed preference for residency districts designed to assure representation of diverse areas of the county).

Add to the final paragraph in Note 1

Cf. U.S. Department of Commerce v. Montana, 503 U.S. 442, 112 S.Ct. 1415, 118 L.Ed.2d 87 (1992) (rejecting challenge to federal statute governing congressional reapportionment even though population numbers within state lines made for differences in the number of voters per representative).

p. 396: Add to Note 2

Freeman v. Pitts, 503 U.S. 467, 112 S.Ct. 1430, 118 L.Ed.2d 108 (1992) (once racial imbalance due to de jure violation has been remedied, school district is under no duty to remedy imbalance caused by demographic factors and federal court, therefore, has discretion to relinquish jurisdiction). Cf. Jenkins v. Missouri, 11 F.3d 755 (8th Cir.1993), cert. granted, ___ U.S. ___, 115 S.Ct. 41, 129 L.Ed.2d 936 (1994) (affirming district court's refusal to conclude that extensive magnet-school efforts had removed last vestiges of discrimination).

p. 396: Add to Note 3, Voter Qualifications, *Property Ownership*

In Southern California Rapid Transit District v. Bolen, 1 Cal.4th 654, 3 Cal.Rptr.2d 843, 822 P.2d 875, cert. denied, ___ U.S. ___, 112 S.Ct. 3031, 120

L.Ed.2d 901 (1992), the court found no Equal Protection violation in a statutory voting plan that restricted the vote in referenda establishing special assessment districts for planned subway stations to owners of nearby commercial property who would be the only ones subject to special assessment levies by the districts to be established.

p. 400: Add after *Quinn*

Note

Whether term limits be considered impositions on the voters' rights of free association and candidate selection or limitations on ballot access, those applicable to municipal and state offices have been upheld while those which state voters wish to apply to Congress have been struck down. Miyazawa v. City of Cincinnati, 825 F.Supp. 816 (S.D.Ohio 1993), affirmed, 45 F.3d 126 (6th Cir.1995) (municipal); Legislature v. Eu, 54 Cal.3d 492, 286 Cal.Rptr. 283, 816 P.2d 1309 (1991), cert. denied, ___ U.S. ___, 112 S.Ct. 1292, 117 L.Ed.2d 516 (1992) (state); U.S. Term Limits, Inc. v. Hill, 316 Ark. 251, 872 S.W.2d 349 (1994) (state and federal); Thorsted v. Gregoire, 841 F.Supp. 1068 (W.D.Wash.1994) (Congress). The Arkansas case has been argued in the U.S. Supreme Court. ___ U.S. ___, 114 S.Ct. 2703, 129 L.Ed.2d 832 (1994) (cert. granted). For articles on the cognate issue of campaign finance reform, see generally Symposium On Campaign Finance Reform, 94 Colum.L.Rev. 1126 (1994).

p. 403: Add new Note 2

2. In first-amendment speech and association challenges to campaign finance laws, term limits, and laws that restrict electoral activity, the courts adjudge whether the states' efforts to establish minimum thresholds to avoid ballot confusion and to promote the desired political independence are legitimately asserted, narrowly tailored, and do not unconstitutionally burden the rights of individuals to speak freely and to associate for political purposes and the rights of qualified voters to cast votes effectively. Strict scrutiny and compelling justification are the norm when the right to vote is severely restricted. In other cases, heightened scrutiny demanding substantial justification is directed to the nature of the injury, the interest asserted by the government, the effect of one on the other, and the necessity for imposing the burden rather than a less burdensome alternative, as set forth in Anderson v. Celebrezze, 460 U.S. 780, 103 S.Ct. 1564, 75 L.Ed.2d 547 (1983). See Burson v. Freeman, 504 U.S. 191, 112 S.Ct. 1846, 119 L.Ed.2d 5 (1992) (law that prohibited campaign activities on election day within 100 feet of the polling place); Burdick v. Takushi, 504 U.S. 428, 112 S.Ct. 2059, 119 L.Ed.2d 245 (1992) (law prohibiting write-in voting); McIntyre v. Ohio Elections Commission, 67 Ohio St.3d 391, 618 N.E.2d 152 (1993), cert. granted, ___ U.S. ___, 114 S.Ct. 1047, 127 L.Ed.2d 370 (1994) (statute prohibiting anonymous campaign literature). Compare Norman v. Reed, 502 U.S. 279, 112 S.Ct. 698, 116 L.Ed.2d 711 (1992) (excessive signature requirements for minor-party ballot access held unconstitutional).

Chapter VI

LOCAL POLICE POWERS

B. DIRECT LEGISLATIVE COMMANDS

1. LOCAL REGULATIONS AND FIRST AMENDMENT FREEDOM OF EXPRESSION

Overview: Classified First Amendment Issues

p. 418–19: Add to a. Forums of Protected and Unprotected Speech

Cf. Irish–American Gay, Lesbian and Bisexual Group of Boston v. Boston, 418 Mass. 238, 636 N.E.2d 1293 (1994), cert. granted, ___ U.S. ___, 115 S.Ct. 714, ___ L.Ed.2d ___ (1995) (because parade organizers never used the St. Patrick's Day parade for expressive purposes, application of Public Accommodation Law to forbid exclusion of gay marching contingent does not violate organizers' first-amendment rights).

p. 419–20: Add to "Nonverbal Expression" at top of 420

Local and state efforts to punish cross burning and other hate crimes have had to walk a careful line between invalid regulation of protected expression and valid regulation aimed at eradicating bias. *Compare* R.A.V. v. City of St. Paul, ___ U.S. ___, 112 S.Ct. 2538, 120 L.Ed.2d 305 (1992) (content-based discrimination among "fighting words"); State v. Sheldon, 332 Md. 45, 629 A.2d 753 (1993) (content based, did not survive strict scrutiny); *and* State v. Vawter, 136 N.J. 56, 642 A.2d 349 (1994) (statute does not increase underlying offense because of bias, but punishes the expression itself), *with* Florida v. Stalder, 630 So.2d 1072 (Fla.1994) (valid enhancement of penalty applying only to bias-related crimes).

p. 420: Add to "Commercial Speech"

Ibanez v. Florida Dept. of Business and Professional Reg., Bd. of Accountancy, ___ U.S. ___, 114 S.Ct. 2084, 129 L.Ed.2d 118 (1994) (attorney's use in advertising of her accountancy licensure and certification is protected commercial speech which the state may ban only if false, deceptive, or misleading).

p. 422: Add after *Young* in *"Begging and Panhandling"*

Loper v. New York City Police Dept., 999 F.2d 699 (2d Cir.1993) found that a penal law prohibiting begging in public place violated the first amendment, and distinguished *Young* which involved a limited subway site, not whole city, and an ordinance that left ample alternative means of communication.

p. 427: After "Notes"

CITY OF CINCINNATI v. DISCOVERY NETWORK, INC.

Supreme Court of the United States, 1993.
___ U.S. ___, 113 S.Ct. 1505, 123 L.Ed.2d 99.

JUSTICE STEVENS delivered the opinion of the Court.

Motivated by its interest in the safety and attractive appearance of its streets and sidewalks, the city of Cincinnati has refused to allow respondents to distribute their commercial publications through free-standing newsracks located on public property. The question presented is whether this refusal is consistent with the First Amendment. In agreement with the District Court and the Court of Appeals, we hold that it is not.

I

Respondent, Discovery Network, Inc., is engaged in the business of providing adult educational, recreational, and social programs to individuals in the Cincinnati area. It advertises those programs in a free magazine that it publishes nine times a year. Although these magazines consist primarily of promotional material pertaining to Discovery's courses, they also include some information about current events of general interest. Approximately one third of these magazines are distributed through the 38 newsracks that the city authorized Discovery to place on public property in 1989.

Respondent, Harmon Publishing Company, Inc., publishes and distributes a free magazine that advertises real estate for sale at various locations throughout the United States. The magazine contains listings and photographs of available residential properties in the greater Cincinnati area, and also includes some information about interest rates, market trends, and other real estate matters. In 1989 Harmon received the city's permission to install 24 newsracks at approved locations. About 15% of its distribution in the Cincinnati area is through those devices.

In March 1990, the city's Director of Public Works notified each of the respondents that its permit to use dispensing devices on public property was revoked, and ordered the newsracks removed within 30 days. Each notice explained that respondent's publication was a "commercial handbill" within the meaning of § 714–1–C of the Municipal Code and therefore § 714–23 of the Code prohibited its distribution on public property. Respondents were granted administrative hearings and review by the Sidewalk Appeals Committee. Although the Committee did not modify the city's position, it agreed to allow the dispensing devices to remain in place pending a judicial determination of the constitutionality of its prohibition. Respondents then commenced this litigation in the United States District Court for the Southern District of Ohio. * * * Applying that test, the Court of Appeals agreed with the District Court that the burden placed on speech "cannot be justified by the paltry gains in safety and beauty achieved by the ordinance." *Ibid.* The importance of the Court of Appeals decision, together with the dramatic growth in the use of newsracks throughout the country, prompted our grant of certiorari. 503 U.S. ___, 112 S.Ct. 1290, 117 L.Ed.2d 514 (1992).

II

There is no claim in this case that there is anything unlawful or misleading about the contents of respondents' publications. Moreover, respondents do not challenge their characterization as "commercial speech." Nor do respondents question the substantiality of the city's interest in safety and esthetics. It was, therefore, proper for the District Court and the Court of Appeals to judge the validity of the city's prohibition under the standard we set forth in *Central Hudson* and *Fox.*[11] It was the city's burden to establish a "reasonable fit" between its legitimate interests in safety and esthetics and its choice of a limited and selective prohibition of newsracks as the means chosen to serve those interests.[12]

There is ample support in the record for the conclusion that the city did not "establish the reasonable fit we require." *Fox,* 492 U.S., at 480, 109 S.Ct., at 3035. The ordinance on which it relied was an outdated prohibition against the distribution of any commercial handbills on

11. While the Court of Appeals ultimately applied the standards set forth in *Central Hudson* and *Fox,* its analysis at least suggested that those standards might not apply to the type of regulation at issue in this case. For if commercial speech is entitled to "lesser protection" only when the regulation is aimed at either the content of the speech or the particular adverse effects stemming from that content, it would seem to follow that a regulation that is not so directed should be evaluated under the standards applicable to regulations on fully protected speech, not the more lenient standards by which we judge regulations on commercial speech. Because we conclude that Cincinnati's ban on commercial newsracks cannot withstand scrutiny under *Central Hudson* and *Fox,* we need not decide whether that policy should be subjected to more exacting review.

12. As we stated in *Fox:*

"[W]hile we have insisted that the free flow of commercial information is valuable enough to justify imposing on would-be regulators the costs of distinguishing * * * the harmless from the harmful, we have not gone so far as to impose upon them the burden of demonstrating that the distinguishment is 100% complete, or that the manner of restriction is absolutely the least severe that will achieve the desired end. What our decisions require is a 'fit' between the legislature's ends and the means chosen to accomplish those ends—a fit that is not necessarily perfect, but reasonable; that represents not necessarily the single best disposition but one whose scope is in proportion to the interest served; that employs not necessarily the least restrictive means but, as we have put it in the other contexts discussed above, a means narrowly tailored to achieve the desired objective. Within those bounds we leave it to governmental decisionmakers to judge what manner of regulation may best be employed * * *.

"Here we require the government goal to be substantial, and the cost to be carefully calculated. Moreover, since the State bears the burden of justifying its restrictions, it must affirmatively establish the reasonable fit we require." *Fox,* 492 U.S., at 480, 109 S.Ct., at 3035 (internal quotation marks and citations omitted).

public property. It was enacted long before any concern about newsracks developed. Its apparent purpose was to prevent the kind of visual blight caused by littering, rather than any harm associated with permanent, freestanding dispensing devices. The fact that the city failed to address its recently developed concern about newsracks by regulating their size, shape, appearance, or number indicates that it has not "carefully calculated" the costs and benefits associated with the burden on speech imposed by its prohibition.[13] The benefit to be derived from the removal of 62 newsracks while about 1,500–2,000 remain in place was considered "minute" by the District Court and "paltry" by the Court of Appeals. We share their evaluation of the "fit" between the city's goal and its method of achieving it.

* * *

III

The city argues that there is a close fit between its ban on newsracks dispensing "commercial handbills" and its interest in safety and esthetics because every decrease in the number of such dispensing devices necessarily effects an increase in safety and an improvement in the attractiveness of the cityscape. In the city's view, the prohibition is thus *entirely* related to its legitimate interests in safety and esthetics.

We accept the validity of the city's proposition, but consider it an insufficient justification for the discrimination against respondents' use of newsracks that are no more harmful than the permitted newsracks, and have only a minimal impact on the overall number of newsracks on the city's sidewalks. The major premise supporting the city's argument is the proposition that commercial speech has only a low value. Based on that premise, the city contends that the fact that assertedly more valuable publications are allowed to use newsracks does not undermine its judgment that its esthetic and safety interests are stronger than the interest in allowing commercial speakers to have similar access to the reading public.

We cannot agree. In our view, the city's argument attaches more importance to the distinction between commercial and non-commercial speech than our cases warrant and seriously underestimates the value of commercial speech.

This very case illustrates the difficulty of drawing bright lines that will clearly cabin commercial speech in a distinct category. For respon-

13. We reject the city's argument that the lower courts' and our consideration of alternative, less drastic measures by which the city could effectuate its interests in safety and esthetics somehow violates *Fox's* holding that regulations on commercial speech are not subject to "least-restrictive-means" analysis. To repeat, see n. 12, *supra,* while we have rejected the "least-restrictive-means" test for judging restrictions on commercial speech, so too have we rejected mere rational basis review. A regulation need not be "absolutely the least severe that will achieve the desired end," *Fox, supra,* 492 U.S., at 480, 109 S.Ct., at 3035, but if there are numerous and obvious less-burdensome alternatives to the restriction on commercial speech, that is certainly a relevant consideration in determining whether the "fit" between ends and means is reasonable.

dents' publications share important characteristics with the publications that the city classifies as "newspapers." Particularly, they are "commercial handbills" within the meaning of § 714–1–C of the city's Code because they contain advertising, a feature that apparently also places ordinary newspapers within the same category. Separate provisions in the code specifically authorize the distribution of "newspapers" on the public right of way, but that term is not defined. Presumably, respondents' publications do not qualify as newspapers because an examination of their content discloses a higher ratio of advertising to other text, such as news and feature stories, than is found in the exempted publications. Indeed, Cincinnati's City Manager has determined that publications that qualify as newspapers and therefore *can* be distributed by newsrack are those that are published daily and or weekly and "*primarily* presen[t] coverage of, and commentary on, current events." App. 230 (emphasis added).

The absence of a categorical definition of the difference between "newspapers" and "commercial handbills" in the city's Code is also a characteristic of our opinions considering the constitutionality of regulations of commercial speech. * * *

Under the *Fox* test it is clear that much of the material in ordinary newspapers is commercial speech and, conversely, that the editorial content in respondents' promotional publications is not what we have described as "core" commercial speech. There is no doubt a "common sense" basis for distinguishing between the two, but under both the city's Code and our cases the difference is a matter of degree.

Nevertheless, for the purpose of deciding this case, we assume that all of the speech barred from Cincinnati's sidewalks is what we have labeled "core" commercial speech and that no such speech is found in publications that are allowed to use newsracks. We nonetheless agree with the Court of Appeals that Cincinnati's actions in this case run afoul of the First Amendment. Not only does Cincinnati's categorical ban on commercial newsracks place too much importance on the distinction between commercial and noncommercial speech, but in this case, the distinction bears no relationship *whatsoever* to the particular interests that the city has asserted. It is therefore an impermissible means of responding to the city's admittedly legitimate interests. Cf. *Simon & Schuster, Inc., v. Members of New York State Crime Victims Bd.,* 502 U.S. ___, ___, 112 S.Ct. 501, 510, 116 L.Ed.2d 476 (1991) (distinction drawn by Son of Sam law between income derived from criminal's descriptions of his crime and other sources "has nothing to do with" State's interest in transferring proceeds of crime from criminals to victims); *Carey v. Brown,* 447 U.S. 455, 465, 100 S.Ct. 2286, 2292, 65 L.Ed.2d 263 (1980) (State's interest in residential privacy cannot sustain statute permitting labor picketing, but prohibiting nonlabor picketing when "nothing in the content-based labor-nonlabor distinction has any bearing whatsoever on privacy").[20]

20. *Metromedia, Inc. v. San Diego,* 453 U.S. 490, 101 S.Ct. 2882, 69 L.Ed.2d 800 (1981), upon which the city heavily relies, is not to the contrary. In that case, a plurali-

The city has asserted an interest in esthetics, but respondent publishers' newsracks are no greater an eyesore than the newsracks permitted to remain on Cincinnati's sidewalks. Each newsrack, whether containing "newspapers" or "commercial handbills," is equally unattractive. While there was some testimony in the District Court that commercial publications are distinct from noncommercial publications in their capacity to proliferate, the evidence of such was exceedingly weak, the Court of Appeals discounted it, 946 F.2d at 466–467, and n. 3, and Cincinnati does not reassert that particular argument in this Court. As we have explained, the city's primary concern, as argued to us, is with the aggregate number of newsracks on its streets. On that score, however, all newsracks, regardless of whether they contain commercial or noncommercial publications, are equally at fault. In fact, the newspapers are arguably the greater culprit because of their superior number.

Cincinnati has not asserted an interest in preventing commercial harms by regulating the information distributed by respondent publishers' newsracks, which is, of course, the typical reason why commercial speech can be subject to greater governmental regulation than noncommercial speech. See, *e.g., Bolger,* 463 U.S., at 81, 103 S.Ct., at 2888 (STEVENS, J., concurring in judgment) ("[T]he commercial aspects of a message may provide a justification for regulation that is not present when the communication has no commercial character"); *Ohralik v. Ohio State Bar Assn.,* 436 U.S. 447, 455–456, 98 S.Ct. 1912, 1918, 56 L.Ed.2d 444 (1978) (commercial speech, unlike other varieties of speech, "occurs in an area traditionally subject to government regulation").[21]

ty of the Court found as a permissible restriction on commercial speech a city ordinance that, for the most part, banned outdoor "offsite" advertising billboards, but permitted "onsite" advertising signs identifying the owner of the premises and the goods sold or manufactured on the site. *Id.,* at 494, 503, 101 S.Ct., at 2885, 2890. Unlike this case, which involves discrimination between commercial and noncommercial speech, the "offsite-onsite" distinction involved disparate treatment of two types of commercial speech. Only the onsite signs served both the commercial and public interest in guiding potential visitors to their intended destinations; moreover, the plurality concluded that a "city may believe that offsite advertising, with its periodically changing content, presents a more acute problem than does onsite advertising," *id.,* at 511–512, 101 S.Ct., at 2894–2895. Neither of these bases has any application to the disparate treatment of newsracks in this case.

The Chief Justice is correct that seven Justices in the *Metromedia* case were of the view that San Diego could completely ban offsite commercial billboards for reasons unrelated to the content of those billboards. *Post,* at 1524–1525. Those seven Justices did not say, however, that San Diego could *distinguish* between commercial and noncommercial offsite billboards that cause the same esthetic and safety concerns. That question was not presented in *Metromedia,* for the regulation at issue in that case did not draw a distinction between commercial and noncommercial offsite billboards; with a few exceptions, it essentially banned *all* offsite billboards.

21. Moreover, the principal reason for drawing a distinction between commercial and noncommercial speech has little, if any, application to a regulation of their distribution practices. As we explained in *Bolger:* "Advertisers should not be permitted to immunize false or misleading product information from government regulation simply by including references to public issues." *Bolger,* 463 U.S., at 68, 103 S.Ct., at 2881. The interest in preventing commercial harms justifies more intensive regulation of commercial speech than noncommercial speech even when they are intermingled in the same publications. On the other hand, the interest in protecting the free flow of information and ideas is still present when

A closer examination of one of the cases we have mentioned, *Bolger v. Youngs Drug Products,* demonstrates the fallacy of the city's argument that a reasonable fit is established by the mere fact that the entire burden imposed on commercial speech by its newsrack policy may in some small way limit the total number of newsracks on Cincinnati's sidewalks. Here, the city contends that safety concerns and visual blight may be addressed by a prohibition that distinguishes between commercial and noncommercial publications that are equally responsible for those problems. In *Bolger,* however, in rejecting the Government's reliance on its interest in protecting the public from "offensive" speech, "[we] specifically declined to recognize a distinction between commercial and noncommercial speech that would render this interest a sufficient justification for a prohibition of commercial speech." 463 U.S., at 71–72, 103 S.Ct., at 2883 (citing *Carey v. Population Services International,* 431 U.S. 678, 701, n. 28, 97 S.Ct. 2010, 2025, n. 28, 52 L.Ed.2d 675 (1977)). Moreover, the fact that the regulation "provide[d] only the most limited incremental support for the interest asserted," 463 U.S., at 73, 103 S.Ct., at 2884—that it achieved only a "marginal degree of protection," *ibid.,* for that interest—supported our holding that the prohibition was invalid. Finally, in *Bolger,* as in this case, the burden on commercial speech was imposed by denying the speaker access to one method of distribution—there the United States mails, and here the placement of newsracks on public property—without interfering with alternative means of access to the audience. As then Justice Rehnquist explained in his separate opinion, that fact did not minimize the significance of the burden:

> "[T]he Postal Service argues that Youngs can communicate with the public otherwise than through the mail. [This argument falls] wide of the mark. A prohibition on the use of the mails is a significant restriction of First Amendment rights. We have noted that ' "[t]he United States may give up the Post Office when it sees fit, but while it carries it on the use of the mails is as much a part of free speech as the right to use our tongues." ' *Blount v. Rizzi,* 400 U.S. [410], at 416 [91 S.Ct. 423, 428, 27 L.Ed.2d 498 (1971)], quoting *Milwaukee Social Democratic Publishing Co. v. Burleson,* 255 U.S. 407, 437 [41 S.Ct. 352, 363, 65 L.Ed. 704] (1921) (Holmes, J., dissenting)." 463 U.S., at 79–80, 103 S.Ct., at 2887 (footnote omitted).

In a similar vein, even if we assume, *arguendo,* that the city might entirely prohibit the use of newsracks on public property, as long as this avenue of communication remains open, these devices continue to play a significant role in the dissemination of protected speech.

In the absence of some basis for distinguishing between "newspapers" and "commercial handbills" that is relevant to an interest asserted by the city, we are unwilling to recognize Cincinnati's bare assertion that the "low value" of commercial speech is a sufficient justification for its selective and categorical ban on newsracks dispensing "commercial handbills." Our holding, however, is narrow. As should be clear from

such expression is found in a commercial context.

the above discussion, we do not reach the question whether, given certain facts and under certain circumstances, a community might be able to justify differential treatment of commercial and noncommercial newsracks. We simply hold that on this record Cincinnati has failed to make such a showing. Because the distinction Cincinnati has drawn has absolutely no bearing on the interests it has asserted, we have no difficulty concluding, as did the two courts below, that the city has not established the "fit" between its goals and its chosen means that is required by our opinion in *Fox*. It remains to consider the city's argument that its prohibition is a permissible time, place, and manner regulation.

IV

The Court has held that government may impose reasonable restrictions on the time, place or manner of engaging in protected speech provided that they are adequately justified " 'without reference to the content of the regulated speech.' " *Ward v. Rock Against Racism,* 491 U.S. 781, 791, 109 S.Ct. 2746, 2753, 105 L.Ed.2d 661 (1989), quoting *Clark v. Community for Creative Non–Violence,* 468 U.S. 288, 293, 104 S.Ct. 3065, 3069, 82 L.Ed.2d 221 (1984). Thus, a prohibition against the use of sound trucks emitting "loud and raucous" noise in residential neighborhoods is permissible if it applies equally to music, political speech, and advertising. See generally *Kovacs v. Cooper,* 336 U.S. 77, 69 S.Ct. 448, 93 L.Ed. 513 (1949). The city contends that its regulation of newsracks qualifies as such a restriction because the interests in safety and esthetics that it serves are entirely unrelated to the content of respondents' publications. Thus, the argument goes, the *justification* for the regulation is content neutral.

The argument is unpersuasive because the very basis for the regulation is the difference in content between ordinary newspapers and commercial speech. True, there is no evidence that the city has acted with animus toward the ideas contained within respondents' publications, but just last Term we expressly rejected the argument that "discriminatory * * * treatment is suspect under the First Amendment only when the legislature intends to suppress certain ideas." *Simon & Schuster v. Members of New York State Crime Victims Bd.,* 502 U.S., at ___, 112 S.Ct., at 509. Regardless of the *mens rea* of the city, it has enacted a sweeping ban on the use of newsracks that distribute "commercial handbills," but not "newspapers." Under the city's newsrack policy, whether any particular newsrack falls within the ban is determined by the content of the publication resting inside that newsrack. Thus, by any commonsense understanding of the term, the ban in this case is "content-based."

Nor are we persuaded that our statements that the test for whether a regulation is content-based turns on the "justification" for the regulation, see, *e.g., Ward,* 491 U.S., at 791, 109 S.Ct., at 2753; *Clark,* 468 U.S., at 293, 104 S.Ct., at 3069, compel a different conclusion. We agree with the city that its desire to limit the total number of newsracks is "justified" by its interest in safety and esthetics. The city has not, however, limited the number of newsracks; it has limited (to zero) the number of newsracks *distributing commercial publications.* As we have explained, there is no justification for that particular regulation other than the city's naked assertion that commercial speech has "low value." It is the absence of a neutral justification for its selective ban on newsracks that prevents the city from defending its newsrack policy as content-neutral.

By the same reasoning, the city's heavy reliance on *Renton v. Playtime Theatres, Inc.,* 475 U.S. 41, 106 S.Ct. 925, 89 L.Ed.2d 29 (1986), is misplaced * * * In contrast to the speech at issue in *Renton,* there are no secondary effects attributable to respondent publishers' newsracks that distinguish them from the newsracks Cincinnati permits to remain on its sidewalks.

In sum, the city's newsrack policy is neither content-neutral nor, as demonstrated in Part III, *supra,* "narrowly tailored." Thus, regardless of whether or not it leaves open ample alternative channels of communication, it cannot be justified as a legitimate time, place, or manner restriction on protected speech.

Cincinnati has enacted a sweeping ban that bars from its sidewalks a whole class of constitutionally protected speech. As did the District Court and the Court of Appeals, we conclude that Cincinnati has failed to justify that policy. The regulation is not a permissible regulation of commercial speech, for on this record it is clear that the interests that Cincinnati has asserted are unrelated to any distinction between "commercial handbills" and "newspapers." Moreover, because the ban is predicated on the content of the publications distributed by the subject newsracks, it is not a valid time, place, or manner restriction on protected speech. For these reasons, Cincinnati's categorical ban on the distribution, via newsrack, of "commercial handbills" cannot be squared with the dictates of the First Amendment.

The judgment of the Court of Appeals is *Affirmed.*

* * *

p. 430: Add to Note 1

Qutb v. Strauss, 11 F.3d 488 (5th Cir.1993), cert. denied sub nom. Qutb v. Bartlett, ___ U.S. ___, 114 S.Ct. 3124, 128 L.Ed.2d 864 (1994) (carefully crafted nocturnal juvenile curfew ordinance, which mandated parental involvement, did not violate either juveniles' or parents' rights under the equal protection provisions of the federal and state constitutions).

p. 435: Note 4—delete sentence referring to the *Naegele* treatment of taking and p. 477, and insert

The district court had also ruled in *Naegele* that the ordinance banning all commercial, off-premises advertising signs except those along interstate or federally aided primary highways after a five and a half year grace period does not effect a taking. The Fourth Circuit affirmed in an unpublished decision, and the Supreme Court denied certiorari. ___ U.S. ___, 115 S.Ct. 317, 130 L.Ed.2d 27 (1994).

p. 435–36: Add to Note 5

See City of Ladue v. Gilleo, ___ U.S. ___, 114 S.Ct. 2038, 129 L.Ed.2d 36 (1994), reported, infra, this supplement.

p. 436: Add to note 6

In a somewhat unusual ruling, the court in Americans United for Separation of Church and State v. Grand Rapids, 980 F.2d 1538 (6th Cir.1992) held that the city's permitting as a display an unattended, privately sponsored 20–foot menorah in a traditional public forum near public buildings and flags did not violate the Establishment Clause; rather it protected free speech.

pp. 438–39: Add to Note 1

Fanelli v. City of Trenton, 135 N.J. 582, 641 A.2d 541 (1994) (municipal ordinance prohibiting hawking, peddling, or vending in statutorily authorized special improvement district did not violate state or federal due process or equal protection provisions or the antitrust laws).

p. 439: Add to Solicitation Ordinances

Edenfield v. Fane, ___ U.S. ___, 113 S.Ct. 1792, 123 L.Ed.2d 543 (1993) (state ban on personal solicitation of potential clients by CPAs is inconsistent with free speech guarantees); New York State Association of Realtors, Inc. v. Shaffer, 27 F.3d 834 (2d Cir.1994), cert. denied, ___ U.S. ___, 115 S.Ct. 511, 130 L.Ed.2d 418 (1994) (ban on real estate solicitation in certain areas was not reasonably tailored to serve substantial government interest in combatting blockbusting and hence was impermissible restriction on commercial speech); Project 80's, Inc. v. City of Pocatello, 942 F.2d 635 (9th Cir.1991) (ordinances banning door-to-door solicitation are neither narrowly tailored nor reasonable time, place, and manner regulations).

Add to Note 4

See Saukstelis v. City of Chicago, 932 F.2d 1171 (7th Cir.1991) (seizure of car with "Denver Boot" applied after tickets were not paid or contested does not violate fourteenth amendment Due Process Clause where city offered hearings upon ticketing of car).

p. 439: Add

2. LOCAL REGULATIONS AND FIRST AMENDMENT'S FREE EXERCISE CLAUSE

CHURCH OF THE LUKUMI BABALU AYE, INC. v. CITY OF HIALEAH

Supreme Court of the United States, 1993.

___ U.S. ___, 113 S.Ct. 2217, 124 L.Ed.2d 472.

JUSTICE KENNEDY delivered the opinion of the Court, except as to Part

II–A–2.*

The principle that government may not enact laws that suppress religious belief or practice is so well understood that few violations are recorded in our opinions. Cf. *McDaniel v. Paty,* 435 U.S. 618, 98 S.Ct. 1322, 55 L.Ed.2d 593 (1978); *Fowler v. Rhode Island,* 345 U.S. 67, 73 S.Ct. 526, 97 L.Ed. 828 (1953). Concerned that this fundamental nonpersecution principle of the First Amendment was implicated here, however, we granted certiorari. 503 U.S. ___, 112 S.Ct. 1472, 117 L.Ed.2d 616 (1992).

Our review confirms that the laws in question were enacted by officials who did not understand, failed to perceive, or chose to ignore the fact that their official actions violated the Nation's essential commitment to religious freedom. The challenged laws had an impermissible object; and in all events the principle of general applicability was violated because the secular ends asserted in defense of the laws were pursued only with respect to conduct motivated by religious beliefs. We invalidate the challenged enactments and reverse the judgment of the Court of Appeals.

I

A

This case involves practices of the Santeria religion, which originated in the nineteenth century. When hundreds of thousands of members of the Yoruba people were brought as slaves from eastern Africa to Cuba, their traditional African religion absorbed significant elements of Roman Catholicism. The resulting syncretion, or fusion, is Santeria, "the way of the saints." The Cuban Yoruba express their devotion to spirits, called *orishas,* through the iconography of Catholic saints, Catholic symbols are often present at Santeria rites, and Santeria devotees attend the Catholic sacraments. 723 F.Supp. 1467, 1469–1470 (SD Fla.1989); 13 The Encyclopedia of Religion 66 (M. Eliade ed. 1987); 1 Encyclopedia of the American Religious Experience 183 (C. Lippy & P. Williams eds. 1988).

The Santeria faith teaches that every individual has a destiny from God, a destiny fulfilled with the aid and energy of the *orishas.* The basis of the Santeria religion is the nurture of a personal relation with the *orishas,* and one of the principal forms of devotion is an animal sacrifice. 13 The Encyclopedia of Religion, *supra,* at 66. The sacrifice of animals as part of religious rituals has ancient roots. See generally 12 *id.,* at 554–556. Animal sacrifice is mentioned throughout the Old Testament, see 14 Encyclopaedia Judaica 600, 600–605 (1971), and it played an important role in the practice of Judaism before destruction of the second Temple in Jerusalem, see *id.,* at 605–612. In modern Islam, there is an annual sacrifice commemorating Abraham's sacrifice of a ram

* The Chief Justice, Justice Scalia, and Justice Thomas join all but Part II–A–2 of this opinion. Justice White joins all but Part II–A of this opinion. Justice Souter joins only Parts I, III, and IV of this opinion.

in the stead of his son. See C. Glassé, The Concise Encyclopedia of Islam 178 (1989); 7 The Encyclopedia of Religion, *supra,* at 456.

According to Santeria teaching, the *orishas* are powerful but not immortal. They depend for survival on the sacrifice. Sacrifices are performed at birth, marriage, and death rites, for the cure of the sick, for the initiation of new members and priests, and during an annual celebration. Animals sacrificed in Santeria rituals include chickens, pigeons, doves, ducks, guinea pigs, goats, sheep, and turtles. The animals are killed by the cutting of the carotid arteries in the neck. The sacrificed animal is cooked and eaten, except after healing and death rituals. See 723 F.Supp., at 1471–1472; 13 The Encyclopedia of Religion, *supra,* at 66; M. Gonzálex–Wippler, The Santeria Experience 105 (1982).

Santeria adherents faced widespread persecution in Cuba, so the religion and its rituals were practiced in secret. The open practice of Santeria and its rites remains infrequent. See 723 F.Supp., at 1470; 13 The Encyclopedia of Religion, *supra,* at 67; M. González–Wippler, Santería: The Religion 3–4 (1989). The religion was brought to this Nation most often by exiles from the Cuban revolution. The District Court estimated that there are at least 50,000 practitioners in South Florida today. See 723 F.Supp., at 1470.

B

Petitioner Church of the Lukumi Babalu Aye, Inc. (Church), is a not-for-profit corporation organized under Florida law in 1973. The Church and its congregants practice the Santeria religion. The president of the Church is petitioner Ernesto Pichardo, who is also the Church's priest and holds the religious title of *Italero,* the second highest in the Santeria faith. In April 1987, the Church leased land in the city of Hialeah, Florida, and announced plans to establish a house of worship as well as a school, cultural center, and museum. Pichardo indicated that the Church's goal was to bring the practice of the Santeria faith, including its ritual of animal sacrifice, into the open. The Church began the process of obtaining utility service and receiving the necessary licensing, inspection, and zoning approvals. Although the Church's efforts at obtaining the necessary licenses and permits were far from smooth, see 723 F.Supp., at 1477–1478, it appears that it received all needed approvals by early August 1987.

The prospect of a Santeria church in their midst was distressing to many members of the Hialeah community, and the announcement of the plans to open a Santeria church in Hialeah prompted the city council to hold an emergency public session on June 9, 1987. The resolutions and ordinances passed at that and later meetings are set forth in the appendix following this opinion.

A summary suffices here, beginning with the enactments passed at the June 9 meeting. First, the city council adopted Resolution 87–66, which noted the "concern" expressed by residents of the city "that certain religions may propose to engage in practices which are inconsistent with public morals, peace or safety," and declared that "[t]he City reiterates its commitment to a prohibition against any and all acts of any and all religious groups which are inconsistent with public morals, peace or safety." Next, the council approved an emergency ordinance, Ordinance 87–40, that incorporated in full, except as to penalty, Florida's animal cruelty laws. Fla.Stat. ch. 828 (1987). Among other things, the incorporated state law subjected to criminal punishment "[w]hoever * * * unnecessarily or cruelly * * * kills any animal." § 828.12.

The city council desired to undertake further legislative action, but Florida law prohibited a municipality from enacting legislation relating to animal cruelty that conflicted with state law. § 828.27(4). To obtain clarification, Hialeah's city attorney requested an opinion from the attorney general of Florida as to whether § 828.12 prohibited "a religious group from sacrificing an animal in a religious ritual or practice" and whether the city could enact ordinances "making religious animal sacrifice unlawful." The attorney general responded in mid-July. He concluded that the "ritual sacrifice of animals for purposes other than food consumption" was not a "necessary" killing and so was prohibited by § 828.12. Fla.Op.Atty.Gen. 87–56, Annual Report of the Atty.Gen. 146, 147, 149 (1988). The attorney general appeared to define "unnecessary" as "done without any useful motive, in a spirit of wanton cruelty or for the mere pleasure of destruction without being in any sense beneficial or useful to the person killing the animal." *Id.,* at 149, n. 11. He advised that religious animal sacrifice was against state law, so that a city ordinance prohibiting it would not be in conflict. *Id.,* at 151.

The city council responded at first with a hortatory enactment, Resolution 87–90, that noted its residents' "great concern regarding the possibility of public ritualistic animal sacrifices" and the state law prohibition. The resolution declared the city policy "to oppose the ritual sacrifices of animals" within Hialeah and announced that any person or organization practicing animal sacrifice "will be prosecuted."

In September 1987, the city council adopted three substantive ordinances addressing the issue of religious animal sacrifice. Ordinance 87–52 defined "sacrifice" as "to unnecessarily kill, torment, torture, or mutilate an animal in a public or private ritual or ceremony not for the primary purpose of food consumption," and prohibited owning or possessing an animal "intending to use such animal for food purposes." It restricted application of this prohibition, however, to any individual or group that "kills, slaughters or sacrifices animals for any type of ritual, regardless of whether or not the flesh or blood of the animal is to be consumed." The ordinance contained an exemption for slaughtering by "licensed establishment[s]" of animals "specifically raised for food purposes." Declaring, moreover, that the city council "has determined that the sacrificing of animals within the city limits is contrary to the public health, safety, welfare and morals of the community," the city council adopted Ordinance 87–71. That ordinance defined sacrifice as had Ordinance 87–52, and then provided that "[i]t shall be unlawful for any person, persons, corporations or associations to sacrifice any animal within the corporate limits of the City of Hialeah, Florida." The final Ordinance, 87–72, defined "slaughter" as "the killing of animals for food" and prohibited slaughter outside of areas zoned for slaughterhouse use. The ordinance provided an exemption, however, for the slaughter or processing for sale of "small numbers of hogs and/or cattle per week in accordance with an exemption provided by state law." All ordinances and resolutions passed the city council by unanimous vote. Violations of each of the four ordinances were punishable by fines not exceeding $500 or imprisonment not exceeding 60 days, or both.

Following enactment of these ordinances, the Church and Pichardo filed this action pursuant to 42 U.S.C. § 1983 in the United States District Court for the Southern District of Florida.

* * *

Balancing the competing governmental and religious interests, the District Court concluded the compelling governmental interests "fully justify the absolute prohibition on ritual sacrifice" accomplished by the ordinances. *Id.,* at 1487. The court also concluded that an exception to the sacrifice prohibition for religious conduct would " 'unduly interfere with fulfillment of the governmental interest' " because any more narrow restrictions—*e.g.,* regulation of disposal of animal carcasses—would be unenforceable as a result of the secret nature of the Santeria religion. *Id.,* at 1486–1487, and nn. 57–59. A religious exemption from the city's ordinances, concluded the court, would defeat the city's compelling interests in enforcing the prohibition. *Id.,* at 1487.

The Court of Appeals for the Eleventh Circuit affirmed in a one-paragraph *per curiam* opinion. Judgt. order reported at 936 F.2d 586 (1991). Choosing not to rely on the District Court's recitation of a compelling interest in promoting the welfare of children, the Court of Appeals stated simply that it concluded the ordinances were consistent with the Constitution. App. to Pet. for Cert. A2. It declined to address the effect of *Employment Div., Dept. of Human Resources of Oregon v. Smith,* 494 U.S. 872, 110 S.Ct. 1595, 108 L.Ed.2d 876 (1990), decided after the District Court's opinion, because the District Court "employed an arguably stricter standard" than that applied in *Smith.* App. to Pet. for Cert. A2, n. 1.

II

The Free Exercise Clause of the First Amendment, which has been applied to the States through the Fourteenth Amendment, see *Cantwell v. Connecticut,* 310 U.S. 296, 303, 60 S.Ct. 900, 903, 84 L.Ed. 1213 (1940), provides that "Congress shall make no law respecting an establishment of religion, or *prohibiting the free exercise thereof* * * *." U.S. Const., Amdt. 1 (emphasis added). The city does not argue that Santeria is not a "religion" within the meaning of the First Amendment. Nor could it. Although the practice of animal sacrifice may seem abhorrent to some, "religious beliefs need not be acceptable, logical, consistent, or comprehensible to others in order to merit First Amendment protection." *Thomas v. Review Bd. of Indiana Employment Security Div.*, 450 U.S. 707, 714, 101 S.Ct. 1425, 1430, 67 L.Ed.2d 624 (1981). Given the historical association between animal sacrifice and religious worship, see *supra,* at 2, petitioners' assertion that animal sacrifice is an integral part of their religion "cannot be deemed bizarre or incredible." *Frazee v. Illinois Dept. of Employment Security,* 489 U.S. 829, 834, n. 2, 109 S.Ct. 1514, 1518, n. 2, 103 L.Ed.2d 914 (1989). Neither the city nor the courts below, moreover, have questioned the sincerity of petitioners' professed desire to conduct animal sacrifices for religious reasons. We must consider petitioners' First Amendment claim.

In addressing the constitutional protection for free exercise of religion, our cases establish the general proposition that a law that is neutral and of general applicability need not be justified by a compelling governmental interest even if the law has the incidental effect of burdening a particular religious practice. *Employment Div., Dept. of Human Resources of Oregon v. Smith, supra.* Neutrality and general applicability are interrelated, and, as becomes apparent in this case, failure to satisfy one requirement is a likely indication that the other has not been satisfied. A law failing to satisfy these requirements must be justified by a compelling governmental interest and must be narrowly tailored to advance that interest. These ordinances fail to satisfy the *Smith* requirements. We begin by discussing neutrality.

A

In our Establishment Clause cases we have often stated the principle that the First Amendment forbids an official purpose to disapprove of a particular religion or of religion in general. * * * These cases, however, for the most part have addressed governmental efforts to benefit religion or particular religions, and so have dealt with a question different, at least in its formulation and emphasis, from the issue here. Petitioners allege an attempt to disfavor their religion because of the religious ceremonies it commands, and the Free Exercise Clause is dispositive in our analysis.

At a minimum, the protections of the Free Exercise Clause pertain if the law at issue discriminates against some or all religious beliefs or regulates or prohibits conduct because it is undertaken for religious reasons. * * *

1

Although a law targeting religious beliefs as such is never permissible, *McDaniel v. Paty, supra,* 435 U.S., at 626, 98 S.Ct., at 1327–28 (plurality opinion); *Cantwell v. Connecticut, supra,* 310 U.S., at 303–304, 60 S.Ct., at 903 if the object of a law is to infringe upon or restrict practices because of their religious motivation, the law is not neutral, see *Employment Div., Dept. of Human Resources of Oregon v. Smith, supra,* 494 U.S., at 878–879, 110 S.Ct., at 1599–1600; and it is invalid unless it is justified by a compelling interest and is narrowly tailored to advance that interest. There are, of course, many ways of demonstrating that the object or purpose of a law is the suppression of religion or religious conduct. To determine the object of a law, we must begin with its text, for the minimum requirement of neutrality is that a law not discriminate on its face. A law lacks facial neutrality if it refers to a religious practice without a secular meaning discernable from the language or context. Petitioners contend that three of the ordinances fail this test of facial neutrality because they use the words "sacrifice" and "ritual," words with strong religious connotations. Brief for Petitioners 16–17. We agree that these words are consistent with the claim of facial discrimination, but the argument is not conclusive. The words "sacrifice" and "ritual" have a religious origin, but current use admits also of secular meanings. See Webster's Third New International Dictionary 1961, 1996 (1971). See also 12 The Encyclopedia of Religion, at 556 ("[T]he word *sacrifice* ultimately became very much a secular term in common usage"). The ordinances, furthermore, define "sacrifice" in secular terms, without referring to religious practices.

We reject the contention advanced by the city, see Brief for Respondent 15, that our inquiry must end with the text of the laws at issue. Facial neutrality is not determinative. The Free Exercise Clause, like the Establishment Clause, extends beyond facial discrimination. The Clause "forbids subtle departures from neutrality," *Gillette v. United States,* 401 U.S. 437, 452, 91 S.Ct. 828, 837, 28 L.Ed.2d 168 (1971), and "covert suppression of particular religious beliefs," *Bowen v. Roy, supra,* 476 U.S., at 703, 106 S.Ct., at 2154 (opinion of Burger, C.J.). Official action that targets religious conduct for distinctive treatment cannot be shielded by mere compliance with the requirement of facial neutrality. The Free Exercise Clause protects against governmental hostility which is masked, as well as overt. "The Court must survey meticulously the circumstances of governmental categories to eliminate, as it were, religious gerrymanders." *Walz v. Tax Comm'n of New York City,* 397 U.S. 664, 696, 90 S.Ct. 1409, 1425, 25 L.Ed.2d 697 (1970) (HARLAN, J., concurring).

The record in this case compels the conclusion that suppression of the central element of the Santeria worship service was the object of the ordinances. First, though use of the words "sacrifice" and "ritual" does not compel a finding of improper targeting of the Santeria religion, the choice of these words is support for our conclusion. There are further respects in which the text of the city council's enactments discloses the improper attempt to target Santeria. Resolution 87–66, adopted June 9, 1987, recited that "residents and citizens of the City of Hialeah have expressed their concern that certain religions may propose to engage in practices which are inconsistent with public morals, peace or safety," and "reiterate[d]" the city's commitment to prohibit "any and all [such] acts of any and all religious groups." No one suggests, and on this record it cannot be maintained, that city officials had in mind a religion other than Santeria.

It becomes evident that these ordinances target Santeria sacrifice when the ordinances' operation is considered. Apart from the text, the effect of a law in its real operation is strong evidence of its object. To be sure, adverse impact will not always lead to a finding of impermissible targeting. For example, a social harm may have been a legitimate concern of government for reasons quite apart from discrimination. *McGowan v. Maryland,* 366 U.S., at 442, 81 S.Ct., at 1113–14. See, *e.g., Reynolds v. United States,* 98 U.S. 145, 25 L.Ed. 244 (1879); *Davis v. Beason,* 133 U.S. 333, 10 S.Ct. 299, 33 L.Ed. 637 (1890). See also Ely, Legislative and Administrative Motivation in Constitutional Law, 79 Yale L.J. 1205, 1319 (1970). The subject at hand does implicate, of course, multiple concerns unrelated to religious animosity, for example, the suffering or mistreatment visited upon the sacrificed animals, and health hazards from improper disposal. But the ordinances when considered together disclose an object remote from these legitimate concerns. The design of these laws accomplishes instead a "religious gerrymander," *Walz v. Tax Comm'n of New York City, supra,* 397 U.S., at 696, 90 S.Ct., at 1425 (Harlan, J., concurring), an impermissible attempt to target petitioners and their religious practices.

* * * It suffices to recite this feature of the law as support for our conclusion that Santeria alone was the exclusive legislative concern. The net result of the gerrymander is that few if any killings of animals are prohibited other than Santeria sacrifice, which is proscribed because it occurs during a ritual or ceremony and its primary purpose is to make an offering to the *orishas,* not food consumption. Indeed, careful drafting ensured that, although Santeria sacrifice is prohibited, killings that are no more necessary or humane in almost all other circumstances are unpunished.

* * * Again, the burden of the ordinance, in practical terms, falls on Santeria adherents but almost no others: If the killing is—unlike most Santeria sacrifices—unaccompanied by the intent to use the animal for food, then it is not prohibited by Ordinance 87–52; if the killing is specifically for food but does not occur during the course of "any type of ritual," it again falls outside the prohibition; and if the killing is for food and occurs during the course of a ritual, it is still exempted if it occurs in a properly zoned and licensed establishment and involves animals "specifically raised for food purposes." A pattern of exemptions parallels the pattern of narrow prohibitions. Each contributes to the gerrymander.

Ordinance 87–40 incorporates the Florida animal cruelty statute, Fla.Stat. § 828.12 (1987). Its prohibition is broad on its face, punishing "[w]hoever * * * unnecessarily * * * kills any animal." The city claims that this ordinance is the epitome of a neutral prohibition. Brief for Respondent 13–14. The problem, however, is the interpretation given to the ordinance by respondent and the Florida attorney general. Killings for religious reasons are deemed unnecessary, whereas most other killings fall outside the prohibition. The city, on what seems to be a *per se* basis, deems hunting, slaughter of animals for food, eradication of insects and pests, and euthanasia as necessary. See *id.,* at 22. There is no indication in the record that respondent has concluded that hunting or fishing for sport is unnecessary. Indeed, one of the few reported Florida cases decided under § 828.12 concludes that the use of live rabbits to train greyhounds is not unnecessary. See *Kiper v. State,* 310 So.2d 42 (Fla.App.), cert. denied, 328 So.2d 845 (Fla.1975). Further, because it requires an evaluation of the particular justification for the killing, this ordinance represents a system of "individualized governmental assessment of the reasons for the relevant conduct," *Employment Div., Dept. of Human Resources of Oregon v. Smith,* 494 U.S., at 884, 110 S.Ct., at 1603. As we noted in *Smith,* in circumstances in which individualized exemptions from a general requirement are available, the government "may not refuse to extend that system to cases of 'religious hardship' without compelling reason." *Id.,* at 884, 110 S.Ct., at 1603 quoting *Bowen v. Roy,* 476 U.S., at 708, 106 S.Ct., at 2156 (opinion of Burger, C.J.). Respondent's application of the ordinance's test of necessity devalues religious reasons for killing by judging them to be of lesser import than nonreligious reasons. Thus, religious practice is being singled out for discriminatory treatment. *Bowen v. Roy, supra,* at 722, and n. 17, 106 S.Ct., at 2164, and n. 17 (Stevens, J., concurring in part and concurring in result); *United States v. Lee,* 455 U.S. 252, 264, n. 3, 102 S.Ct. 1051, 1059, n. 3, 71 L.Ed.2d 127 (1982) (Stevens, J., concurring in judgment); *Bowen v. Roy, supra,* 476 U.S., at 708, 106 S.Ct., at 2156 (opinion of Burger, C.J.).

We also find significant evidence of the ordinances' improper targeting of Santeria sacrifice in the fact that they proscribe more religious conduct than is necessary to achieve their stated ends. It is not unreasonable to infer, at least when there are no persuasive indications to the contrary, that a law which visits "gratuitous restrictions" on religious conduct, *McGowan v. Maryland,* 366 U.S., at 520, 81 S.Ct., at 1186 (opinion of Frankfurter, J.), seeks not to effectuate the stated governmental interests, but to suppress the conduct because of its religious motivation.

The legitimate governmental interests in protecting the public health and preventing cruelty to animals could be addressed by restrictions stopping far short of a flat prohibition of all Santeria sacrificial practice.† If improper disposal, not the sacrifice itself, is the harm to be prevented, the city could have imposed a general regulation on the disposal of organic garbage. It did not do so. Indeed, counsel for the city conceded at oral argument that, under the ordinances, Santeria sacrifices would be illegal even if they occurred in licensed, inspected, and zoned slaughterhouses. Tr. of Oral Arg. 45. See also *id.,* at 42, 48. Thus, these broad ordinances prohibit Santeria sacrifice even when it does not threaten the city's interest in the public health. The District Court accepted the argument that narrower regulation would be unen-

† Respondent advances the additional governmental interest in prohibiting the slaughter or sacrifice of animals in areas of the city not zoned for slaughterhouses, see Brief for Respondent 28–31, and the District Court found this interest to be compelling, see 723 F.Supp. 1467, 1486 (SD Fla. 1989). This interest cannot justify Ordinances 87–40, 87–52, and 87–71, for they apply to conduct without regard to where it occurs. Ordinance 87–72 does impose a locational restriction, but this asserted governmental interest is a mere restatement of the prohibition itself, not a justification for it. In our discussion, therefore, we put aside this asserted interest.

forceable because of the secrecy in the Santeria rituals and the lack of any central religious authority to require compliance with secular disposal regulations. See 723 F.Supp., at 1486–1487, and nn. 58–59. It is difficult to understand, however, how a prohibition of the sacrifices themselves, which occur in private, is enforceable if a ban on improper disposal, which occurs in public, is not. The neutrality of a law is suspect if First Amendment freedoms are curtailed to prevent isolated collateral harms not themselves prohibited by direct regulation. See, *e.g., Schneider v. State,* 308 U.S. 147, 162, 60 S.Ct. 146, 151–52, 84 L.Ed. 155 (1939).

Under similar analysis, narrower regulation would achieve the city's interest in preventing cruelty to animals. With regard to the city's interest in ensuring the adequate care of animals, regulation of conditions and treatment, regardless of why an animal is kept, is the logical response to the city's concern, not a prohibition on possession for the purpose of sacrifice. The same is true for the city's interest in prohibiting cruel methods of killing. Under federal and Florida law and Ordinance 87–40, which incorporates Florida law in this regard, killing an animal by the "simultaneous and instantaneous severance of the carotid arteries with a sharp instrument"—the method used in Kosher slaughter—is approved as humane. See 7 U.S.C. § 1902(b); Fla.Stat. § 828.23(7)(b) (1991); Ordinance 87–40, § 1. The District Court found that, though Santeria sacrifice also results in severance of the carotid arteries, the method used during sacrifice is less reliable and therefore not humane. See 723 F.Supp., at 1472–1473. If the city has a real concern that other methods are less humane, however, the subject of the regulation should be the method of slaughter itself, not a religious classification that is said to bear some general relation to it.

Ordinance 87–72—unlike the three other ordinances—does appear to apply to substantial nonreligious conduct and not to be overbroad. For our purposes here, however, the four substantive ordinances may be treated as a group for neutrality purposes. Ordinance 87–72 was passed the same day as Ordinance 87–71 and was enacted, as were the three others, in direct response to the opening of the Church. It would be implausible to suggest that the three other ordinances, but not Ordinance 87–72, had as their object the suppression of religion. We need not decide whether the Ordinance 87–72 could survive constitutional scrutiny if it existed separately; it must be invalidated because it functions, with the rest of the enactments in question, to suppress Santeria religious worship.

2

* * *

3

In sum, the neutrality inquiry leads to one conclusion: The ordinances had as their object the suppression of religion. The pattern we have recited discloses animosity to Santeria adherents and their religious practices; the ordinances by their own terms target this religious exercise; the texts of the ordinances were gerrymandered with care to proscribe religious killings of animals but to exclude almost all secular killings; and the ordinances suppress much more religious conduct than is necessary in order to achieve the legitimate ends asserted in their defense. These ordinances are not neutral, and the court below committed clear error in failing to reach this conclusion.

B

We turn next to a second requirement of the Free Exercise Clause, the rule that laws burdening religious practice must be of general applicability. *Employment Div., Dept. of Human Resources of Oregon v. Smith,* 494 U.S., at 879–881, 110 S.Ct., at 1600–01. All laws are selective to some extent, but categories of selection are of paramount concern when a law has the incidental effect of burdening religious practice. The Free Exercise Clause "protect[s] religious observers against unequal treatment," *Hobbie v. Unemployment Appeals Comm'n of Florida,* 480 U.S. 136, 148, 107 S.Ct. 1046, 1053, 94 L.Ed.2d 190 (1987) (STEVENS, J., concurring in judgment), and inequality results when a legislature decides that the governmental interests it seeks to advance are worthy of being pursued only against conduct with a religious motivation.

The principle that government, in pursuit of legitimate interests, cannot in a selective manner impose burdens only on conduct motivated by religious belief is essential to the protection of the rights guaranteed by the Free Exercise Clause. The principle underlying the general applicability requirement has parallels in our First Amendment jurisprudence. * * * In this case we need not define with precision the standard used to evaluate whether a prohibition is of general application, for these ordinances fall well below the minimum standard necessary to protect First Amendment rights.

Respondent claims that Ordinances 87–40, 87–52, and 87–71 advance two interests: protecting the public health and preventing cruelty to animals. The ordinances are underinclusive for those ends. They fail to prohibit non-religious conduct that endangers these interests in a similar or greater degree than Santeria sacrifice does. The underinclusion is substantial, not inconsequential. Despite the city's proffered interest in preventing cruelty to animals, the ordinances are drafted with care to forbid few killings but those occasioned by religious sacrifice. Many types of animal deaths or kills for nonreligious reasons are either not prohibited or approved by express provision. For example, fishing—which occurs in Hialeah, see A. Khedouri & F. Khedouri, South Florida Inside Out 57 (1991)—is legal. Extermination of mice and rats within a home is also permitted. Florida law incorporated by Ordinance 87–40 sanctions euthanasia of "stray, neglected, abandoned, or unwanted animals," Fla.Stat. § 828.058 (1987); destruction of animals judicially removed from their owners "for humanitarian reasons" or when the animal "is of no commercial value," § 828.073(4)(c)(2); the infliction of pain or suffering "in the interest of medical science," § 828.02; the placing of poison in one's yard or enclosure, § 828.08; and the use of a live animal "to pursue or take wildlife or to participate in any hunting," § 828.122(6)(b), and "to hunt wild hogs," § 828.122(6)(e).

The city concedes that "neither the State of Florida nor the City has enacted a generally applicable ban on the killing of animals." Brief for Respondent 21. It asserts, however, that animal sacrifice is "different" from the animal killings that are permitted by law. *Ibid.* According to the city, it is "self-evident" that killing animals for food is "important"; the eradication of insects and pests is "obviously justified"; and the euthanasia of excess animals "makes sense." *Id.,* at 22. These *ipse dixits* do not explain why religion alone must bear the burden of the ordinances, when many of these secular killings fall within the city's interest in preventing the cruel treatment of animals.

The ordinances are also underinclusive with regard to the city's interest in public health, which is threatened by the disposal of animal carcasses in open public places and the consumption of uninspected meat, see Brief for Respondent 32, citing 723 F.Supp., at 1474–1475, 1485. Neither interest is pursued by respondent with regard to conduct that is not motivated by religious conviction. The health risks posed by the improper disposal of animal carcasses are the same whether Santeria sacrifice or some nonreligious killing preceded it. The city does not, however, prohibit hunters from bringing their kill to their houses, nor does it regulate disposal after their activity. Despite substantial testimony at trial that the same public health hazards result from improper disposal of garbage by restaurants, see 11 Record 566, 590–591, restaurants are outside the scope of the ordinances. Improper disposal is a general problem that causes substantial health risks, 723 F.Supp., at 1485, but which respondent addresses only when it results from religious exercise.

The ordinances are underinclusive as well with regard to the health risk posed by consumption of uninspected meat. Under the city's ordinances, hunters may eat their kill and fisherman may eat their catch without undergoing governmental inspection. Likewise, state law requires inspection of meat that is sold but exempts meat from animals raised for the use of the owner and "members of his household and nonpaying guests and employees." Fla.Stat. § 585.88(1)(a) (1991). The asserted interest in inspected meat is not pursued in contexts similar to that of religious animal sacrifice.

Ordinance 87–72, which prohibits the slaughter of animals outside of areas zoned for slaughterhouses, is underinclusive on its face. The ordinance includes an exemption for "any person, group, or organization" that "slaughters or processes for sale, small numbers of hogs and/or cattle per week in accordance with an exemption provided by state law." See Fla.Stat. § 828.24(3) (1991). Respondent has not explained why commercial operations that slaughter "small numbers" of hogs and cattle do not implicate its professed desire to prevent cruelty to animals and preserve the public health. Although the city has classified Santeria sacrifice as slaughter, subjecting it to this ordinance, it does not regulate other killings for food in like manner.

We conclude, in sum, that each of Hialeah's ordinances pursues the city's governmental interests only against conduct motivated by religious belief. The ordinances "ha[ve] every appearance of a prohibition that society is prepared to impose upon [Santeria worshippers] but not upon itself." *The Florida Star v. B.J.F.,* 491 U.S. 524, 542, 109 S.Ct. 2603, 2614, 105 L.Ed.2d 443 (1989) (SCALIA, J., concurring in part and concurring in judgment). This precise evil is what the requirement of general applicability is designed to prevent.

III

A law burdening religious practice that is not neutral or not of general application must undergo the most rigorous of scrutiny. To satisfy the commands of the First Amendment, a law restrictive of religious practice must advance " 'interests of the highest order' " and must be narrowly tailored in pursuit of those interests. *McDaniel v. Paty,* 435 U.S., at 628, 98 S.Ct., at 1328, quoting *Wisconsin v. Yoder,* 406 U.S. 205, 215, 92 S.Ct. 1526, 1533, 32 L.Ed.2d 15 (1972). The compelling interest standard that we apply once a law fails to meet the *Smith* requirements is not "water[ed] * * * down" but "really means what it says." *Employment Div., Dept. of Human Resources of Oregon v. Smith,* 494 U.S., at 888, 110 S.Ct., at 1605. A law that targets religious conduct for distinctive treatment or advances legitimate governmental interests only against conduct with a religious motivation will survive strict scrutiny only in rare cases. It follows from what we have already said that these ordinances cannot withstand this scrutiny.

First, even were the governmental interests compelling, the ordinances are not drawn in narrow terms to accomplish those interests. As we have discussed, see *supra,* at 16–18, 21–24, all four ordinances are overbroad or underinclusive in substantial respects. The proffered objectives are not pursued with respect to analogous non-religious conduct, and those interests could be achieved by narrower ordinances that burdened religion to a far lesser degree. The absence of narrow tailoring suffices to establish the invalidity of the ordinances. See *Arkansas Writers' Project, Inc. v. Ragland,* 481 U.S. 221, 232, 107 S.Ct. 1722, 1729, 95 L.Ed.2d 209 (1987).

Respondent has not demonstrated, moreover, that, in the context of these ordinances, its governmental interests are compelling. Where government restricts only conduct protected by the First Amendment and fails to enact feasible measures to restrict other conduct producing substantial harm or alleged harm of the same sort, the interest given in justification of the restriction is not compelling. It is established in our strict scrutiny jurisprudence that "a law cannot be regarded as protecting an interest 'of the highest order' * * * when it leaves appreciable damage to that supposedly vital interest unprohibited." * * * As we show above, see *supra,* at 21–24, the ordinances are underinclusive to a substantial extent with respect to each of the interests that respondent has asserted, and it is only conduct motivated by religious conviction that bears the weight of the governmental restrictions. There can be no serious claim that those interests justify the ordinances.

IV

The Free Exercise Clause commits government itself to religious tolerance, and upon even slight suspicion that proposals for state intervention stem from animosity to religion or distrust of its practices, all officials must pause to remember their own high duty to the Constitution and to the rights it secures. Those in office must be resolute in resisting importunate demands and must ensure that the sole reasons for imposing the burdens of law and regulation are secular. Legislators may not devise mechanisms, overt or disguised, designed to persecute or oppress a religion or its practices. The laws here in question were enacted contrary to these constitutional principles, and they are void.

Reversed.

* * *

C. ADMINISTRATIVE REGULATIONS—LICENSES AND PERMITS

2. REVENUE AND REGULATORY CHARGES

p. 459: Add to Note 3

Where a county ordinance required applicants for a permit to parade or assemble on public property to pay in advance a fee of up to one thousand dollars but allowed the permit administrator to adjust the fee on a case-by-case basis to meet security expenses, the ordinance was held facially invalid for lack of adequate standards to guide or control administrative discretion. Forsyth County v. Nationalist Movement, ___ U.S. ___, 112 S.Ct. 2395, 120 L.Ed.2d 101 (1992). Compare Center for Auto Safety v. Athey, 37 F.3d 139 (4th Cir.1994) (state statute requiring charities to pay sliding-scale fee based on nationwide contribution level imposes user fee, not tax, does not violate Commerce Clause, and survives first-amendment scrutiny because content-neutral and narrowly tailored).

D. SPECIAL SUBJECTS OF FEDERAL AND LOCAL INTEREST

p. 477: Add after *City of Boston v. Harris* opinion

Note

Public housing tenants combine the roles of tenant and of the subjects of state action, and may be accorded "rights" under both statuses. For example, in Doe v. New Bedford Housing Authority, 417 Mass. 273, 630 N.E.2d 248 (1994), the court found that while the housing authority's failure to make any effort to rid the common areas of non-tenant drug dealers and buyers, may not have constituted an actionable breach of the implied warranty of habitability, or an actionable nuisance, it did violate the tenants' rights under pertinent statutes and the covenant of quiet enjoyment. In Pratt v. Chicago Housing Authority, 848 F.Supp. 792 (N.D.Ill.1994), the District Court granted temporary injunctive relief in response to a predictably successful challenge on fourth amendment grounds of the Authority's program in which a warrantless search of every apartment, closet, drawer, and refrigerator in an entire, high-rise building would be pursued in response to gunfire from a building or if one ran into the building after firing a gun.

p. 483: Add new title to Note 1

1. Local Rent Control As Not Constituting Fifth Amendment Taking.

Add to note

Subsequently, the Supreme Court was asked to consider rent control and eviction limits as the equivalent of a physical invasion under the Court's regulatory-takings jurisprudence. In Yee v. City of Escondido, 503 U.S. 519, 112 S.Ct. 1522, 118 L.Ed.2d 153 (1992), the Court rejected the argument; the mobile pad rental that led to imposition of the controls was voluntary, not compelled.

p. 492: Add to Note 1

Congress passed the Cable Television Consumer Protection and Competition Act of 1992, P.L. 102–85, 106 Stat. 1460, which subjects the industry to rate regulation by the F.C.C., and by municipal franchising authorities, prohibits municipalities from awarding exclusive franchises, imposes various restrictions, and directs the F.C.C. to impose technical standards. The "must carry" provisions of the Act, which required operators to carry a specified number of local stations, were challenged as violating first amendment freedoms. With a number of opinions, none gathering a majority, the Supreme Court vacated a district court judgment that ruled that the provisions were consistent with the first amendment, and remanded for further proceedings consistent with the ruling. Turner Broadcasting System, Inc. v. F.C.C., ___ U.S. ___, 114 S.Ct. 2445, 129 L.Ed.2d 497 (1994).

Chapter VII

LOCAL GOVERNMENT MANAGEMENT OF LAND

I. LAND USE PLANNING AND REGULATION

B. PUBLIC REGULATION OF LAND USE

2. OTHER LAND USE CONTROLS

b. Landmark and Historic Preservation

p. 504: Add to the first paragraph discussion of *United Artists*

The Supreme Court of Pennsylvania reversed its prior *United Artists* decision and held that the designation, without the consent of its owner, of a private building as historic did not constitute a taking. The court found, however, that the ordinance in question did not authorize designation of the interior of the building. United Artists' Theater Circuit, Inc. v. City of Philadelphia, 535 Pa. 370, 635 A.2d 612 (1993).

Religious freedoms limit landmark designation authority. In First Covenant Church of Seattle v. Seattle, 120 Wash.2d 203, 840 P.2d 174 (1992) the court voided an ordinance permitting alteration of church exterior only if the church's "liturgy" demands because it burdens the free exercise of religion administratively and financially, and is not compellingly justified by the city's interest in preserving aesthetic and historic structures. The decision also rested on independent state constitutional grounds.

c. Environmental

p. 510: Add to Note 1

But municipal efforts to impose environmentally protective requirements under building-code permit authority might have difficulty. For example, in New York, a village was held to lack the type of discretion that would enable it to tie permit approval to the land use or environmental information contained in an environmental impact statement which it attempted to demand of a developer under the state's Environmental Quality Review Act. Incorporated Village of Atlantic Beach v. Gavalas, 81 N.Y.2d 322, 599 N.Y.S.2d 218, 615 N.E.2d 608 (1993).

d. *Group Occupancy Restrictions*

p. 511: Add to first full paragraph

Compare County of Dane v. Norman, 174 Wis.2d 683, 497 N.W.2d 714 (1993) (living together is conduct not status and thus ordinance prohibiting discrimination on the basis of marital status was not applicable where landlord refused to rent to unmarried, unrelated groups) with Swanner v. Anchorage Equal Rights Com'n, 874 P.2d 274 (Alaska 1994), cert. denied, ___ U.S. ___, 115 S.Ct. 460, 130 L.Ed.2d 368 (1994) (Landlord's refusal on religious grounds to rent to unmarrieds held to violate state and local anti-discrimination laws).

Add to second full paragraph

In Kirsch v. Prince George's County, 331 Md. 89, 626 A.2d 372, cert. denied, ___ U.S. ___, 114 S.Ct. 600, 126 L.Ed.2d 565 (1993), a county zoning ordinance that placed restrictions on the rental of housing to groups of students, but not to other groups, was overturned as lacking a rational basis. Unlike the *Belle Terre* ordinance, this ordinance differentiated on the basis of occupation (only students were regulated) and did not advance the county's goals of limiting noise, litter, and parking congestion as there was no proof that groups of unrelated non-students would not cause similar problems.

Add after second full paragraph

Group home cases, especially with regard to retarded and other disabled groups, have begun to experience the impact of the Fair Housing Act Amendments of 1988 directed toward disabilities, and of other federal reasonable-accommodation statutes. Compare City of Edmonds v. Washington State Building Code Council, 18 F.3d 802 (9th Cir.1994), cert. granted, ___ U.S. ___, 115 S.Ct. 417, 130 L.Ed.2d 332 (1994) with Elliott v. Athens, Ga., 960 F.2d 975 (11th Cir.1992), cert. denied, ___ U.S. ___, 113 S.Ct. 376, 121 L.Ed.2d 287 (1992) and Familystyle of St. Paul, Inc. v. City of St. Paul, 923 F.2d 91 (8th Cir.1991). And see Smith & Lee Assoc. v. City of Taylor, 13 F.3d 920 (6th Cir.1993); Pentel v. City of Mendota Heights, 13 F.3d 1261 (8th Cir.1994).

e. *Aesthetics and Sign Regulation*

p. 513: Add after the text

The *Gilleo* case, cited above, was affirmed by the Supreme Court in the following opinion:

CITY OF LADUE v. GILLEO

Supreme Court of the United States, 1994.
___ U.S. ___, 114 S.Ct. 2038, 129 L.Ed.2d 36.

JUSTICE STEVENS delivered the opinion of the Court.

An ordinance of the City of Ladue prohibits homeowners from displaying any signs on their property except "residence identification" signs, "for sale" signs, and signs warning of safety hazards. The ordinance permits commercial establishments, churches, and nonprofit organizations to erect certain signs that are not allowed at residences. The question presented is whether the ordinance violates a Ladue resident's right to free speech.

I

Respondent Margaret P. Gilleo owns one of the 57 single-family homes in the Willow Hill subdivision of Ladue. On December 8, 1990, she placed on her front lawn a 24– by 36–inch sign printed with the words "Say No to War in the Persian Gulf, Call Congress Now." After that sign disappeared, Gilleo put up another but it was knocked to the ground. When Gilleo reported these incidents to the police, they advised her that such signs were prohibited in Ladue. The City Council denied her petition for a variance. Gilleo then filed this action under 42 U.S.C. § 1983 against the City, the Mayor, and members of the City Council, alleging that Ladue's sign ordinance violated her First Amendment right of free speech.

The District Court issued a preliminary injunction against enforcement of the ordinance. 774 F.Supp. 1559 (E.D.Mo.1991). Gilleo then placed an 8.5– by 11–inch sign in the second story window of her home stating, "For Peace in the Gulf." The Ladue City Council responded to the injunction by repealing its ordinance and enacting a replacement. Like its predecessor, the new ordinance contains a general prohibition of "signs" and defines that term broadly. The ordinance prohibits all signs except those that fall within one of ten exemptions. Thus, "residential identification signs" no larger than one square foot are allowed, as are signs advertising "that the property is for sale, lease or exchange" and identifying the owner or agent. § 35–10, App. to Pet. for Cert. 45a. Also exempted are signs "for churches, religious institutions, and schools," "[c]ommercial signs in commercially or industrial zoned districts," and on-site signs advertising "gasoline filling stations." Unlike its predecessor, the new ordinance contains a lengthy "Declaration of Findings, Policies, Interests, and Purposes," part of which recites that the

> "proliferation of an unlimited number of signs in private, residential, commercial, industrial, and public areas of the City of Ladue would create ugliness, visual blight and clutter, tarnish the natural beauty of the landscape as well as the residential and commercial architecture, impair property values, substantially impinge upon the

privacy and special ambience of the community, and may cause safety and traffic hazards to motorists, pedestrians, and children[.]" *Id.,* at 36a.

Gilleo amended her complaint to challenge the new ordinance, which explicitly prohibits window signs like hers. The District Court held the ordinance unconstitutional, and the Court of Appeals affirmed. 986 F.2d 1180 (CA8 1993). Relying on the plurality opinion in *Metromedia, Inc. v. San Diego,* 453 U.S. 490, 101 S.Ct. 2882, 69 L.Ed.2d 800 (1981), the Court of Appeals held the ordinance invalid as a "content based" regulation because the City treated commercial speech more favorably than noncommercial speech and favored some kinds of noncommercial speech over others. *Id.,* at 1182. Acknowledging that "Ladue's interests in enacting its ordinance are substantial," the Court of Appeals nevertheless concluded that those interests were "not sufficiently 'compelling' to support a content-based restriction." *Id.,* at 1183–1184 (citing *Simon & Schuster, Inc. v. New York Crime Victims Bd.,* 502 U.S. ___, ___, 112 S.Ct. 501, 513, 116 L.Ed.2d 476 (1991)).

We granted the City of Ladue's petition for certiorari, 510 U.S. ___, 114 S.Ct. 55, 126 L.Ed.2d 24 (1993), and now affirm.

II

While signs are a form of expression protected by the Free Speech Clause, they pose distinctive problems that are subject to municipalities' police powers. Unlike oral speech, signs take up space and may obstruct views, distract motorists, displace alternative uses for land, and pose other problems that legitimately call for regulation. It is common ground that governments may regulate the physical characteristics of signs—just as they can, within reasonable bounds and absent censorial purpose, regulate audible expression in its capacity as noise. See, *e.g., Ward v. Rock Against Racism,* 491 U.S. 781, 109 S.Ct. 2746, 105 L.Ed.2d 661 (1989); *Kovacs v. Cooper,* 336 U.S. 77, 69 S.Ct. 448, 93 L.Ed. 513 (1949). However, because regulation of a medium inevitably affects communication itself, it is not surprising that we have had occasion to review the constitutionality of municipal ordinances prohibiting the display of certain outdoor signs.

In *Linmark Associates, Inc. v. Willingboro,* 431 U.S. 85, 97 S.Ct. 1614, 52 L.Ed.2d 155 (1977), we addressed an ordinance that sought to maintain stable, integrated neighborhoods by prohibiting homeowners from placing "For Sale" or "Sold" signs on their property. Although we recognized the importance of Willingboro's objective, we held that the First Amendment prevented the township from "achieving its goal by restricting the free flow of truthful information." *Id.,* at 95, 97 S.Ct., at 1619. In some respects *Linmark* is the mirror image of this case. For instead of prohibiting "For Sale" signs without banning any other signs, Ladue has exempted such signs from an otherwise virtually complete ban. Moreover, whereas in *Linmark* we noted that the ordinance was not concerned with the promotion of aesthetic values unrelated to the content of the prohibited speech, *id.,* at 93–94, 97 S.Ct., at 1618–1619, here Ladue relies squarely on that content-neutral justification for its ordinance.

In *Metromedia,* we reviewed an ordinance imposing substantial prohibitions on outdoor advertising displays within the City of San Diego in the interest of traffic safety and aesthetics. The ordinance generally banned all except those advertising "on-site" activities. The Court concluded that the City's interest in traffic safety and its aesthetic interest in preventing "visual clutter" could justify a prohibition of off-site commercial billboards even though similar on-site signs were allowed. 453 U.S., at 511–512, 101 S.Ct., at 2894–2895. Nevertheless, the Court's judgment in *Metromedia,* supported by two different lines of reasoning, invalidated the San Diego ordinance in its entirety. According to Justice White's plurality opinion, the ordinance impermissibly discriminated on the basis of content by permitting on-site commercial speech while broadly prohibiting noncommercial messages. *Id.,* at 514–515, 101 S.Ct., at 2896–2897. On the other hand, Justice Brennan, joined by Justice Blackmun, concluded "that the *practical* effect of the San Diego ordinance [was] to eliminate the billboard as an effective medium of communication" for noncommercial messages, and that the city had failed to make the strong showing needed to justify such "content-neutral prohibitions of particular media of communication." *Id.,* at 525–527, 101 S.Ct., at 2902. The three dissenters also viewed San Diego's ordinance as tantamount to a blanket prohibition of billboards, but would have upheld it because they did not perceive "even a hint of bias or censorship in the city's actions" nor "any reason to believe that the overall communications market in San Diego is inadequate." *Id.,* at 552–553, 101 S.Ct., at 2915–2916 (STEVENS, J., dissenting in part). See also *id.,* at 563, 566, 101 S.Ct., at 2921, 2922–2923 (BURGER, C.J., dissenting); *Id.,* at 569–570, 101 S.Ct., at 2924–2925 (REHNQUIST, J., dissenting).

In *City Council of Los Angeles v. Taxpayers for Vincent,* 466 U.S. 789, 104 S.Ct. 2118, 80 L.Ed.2d 772 (1984), we upheld a Los Angeles ordinance that prohibited the posting of signs on public property. Noting the conclusion shared by seven Justices in *Metromedia* that San Diego's "interest in avoiding visual clutter" was sufficient to justify a prohibition of commercial billboards, *id.,* at 806–807, 104 S.Ct., at 2130 in *Vincent* we upheld the Los Angeles ordinance, which was justified on the same grounds. We rejected the argument that the validity of the City's aesthetic interest had been compromised by failing to extend the ban to private property, reasoning that the "private citizen's interest in controlling the use of his own property justifies the disparate treatment." *Id.,* at 811, 104 S.Ct., at 2132. We also rejected as "misplaced" respondents' reliance on public forum principles, for they had "fail[ed] to demonstrate the existence of a traditional right of access respecting such items as utility poles * * * comparable to that recognized for public streets and parks." *Id.,* at 814, 104 S.Ct., at 2133.

These decisions identify two analytically distinct grounds for challenging the constitutionality of a municipal ordinance regulating the display of signs. One is that the measure in effect restricts too little speech because its exemptions discriminate on the basis of the signs' messages. See *Metromedia,* 453 U.S., at 512–517, 101 S.Ct., at 2895–2897 (opinion of White, J.). Alternatively, such provisions are subject to attack on the ground that they simply prohibit too much protected speech. See *id.,* at 525–534, 101 S.Ct., at 2901–2906 (Brennan, J., concurring in judgment). The City of Ladue contends, first, that the Court of Appeals' reliance on the former rationale was misplaced because the City's regulatory purposes are content-neutral, and, second, that those purposes justify the comprehensiveness of the sign prohibition. A comment on the former contention will help explain why we ultimately base our decision on a rejection of the latter.

III

While surprising at first glance, the notion that a regulation of speech may be impermissibly *underinclusive* is firmly grounded in basic First Amendment principles. Thus, an exemption from an otherwise permissible regulation of speech may represent a governmental "attempt to give one side of a debatable public question an advantage in expressing its views to the people." *First Nat. Bank of Boston v. Belloti,* 435 U.S. 765, 785–786, 98 S.Ct. 1407, 1420–1421, 55 L.Ed.2d 707 (1978). Alternatively, through the combined operation of a general speech restriction and its exemptions, the government might seek to select the "permissible subjects for public debate" and thereby to "control * * * the search for political truth." *Consolidated Edison Co. of N.Y. v. Public Service Comm'n of N.Y.,* 447 U.S. 530, 538, 100 S.Ct. 2326, 2333, 65 L.Ed.2d 319 (1980).

* * *

Under the Court of Appeals' content discrimination rationale, the City might theoretically remove the defects in its ordinance by simply repealing all of the exemptions. If, however, the ordinance is also vulnerable because it prohibits too much speech, that solution would not save it. Moreover, if the prohibitions in Ladue's ordinance are impermissible, resting our decision on its exemptions would afford scant relief for respondent Gilleo. She is primarily concerned not with the scope of the exemptions available in other locations, such as commercial areas and on church property. She asserts a constitutional right to display an antiwar sign at her own home. Therefore, we first ask whether Ladue may properly *prohibit* Gilleo from displaying her sign, and then, only if necessary, consider the separate question whether it was improper for the City simultaneously to *permit* certain other signs. In examining the propriety of Ladue's near-total prohibition of residential signs, we will assume, *arguendo,* the validity of the City's submission that the various exemptions are free of impermissible content or viewpoint discrimination.

IV

In *Linmark* we held that the City's interest in maintaining a stable, racially integrated neighborhood was not sufficient to support a prohibition of residential "For Sale" signs. We recognized that even such a narrow sign prohibition would have a deleterious effect on residents' ability to convey important information because alternatives were "far from satisfactory." 431 U.S., at 93, 97 S.Ct., at 1618. Ladue's sign ordinance is supported principally by the City's interest in minimizing the visual clutter associated with signs, an interest that is concededly valid but certainly no more compelling than the interests at stake in *Linmark*. Moreover, whereas the ordinance in *Linmark* applied only to a form of commercial speech, Ladue's ordinance covers even such absolutely pivotal speech as a sign protesting an imminent governmental decision to go to war.

The impact on free communication of Ladue's broad sign prohibition, moreover, is manifestly greater than in *Linmark*. Gilleo and other residents of Ladue are forbidden to display virtually any "sign" on their property. The ordinance defines that term sweepingly. A prohibition is not always invalid merely because it applies to a sizeable category of speech; the sign ban we upheld in *Vincent,* for example, was quite broad. But in *Vincent* we specifically noted that the category of speech in question—signs placed on public property—was not a "uniquely valuable or important mode of communication," and that there was no evidence that "appellees' ability to communicate effectively is threatened by ever-increasing restrictions on expression." 466 U.S., at 812, 104 S.Ct., at 2133.

Here, in contrast, Ladue has almost completely foreclosed a venerable means of communication that is both unique and important. It has totally foreclosed that medium to political, religious, or personal messages. Signs that react to a local happening or express a view on a controversial issue both reflect and animate change in the life of a community. Often placed on lawns or in windows, residential signs play an important part in political campaigns, during which they are displayed to signal the resident's support for particular candidates, parties, or causes. They may not afford the same opportunities for conveying complex ideas as do other media, but residential signs have long been an important and distinct medium of expression.

Our prior decisions have voiced particular concern with laws that foreclose an entire medium of expression. Thus, we have held invalid ordinances that completely banned the distribution of pamphlets within the municipality, *Lovell v. Griffin,* 303 U.S. 444, 451–452, 58 S.Ct. 666, 669, 82 L.Ed. 949 (1938); handbills on the public streets, *Jamison v. Texas,* 318 U.S. 413, 416, 63 S.Ct. 669, 672, 87 L.Ed. 869 (1943); the door-to-door distribution of literature, *Martin v. Struthers,* 319 U.S. 141, 145–149, 63 S.Ct. 862, 864–866, 87 L.Ed. 1313 (1943); *Schneider v. State,* 308 U.S. 147, 164–165, 60 S.Ct. 146, 152, 84 L.Ed. 155 (1939), and live entertainment, *Schad v. Mount Ephraim,* 452 U.S. 61, 75–76, 101 S.Ct. 2176, 2186, 68 L.Ed.2d 671 (1981). See also *Frisby v. Schultz,* 487 U.S. 474, 486, 108 S.Ct. 2495, 2503, 101 L.Ed.2d 420 (1988) (picketing focused upon individual residence is "fundamentally different from more generally directed means of communication that may not be completely banned in residential areas"). Although prohibitions foreclosing entire media may be completely free of content or viewpoint discrimination, the danger they pose to the freedom of speech is readily apparent—by eliminating a common means of speaking, such measures can suppress too much speech.

Ladue contends, however, that its ordinance is a mere regulation of the "time, place, or manner" of speech because residents remain free to convey their desired messages by other means, such as *hand-held* signs, "letters, handbills, flyers, telephone calls, newspaper advertisements, bumper stickers, speeches, and neighborhood or community meetings." Brief for Petitioners 41. However, even regulations that do not foreclose an entire medium of expression, but merely shift the time, place, or manner of its use, must "leave open ample alternative channels for communication." *Clark v. Community for Creative Non–Violence,* 468 U.S. 288, 293, 104 S.Ct. 3065, 3069, 82 L.Ed.2d 221 (1984). In this case, we are not persuaded that adequate substitutes exist for the important medium of speech that Ladue has closed off.

Displaying a sign from one's own residence often carries a message quite distinct from placing the same sign someplace else, or conveying the same text or picture by other means. Precisely because of their location, such signs provide information about the identity of the "speaker." As an early and eminent student of rhetoric observed, the identity of the speaker is an important component of many attempts to persuade. A sign advocating "Peace in the Gulf" in the front lawn of a retired general or decorated war veteran may provoke a different reaction than the same sign in a 10–year–old child's bedroom window or the same message on a bumper sticker of a passing automobile. An espousal of socialism may carry different implications when displayed on the grounds of a stately mansion than when pasted on a factory wall or an ambulatory sandwich board.

Residential signs are an unusually cheap and convenient form of communication. Especially for persons of modest means or limited mobility, a yard or window sign may have no practical substitute. Cf. *Vincent,* 466 U.S., at 812–813, n. 30, 104 S.Ct., at 2132–2133, n. 30; *Anderson v. Celebrezze,* 460 U.S. 780, 793–794, 103 S.Ct. 1564, 1572–1573, 75 L.Ed.2d 547 (1983); *Martin v. Struthers,* 319 U.S., at 146, 63 S.Ct. at 865; *Milk Wagon Drivers v. Meadowmoor Dairies, Inc.,* 312 U.S. 287, 293, 61 S.Ct. 552, 555, 85 L.Ed. 836 (1941). Even for the affluent, the added costs in money or time of taking out a newspaper advertisement, handing out leaflets on the street, or standing in front of one's house with a handheld sign may make the difference between participating and not participating in some public debate. Furthermore, a person who puts up a sign at her residence often intends to reach *neighbors,* an audience that could not be reached nearly as well by other means.

A special respect for individual liberty in the home has long been part of our culture and our law, see, *e.g., Payton v. New York,* 445 U.S. 573, 596–597, and nn. 44–45, 100 S.Ct. 1371, 1385–1386, and nn. 44–45,

63 L.Ed.2d 639 (1980); that principle has special resonance when the government seeks to constrain a person's ability to *speak* there. See *Spence v. Washington,* 418 U.S. 405, 406, 409, 411, 94 S.Ct. 2727, 2728, 2729–2730, 41 L.Ed.2d 842 (1974) (*per curiam*). Most Americans would be understandably dismayed, given that tradition, to learn that it was illegal to display from their window an 8– by 11–inch sign expressing their political views. Whereas the government's need to mediate among various competing uses, including expressive ones, for public streets and facilities is constant and unavoidable, see *Cox v. New Hampshire,* 312 U.S. 569, 574, 576, 61 S.Ct. 762, 765, 765, 85 L.Ed. 1049 (1941); see also *Widmar v. Vincent,* 454 U.S. 263, 278, 102 S.Ct. 269, 278–279, 70 L.Ed.2d 440 (1981) (STEVENS, J., concurring in judgment), its need to regulate temperate speech from the home is surely much less pressing, see *Spence,* 418 U.S., at 409, 94 S.Ct., at 2729–2730.

Our decision that Ladue's ban on almost all residential signs violates the First Amendment by no means leaves the City powerless to address the ills that may be associated with residential signs.[17] It bears mentioning that individual residents themselves have strong incentives to keep their own property values up and to prevent "visual clutter" in their own yards and neighborhoods—incentives markedly different from those of persons who erect signs on others' land, in others' neighborhoods, or on public property. Residents' self-interest diminishes the danger of the "unlimited" proliferation of residential signs that concerns the City of Ladue. We are confident that more temperate measures could in large part satisfy Ladue's stated regulatory needs without harm to the First Amendment rights of its citizens. As currently framed, however, the ordinance abridges those rights.

Accordingly, the judgment of the Court of Appeals is

Affirmed.

* * *

f. Control of "Adult" Establishments

p. 518: Add to note

International Eateries of America v. Broward County, Florida, 941 F.2d 1157 (11th Cir.1991), cert. denied, ___ U.S. ___, 112 S.Ct. 1294, 117 L.Ed.2d 517 (1992) (upholding county ordinance regulating location of adult nightclubs).

17. Nor do we hold that every kind of sign must be permitted in residential areas. Different considerations might well apply, for example, in the case of signs (whether political or otherwise) displayed by residents for a fee, or in the case of off-site commercial advertisements on residential property. We also are not confronted here with mere regulations short of a ban.

C. ZONING

1. GENERAL STANDARDS

d. Conditional Zoning

p. 534: Add to Note

In Dacy v. Village of Ruidoso, 114 N.M. 699, 845 P.2d 793 (1992), the court held that contract zoning was illegal when a city does not follow legislative procedure prescribed for zoning changes. The court distinguished a situation where a city does not commit itself to a zoning change before a hearing. A party's unilateral promise in return for a municipality's rezoning would be a legal unilateral contract because the municipality made no bilateral or reciprocal promise to effect the rezoning.

2. EXCEPTIONAL STANDARDS

a. Nonconforming Uses

p. 542: Add to Note 1

The Pennsylvania Supreme Court has ruled that a legal, nonconforming use (there an adult bookstore) could not be terminated by amortization under that state's constitution. "If government decides to interfere with the owner's use, where the use is lawful and is not a nuisance nor is it abandoned, it must compensate the owner for the resulting loss * * *. Thus, we hold that the amortization and discontinuance of lawful, pre-existing, non-conforming use is per se confiscatory and violative of the constitution." PA Northwestern Distributors, Inc. v. Zoning Hearing Board of Moon Township, 526 Pa. 186, 584 A.2d 1372 (1991), noted, supra, at p. 518.

d. Special Exceptions

p. 552: Add to Note 3

See In re Kostenblatt, 161 Vt. 292, 640 A.2d 39 (1994) (conditions not stated in conditional use permit are not enforceable; however, requirements of town by-laws are enforceable even though they are not expressly included in the conditional use permit).

Add to Note 4

See Western Presbyterian Church v. Board of Zoning Adjustment, 862 F.Supp. 538 (D.D.C.1994) (where a church's interest in feeding the homeless was substantially and improperly burdened by being in split zone, one part of which *prohibited* the use and the other part of which *did not include* it, the denial of a permit violated the church's freedom of religion under the first amendment and the federal 1993 Religious Freedom Restoration Act).

D. SUBDIVISION CONTROLS

1. OFFICIAL MAPS

p. 558: Add to citations in text

Joint Ventures, Inc. v. Department of Transportation, 563 So.2d 622, 626 (Fla.1990) (official map reservation constitutes a taking under both the federal and state constitutions; there is "no valid distinction between 'freezing' property in this fashion and deliberately attempting to depress land values in anticipation of eminent domain proceedings.")

2. SUBDIVISION BY PRIVATE DEVELOPERS

p. 569: Add to Note 3

The Supreme Court has required that such regulatory exercises have an essential nexus to legitimate public purposes, and that the required exactions must be thus justified by their relation to the projected impact of the proposed development. In determining the closeness of that relationship, the Court considered the three standards developed by the state courts—broadly reasonable; rational nexus; specifically and uniquely attributable—and seemed to prefer rational nexus, rephrased as "roughly proportional." Underscoring *Nollan,* the Court drew distinctions between land use regulations that enjoy presumptions of rationality, on the one hand, and government actions that pass upon the individual circumstances of a building-permit request. Dolan v. City of Tigard, ___ U.S. ___, 114 S.Ct. 2309, 129 L.Ed.2d 304 (1994), reported infra in this Supplement.

E. CONTROL OF GROWTH AND DEVELOPMENT

1. EXCLUSIONARY ZONING

pp. 575–76: Add to Note 2

The resurgence of judicial interest in fair share standards, illustrated by *Britton,* has encouraged like initiatives from other sources. The federal government warned state and local governments that failure to amend restrictive zoning and building codes would risk loss of federal funds. "Governments Warned On Restrictive Housing Codes," The Washington Post, February 1, 1992, at F6. States such as Connecticut and Massachusetts had added statutory impetus to full consideration in the land-use permit processes. See West Hartford Interfaith Coalition, Inc. v. Town Council, 228 Conn. 498, 636 A.2d 1342 (1994) (procedure governing affordable housing land-use appeals applied to legislative decision to deny zoning changes; court could grant application instead of remand to allow submission of modified application); George Hudson, "Housing Law Challenges Power of Zoning Boards," The New York Times, November 5, 1991, at B5.

3. COST CONTROL; EXACTIONS, IMPACT AND OTHER FEES

a. Transferable Development Rights

p. 588: Add to Note

The protection of farmland has motivated at least one area, the Old Mission Peninsula of Michigan, to impose taxes on itself to provide funds whereby the township might purchase landowner's development rights. Keith Schneider, "Town Finds Rare Way To Protect Farms: Tax," The New York Times, September 11, 1994, at 16; Amy Hamilton, "Michigan Voters Hike Property Tax To Fund Conservation," 7 State Tax Notes 846 (1994). A farmer who could not afford a $50,000 fine for causing a severe fish kill, "paid" the fine by transferring to a state preservation foundation the development rights to his property. "Va. Farmer Settles Fine By Giving Up Land Rights," The Washington Post, April 4, 1992, at F6.

b. Impact and Linkage Fees and Taxes

p. 596: Add new Note 1

1. Administrative Regulation. Illustrative of the hurdles facing COAH's administrative regulation in the wake of *Mount Laurel* is In re Township of Warren, 132 N.J. 1, 622 A.2d 1257 (1993). There the court invalidated a COAH regulation authorizing municipalities that seek substantive certification of regional fair-share plans to make available an occupancy preference for 50% of such housing to income-eligible households that reside or work in the municipality. See generally, Timothy J. Choppin, *Breaking the Exclusionary Land Use Regulation Barrier: Policies to Promote Affordable Housing in the Suburbs,* 82 Geo.L.J. 2039 (1994).

Add to what now becomes Note 2, Impact Fees

To *Commercial Builders:* Certiorari was denied, ___ U.S. ___, 112 S.Ct. 1997, 118 L.Ed.2d 593 (1992).

To the Schukoske article: The page is 1011.

Add after the *Eastern Diversified Properties* and *New Jersey Builders Assoc.* citations: Compare Waters Landing Limited Partnership v. Montgomery County, 337 Md. 15, 650 A.2d 712 (1994) (county may impose development impact *taxes* retroactively to encompass charges earlier levied as development impact "fees").

To the end of the note

The question whether the Supreme Court's ruling in *Nollan* would have a limiting effect on this area has been answered by the Court in *Dolan v. City of Tigard,* reported infra in this Supplement. The reader is invited to refer back to this supplement's addition to the note on p. 569.

G. ADDITIONAL CONSTITUTIONAL CHALLENGES: DUE PROCESS; REGULATORY TAKING

1. ZONING PROCEDURE AND DUE PROCESS

p. 605: Add to Notes, paragraph 1

See also, L.A. Ray Realty v. Town of Cumberland, 603 A.2d 311 (R.I.1992) (voiding zoning amendment establishing minimum lot size, adopted by referendum but without notice to, and hearing of, affected landowners, because referendum and initiative processes were inconsistent with procedural safeguards in the general enabling statutes); The Great Atlantic and Pacific Tea Co. v. Borough of Point Pleasant, 137 N.J. 136, 644 A.2d 598 (1944) (prohibition in the Municipal Land Use Law against adoption of zoning ordinance by referendum does not include a non-binding referendum expressing voter preference).

2. REGULATORY TAKING

p. 605: Add to introduction before Bosselman article

See generally, David J. McCarthy, Jr., *Ruminations On Regulation and the Takings Clause,* Home Rule and Civil Society, March 1994, at 27.

p. 619: Add to Note 2

The New York Court of Appeals invalidated as a regulatory taking a narrow rent control regulation requiring some Manhattan building owners to offer renewals to non-profit-hospital lessees who in turn sublet the apartments to hospital employees. Manocherian v. Lenox Hill Hosp., 84 N.Y.2d 385, 618 N.Y.S.2d 857, 643 N.E.2d 479 (1994).

The U.S. Supreme Court has recently added three opinions that dramatically advance the evolution of the regulatory-takings doctrine: Yee v. City of Escondido, 503 U.S. 519, 112 S.Ct. 1522, 118 L.Ed.2d 153 (1992); Lucas v. South Carolina Coastal Council, reported below; and Dolan v. City of Tigard, reported below.

p. 619: Substitute for the Presbytery of Seattle case the following comment

DAVID J. MCCARTHY, JR., RUMINATIONS ON REGULATION AND THE TAKINGS CLAUSE

Home Rule and Civil Society, March 1994, at 27, 55–57 (footnotes omitted).

What of *Yee v. City of Escondido?* With all the questions resulting from the *Lucas* decision, *Yee* has gone much unremarked. But it has things to teach us. Remember what was at issue. Before *Lucas'* elaboration, one apparently "sure thing" was that a regulation that involved a physical invasion seemed to be a *per se* taking. Analyzing the problem of rent control applied to mobile-home sites, U.S. Circuit Judge Alex Kozinski, in *Hall v. City of Santa Barbara,* thought that, while the typical rent-control ordinance may not have inherent incentives leading tenants to "overstay" in the controlled premises, the same could not be said of controls on mobile-home sites. The ordinance that imposed controls on the rental of mobile-home sites effectively permitted the tenants to profit from the controls in the selling prices to mobile-unit buyers who would continue to use the home on the controlled site. (Buyers normally did just that.) Economic studies at the time demonstrated that the resale value of mobile units sold on rent-controlled sites was one-third higher than units sold elsewhere. The combined effect of the Santa Barbara rent-control ordinance and a California statute that prohibited tenant evictions without just cause was to transfer a possessory interest from park owner to mobile unit owner, a transfer that amounted to a physical invasion like the one invalidated in *Loretto.*

The *Yee* California courts disagreed with Judge Kozinski's *Hall* rationale, asserting that neither the rent controls nor the eviction restrictions constituted regulatory takings, separately or in toto. Meanwhile, in another federal circuit, in *Pinewood Estates v. Barnegat Tp.*

Leveling Board, the court, like Judge Kozinski, found a taking. The California *Yee* opinion offered merely the economic observation that when the price of goods is lowered, the price of complementary goods increases. However, interim economic commentary disagreed and looked approvingly at the Kozinski effort as more faithful to the balancing approach of *Penn Central.* The U.S. Supreme Court attempted to resolve the conflict between the circuits and the state case.

In the U.S. Supreme Court, Justice O'Connor and the majority continued the effort to bring order to the area of regulatory taking. The Kozinski argument "while perhaps within the scope of our regulatory taking cases, cannot be squared easily with our cases on physical takings." Many ordinary land-use regulations transfer wealth and are not objectionable for that reason. The arguments that the one-time premium earned by the rent-controlled tenant's sale distinguish the mobile-home-site controls from ordinary rent controls, and that the combined effect of the California just-cause eviction statute and city rent control ordinance is to deprive landlords of the ability to choose their incoming tenants, may bear upon whether there is a regulatory taking, a taking the cost of which should not be visited upon one person but should be spread among the taxpayers. But those arguments do not "convert regulation into the unwanted physical occupation of land." The landlords' choices to rent their lands for these purposes were voluntary choices subsequent aspects of which are regulated; they were not compelled choices.

The Court recognized as arguments *conceptually separate* from the physical invasion challenge assertions that the ordinance also constitutes a denial of substantive due process and a regulatory taking. It did not address either one because substantive due process was not appropriately raised below and the other was not within the grant of certiorari. In discussing the latter point, the Court attempted some further clarification.

To the argument that a regulatory-taking challenge would be unripe without an effort to seek rent increases in Escondido, the Court responded that the *Yee* challenge was a facial challenge, an assertion that the ordinance "does not 'substantially advance' a 'legitimate state interest' no matter how it is applied" and did not depend on the extent to which the landowners were deprived of the economic use of the property or the extent to which they have been compensated.

As to the relationship between physical takings and regulatory takings, the Court said, "Consideration of whether a regulatory taking occurred would not assist in resolving whether a physical taking occurred as well; neither of the two questions is subsidiary to the other. Both might be subsidiary to a question embracing both—Was there a taking?—but they exist side by side, neither encompassing the other." Quoting *Loretto,* the Court went on to say, "Our holding today is very narrow. We affirm the traditional rule that a permanent physical occupation of property is a taking. In such a case, the property owner entertains a historically rooted expectation of compensation, and the character of the invasion is qualitatively more intrusive than perhaps any other category of property regulation. We do not, however, question the equally substantial authority upholding a State's broad power to impose appropriate restrictions upon an owner's use of his property." Here, the Court held, the rent control ordinance did not compel a landowner to suffer the physical occupation of the property.

Some "sorting out" had occurred as a result of the *Yee* opinion. Regulations could result in compelled physical occupation and would then be *per se* takings. Regulatory physical invasions are a subspecies of the broad takings question as are the complementary assertions of regulatory takings that do not compel physical occupation. Facial challenges are recognized, and the ripeness requirements do not then apply. The takings arguments are separate from substantive due process arguments. The assertion that an ordinance does not substantially advance a legitimate state interest is a facial challenge that, lest there have been any doubt, need not be accompanied by an assertion that the ordinance has denied all economic value. The recognition of an appropriate state role in regulating land use without compensation does not augur well for the development of a plethora of *per se* takings in the regulatory field. And finally, *compelled* physical occupation is the essence of a *Loretto* problem, whatever the economic analysis, as *Nollan* had suggested.

* * *

LUCAS v. SOUTH CAROLINA COASTAL COUNCIL

Supreme Court of the United States, 1992.
___ U.S. ___, 112 S.Ct. 2886, 120 L.Ed.2d 798.

JUSTICE SCALIA delivered the opinion of the Court.

In 1986, petitioner David H. Lucas paid $975,000 for two residential lots on the Isle of Palms in Charleston County, South Carolina, on which he intended to build single-family homes. In 1988, however, the South Carolina Legislature enacted the Beachfront Management Act, S.C.Code § 48–39–250 *et seq.* (Supp.1990) (Act), which had the direct effect of barring petitioner from erecting any permanent habitable structures on his two parcels. See § 48–39–290(A). A state trial court found that this prohibition rendered Lucas's parcels "valueless." App. to Pet. for Cert. 37. This case requires us to decide whether the Act's dramatic effect on the economic value of Lucas's lots accomplished a taking of private property under the Fifth and Fourteenth Amendments requiring the payment of "just compensation." U.S. Const., Amdt. 5.

I

A

South Carolina's expressed interest in intensively managing development activities in the so-called "coastal zone" dates from 1977 when, in the aftermath of Congress's passage of the federal Coastal Zone Management Act of 1972, 86 Stat. 1280, as amended, 16 U.S.C. § 1451 *et seq.*, the legislature enacted a Coastal Zone Management Act of its own. See S.C.Code § 48–39–10 *et seq.* (1987). In its original form, the South Carolina Act required owners of coastal zone land that qualified as a "critical area" (defined in the legislation to include beaches and immediately adjacent sand dunes, § 48–39–10(J)) to obtain a permit from the newly created South Carolina Coastal Council (respondent here) prior to committing the land to a "use other than the use the critical area was devoted to on [September 28, 1977]." § 48–39–130(A).

In the late 1970's, Lucas and others began extensive residential development of the Isle of Palms, a barrier island situated eastward of the City of Charleston. Toward the close of the development cycle for one residential subdivision known as "Beachwood East," Lucas in 1986 purchased the two lots at issue in this litigation for his own account. No portion of the lots, which were located approximately 300 feet from the beach, qualified as a "critical area" under the 1977 Act; accordingly, at the time Lucas acquired these parcels, he was not legally obliged to obtain a permit from the Council in advance of any development activity. His intention with respect to the lots was to do what the owners of the immediately adjacent parcels had already done: erect single-family residences. He commissioned architectural drawings for this purpose.

The Beachfront Management Act brought Lucas's plans to an abrupt end. Under that 1988 legislation, the Council was directed to establish a "baseline" connecting the landward-most "point[s] of erosion * * * during the past forty years" in the region of the Isle of Palms that includes Lucas's lots. § 48–39–280(A)(2) (Supp.1988).[1] In action not challenged here, the Council fixed this baseline landward of Lucas's parcels. That was significant, for under the Act construction of occupiable improvements [2] was flatly prohibited seaward of a line drawn 20 feet landward of, and parallel to, the baseline, § 48–39–290(A) (Supp.1988). The Act provided no exceptions.

B

Lucas promptly filed suit in the South Carolina Court of Common Pleas, contending that the Beachfront Management Act's construction bar effected a taking of his property without just compensation. Lucas did not take issue with the validity of the Act as a lawful exercise of South Carolina's police power, but contended that the Act's complete

1. This specialized historical method of determining the baseline applied because the Beachwood East subdivision is located adjacent to a so-called "inlet erosion zone" (defined in the Act to mean "a segment of shoreline along or adjacent to tidal inlets which is influenced directly by the inlet and its associated shoals," S.C.Code § 48–39–270(7) (Supp.1988)) that is "not stabilized by jetties, terminal groins, or other structures," § 48–39–280(A)(2). For areas other than these unstabilized inlet erosion zones, the statute directs that the baseline be established "along the crest of the primary oceanfront sand dune." § 48–39–280(A)(1).

2. The Act did allow the construction of certain nonhabitable improvements, *e.g.*, "wooden walkways no larger in width than six feet," and "small wooden decks no larger than one hundred forty-four square feet." §§ 48–39–290(A)(1) and (2) (Supp. 1988).

extinguishment of his property's value entitled him to compensation regardless of whether the legislature had acted in furtherance of legitimate police power objectives. Following a bench trial, the court agreed. Among its factual determinations was the finding that "at the time Lucas purchased the two lots, both were zoned for single-family residential construction and * * * there were no restrictions imposed upon such use of the property by either the State of South Carolina, the County of Charleston, or the Town of the Isle of Palms." App. to Pet. for Cert. 36. The trial court further found that the Beachfront Management Act decreed a permanent ban on construction insofar as Lucas's lots were concerned, and that this prohibition "deprive[d] Lucas of any reasonable economic use of the lots, * * * eliminated the unrestricted right of use, and render[ed] them valueless." *Id.,* at 37. The court thus concluded that Lucas's properties had been "taken" by operation of the Act, and it ordered respondent to pay "just compensation" in the amount of $1,232,387.50. *Id.,* at 40.

The Supreme Court of South Carolina reversed. It found dispositive what it described as Lucas's concession "that the Beachfront Management Act [was] properly and validly designed to preserve * * * South Carolina's beaches." 304 S.C. 376, 379, 404 S.E.2d 895, 896 (1991). Failing an attack on the validity of the statute as such, the court believed itself bound to accept the "uncontested * * * findings" of the South Carolina legislature that new construction in the coastal zone—such as petitioner intended—threatened this public resource. *Id.,* at 383, 404 S.E.2d, at 898. The Court ruled that when a regulation respecting the use of property is designed "to prevent serious public harm," *id.,* at 383, 404 S.E.2d, at 899 (citing, *inter alia, Mugler v. Kansas,* 123 U.S. 623, 8 S.Ct. 273, 31 L.Ed. 205 (1887)), no compensation is owing under the Takings Clause regardless of the regulation's effect on the property's value.

Two justices dissented. They acknowledged that our *Mugler* line of cases recognizes governmental power to prohibit "noxious" uses of property—*i.e.,* uses of property akin to "public nuisances"—without having to pay compensation. But they would not have characterized the Beachfront Management Act's "*primary* purpose [as] the prevention of a nuisance." 304 S.C., at 395, 404 S.E.2d, at 906 (Harwell, J., dissenting). To the dissenters, the chief purposes of the legislation, among them the promotion of tourism and the creation of a "habitat for indigenous flora and fauna," could not fairly be compared to nuisance abatement. *Id.,* at 396, 404 S.E.2d, at 906. As a consequence, they would have affirmed the trial court's conclusion that the Act's obliteration of the value of petitioner's lots accomplished a taking.

We granted certiorari. 502 U.S. ___, 112 S.Ct. 436, 116 L.Ed.2d 455 (1991).

II

* * *

III

A

Prior to Justice Holmes' exposition in *Pennsylvania Coal Co. v. Mahon,* 260 U.S. 393, 43 S.Ct. 158, 67 L.Ed. 322 (1922), it was generally thought that the Takings Clause reached only a "direct appropriation" of property, *Legal Tender Cases,* 12 Wall. 457, 551, 20 L.Ed. 287 (1871), or the functional equivalent of a "practical ouster of [the owner's] possession." *Transportation Co. v. Chicago,* 99 U.S. 635, 642, 25 L.Ed. 336 (1879). See also *Gibson v. United States,* 166 U.S. 269, 275–276, 17 S.Ct. 578, 580, 41 L.Ed. 996 (1897). Justice Holmes recognized in *Mahon,* however, that if the protection against physical appropriations of private property was to be meaningfully enforced, the government's power to redefine the range of interests included in the ownership of property was necessarily constrained by constitutional limits. 260 U.S., at 414–415, 43 S.Ct., at 160. If, instead, the uses of private property were subject to unbridled, uncompensated qualification under the police power, "the natural tendency of human nature [would be] to extend the qualification more and more until at last private property disappear[ed]." *Id.,* at 415, 43 S.Ct., at 160. These considerations gave birth in that case to the oft-cited maxim that, "while property may be regulated to a certain extent, if regulation goes too far it will be recognized as a taking." *Ibid.*

Nevertheless, our decision in *Mahon* offered little insight into when, and under what circumstances, a given regulation would be seen as going "too far" for purposes of the Fifth Amendment. In 70–odd years of succeeding "regulatory takings" jurisprudence, we have generally eschewed any " 'set formula' " for determining how far is too far, preferring to "engag[e] in * * * essentially ad hoc, factual inquiries," *Penn Central Transportation Co. v. New York City,* 438 U.S. 104, 124, 98 S.Ct. 2646, 2659, 57 L.Ed.2d 631 (1978) (quoting *Goldblatt v. Hempstead,* 369 U.S. 590, 594, 82 S.Ct. 987, 990, 8 L.Ed.2d 130 (1962)). See Epstein, Takings: Descent and Resurrection, 1987 Sup.Ct.Rev. 1, 4. We have, however, described at least two discrete categories of regulatory action as compensable without case-specific inquiry into the public interest advanced in support of the restraint. The first encompasses regulations that compel the property owner to suffer a physical "invasion" of his property. In general (at least with regard to permanent invasions), no matter how minute the intrusion, and no matter how weighty the public purpose behind it, we have required compensation. For example, in *Loretto v. Teleprompter Manhattan CATV Corp.,* 458 U.S. 419, 102 S.Ct. 3164, 73 L.Ed.2d 868 (1982), we determined that New York's law requiring landlords to allow television cable companies to emplace cable facilities in their apartment buildings constituted a taking, *id.,* at 435–440, 102 S.Ct., at 3175–3178, even though the facilities occupied at most only 1½ cubic feet of the landlords' property, see *id.,* at 438, n. 16, 102 S.Ct., at 3177. See also *United States v. Causby,* 328 U.S. 256, 265, and n. 10, 66 S.Ct. 1062, 1067, and n. 10, 90 L.Ed. 1206 (1946) (physical invasions of airspace); cf. *Kaiser Aetna v.*

United States, 444 U.S. 164, 100 S.Ct. 383, 62 L.Ed.2d 332 (1979) (imposition of navigational servitude upon private marina).

The second situation in which we have found categorical treatment appropriate is where regulation denies all economically beneficial or productive use of land. See *Agins,* 447 U.S., at 260, 100 S.Ct., at 2141; see also *Nollan v. California Coastal Comm'n,* 483 U.S. 825, 834, 107 S.Ct. 3141, 3147, 97 L.Ed.2d 677 (1987); *Keystone Bituminous Coal Assn. v. DeBenedictis,* 480 U.S. 470, 495, 107 S.Ct. 1232, 1247, 94 L.Ed.2d 472 (1987); *Hodel v. Virginia Surface Mining & Reclamation Assn., Inc.,* 452 U.S. 264, 295–296, 101 S.Ct. 2352, 2370, 69 L.Ed.2d 1 (1981). As we have said on numerous occasions, the Fifth Amendment is violated when land-use regulation "does not substantially advance legitimate state interests *or denies an owner economically viable use of his land.*" *Agins, supra,* 447 U.S., at 260, 100 S.Ct., at 2141 (citations omitted) (emphasis added).[7]

We have never set forth the justification for this rule. Perhaps it is simply, as Justice Brennan suggested, that total deprivation of beneficial use is, from the landowner's point of view, the equivalent of a physical appropriation. See *San Diego Gas & Electric Co. v. San Diego,* 450 U.S., at 652, 101 S.Ct., at 1304 (Brennan, J., dissenting). "[F]or what is the land but the profits thereof[?]" 1 E. Coke, Institutes ch. 1, § 1 (1st Am. ed. 1812). Surely, at least, in the extraordinary circumstance when *no* productive or economically beneficial use of land is permitted, it is less realistic to indulge our usual assumption that the legislature is simply "adjusting the benefits and burdens of economic life," *Penn Central*

7. Regrettably, the rhetorical force of our "deprivation of all economically feasible use" rule is greater than its precision, since the rule does not make clear the "property interest" against which the loss of value is to be measured. When, for example, a regulation requires a developer to leave 90% of a rural tract in its natural state, it is unclear whether we would analyze the situation as one in which the owner has been deprived of all economically beneficial use of the burdened portion of the tract, or as one in which the owner has suffered a mere diminution in value of the tract as a whole. (For an extreme—and, we think, unsupportable—view of the relevant calculus, see *Penn Central Transportation Co. v. New York City,* 42 N.Y.2d 324, 333–334, 397 N.Y.S.2d 914, 920, 366 N.E.2d 1271, 1276–1277 (1977), aff'd, 438 U.S. 104, 98 S.Ct. 2646, 57 L.Ed.2d 631 (1978), where the state court examined the diminution in a particular parcel's value produced by a municipal ordinance in light of total value of the taking claimant's other holdings in the vicinity.) Unsurprisingly, this uncertainty regarding the composition of the denominator in our "deprivation" fraction has produced inconsistent pronouncements by the Court. Compare *Pennsylvania Coal Co. v. Mahon,* 260 U.S. 393, 414, 43 S.Ct. 158, 160, 67 L.Ed. 322 (1922) (law restricting subsurface extraction of coal held to effect a taking), with *Keystone Bituminous Coal Assn. v. DeBenedictis,* 480 U.S. 470, 497–502, 107 S.Ct. 1232, 1248–1251, 94 L.Ed.2d 472 (1987) (nearly identical law held not to effect a taking); see also *id.,* at 515–520, 107 S.Ct., at 1257–1260 (Rehnquist, C.J., dissenting); Rose, *Mahon* Reconstructed: Why the Takings Issue is Still a Muddle, 57 S.Cal.L.Rev. 561, 566–569 (1984). The answer to this difficult question may lie in how the owner's reasonable expectations have been shaped by the State's law of property—*i.e.,* whether and to what degree the State's law has accorded legal recognition and protection to the particular interest in land with respect to which the takings claimant alleges a diminution in (or elimination of) value. In any event, we avoid this difficulty in the present case, since the "interest in land" that Lucas has pleaded (a fee simple interest) is an estate with a rich tradition of protection at common law, and since the South Carolina Court of Common Pleas found that the Beachfront Management Act left each of Lucas's beachfront lots without economic value.

Transportation Co., 438 U.S., at 124, 98 S.Ct., at 2659, in a manner that secures an "average reciprocity of advantage" to everyone concerned. *Pennsylvania Coal Co. v. Mahon,* 260 U.S., at 415, 43 S.Ct., at 160. And the *functional* basis for permitting the government, by regulation, to affect property values without compensation—that "Government hardly could go on if to some extent values incident to property could not be diminished without paying for every such change in the general law," *id.,* at 413, 43 S.Ct., at 159—does not apply to the relatively rare situations where the government has deprived a landowner of all economically beneficial uses.

On the other side of the balance, affirmatively supporting a compensation requirement, is the fact that regulations that leave the owner of land without economically beneficial or productive options for its use—typically, as here, by requiring land to be left substantially in its natural state—carry with them a heightened risk that private property is being pressed into some form of public service under the guise of mitigating serious public harm. See, *e.g., Annicelli v. South Kingstown,* 463 A.2d 133, 140–141 (R.I.1983) (prohibition on construction adjacent to beach justified on twin grounds of safety and "conservation of open space"); *Morris County Land Improvement Co. v. Parsippany–Troy Hills Township,* 40 N.J. 539, 552–553, 193 A.2d 232, 240 (1963) (prohibition on filling marshlands imposed in order to preserve region as water detention basin and create wildlife refuge). As Justice Brennan explained: "From the government's point of view, the benefits flowing to the public from preservation of open space through regulation may be equally great as from creating a wildlife refuge through formal condemnation or increasing electricity production through a dam project that floods private property." *San Diego Gas & Elec. Co., supra,* 450 U.S., at 652, 101 S.Ct., at 1304 (Brennan, J., dissenting). The many statutes on the books, both state and federal, that provide for the use of eminent domain to impose servitudes on private scenic lands preventing developmental uses, or to acquire such lands altogether, suggest the practical equivalence in this setting of negative regulation and appropriation. See, *e.g.,* 16 U.S.C. § 410ff–1(a) (authorizing acquisition of "lands, waters, or interests [within Channel Islands National Park] (including but not limited to scenic easements)"); § 460aa–2(a) (authorizing acquisition of "any lands, or lesser interests therein, including mineral interests and scenic easements" within Sawtooth National Recreation Area); §§ 3921–3923 (authorizing acquisition of wetlands); N.C.Gen.Stat. § 113A–38 (1990) (authorizing acquisition of, *inter alia,* " 'scenic easements' " within the North Carolina natural and scenic rivers system); Tenn.Code Ann. §§ 11–15–101—11–15–108 (1987) (authorizing acquisition of "protective easements" and other rights in real property adjacent to State's historic, architectural, archaeological, or cultural resources).

We think, in short, that there are good reasons for our frequently expressed belief that when the owner of real property has been called upon to sacrifice *all* economically beneficial uses in the name of the common good, that is, to leave his property economically idle, he has suffered a taking.[8]

* * *

It is correct that many of our prior opinions have suggested that "harmful or noxious uses" of property may be proscribed by government regulation without the requirement of compensation. For a number of reasons, however, we think the South Carolina Supreme Court was too quick to conclude that that principle decides the present case. The "harmful or noxious uses" principle was the Court's early attempt to describe in theoretical terms why government may, consistent with the Takings Clause, affect property values by regulation without incurring an obligation to compensate—a reality we nowadays acknowledge explicitly with respect to the full scope of the State's police power. See, *e.g., Penn Central Transportation Co.,* 438 U.S., at 125, 98 S.Ct., at 2659 (where State "reasonably conclude[s] that 'the health, safety, morals, or general welfare' would be promoted by prohibiting particular contemplated uses of land," compensation need not accompany prohibition); see also *Nollan v. California Coastal Commission,* 483 U.S., at 834–835, 107 S.Ct., at 3147 ("Our cases have not elaborated on the standards for determining what constitutes a 'legitimate state interest[,]' [but] [t]hey have made clear * * * that a broad range of governmental purposes and regulations satisfy these requirements"). We made this very point in *Penn Central Transportation Co.,* where, in the course of sustaining New York City's landmarks preservation program against a takings challenge, we rejected the petitioner's suggestion that *Mugler* and the cases following it were premised on, and thus limited by, some objective conception of "noxiousness":

8. Justice Stevens criticizes the "deprivation of all economically beneficial use" rule as "wholly arbitrary", in that "[the] landowner whose property is diminished in value 95% recovers nothing," while the landowner who suffers a complete elimination of value "recovers the land's full value." *Post,* at 2919. This analysis errs in its assumption that the landowner whose deprivation is one step short of complete is not entitled to compensation. Such an owner might not be able to claim the benefit of our categorical formulation, but, as we have acknowledged time and again, "[t]he economic impact of the regulation on the claimant and * * * the extent to which the regulation has interfered with distinct investment-backed expectations" are keenly relevant to takings analysis generally. *Penn Central Transportation Co. v. New York City,* 438 U.S. 104, 124, 98 S.Ct. 2646, 2659, 57 L.Ed.2d 631 (1978). It is true that in at least *some* cases the landowner with 95% loss will get nothing, while the landowner with total loss will recover in full. But that occasional result is no more strange than the gross disparity between the landowner whose premises are taken for a highway (who recovers in full) and the landowner whose property is reduced to 5% of its former value by the highway (who recovers nothing). Takings law is full of these "all-or-nothing" situations.

Justice Stevens similarly misinterprets our focus on "developmental" uses of property (the uses proscribed by the Beachfront Management Act) as betraying an "assumption that the only uses of property cognizable under the Constitution are *developmental* uses." *Post,* at 2919, n. 3. We make no such assumption. Though our prior takings cases evince an abiding concern for the productive use of, and economic investment in, land, there are plainly a number of noneconomic interests in land whose impairment will invite exceedingly close scrutiny under the Takings Clause. See, *e.g., Loretto v. Teleprompter Manhattan CATV Corp.,* 458 U.S. 419, 436, 102 S.Ct. 3164, 3176, 73 L.Ed.2d 868 (1982) (interest in excluding strangers from one's land).

"[T]he uses in issue in *Hadacheck, Miller,* and *Goldblatt* were perfectly lawful in themselves. They involved no 'blameworthiness, * * * moral wrongdoing or conscious act of dangerous risk-taking which induce[d society] to shift the cost to a pa[rt]icular individual.' Sax, Takings and the Police Power, 74 Yale L.J. 36, 50 (1964). These cases are better understood as resting not on any supposed 'noxious' quality of the prohibited uses but rather on the ground that the restrictions were reasonably related to the implementation of a policy—not unlike historic preservation—expected to produce a widespread public benefit and applicable to all similarly situated property." 438 U.S., at 133–134, n. 30, 98 S.Ct., at 2664, n. 30.

"Harmful or noxious use" analysis was, in other words, simply the progenitor of our more contemporary statements that "land-use regulation does not effect a taking if it 'substantially advance[s] legitimate state interests' * * *." *Nollan, supra,* 483 U.S., at 834, 107 S.Ct., at 3147 (quoting *Agins v. Tiburon,* 447 U.S., at 260, 100 S.Ct., at 2141); see also *Penn Central Transportation Co., supra,* 438 U.S., at 127, 98 S.Ct., at 2660; *Euclid v. Ambler Realty Co.,* 272 U.S. 365, 387–388, 47 S.Ct. 114, 118, 71 L.Ed. 303 (1926).

The transition from our early focus on control of "noxious" uses to our contemporary understanding of the broad realm within which government may regulate without compensation was an easy one, since the distinction between "harm-preventing" and "benefit-conferring" regulation is often in the eye of the beholder. It is quite possible, for example, to describe in *either* fashion the ecological, economic, and aesthetic concerns that inspired the South Carolina legislature in the present case. One could say that imposing a servitude on Lucas's land is necessary in order to prevent his use of it from "harming" South Carolina's ecological resources; or, instead, in order to achieve the "benefits" of an ecological preserve.[11] Compare, *e.g., Claridge v. New Hampshire Wetlands Board,*

11. In the present case, in fact, some of the "[South Carolina] legislature's 'findings' " to which the South Carolina Supreme Court purported to defer in characterizing the purpose of the Act as "harm-preventing," 304 S.C. 376, 385, 404 S.E.2d 895, 900 (1991), seem to us phrased in "benefit-conferring" language instead. For example, they describe the importance of a construction ban in enhancing "South Carolina's annual tourism industry revenue," S.C.Code § 48–39–250(1)(b) (Supp.1991), in "provid[ing] habitat for numerous species of plants and animals, several of which are threatened or endangered," § 48–39–250(1)(c), and in "provid[ing] a natural healthy environment for the citizens of South Carolina to spend leisure time which serves their physical and mental well-being." § 48–39–250(1)(d). It would be pointless to make the outcome of this case hang upon this terminology, since the same interests could readily be described in "harm-preventing" fashion.

Justice Blackmun, however, apparently insists that we *must* make the outcome hinge (exclusively) upon the South Carolina Legislature's other, "harm-preventing" characterizations, focusing on the declaration that "prohibitions on building in front of the setback line are necessary to protect people and property from storms, high tides, and beach erosion." *Post,* at 2906. He says "[n]othing in the record undermines [this] assessment," *ibid.,* apparently seeing no significance in the fact that the statute permits owners of *existing* structures to remain (and even to rebuild if their structures are not "destroyed beyond repair," S.C.Code Ann. § 48–39–290(B)), and in the fact that the 1990 amendment authorizes the Council to issue permits for new construction in violation of the uniform prohibition, see S.C.Code § 48–39–290(D)(1) (Supp.1991).

125 N.H. 745, 752, 485 A.2d 287, 292 (1984) (owner may, without compensation, be barred from filling wetlands because landfilling would deprive adjacent coastal habitats and marine fisheries of ecological support), with, *e.g., Bartlett v. Zoning Comm'n of Old Lyme,* 161 Conn. 24, 30, 282 A.2d 907, 910 (1971) (owner barred from filling tidal marshland must be compensated, despite municipality's "laudable" goal of "preserv[ing] marshlands from encroachment or destruction"). Whether one or the other of the competing characterizations will come to one's lips in a particular case depends primarily upon one's evaluation of the worth of competing uses of real estate. See Restatement (Second) of Torts § 822, Comment *g,* p. 112 (1979) ("[p]ractically all human activities unless carried on in a wilderness interfere to some extent with others or involve some risk of interference"). A given restraint will be seen as mitigating "harm" to the adjacent parcels or securing a "benefit" for them, depending upon the observer's evaluation of the relative importance of the use that the restraint favors. See Sax, Takings and the Police Power, 74 Yale L.J. 36, 49 (1964) ("[T]he problem [in this area] is not one of noxiousness or harm-creating activity at all; rather it is a problem of inconsistency between perfectly innocent and independently desirable uses"). Whether Lucas's construction of single-family residences on his parcels should be described as bringing "harm" to South Carolina's adjacent ecological resources thus depends principally upon whether the describer believes that the State's use interest in nurturing those resources is so important that *any* competing adjacent use must yield.[12]

When it is understood that "prevention of harmful use" was merely our early formulation of the police power justification necessary to sustain (without compensation) *any* regulatory diminution in value; and that the distinction between regulation that "prevents harmful use" and that which "confers benefits" is difficult, if not impossible, to discern on an objective, value-free basis; it becomes self-evident that noxious-use logic cannot serve as a touch-stone to distinguish regulatory "takings"—which require compensation—from regulatory deprivations that do not require compensation. *A fortiori* the legislature's recitation of a noxious-use justification cannot be the basis for departing from our categorical rule that total regulatory takings must be compensated. If it were, departure would virtually always be allowed. The South Carolina Supreme Court's approach would essentially nullify *Mahon* 's affirmation of limits to the noncompensable exercise of the police power. Our cases provide no support for this: None of them that employed the logic of "harmful use" prevention to sustain a regulation involved an allegation that the regulation wholly eliminated the value of the claimant's land.

12. In Justice Blackmun's view, even with respect to regulations that deprive an owner of all developmental or economically beneficial land uses, the test for required compensation is whether the legislature has recited a harm-preventing justification for its action. See *post,* at 2906, 2910–2912. Since such a justification can be formulated in practically every case, this amounts to a test of whether the legislature has a stupid staff. We think the Takings Clause requires courts to do more than insist upon artful harm-preventing characterizations.

See *Keystone Bituminous Coal Assn.,* 480 U.S., at 513–514, 107 S.Ct., at 1257 (REHNQUIST, C.J., dissenting).[13]

Where the State seeks to sustain regulation that deprives land of all economically beneficial use, we think it may resist compensation only if the logically antecedent inquiry into the nature of the owner's estate shows that the proscribed use interests were not part of his title to begin with.[14] This accords, we think, with our "takings" jurisprudence, which has traditionally been guided by the understandings of our citizens regarding the content of, and the State's power over, the "bundle of rights" that they acquire when they obtain title to property. It seems to us that the property owner necessarily expects the uses of his property to be restricted, from time to time, by various measures newly enacted by the State in legitimate exercise of its police powers; "[a]s long recognized, some values are enjoyed under an implied limitation and must yield to the police power." *Pennsylvania Coal Co. v. Mahon,* 260 U.S., at 413, 43 S.Ct., at 159. And in the case of personal property, by reason of the State's traditionally high degree of control over commercial dealings, he ought to be aware of the possibility that new regulation might even render his property economically worthless (at least if the property's only economically productive use is sale or manufacture for sale), see *Andrus v. Allard,* 444 U.S. 51, 66–67, 100 S.Ct. 318, 327, 62 L.Ed.2d 210 (1979) (prohibition on sale of eagle feathers). In the case of land, however, we think the notion pressed by the Council that title is somehow held subject to the "implied limitation" that the State may subsequently eliminate all economically valuable use is inconsistent with the historical compact recorded in the Takings Clause that has become

13. *E.g., Mugler v. Kansas,* 123 U.S. 623, 8 S.Ct. 273, 31 L.Ed. 205 (1887) (prohibition upon use of a building as a brewery; other uses permitted); *Plymouth Coal Co. v. Pennsylvania,* 232 U.S. 531, 34 S.Ct. 359, 58 L.Ed. 713 (1914) (requirement that "pillar" of coal be left in ground to safeguard mine workers; mineral rights could otherwise be exploited); *Reinman v. Little Rock,* 237 U.S. 171, 35 S.Ct. 511, 59 L.Ed. 900 (1915) (declaration that livery stable constituted a public nuisance; other uses of the property permitted); *Hadacheck v. Sebastian,* 239 U.S. 394, 36 S.Ct. 143, 60 L.Ed. 348 (1915) (prohibition of brick manufacturing in residential area; other uses permitted); *Goldblatt v. Hempstead,* 369 U.S. 590, 82 S.Ct. 987, 8 L.Ed.2d 130 (1962) (prohibition on excavation; other uses permitted).

14. Drawing on our First Amendment jurisprudence, see, *e.g., Employment Division, Department of Human Resources of Oregon v. Smith,* 494 U.S. 872, 878–879, 110 S.Ct. 1595, 1600, 108 L.Ed.2d 876 (1990), Justice Stevens would "loo[k] to the *generality* of a regulation of property" to determine whether compensation is owing. *Post,* at 2923. The Beachfront Management Act is general, in his view, because it "regulates the use of the coastline of the entire state." *Post,* at 2924. There may be some validity to the principle Justice Stevens proposes, but it does not properly apply to the present case. The equivalent of a law of general application that inhibits the practice of religion without being aimed at religion, see *Oregon v. Smith, supra,* is a law that destroys the value of land without being aimed at land. Perhaps such a law—the generally applicable criminal prohibition on the manufacturing of alcoholic beverages challenged in *Mugler* comes to mind—cannot constitute a compensable taking. See 123 U.S., at 655–656, 8 S.Ct., at 293–294. But a regulation *specifically directed to land use* no more acquires immunity by plundering landowners generally than does a law specifically directed at religious practice acquire immunity by prohibiting all religions. Justice Stevens' approach renders the Takings Clause little more than a particularized restatement of the Equal Protection Clause.

part of our constitutional culture.[15]

Where "permanent physical occupation" of land is concerned, we have refused to allow the government to decree it anew (without compensation), no matter how weighty the asserted "public interests" involved, *Loretto v. Teleprompter Manhattan CATV Corp.*, 458 U.S., at 426, 102 S.Ct., at 3171—though we assuredly *would* permit the government to assert a permanent easement that was a pre-existing limitation upon the landowner's title. Compare *Scranton v. Wheeler,* 179 U.S. 141, 163, 21 S.Ct. 48, 57, 45 L.Ed. 126 (1900) (interests of "riparian owner in the submerged lands * * * bordering on a public navigable water" held subject to Government's navigational servitude), with *Kaiser Aetna v. United States,* 444 U.S., at 178–180, 100 S.Ct., at 392–393 (imposition of navigational servitude on marina created and rendered navigable at private expense held to constitute a taking). We believe similar treatment must be accorded confiscatory regulations, *i.e.,* regulations that prohibit all economically beneficial use of land: Any limitation so severe cannot be newly legislated or decreed (without compensation), but must inhere in the title itself, in the restrictions that background principles of the State's law of property and nuisance already place upon land ownership. A law or decree with such an effect must, in other words, do no more than duplicate the result that could have been achieved in the courts—by adjacent landowners (or other uniquely affected persons) under the State's law of private nuisance, or by the State under its complementary power to abate nuisances that affect the public generally, or otherwise.[16]

On this analysis, the owner of a lake bed, for example, would not be entitled to compensation when he is denied the requisite permit to engage in a landfilling operation that would have the effect of flooding

15. After accusing us of "launch[ing] a missile to kill a mouse," *post,* at 2904, Justice Blackmun expends a good deal of throw-weight of his own upon a noncombatant, arguing that our description of the "understanding" of land ownership that informs the Takings Clause is not supported by early American experience. That is largely true, but entirely irrelevant. The practices of the States *prior* to incorporation of the Takings and Just Compensation Clauses, see *Chicago, B. & Q.R. Co. v. Chicago,* 166 U.S. 226, 17 S.Ct. 581, 41 L.Ed. 979 (1897)—which, as Justice Blackmun acknowledges, occasionally included *outright physical appropriation* of land without compensation, see *post,* at 2915—were out of accord with *any* plausible interpretation of those provisions. Justice Blackmun is correct that early constitutional theorists did not believe the Takings Clause embraced regulations of property at all, see *post,* at 2915, and n. 23, but even he does not suggest (explicitly, at least) that we renounce the Court's contrary conclusion in *Mahon.* Since the text of the Clause can be read to encompass regulatory as well as physical deprivations (in contrast to the text originally proposed by Madison, see Speech Proposing Bill of Rights (June 8, 1789), in 12 J. Madison, The Papers of James Madison 201 (C. Hobson, R. Rutland, W. Rachal, & J. Sisson ed. 1979) ("No person shall be * * * obliged to relinquish his property, where it may be necessary for public use, without a just compensation"), we decline to do so as well.

16. The principal "otherwise" that we have in mind is litigation absolving the State (or private parties) of liability for the destruction of "real and personal property, in cases of actual necessity, to prevent the spreading of a fire" or to forestall other grave threats to the lives and property of others. *Bowditch v. Boston,* 101 U.S. 16, 18–19, 25 L.Ed. 980 (1880); see *United States v. Pacific Railroad,* 120 U.S. 227, 238–239, 7 S.Ct. 490, 495–496, 30 L.Ed. 634 (1887).

others' land. Nor the corporate owner of a nuclear generating plant, when it is directed to remove all improvements from its land upon discovery that the plant sits astride an earthquake fault. Such regulatory action may well have the effect of eliminating the land's only economically productive use, but it does not proscribe a productive use that was previously permissible under relevant property and nuisance principles. The use of these properties for what are now expressly prohibited purposes was *always* unlawful, and (subject to other constitutional limitations) it was open to the State at any point to make the implication of those background principles of nuisance and property law explicit. See Michelman, Property, Utility, and Fairness, Comments on the Ethical Foundations of "Just Compensation" Law, 80 Harv.L.Rev. 1165, 1239–1241 (1967). In light of our traditional resort to "existing rules or understandings that stem from an independent source such as state law" to define the range of interests that qualify for protection as "property" under the Fifth (and Fourteenth) amendments, *Board of Regents of State Colleges v. Roth,* 408 U.S. 564, 577, 92 S.Ct. 2701, 2709, 33 L.Ed.2d 548 (1972); see, *e.g., Ruckelshaus v. Monsanto Co.,* 467 U.S. 986, 1011–1012, 104 S.Ct. 2862, 2877, 81 L.Ed.2d 815 (1984); *Hughes v. Washington,* 389 U.S. 290, 295, 88 S.Ct. 438, 441, 19 L.Ed.2d 530 (1967) (STEWART, J., concurring), this recognition that the Takings Clause does not require compensation when an owner is barred from putting land to a use that is proscribed by those "existing rules or understandings" is surely unexceptional. When, however, a regulation that declares "off-limits" all economically productive or beneficial uses of land goes beyond what the relevant background principles would dictate, compensation must be paid to sustain it.[17]

The "total taking" inquiry we require today will ordinarily entail (as the application of state nuisance law ordinarily entails) analysis of, among other things, the degree of harm to public lands and resources, or adjacent private property, posed by the claimant's proposed activities, see, *e.g.,* Restatement (Second) of Torts §§ 826, 827, the social value of the claimant's activities and their suitability to the locality in question, see, *e.g., id.,* §§ 828(a) and (b), 831, and the relative ease with which the alleged harm can be avoided through measures taken by the claimant and the government (or adjacent private landowners) alike, see, *e.g., id.,* §§ 827(e), 828(c), 830. The fact that a particular use has long been engaged in by similarly situated owners ordinarily imports a lack of any common-law prohibition (though changed circumstances or new knowledge may make what was previously permissible no longer so, see Restatement (Second) of Torts, *supra,* § 827, comment *g.* So also does the fact that other landowners, similarly situated, are permitted to continue the use denied to the claimant.

17. Of course, the State may elect to rescind its regulation and thereby avoid having to pay compensation for a permanent deprivation. See *First English Evangelical Lutheran Church,* 482 U.S., at 321, 107 S.Ct., at 2389. But "where the [regulation has] already worked a taking of all use of property, no subsequent action by the government can relieve it of the duty to provide compensation for the period during which the taking was effective." *Ibid.*

It seems unlikely that common-law principles would have prevented the erection of any habitable or productive improvements on petitioner's land; they rarely support prohibition of the "essential use" of land, *Curtin v. Benson,* 222 U.S. 78, 86, 32 S.Ct. 31, 33, 56 L.Ed. 102 (1911). The question, however, is one of state law to be dealt with on remand. We emphasize that to win its case South Carolina must do more than proffer the legislature's declaration that the uses Lucas desires are inconsistent with the public interest, or the conclusory assertion that they violate a common-law maxim such as *sic utere tuo ut alienum non laedas.* As we have said, a "State, by *ipse dixit,* may not transform private property into public property without compensation * * *." *Webb's Fabulous Pharmacies, Inc. v. Beckwith,* 449 U.S. 155, 164, 101 S.Ct. 446, 452, 66 L.Ed.2d 358 (1980). Instead, as it would be required to do if it sought to restrain Lucas in a common-law action for public nuisance, South Carolina must identify background principles of nuisance and property law that prohibit the uses he now intends in the circumstances in which the property is presently found. Only on this showing can the State fairly claim that, in proscribing all such beneficial uses, the Beachfront Management Act is taking nothing.

* * *

The judgment is reversed and the cause remanded for proceedings not inconsistent with this opinion.

So ordered.

* * *

DAVID J. McCARTHY, JR., RUMINATIONS ON REGULATION AND THE TAKINGS CLAUSE

Home Rule and Civil Society, March 1994, at 27, 28–30, 35, 36, 49, 68–73 (footnotes omitted).

First, let us see where we are. The federal constitutional clause says: "nor shall private property be taken for public use without just compensation." It should be noted, as will appear later, that societies with newer constitutions have included in provisions recognizing private property rights the concomitant obligations of that property to serve the common weal, an express recognition not found in the Takings Clause of the U.S. Constitution. Does that ease the tension described above? Will such clauses give freer reign to government land-use regulation designed both to avoid harm and to gain benefit?

Until the late 1800s, the U.S. clause was invoked only in response to formal condemnation by the federal, and then through the Fourteenth Amendment, state government. At the end of the nineteenth century, the U.S. Supreme Court extended its reach to what has been called "inverse condemnation," suit by the property owner against the government asserting that a taking has occurred. The takings thus recognized tended to be appropriations and physical invasions (flooding from water projects, for example).

In 1922, Justice Holmes' opinion for the Court in *Pennsylvania Coal v. Mahon,* recognized Takings Clause applicability to *regulatory* excess. In the years that followed, little flesh was put on that skeleton. The Court seemed more comfortable with the customary due process evaluation of regulatory exercise that permitted a balancing of the respective governmental and private interests through the use of such classifications as "reasonable." and "noxious." Then, in 1978, the Court began its present effort to construct the jurisprudential underpinnings of the modern theory of regulatory takings.

At risk of oversimplification and of giving a sense of predictability to an area defined in *Penn Central* as "ad hoc," we may suggest that at present the genus, regulatory taking, can be divided into four species. The first two do not require exploration of the merit of the government's purpose. The second pair obviously does require such evaluation. The Supreme Court has defined the genus, regulatory taking, as involving a regulation that denies economically viable use of the property or fails substantially to advance a legitimate state interest. The four species are:

1. Compelled [permanent] physical invasion as a result of government's regulatory activity. Where the property owner has choices—whether to rent, perhaps whether to seek more intensive development, for example—the needed compulsion is not present. The Court has rejected artful arguments seeking to portray the results of economic regulation as the sort of physical invasion that would be included in this *per se* category.

2. Regulation that deprives the property of all economically beneficial or productive use. This species inevitably raises the question, "What property." If the property is always to be the full bundle of sticks we call ownership, then this deprivation will be necessarily significant indeed, and government will have more room in which to regulate without paying compensation.

If, contrary to Justice Brandeis' dissent in *Pennsylvania Coal,* what Professor Radin calls "conceptual severance" predominates in judicial thinking, then the regulatory authority of government will be narrowed. In addition, in determining what are the protected property interests or sticks in the bundle, does one use "layman's" understanding or scientific analysis? Finally, in defining this property, the enforceable "property-rights" expectations of the owner must be tempered by state land-use and nuisance law, how fixed or evolving is yet to be seen.

3. Regulation that fails substantially to advance a legitimate state interest. This is an obvious due process failure, but we shall see reasons for considering it in the context of the Takings Clause as well. * * * Questions include the degree of deference to the legislature, the level of judicial scrutiny, and the strictness of the required nexus between the regulatory objective and the regulated use.

4. Regulation that does not survive *Penn Central's* ad hoc analysis, that imposes on the private property owner burdens that should be imposed on the public, when judged in the light of the asserted property interest (without "conceptual severance"), distinct investment-backed expectations, and the character of the government action.

To the species have been added remedial concepts that on the one hand respect the appropriate role of the state or local legislature by permitting government to respond to judicial finding of a taking by repeal or appropriate modification of the regulation or by compensation, while on the other hand insist on compensation for the preceding period during which the ordinance's application constituted a taking, albeit a temporary one. There is also less judicial enthusiasm for facial attacks on government regulation asserting Takings Clause arguments than there is for challenges to the ordinance as applied. Finally, there is, by virtue of the takings argument's constitutional basis, the necessary link to the separate damages and equitable remedies provided by the Civil Rights Act of 1871, 42 U.S.C. § 1983.

* * *

Whether or not the Holmes–Brandeis debate intentionally reflected the tension between individual property rights and the communitarian needs of the public, their opinions have spawned many efforts to resolve that tension. The issue lurks in the United States' constitutional structure. As we have said, the U.S. Constitution manifests the framers' perception of the importance of individual property rights to personal individuality and liberty. It is against that reality that communitarian needs must compete.

Constitutions designed later than that of the United States have recognized that eminent domain alone—both coercive and thereby counterproductive to the individual-liberty goals, and also expensive and thereby counterproductive to protective government—would not resolve the tension. While no constitution answers all questions, the later charters expressly limit individual property ownership to bounds reflecting the public welfare. They invite consideration of the public good in the very framing of the individual's protected expectations. * * *:

But the American tension had to be resolved by reconciling the police power of the states with the individual-rights protections of the U.S. Constitution and possibly even more protective state constitutions, by finding some manner of identifying respectively appropriate public and private burdens. And just as the Cardozo–Andrews debate framed the evolving issues in American negligence doctrine, so too have Holmes and Brandeis defined the terms of the evolving case law on regulatory takings. One can see in their discussion the seeds of facial and as applied challenges (*Keystone Bituminous, Pennell,* e.g.); the rightness of making the property owner bear the burden; unwillingness to segment property for takings purposes (*Penn Central,* e.g.); the necessity of identifying a public purpose presently to be served (*Nollan,* e.g.); and, coming full circle, *Lucas'* effort to marry Holmes' taking position on diminution with a property owner's expectations tied to the nuisance law highlighted by Brandeis.

But from 1922 until 1978, the Supreme Court and other courts vacillated on the matter, ready like their predecessors to find *de facto* takings in government appropriational actions, but when faced with regulatory actions, more inclined to use due process analysis while paying lip service to Holmes.

During this period, state court results were similarly mixed. While constitutional takings clauses in several states included the phrase "and damaging" in describing government actions that would lead to the compensation requirement, state courts were reluctant to give the phrase independent meaning. "[S]ubtle efforts at legal refinement * * * can be expected to be more difficult and treacherous than convincing or utilitarian." Some state courts moved "ahead" of the U.S. Supreme Court in their contemplation of what was a taking, or, indeed, in their rejection of a takings jurisprudence too tilted toward individual land uses and away from communitarian needs. As one can imagine, the results and the directions of evolutionary doctrinal development were unpredictable and inconsistent.

"Contributing Strands"

As the 1970s progressed, several strands were added to the Holmes–Brandeis debate to form the "Bayeux Tapestry" we now examine. They included: (1) the dramatic expansion of land-use regulation; (2) the significant contributions from the academic community; (3) the explosion of civil rights litigation and accompanying development of jurisprudence under 42 U.S.C. § 1983; and (4) Justice Brennan's formative opinions, for the Court in *Penn Central,* and in dissent in *San Diego Gas and Electric.*

* * *

Given dramatically expanding land-use regulation, deeply divided views of the nature of regulatory taking, independent remedies and attorneys' fees provided by the civil rights laws, and roadmaps of the arguments provided by the Brennan and other opinions, little additional impetus was needed for litigators to adopt almost as routine the strategy of challenging regulations, not only under the customary due process and equal protection rubrics, but also under the Fifth Amendment, incorporated through the Fourteenth. The Court's effort to define a takings challenge and the apparent, continued validity of the Holmes application to regulation constituted all the invitation that was needed. * * *

The Supreme Court was not immune to the chase. While it appeared initially hesitant to find a taking in regulatory challenges, it was impatient to put Justice Brennan's temporary-taking compensation principles into effect. Justice Brennan and those who agreed with him, whatever their position on compensation, found themselves attempting to restrain the Court from too readily finding takings, while other members of the Court, notably Chief Justice Rehnquist, and lately,

Justice Scalia, have been strongly asserting the prominence of the property owner's rights.

The Court's efforts were, of course, not limited to the Fifth Amendment as applied to the states. The Amendment's direct applicability to the federal government prompted challenges as well to federal regulatory and spending laws. Like some of the state courts in the post-*Mahon* period, lower federal courts, especially the Court of [Federal] Claims, with some applause in Congress, were responsive to the individual property owner.

* * *

ANOTHER LOOK AT REMEDIES

The matter of remedies in regulatory-takings cases is less developed—or, perhaps, more taken for granted judicially—than even the fluid theories underlying the substantive challenge itself.

First, the basics should be reiterated. When the government seeks to appropriate a privately held property interest through exercise of its power of eminent domain, it becomes the plaintiff in a condemnation action and the private owner is the defendant. The burden of showing the public-purpose and compensation aspects of the taking thus falls on the government. When, instead, the private owner is the plaintiff, with the burden of showing a taking by the defendant government, the action is frequently one styled in *inverse condemnation*. This classification, however, tells only that the "normal" order of the parties has been reversed: it does not tell much about the nature of the cause of action.

For that, it is necessary to examine the gravamen of the complaint. Where the inverse-condemnation action seeks compensation because a government that has eminent-domain power has, without using that power, appropriated a privately held property interest, this is the classic *de facto* condemnation case.

The complaint, however, may be based not on entrepreneurial or acquisitional government activity, but rather on its regulatory efforts. As we have seen again and again, the regulatory exercises may, whether they are asserted in an inverse condemnation action or not, fall into one or more of our four classifications of *regulatory* takings.

The fact that inverse-condemnation cases differ from formal condemnation efforts and may include either *de facto* takings challenges or regulatory takings challenges does not exhaust the universe of takings challenges if one assumes, as one normally does, that inverse-condemnation actions, whatever the gravamen, seek the compensation remedy customarily associated with condemnation. The landowner may instead be asserting a takings argument in resisting enforcement of a regulatory ordinance and may not want compensation. Like its cousin, the Fourteenth-Amendment challenge to taking property without due process, the Fifth-Amendment takings challenge may seek to invalidate the government's regulatory exercise.

The court may think it the appropriate role of the judiciary to leave the taking-and-compensation question to the legislative branch. Thus, by invalidating the ordinance or statute, the court will leave to the legislature the choice whether to insist on the ordinance and pay compensation, to modify the ordinance to avoid the constitutional difficulty, or to repeal and start again, thereby mitigating damages.

In short and in theory then, there may be regulatory-taking cases where compensation is not the objective and where the term "inverse condemnation" might thus be inappropriately used. But the matter is even more complex, for damages for temporary taking, 42 U.S.C. § 1983, challenges under due process, and concepts of ripeness must be added to the mixture.

First English held that a remedial scheme for regulatory takings which did not include the possibility of damages for a temporary taking during the challenged ordinance's invalid operation was not constitutionally sufficient. Thus, even if the court were moved to invalidate the regulatory exercise as a taking without compensation, thereby giving the legislature the three choices earlier described, the possibility of a damage award for temporary taking would still be present.

A property owner who believes that her constitutionally protected property rights have been deliberately violated by government regulatory action may choose as her remedy the Civil Rights Act of 1871, 42 U.S.C. § 1983 and seek to collect damages. If a regulatory taking is proved, the measure of damages will undoubtedly have property overtones whatever else may be included.

Given *First English* and § 1983, the damages remedy does not really distinguish the takings challenge from the substantive due process challenge, which, we have seen, may assert the regulation's confiscatory nature too. Nor are they distinguished by the fact that § 1983's remedy is an independent one; both clauses might lead to damages and the measure might relate to property values.

Two things do distinguish them: the availability of damages for temporary taking; and the respective ripeness requirements imposed by the Court. The temporary-takings compensation requirement requires a successful challenge to the regulation as a taking. It also requires some delineation of the beginning of the period of the temporary taking. Is it passage of the ordinance or its application to the property? Is it the first administrative implementation or insistent application in the face of an incontrovertible assertion that implementation constitutes a taking? Is it limited to improper delay in the challenge procedures, brought about by the government, or frivolous obstruction by the government? We have seen that these questions remain to be answered. Unless the challenge is a facial attack, "as applied" necessarily imports the facts that lead to the conclusion that a taking without compensation has occurred.

So, the onset of the temporary-taking period is necessarily related to the Court's rulings on ripeness of the challenge. For an "as applied" challenge to be ripe, it must follow an attempt to seek variances or other possibilities of avoiding the taking. For there to be a taking—unless the ordinance failed substantially to advance a legitimate state interest, a facial attack—economic viability had to be impeded. For it to be impeded, economically productive uses had to be denied. This requirement applies to substantive due-process attacks as well. But for the takings challenge, the cause of action—a taking *without compensation*—must have matured. The challenger, though not relegated to piecemeal litigation, must attempt pursuant to state procedures to seek compensation and have it denied. The courts have engrafted futility to this, relieving the challenger of the prerequisite efforts that would have been demonstratively unavailing.

If takings ripeness requires both the showing that there is no way to avoid the confiscatory regulatory effect and that compensation has been sought unsuccessfully, then, in the absence of futility, it would follow that the challenger must first have effectively sought inverse condemnation. This will blur the remedy distinction so carefully set forth in *First English* and in Valente and McCarthy, but it will help to demarcate the line between substantive due process challenges and attacks under the Takings Clause. If compensation were not denied under the state processes, one could hardly (given the tenets of our federalism) complain of a taking without compensation. Thus, when the attack is under the Takings Clause, even where § 1983 is not involved, where the plaintiff would be seeking invalidation of the ordinance, where *First English* would suggest that the legislature be given the three choices, the ripeness doctrine would seem to demand that the plaintiff unsuccessfully have sought compensation pursuant to the state processes therefor.

First English is both helpful and unhelpful here. It seems to suggest that ripeness governs the onset of the compensable partial taking and underscores the possibility of a futility exception to the ripeness requirements, an exception adopted by the lower courts. Indeed, aberrations in the normal processes that delay the onset of ripeness may arguably create the futility. That very futility, however, eliminates any help the case might have given in resolving the three-legislative-choices versus the compensation-ripeness dilemma. * * *

CONCLUSION

The tapestry is far from complete, but substantial elements of the design are in place. The terse Holmesian phraseology has spawned a complex set of ripeness, definition, and remedy rules. But hints in the dissents, comments in the literature, efforts to demarcate the different takings and due process spheres, and, perhaps, the very struggle to put flesh on the Holmesian skeleton, all prompt the unthinkable question: was this trip necessary. Is not the Due Process Clause, in both its procedural and substantive manifestations, precisely intended to restrain abusive, overreaching, unreasonable, arbitrary and capricious, governmental police-power exercises? Or are the dual, individual and constitutionally protective purposes of our concept of property only appropriately safeguarded by a combination of the Takings and Due Process Clauses?

Are the two clauses complementary safeguards because of damages? Yes and no. "No," because, given the availability of 42 U.S.C. § 1983, the damages remedy for due process violations will be available. "Yes," because by using the Takings Clause the Court will be able to refer to the ultimate judgment of the legislature—to a voter-accountable entity exercising legislative power in our political system—the questions whether to expend public funds to achieve a public good, and what political priorities will enter into the legislative choice. While deference to the legislature may not be the hallmark of developing takings jurisprudence, it may be at root the raison dètre for invoking the Takings Clause.

But as we look at the matter today, it is not the only reason. The Court may be in this area, as in so many other matters, the stabilizer of the pendulum which historically swings from near-extreme to near-extreme. When government land regulation was minimal and largely undebatable, the Court was unlikely to uphold the landowner's challenge. When, as the pendulum has swung, government regulation has become dramatically more intrusive on the choices available to a property owner—indeed, when it has combined with the growing impact of private government—the Court has become more sensitive to the individual's need for counterweight.

For both of these purposes, the subtleties of due process may not work. Indeed, the clause is, in these two contexts, a blunt instrument. Either the government will be upheld, or its efforts will be invalidated. The Takings Clause offers an alternative. It not only permits a judicial decision that incorporates the fluidity of the due process concept and recognizes changing circumstances, but, where it finds that government has crossed the line, has imposed on the individual a burden that should have been borne by the public as a whole, the Court is able to offer the voter-accountable legislature not only the two customary choices of due process—invalidation and subsequent abandonment or modification—but the Takings–Clause–dramatized third choice: decide whether to compensate for that burden thereby spreading its cost across the benefited public through the tax or borrowing methods available to the legislature. Whatever ultimate choice the legislature may make, a counterweight is available to offset the individual pain caused by the temporary imposition of the public burden.

* * *

DOLAN v. CITY OF TIGARD

Supreme Court of the United States, 1994.
— U.S. —, 114 S.Ct. 2309, 129 L.Ed.2d 304.

CHIEF JUSTICE REHNQUIST delivered the opinion of the Court.

Petitioner challenges the decision of the Oregon Supreme Court which held that the city of Tigard could condition the approval of her building permit on the dedication of a portion of her property for flood control and traffic improvements. 317 Ore. 110, 854 P.2d 437 (1993). We granted certiorari to resolve a question left open by our decision in *Nollan v. California Coastal Comm'n,* 483 U.S. 825, 107 S.Ct. 3141, 97 L.Ed.2d 677 (1987), of what is the required degree of connection between the exactions imposed by the city and the projected impacts of the proposed development.

I

The State of Oregon enacted a comprehensive land use management program in 1973. Ore.Rev.Stat. §§ 197.005–197.860 (1991). The program required all Oregon cities and counties to adopt new comprehensive land use plans that were consistent with the statewide planning goals. §§ 197.175(1), 197.250. The plans are implemented by land use regulations which are part of an integrated hierarchy of legally binding goals, plans, and regulations. §§ 197.175, 197.175(2)(b). Pursuant to the State's requirements, the city of Tigard, a community of some 30,000 residents on the southwest edge of Portland, developed a comprehensive plan and codified it in its Community Development Code (CDC). The CDC requires property owners in the area zoned Central Business District to comply with a 15% open space and landscaping requirement, which limits total site coverage, including all structures and paved parking, to 85% of the parcel. CDC, ch. 18.66, App. to Pet. for Cert. G16–G17. After the completion of a transportation study that identified congestion in the Central Business District as a particular problem, the city adopted a plan for a pedestrian/bicycle pathway intended to encourage alternatives to automobile transportation for short trips. The CDC requires that new development facilitate this plan by dedicating land for pedestrian pathways where provided for in the pedestrian/bicycle pathway plan.

The city also adopted a Master Drainage Plan (Drainage Plan). The Drainage Plan noted that flooding occurred in several areas along Fanno Creek, including areas near petitioner's property. Record, Doc. No. F, ch. 2, pp. 2–5 to 2–8; 4–2 to 4–6; Figure 4–1. The Drainage Plan also established that the increase in impervious surfaces associated with continued urbanization would exacerbate these flooding problems. To combat these risks, the Drainage Plan suggested a series of improvements to the Fanno Creek Basin, including channel excavation in the area next to petitioner's property. App. to Pet. for Cert. G13, G38. Other recommendations included ensuring that the floodplain remains free of structures and that it be preserved as greenways to minimize flood damage to structures. Record, Doc. No. F, ch. 5, pp. 5–16 to 5–21. The Drainage Plan concluded that the cost of these improvements should be shared based on both direct and indirect benefits, with property owners along the waterways paying more due to the direct benefit that they would receive. *Id.,* ch. 8, p. 8–11. CDC Chapters 18.84, 18.86 and CDC § 18.164.100 and the Tigard Park Plan carry out these recommendations.

Petitioner Florence Dolan owns a plumbing and electric supply store located on Main Street in the Central Business District of the city. The store covers approximately 9,700 square feet on the eastern side of a 1.67–acre parcel, which includes a gravel parking lot. Fanno Creek flows through the southwestern corner of the lot and along its western boundary. The year-round flow of the creek renders the area within the creek's 100–year floodplain virtually unusable for commercial development. The city's comprehensive plan includes the Fanno Creek floodplain as part of the city's greenway system.

Petitioner applied to the city for a permit to redevelop the site. Her proposed plans called for nearly doubling the size of the store to 17,600 square feet, and paving a 39–space parking lot. The existing store, located on the opposite side of the parcel, would be razed in sections as construction progressed on the new building. In the second phase of the project, petitioner proposed to build an additional structure on the northeast side of the site for complementary businesses, and to provide more parking. The proposed expansion and intensified use are consistent with the city's zoning scheme in the Central Business District. CDC § 18.66.030. App. to Brief for Petitioner C1–C2.

The City Planning Commission granted petitioner's permit application subject to conditions imposed by the city's CDC. The CDC establishes the following standard for site development review approval:

> "Where landfill and/or development is allowed within and adjacent to the 100–year floodplain, the city shall require the dedication of sufficient open land area for greenway adjoining and within the floodplain. This area shall include portions at a suitable elevation for the construction of a pedestrian/bicycle pathway within the floodplain in accordance with the adopted pedestrian/bicycle plan." CDC § 18.120–180.A.8, App. to Brief for Respondent.

Thus, the Commission required that petitioner dedicate the portion of her property lying within the 100–year floodplain for improvement of a storm drainage system along Fanno Creek and that she dedicate an additional 15–foot strip of land adjacent to the floodplain as a pedestrian/bicycle pathway. The dedication required by that condition encompasses approximately 7,000 square feet, or roughly 10% of the property. In accordance with city practice, petitioner could rely on the dedicated property to meet the 15% open space and landscaping requirement mandated by the city's zoning scheme. App. to Pet. for Cert. G28–G29. The city would bear the cost of maintaining a landscaped buffer between the dedicated area and the new store. *Id.*, at G44–G45.

Petitioner requested variances from the CDC standards. Variances are granted only where it can be shown that, owing to special circumstances related to a specific piece of the land, the literal interpretation of the applicable zoning provisions would cause "an undue or unnecessary hardship" unless the variance is granted. CDC § 18.134.010. App. to Brief for Respondent B–47. Rather than posing alternative mitigating measures to offset the expected impacts of her proposed development, as allowed under the CDC, petitioner simply argued that her proposed development would not conflict with the policies of the comprehensive plan. *Id.,* at E–4. The Commission denied the request.

The Commission made a series of findings concerning the relationship between the dedicated conditions and the projected impacts of petitioner's project. First, the Commission noted that "[i]t is reasonable to assume that customers and employees of the future uses of this site could utilize a pedestrian/bicycle pathway adjacent to this development for their transportation and recreational needs." City of Tigard Planning Commission Final Order No. 91–09 PC, App. to Pet. for Cert. G24. The Commission noted that the site plan has provided for bicycle parking in a rack in front of the proposed building and "[i]t is reasonable to expect that some of the users of the bicycle parking provided for by the site plan will use the pathway adjacent to Fanno Creek if it is constructed." *Ibid.* In addition, the Commission found that creation of a convenient, safe pedestrian/bicycle pathway system as an alternative means of transportation "could offset some of the traffic demand on [nearby] streets and lessen the increase in traffic congestion." *Ibid.*

The Commission went on to note that the required floodplain dedication would be reasonably related to petitioner's request to intensify the use of the site given the increase in the impervious surface. The Commission stated that the "anticipated increased storm water flow from the subject property to an already strained creek and drainage basin can only add to the public need to manage the stream channel and floodplain for drainage purposes." *Id.,* at G37. Based on this anticipated increased storm water flow, the Commission concluded that "the requirement of dedication of the floodplain area on the site is related to the applicant's plan to intensify development on the site." *Ibid.* The Tigard City Council approved the Commission's final order, subject to one minor modification; the City Council reassigned the responsibility for surveying and marking the floodplain area from petitioner to the city's engineering department. *Id.,* at G–7.

* * *

II

The Takings Clause of the Fifth Amendment of the United States Constitution, made applicable to the States through the Fourteenth Amendment, *Chicago, B. & Q.R. Co. v. Chicago,* 166 U.S. 226, 239, 17 S.Ct. 581, 585, 41 L.Ed. 979 (1897), provides: "[N]or shall private property be taken for public use, without just compensation." [5] One of

5. Justice Stevens' dissent suggests that this case is actually grounded in "substantive" due process, rather than in the view that the Takings Clause of the Fifth Amendment was made applicable to the States by the Fourteenth Amendment. But there is no doubt that later cases have held that the Fourteenth Amendment does make the Takings Clause of the Fifth Amendment applicable to the States, see *Penn Central Transp. Co. v. New York City,* 438 U.S. 104, 122, 98 S.Ct. 2646, 2658, 57 L.Ed.2d 631 (1978); *Nollan v. California Coastal Comm'n,* 483 U.S. 825, 827, 107 S.Ct. 3141, 3143, 97 L.Ed.2d 677 (1987). Nor is there any doubt that these cases have relied upon

the principal purposes of the Takings Clause is "to bar Government from forcing some people alone to bear public burdens which, in all fairness and justice, should be borne by the public as a whole." *Armstrong v. United States,* 364 U.S. 40, 49, 80 S.Ct. 1563, 1569, 4 L.Ed.2d 1554 (1960). Without question, had the city simply required petitioner to dedicate a strip of land along Fanno Creek for public use, rather than conditioning the grant of her permit to redevelop her property on such a dedication, a taking would have occurred. *Nollan, supra,* 483 U.S., at 831, 107 S.Ct., at 3145. Such public access would deprive petitioner of the right to exclude others, "one of the most essential sticks in the bundle of rights that are commonly characterized as property." *Kaiser Aetna v. United States,* 444 U.S. 164, 176, 100 S.Ct. 383, 391, 62 L.Ed.2d 332 (1979).

On the other side of the ledger, the authority of state and local governments to engage in land use planning has been sustained against constitutional challenge as long ago as our decision in *Euclid v. Ambler Realty Co.,* 272 U.S. 365, 47 S.Ct. 114, 71 L.Ed. 303 (1926). "Government hardly could go on if to some extent values incident to property could not be diminished without paying for every such change in the general law." *Pennsylvania Coal Co. v. Mahon,* 260 U.S. 393, 413, 43 S.Ct. 158, 159, 67 L.Ed. 322 (1922). A land use regulation does not effect a taking if it "substantially advance[s] legitimate state interests" and does not "den[y] an owner economically viable use of his land." *Agins v. Tiburon,* 447 U.S. 255, 260, 100 S.Ct. 2138, 2141, 65 L.Ed.2d 106 (1980).[6]

The sort of land use regulations discussed in the cases just cited, however, differ in two relevant particulars from the present case. First, they involved essentially legislative determinations classifying entire areas of the city, whereas here the city made an adjudicative decision to condition petitioner's application for a building permit on an individual parcel. Second, the conditions imposed were not simply a limitation on the use petitioner might make of her own parcel, but a requirement that she deed portions of the property to the city. In *Nollan, supra,* we held that governmental authority to exact such a condition was circumscribed by the Fifth and Fourteenth Amendments. Under the well-settled doctrine of "unconstitutional conditions," the government may not

Chicago, B. & Q.R. Co. v. Chicago, 166 U.S. 226, 17 S.Ct. 581, 41 L.Ed. 979 (1897), to reach that result. See, *e.g., Penn Central, supra,* 438 U.S., at 122, 98 S.Ct., at 2658 ("The issu[e] presented . . . [is] whether the restrictions imposed by New York City's law upon appellants' exploitation of the Terminal site effect a 'taking' of appellants' property for a public use within the meaning of the Fifth Amendment, which of course is made applicable to the States through the Fourteenth Amendment, see *Chicago, B. & Q.R. Co. v. Chicago,* 166 U.S. 226, 239, 17 S.Ct. 581, 585, 41 L.Ed. 979 (1897)").

6. There can be no argument that the permit conditions would deprive petitioner "economically beneficial us[e]" of her property as she currently operates a retail store on the lot. Petitioner assuredly is able to derive *some* economic use from her property. See, *e.g., Lucas v. South Carolina,* 505 U.S. ___, ___, 112 S.Ct. 2886, 2893, 120 L.Ed.2d 798 (1992); *Kaiser Aetna v. United States,* 444 U.S. 164, 175, 100 S.Ct. 383, 390, 62 L.Ed.2d 332 (1979); *Penn Central Transportation Co. v. New York City,* 438 U.S. 104, 124, 98 S.Ct. 2646, 2659, 57 L.Ed.2d 631 (1978).

require a person to give up a constitutional right—here the right to receive just compensation when property is taken for a public use—in exchange for a discretionary benefit conferred by the government where the property sought has little or no relationship to the benefit. See *Perry v. Sindermann,* 408 U.S. 593, 92 S.Ct. 2694, 33 L.Ed.2d 570 (1972); *Pickering v. Board of Ed. of Township High School Dist.,* 391 U.S. 563, 568, 88 S.Ct. 1731, 1734, 20 L.Ed.2d 811 (1968).

Petitioner contends that the city has forced her to choose between the building permit and her right under the Fifth Amendment to just compensation for the public easements. Petitioner does not quarrel with the city's authority to exact some forms of dedication as a condition for the grant of a building permit, but challenges the showing made by the city to justify these exactions. She argues that the city has identified "no special benefits" conferred on her, and has not identified any "special quantifiable burdens" created by her new store that would justify the particular dedications required from her which are not required from the public at large.

III

In evaluating petitioner's claim, we must first determine whether the "essential nexus" exists between the "legitimate state interest" and the permit condition exacted by the city. *Nollan,* 483 U.S., at 837, 107 S.Ct., at 3148. If we find that a nexus exists, we must then decide the required degree of connection between the exactions and the projected impact of the proposed development. We were not required to reach this question in *Nollan,* because we concluded that the connection did not meet even the loosest standard. 483 U.S., at 838, 107 S.Ct., at 3149. Here, however, we must decide this question.

A

We addressed the essential nexus question in *Nollan.* The California Coastal Commission demanded a lateral public easement across the Nollan's beachfront lot in exchange for a permit to demolish an existing bungalow and replace it with a three-bedroom house. 483 U.S., at 828, 107 S.Ct., at 3144. The public easement was designed to connect two public beaches that were separated by the Nollan's property. The Coastal Commission had asserted that the public easement condition was imposed to promote the legitimate state interest of diminishing the "blockage of the view of the ocean" caused by construction of the larger house.

We agreed that the Coastal Commission's concern with protecting visual access to the ocean constituted a legitimate public interest. *Id.,* at 835, 107 S.Ct., at 3148. We also agreed that the permit condition would have been constitutional "even if it consisted of the requirement that the Nollans provide a viewing spot on their property for passersby with whose sighting of the ocean their new house would interfere." *Id.,* at 836, 107 S.Ct., at 3148. We resolved, however, that the Coastal Commission's regulatory authority was set completely adrift from its constitutional moorings when it claimed that a nexus existed between visual access to the ocean and a permit condition requiring lateral public access along the Nollan's beachfront lot. *Id.,* at 837, 107 S.Ct., at 3148. How enhancing the public's ability to "traverse to and along the shorefront" served the same governmental purpose of "visual access to the ocean" from the roadway was beyond our ability to countenance. The absence of a nexus left the Coastal Commission in the position of simply trying to obtain an easement through gimmickry, which converted a valid regulation of land use into "an out-and-out plan of extortion." *Ibid.,* quoting *J.E.D. Associates, Inc. v. Atkinson,* 121 N.H. 581, 584, 432 A.2d 12, 14–15 (1981).

No such gimmicks are associated with the permit conditions imposed by the city in this case. Undoubtedly, the prevention of flooding along Fanno Creek and the reduction of traffic congestion in the Central Business District qualify as the type of legitimate public purposes we have upheld. *Agins, supra,* 447 U.S., at 260–262, 100 S.Ct., at 2141–2142. It seems equally obvious that a nexus exists between preventing flooding along Fanno Creek and limiting development within the creek's 100–year floodplain. Petitioner proposes to double the size of her retail store and to pave her now-gravel parking lot, thereby expanding the impervious surface on the property and increasing the amount of stormwater run-off into Fanno Creek.

The same may be said for the city's attempt to reduce traffic congestion by providing for alternative means of transportation. In theory, a pedestrian/bicycle pathway provides a useful alternative means of transportation for workers and shoppers: "Pedestrians and bicyclists occupying dedicated spaces for walking and/or bicycling * * * remove potential vehicles from streets, resulting in an overall improvement in total transportation system flow." A. Nelson, Public Provision of Pedestrian and Bicycle Access Ways: Public Policy Rationale and the Nature of Private Benefits 11, Center for Planning Development, Georgia Institute of Technology, Working Paper Series (Jan. 1994). See also, Intermodal Surface Transportation Efficiency Act of 1991, Pub.L. 102–240, 105 Stat. 1914; (recognizing pedestrian and bicycle facilities as necessary components of any strategy to reduce traffic congestion).

B

The second part of our analysis requires us to determine whether the degree of the exactions demanded by the city's permit conditions bear the required relationship to the projected impact of petitioner's proposed development. *Nollan, supra,* 483 U.S., at 834, 107 S.Ct., at 3147, quoting *Penn Central,* 438 U.S. 104, 127, 98 S.Ct. 2646, 2660, 57 L.Ed.2d 631 (1978) (" '[A] use restriction may constitute a taking if not reasonably necessary to the effectuation of a substantial government purpose' "). Here the Oregon Supreme Court deferred to what it termed the "city's unchallenged factual findings" supporting the dedication conditions and found them to be reasonably related to the impact of the expansion of petitioner's business. 317 Ore., at 120–121, 854 P.2d, at 443.

The city required that petitioner dedicate "to the city as Greenway all portions of the site that fall within the existing 100-year floodplain [of Fanno Creek] ... and all property 15 feet above [the floodplain] boundary." In addition, the city demanded that the retail store be designed so as not to intrude into the greenway area. The city relies on the Commission's rather tentative findings that increased stormwater flow from petitioner's property "can only add to the public need to manage the [floodplain] for drainage purposes" to support its conclusion that the "requirement of dedication of the floodplain area on the site is related to the applicant's plan to intensify development on the site." City of Tigard Planning Commission Final Order No. 91–09 PC, App. to Pet. for Cert. G37.

The city made the following specific findings relevant to the pedestrian/bicycle pathway:

> "In addition, the proposed expanded use of this site is anticipated to generate additional vehicular traffic thereby increasing congestion on nearby collector and arterial streets. Creation of a convenient, safe pedestrian/bicycle pathway system as an alternative means of transportation could offset some of the traffic demand on these nearby streets and lessen the increase in traffic congestion." *Id.,* at 24.

The question for us is whether these findings are constitutionally sufficient to justify the conditions imposed by the city on petitioner's building permit. Since state courts have been dealing with this question a good deal longer than we have, we turn to representative decisions made by them.

In some States, very generalized statements as to the necessary connection between the required dedication and the proposed development seem to suffice. See, *e.g., Billings Properties, Inc. v. Yellowstone County,* 144 Mont. 25, 394 P.2d 182 (1964); *Jenad, Inc. v. Scarsdale,* 18 N.Y.2d 78, 271 N.Y.S.2d 955, 218 N.E.2d 673 (1966). We think this standard is too lax to adequately protect petitioner's right to just compensation if her property is taken for a public purpose.

Other state courts require a very exacting correspondence, described as the "specifi[c] and uniquely attributable" test. The Supreme Court of Illinois first developed this test in *Pioneer Trust & Savings Bank v. Mount Prospect,* 22 Ill.2d 375, 380, 176 N.E.2d 799, 802 (1961).[7] Under this standard, if the local government cannot demonstrate that its exaction is directly proportional to the specifically created need, the exaction becomes "a veiled exercise of the power of eminent domain and a confiscation of private property behind the defense of police regulations." *Id.,* at 381, 176 N.E.2d, at 802. We do not think the Federal

7. The "specifically and uniquely attributable" test has now been adopted by a minority of other courts. See, *e.g., J.E.D. Associates, Inc. v. Atkinson,* 121 N.H. 581, 585, 432 A.2d 12, 15 (1981); *Divan Builders, Inc. v. Planning Bd. of Twp. of Wayne,* 66 N.J. 582, 600–601, 334 A.2d 30, 40 (1975); *McKain v. Toledo City Plan Comm'n,* 26 Ohio App.2d 171, 176, 270 N.E.2d 370, 374 (1971); *Frank Ansuini, Inc. v. Cranston,* 107 R.I. 63, 69, 264 A.2d 910, 913 (1970).

Constitution requires such exacting scrutiny, given the nature of the interests involved.

A number of state courts have taken an intermediate position, requiring the municipality to show a "reasonable relationship" between the required dedication and the impact of the proposed development. Typical is the Supreme Court of Nebraska's opinion in *Simpson v. North Platte,* 206 Neb. 240, 245, 292 N.W.2d 297, 301 (1980), where that court stated:

> "The distinction, therefore, which must be made between an appropriate exercise of the police power and an improper exercise of eminent domain is whether the requirement has some reasonable relationship or nexus to the use to which the property is being made or is merely being used as an excuse for taking property simply because at that particular moment the landowner is asking the city for some license or permit."

Thus, the court held that a city may not require a property owner to dedicate private property for some future public use as a condition of obtaining a building permit when such future use is not "occasioned by the construction sought to be permitted." *Id.,* at 248, 292 N.W.2d, at 302.

Some form of the reasonable relationship test has been adopted in many other jurisdictions. See, *e.g., Jordan v. Menomonee Falls,* 28 Wis.2d 608, 137 N.W.2d 442 (1965); *Collis v. Bloomington,* 310 Minn. 5, 246 N.W.2d 19 (1976) (requiring a showing of a reasonable relationship between the planned subdivision and the municipality's need for land); *College Station v. Turtle Rock Corp.,* 680 S.W.2d 802, 807 (Tex.1984); *Call v. West Jordan,* 606 P.2d 217, 220 (Utah 1979) (affirming use of the reasonable relation test). Despite any semantical differences, general agreement exists among the courts "that the dedication should have some reasonable relationship to the needs created by the [development]." *Ibid.* See generally, Morosoff, Take My Beach Please!: Nollan v. California Coastal Commission and a Rational–Nexus Constitutional Analysis of Development Exactions, 69 B.U.L.Rev. 823 (1989); see also *Parks v. Watson,* 716 F.2d 646, 651–653 (CA9 1983).

We think the "reasonable relationship" test adopted by a majority of the state courts is closer to the federal constitutional norm than either of those previously discussed. But we do not adopt it as such, partly because the term "reasonable relationship" seems confusingly similar to the term "rational basis" which describes the minimal level of scrutiny under the Equal Protection Clause of the Fourteenth Amendment. We think a term such as "rough proportionality" best encapsulates what we hold to be the requirement of the Fifth Amendment. No precise mathematical calculation is required, but the city must make some sort of individualized determination that the required dedication is related both in nature and extent to the impact of the proposed development.[8]

8. Justice Stevens' dissent takes us to task for placing the burden on the city to justify the required dedication. He is correct in arguing that in evaluating most gen-

Justice Stevens' dissent relies upon a law review article for the proposition that the city's conditional demands for part of petitioner's property are "a species of business regulation that heretofore warranted a strong presumption of constitutional validity." *Post,* at 2325. But simply denominating a governmental measure as a "business regulation" does not immunize it from constitutional challenge on the grounds that it violates a provision of the Bill of Rights. In *Marshall v. Barlow's, Inc.,* 436 U.S. 307, 98 S.Ct. 1816, 56 L.Ed.2d 305 (1978), we held that a statute authorizing a warrantless search of business premises in order to detect OSHA violations violated the Fourth Amendment. See also *Air Pollution Variance Board of Colo. v. Western Alfalfa Corp.,* 416 U.S. 861, 94 S.Ct. 2114, 40 L.Ed.2d 607 (1974); *New York v. Burger,* 482 U.S. 691, 107 S.Ct. 2636, 96 L.Ed.2d 601 (1982). And in *Central Hudson Gas & Electric Corp. v. Public Service Comm'n of N.Y.,* 447 U.S. 557, 100 S.Ct. 2343, 65 L.Ed.2d 341 (1980), we held that an order of the New York Public Service Commission, designed to cut down the use of electricity because of a fuel shortage, violated the First Amendment insofar as it prohibited advertising by a utility company to promote the use of electricity. We see no reason why the Takings Clause of the Fifth Amendment, as much a part of the Bill of Rights as the First Amendment or Fourth Amendment, should be related to the status of a poor relation in these comparable circumstances. We turn now to analysis of whether the findings relied upon by the city here, first with respect to the floodplain easement, and second with respect to the pedestrian/bicycle path, satisfied these requirements.

It is axiomatic that increasing the amount of impervious surface will increase the quantity and rate of storm-water flow from petitioner's property. Record, Dec. No. F, ch. 4, p. 4–29. Therefore, keeping the floodplain open and free from development would likely confine the pressures on Fanno Creek created by petitioner's development. In fact, because petitioner's property lies within the Central Business District, the Community Development Code already required that petitioner leave 15% of it as open space and the undeveloped floodplain would have nearly satisfied that requirement. App. to Pet. for Cert. G16–G17. But the city demanded more—it not only wanted petitioner not to build in the floodplain, but it also wanted petitioner's property along Fanno Creek for its Greenway system. The city has never said why a public

erally applicable zoning regulations, the burden properly rests on the party challenging the regulation to prove that it constitutes an arbitrary regulation of property rights. See, *e.g., Euclid v. Ambler Realty Co.,* 272 U.S. 365, 47 S.Ct. 114, 71 L.Ed. 303 (1926). Here, by contrast, the city made an adjudicative decision to condition petitioner's application for a building permit on an individual parcel. In this situation, the burden properly rests on the city. See *Nollan,* 483 U.S., at 836, 107 S.Ct., at 3148. This conclusion is not, as he suggests, undermined by our decision in *Moore v. East Cleveland,* 431 U.S. 494, 97 S.Ct. 1932, 52 L.Ed.2d 531 (1977), in which we struck down a housing ordinance that limited occupancy of a dwelling unit to members of a single family as violating the Due Process Clause of the Fourteenth Amendment. The ordinance at issue in *Moore* intruded on choices concerning family living arrangements, an area in which the usual deference to the legislature was found to be inappropriate. *Id.,* at 499, 97 S.Ct., at 1935.

greenway, as opposed to a private one, was required in the interest of flood control.

The difference to petitioner, of course, is the loss of her ability to exclude others. As we have noted, this right to exclude others is "one of the most essential sticks in the bundle of rights that are commonly characterized as property." *Kaiser Aetna,* 444 U.S., at 176, 100 S.Ct., at 391. It is difficult to see why recreational visitors trampling along petitioner's floodplain easement are sufficiently related to the city's legitimate interest in reducing flooding problems along Fanno Creek, and the city has not attempted to make any individualized determination to support this part of its request.

* * *

Admittedly, petitioner wants to build a bigger store to attract members of the public to her property. She also wants, however, to be able to control the time and manner in which they enter. The recreational easement on the Greenway is different in character from the exercise of state-protected rights of free expression and petition that we permitted in *PruneYard.* In *PruneYard,* we held that a major private shopping center that attracted more than 25,000 daily patrons had to provide access to persons exercising their state constitutional rights to distribute pamphlets and ask passersby to sign their petitions. *Id.,* at 85, 100 S.Ct., at 2042. We based our decision, in part, on the fact that the shopping center "may restrict expressive activity by adopting time, place, and manner regulations that will minimize any interference with its commercial functions." *Id.,* at 83, 100 S.Ct., at 2042. By contrast, the city wants to impose a permanent recreational easement upon petitioner's property that borders Fanno Creek. Petitioner would lose all rights to regulate the time in which the public entered onto the Greenway, regardless of any interference it might pose with her retail store. Her right to exclude would not be regulated, it would be eviscerated.

If petitioner's proposed development had somehow encroached on existing greenway space in the city, it would have been reasonable to require petitioner to provide some alternative greenway space for the public either on her property or elsewhere. See *Nollan,* 483 U.S., at 836, 107 S.Ct., at 3148 ("Although such a requirement, constituting a permanent grant of continuous access to the property, would have to be considered a taking if it were not attached to a development permit, the Commission's assumed power to forbid construction of the house in order to protect the public's view of the beach must surely include the power to condition construction upon some concession by the owner, even a concession of property rights, that serves the same end"). But that is not the case here. We conclude that the findings upon which the city relies do not show the required reasonable relationship between the floodplain easement and the petitioner's proposed new building.

With respect to the pedestrian/bicycle pathway, we have no doubt that the city was correct in finding that the larger retail sales facility proposed by petitioner will increase traffic on the streets of the Central Business District. The city estimates that the proposed development would generate roughly 435 additional trips per day. Dedications for streets, sidewalks, and other public ways are generally reasonable exactions to avoid excessive congestion from a proposed property use. But on the record before us, the city has not met its burden of demonstrating that the additional number of vehicle and bicycle trips generated by the petitioner's development reasonably relate to the city's requirement for a dedication of the pedestrian/bicycle pathway easement. The city simply found that the creation of the pathway "could offset some of the traffic demand * * * and lessen the increase in traffic congestion."

As Justice Peterson of the Supreme Court of Oregon explained in his dissenting opinion, however, "[t]he findings of fact that the bicycle pathway system '*could* offset some of the traffic demand' is a far cry from a finding that the bicycle pathway system *will,* or is *likely to,* offset some of the traffic demand." 317 Ore., at 127, 854 P.2d, at 447 (emphasis in original). No precise mathematical calculation is required, but the city must make some effort to quantify its findings in support of the dedication for the pedestrian/bicycle pathway beyond the conclusory statement that it could offset some of the traffic demand generated.

IV

Cities have long engaged in the commendable task of land use planning, made necessary by increasing urbanization particularly in metropolitan areas such as Portland. The city's goals of reducing flooding hazards and traffic congestion, and providing for public greenways, are laudable, but there are outer limits to how this may be done. "A strong public desire to improve the public condition [will not] warrant achieving the desire by a shorter cut than the constitutional way of paying for the change." *Pennsylvania Coal,* 260 U.S., at 416, 43 S.Ct., at 160.

The judgment of the Supreme Court of Oregon is reversed, and the case is remanded for further proceedings consistent with this opinion.

It is so ordered. * * *

p. 625: Omit note 1.

p. 626: Add before Note 2 new Note 1 following *Dolan.* Retain note 2.

1. Congress and state legislatures are also giving increased attention to regulatory takings. See, e.g., Private Property Protection Act of 1995, H.R. 925, passed House Mar. 3, 1995, 141 Cong.Rec. H 2607; S. 605, Omnibus Property Rights Act of 1995, 1995 WL 123885, pp. 42–78; "32 States Introduce 'Takings' Bills This Year," State Legislatures, September 1994, at 11.

II. PUBLIC PROPERTY: ACQUISITION, OWNERSHIP AND USE

B. LIMITATIONS ON USE AND DISPOSITION

1. CONSTITUTIONAL LIMITATIONS

p. 632: Add to the Note's citations

City of Cincinnati v. Discovery Network, Inc., ___ U.S. ___, 113 S.Ct. 1505, 123 L.Ed.2d 99 (1993), reported, supra, this Supplement (overturning city's selective, categorical ban on the newsrack distribution of what it classified as commercial handbills); Lamb's Chapel v. Center Moriches Union Free Sch. Dist., ___ U.S. ___, 113 S.Ct. 2141, 124 L.Ed.2d 352 (1993) (school's refusal to permit on school grounds non-school-sponsored showing of film on family values and child rearing offered by evangelical church and pastor, on the terms whereby it has permitted other private, after-school-hours programs violated free speech and was not required by the Establishment Clause); Kreisner v. City of San Diego, 1 F.3d 775 (9th Cir.1993), cert. denied, ___ U.S. ___, 114 S.Ct. 690, 126 L.Ed.2d 657 (1994) (city permission for private group to show scenes from life of Christ during Christmas season in a public park, a public forum open to all speakers, was not an endorsement of religion in violation of Establishment Clause); Chabad–Lubavitch of Georgia v. Miller, 5 F.3d 1383 (11th Cir.1993) (denial of permission for privately sponsored display of 15–foot menorah in rotunda of state capitol designated as public forum would implicate free speech burdens); Americans United for Separation of Church and State v. City of Grand Rapids, 980 F.2d 1538 (6th Cir.1992) (unattended display of privately funded menorah in city's principal plaza, near government buildings and flags, but with small sign disclaiming government endorsement, during holiday season, unaccompanied by other seasonal decorations, did not violate Establishment Clause).

With regard to constitutional and statutory limitations on municipal regulation of waste disposal, see this Supplement, supra, with regard to Note 3, p. 376 of the casebook.

C. EMINENT DOMAIN

1. DE FACTO TAKINGS

P. 635: Add to first introductory paragraph

Apparently, the courts will apply the following tests in cases seeking compensation for a period earlier than the de jure taking time. As noted above, landowners may seek to have the time of taking moved back (see *J.W. Clement Co.,* supra), or they may counterclaim in inverse condemnation seeking lost profits for the earlier time period (see Westgate, Ltd. v. State, 843 S.W.2d 448 (Tex.1992)). In the latter instance, the court held that no cause of action existed absent an allegation that the government acted in bad faith in permitting construction to proceed while the highway plan was being completed. The dissenters cited authorities from other jurisdictions which hold that bad faith is shown where the government delay of condemnation is unreasonable.

Police damage or destruction of an innocent party's property in the course of apprehending a suspect may constitute a de facto taking. Wegner v. Milwaukee Mutual Insurance Co., 479 N.W.2d 38 (Minn. 1991).

5. JUST COMPENSATION

p. 660: Add to Notes, 2(a)

Appeal of Marple Springfield Center, Inc., 530 Pa. 122, 607 A.2d 708 (1992) (capitalization-of-income approach appropriate to determine fair market value where lease rental was lower than current market rental owing to long term of the commercial lease); State v. Caoili, 135 N.J. 252, 639 A.2d 275 (1994) (value of property is its price if zoning change to commercial is granted, discounted by the probability of that rezoning occurring).

Add to Notes, 2(c)

Capital Properties, Inc. v. State, 636 A.2d 319 (R.I.1994) (court improperly deducted special benefits to the remainder from the compensation for the land taken).

Chapter VIII

FINANCING LOCAL GOVERNMENT

A. BUDGETING, APPROPRIATIONS, AUDITING, EARMARKING

p. 676: Add to Note 2

In their popular book, Reinventing Government: How the Entrepreneurial Spirit Is Transforming the Public Sector, David Osbourne and Ted Gaebler proposed, inter alia, that individual local government departments be permitted to add savings from the present year to their individual budgets for the next year, thus giving more incentive for efficiency.

B. REVENUE

p. 687: Add to text at bottom of page

At the state level, because other revenues may include those resulting from escheat, and because the Supreme Court has held that the places of dividend payers' incorporation, primarily Delaware and New York, are entitled to the proceeds of escheated, unclaimed dividends, Delaware v. New York, ___ U.S. ___, 113 S.Ct. 1550, 123 L.Ed.2d 211 (1993), the rest of the states have sought from Congress legislation that will permit states of shareholders' last known address or stockbrokers' actual places of business to share in those proceeds. The states have settled their dispute with Delaware and New York without federal legislation.

p. 688: Add to the end of the introductory text

See generally Steven D. Gold and Jennifer McCormick, State Tax Reform in the Early 1990s, 6 State Tax Notes 1146 (1994); see also Harold Hovey, *Financing State Government In the 1990s,* 13 State Budget & Tax News 1 (March 7, 1994).

1. PROPERTY TAXATION

p. 690: Add to text

See generally, ACIR, Symposium on the Property Tax, 19 Intergovernmental Perspective 10 (1993).

a. Property Tax Reform

p. 703: Add to Note

See also, e.g., Claremont School District v. Governor, 138 N.H. 183, 635 A.2d 1375 (1993) (system of property tax funding of public education held to violate state constitution's encouragement of literature clause); semble, McDuffy v. Secretary of the Executive Office of Education, 415 Mass. 545, 615 N.E.2d 516 (1993); Steven D. Gold, School Property Taxes Under Fire, 6 State Tax Notes 1280 (1994). Because states and their local governments continue to share the costs, both may have funding problems. See New Haven v. State Board of Education, 228 Conn. 699, 638 A.2d 589 (1994) (on review of state board ruling, court found that city did not adequately provide its share of school system funds).

b. Property Tax Assessment

p. 710: Replace the *Allegheny Pittsburgh Coal* case with the following

NORDLINGER v. HAHN

Supreme Court of the United States, 1992.
___ U.S. ___, 112 S.Ct. 2326, 120 L.Ed.2d 1.

JUSTICE BLACKMUN delivered the opinion of the Court.

In 1978, California voters staged what has been described as a property tax revolt by approving a statewide ballot initiative known as Proposition 13. The adoption of Proposition 13 served to amend the California Constitution to impose strict limits on the rate at which real property is taxed and on the rate at which real property assessments are increased from year to year. In this litigation, we consider a challenge under the Equal Protection Clause of the Fourteenth Amendment to the manner in which real property now is assessed under the California Constitution.

I

A

Proposition 13 followed many years of rapidly rising real property taxes in California. From fiscal years 1967–1968 to 1971–1972, revenues from these taxes increased on an average of 11.5 percent per year. See Report of the Senate Commission on Property Tax Equity and Revenue to the California State Senate 23 (1991). In response, the California Legislature enacted several property tax relief measures, including a cap on tax rates in 1972. *Id.,* at 23–24. The boom in the State's real estate market persevered, however, and the median price of an existing home doubled from $31,530 in 1973 to $62,430 in 1977. As a result, tax levies continued to rise because of sharply increasing assessment values. *Id.,* at 23. Some homeowners saw their tax bills double or triple during this period, well outpacing any growth in their income and ability to pay. *Id.,* at 25. See also Oakland, Proposition 13—Genesis and Consequences, 32 Nat.Tax J. 387, 392 (Supp. June 1979).

By 1978, property tax relief had emerged as a major political issue in California. In only one month's time, tax relief advocates collected over 1.2 million signatures to qualify Proposition 13 for the June 1978 ballot. See Lefcoe & Allison, The Legal Aspects of Proposition 13: The *Amador Valley* Case, 53 S.Cal.L.Rev. 173, 174 (1978). On election day, Proposition 13 received a favorable vote of 64.8 percent and carried 55 of the State's 58 counties. California Secretary of State, Statement of Vote and Supplement, Primary Election, June 6, 1978, p. 39. California thus had a novel constitutional amendment that led to a property tax cut of approximately $7 billion in the first year. Senate Commission Report, at 28. A California homeowner with a $50,000 home enjoyed an immediate reduction of about $750 per year in property taxes. *Id.,* at 26.

As enacted by Proposition 13, Article XIIIA of the California Constitution caps real property taxes at 1% of a property's "full cash value." § 1(a). "Full cash value" is defined as the assessed valuation as of the 1975–1976 tax year or, "thereafter, the appraised value of real property when purchased, newly constructed, or a change in ownership has occurred after the 1975 assessment." § 2(a). The assessment "may reflect from year to year the inflationary rate not to exceed 2 percent for any given year." § 2(b).

Article XIIIA also contains several exemptions from this reassessment provision. One exemption authorizes the legislature to allow homeowners over the age of 55 who sell their principal residences to carry their previous base-year assessments with them to replacement residences of equal or lesser value. § 2(a). A second exemption applies to transfers of a principal residence (and up to $1 million of other real property) between parents and children. § 2(h).

In short, Article XIIIA combines a 1% ceiling on the property tax rate with a 2% cap on annual increases in assessed valuations. The assessment limitation, however, is subject to the exception that new construction or a change of ownership triggers a reassessment up to current appraised value. Thus, the assessment provisions of Article XIIIA essentially embody an "acquisition value" system of taxation rather than the more commonplace "current value" taxation. Real property is assessed at values related to the value of the property at the time it is acquired by the taxpayer rather than to the value it has in the current real estate market.

Over time, this acquisition-value system has created dramatic disparities in the taxes paid by persons owning similar pieces of property. Property values in California have inflated far in excess of the allowed 2% cap on increases in assessments for property that is not newly constructed or that has not changed hands. See Senate Commission Report, at 31–32. As a result, longer-term property owners pay lower property taxes reflecting historic property values, while newer owners pay higher property taxes reflecting more recent values. For that reason, Proposition 13 has been labeled by some as a "welcome stranger" system—the newcomer to an established community is "welcome" in anticipation that he will contribute a larger percentage of support for local government than his settled neighbor who owns a comparable home. Indeed, in dollar terms, the differences in tax burdens are staggering. By 1989, the 44% of California home owners who have owned their homes since enactment of Proposition 13 in 1978 shouldered only 25% of the more than $4 billion in residential property taxes paid by homeowners statewide. *Id.*, at 33. If property values continue to rise more than the annual 2% inflationary cap, this disparity will continue to grow.

B

According to her amended complaint, petitioner Stephanie Nordlinger in November 1988 purchased a house in the Baldwin Hills neighborhood of Los Angeles County for $170,000. App. 5. The prior owners bought the home just two years before for $121,500. *Id.*, at 6. Before her purchase, petitioner had lived in a rented apartment in Los Angeles and had not owned any real property in California. *Id.*, at 5; Tr. of Oral Arg. 12.

In early 1989, petitioner received a notice from the Los Angeles County Tax Assessor, who is a respondent here, informing her that her home had been reassessed upward to $170,100 on account of its change in ownership. App. 7. She learned that the reassessment resulted in a property tax increase of $453.60, up 36% to $1,701, for the 1988–1989 fiscal year. *Ibid.*

Petitioner later discovered she was paying about five times more in taxes than some of her neighbors who owned comparable homes since 1975 within the same residential development. For example, one block away, a house of identical size on a lot slightly larger than petitioner's was subject to a general tax levy of only $358.20 (based on an assessed valuation of $35,820, which reflected the home's value in 1975 plus the up-to-2% per year inflation factor). *Id.*, at 9–10. According to petitioner, her total property taxes over the first 10 years in her home will approach $19,000, while any neighbor who bought a comparable home in 1975 stands to pay just $4,100. Brief for Petitioner 3. The general tax levied against her modest home is only a few dollars short of that paid by a pre–1976 owner of a $2.1 million Malibu beachfront home. App. 24. * * *

II

The Equal Protection Clause of the Fourteenth Amendment, § 1, commands that no State shall "deny to any person within its jurisdiction the equal protection of the laws." Of course, most laws differentiate in some fashion between classes of persons. The Equal Protection Clause does not forbid classifications. It simply keeps governmental decisionmakers from treating differently persons who are in all relevant respects alike. *F.S. Royster Guano Co. v. Virginia,* 253 U.S. 412, 415, 40 S.Ct. 560, 561, 64 L.Ed. 989 (1920).

As a general rule, "legislatures are presumed to have acted within their constitutional power despite the fact that, in practice, their laws result in some inequality." *McGowan v. Maryland,* 366 U.S. 420, 425–426, 81 S.Ct. 1101, 1105, 6 L.Ed.2d 393 (1961). Accordingly, this Court's cases are clear that, unless a classification warrants some form of heightened review because it jeopardizes exercise of a fundamental right or categorizes on the basis of an inherently suspect characteristic, the Equal Protection Clause requires only that the classification rationally further a legitimate state interest. See, *e.g., Cleburne v. Cleburne Living Center, Inc.,* 473 U.S. 432, 439–441, 105 S.Ct. 3249, 3254–3255, 87 L.Ed.2d 313 (1985); *New Orleans v. Dukes,* 427 U.S. 297, 303, 96 S.Ct. 2513, 2517, 49 L.Ed.2d 511 (1976).

A

At the outset, petitioner suggests that her challenge to Article XIIIA qualifies for heightened scrutiny because it infringes upon the constitutional right to travel. See, *e.g., Zobel v. Williams,* 457 U.S. 55, 60, n. 6, 102 S.Ct. 2309, 2312, n. 6, 72 L.Ed.2d 672 (1982); *Memorial Hospital v. Maricopa County,* 415 U.S. 250, 254–256, 94 S.Ct. 1076, 1080–1081, 39 L.Ed.2d 306 (1976). In particular, petitioner alleges that the exemptions to reassessment for transfers by owners over 55 and for transfers between parents and children run afoul of the right to travel, because they classify directly on the basis of California residency. But the complaint does not allege that petitioner herself has been impeded from traveling or from settling in California because, as has been noted, prior to purchasing her home, petitioner lived in an apartment in Los Angeles. This Court's prudential standing principles impose a "general prohibition on a litigant's raising another person's legal rights." *Allen v. Wright,* 468 U.S. 737, 751, 104 S.Ct. 3315, 3324, 82 L.Ed.2d 556 (1984). See also *Moose Lodge No. 107 v. Irvis,* 407 U.S. 163, 166, 92 S.Ct. 1965, 1968, 32 L.Ed.2d 627 (1972). Petitioner has not identified any obstacle preventing others who wish to travel or settle in California from asserting claims on their own behalf, nor has she shown any special relationship with those whose rights she seeks to assert, such that we might overlook this prudential limitation. *Caplin & Drysdale v. United States,* 491 U.S. 617, 623, n. 3, 109 S.Ct. 2646, 2651, n. 3, 105 L.Ed.2d 528 (1989). Accordingly, petitioner may not assert the constitutional right to travel as a basis for heightened review.

B

The appropriate standard of review is whether the difference in treatment between newer and older owners rationally furthers a legitimate state interest. In general, the Equal Protection Clause is satisfied so long as there is a plausible policy reason for the classification, see *United States Railroad Retirement Bd. v. Fritz,* 449 U.S. 166, 174, 179, 101 S.Ct. 453, 459, 461, 66 L.Ed.2d 368 (1980), the legislative facts on which the classification is apparently based rationally may have been considered to be true by the governmental decisionmaker, see *Minnesota v. Clover Leaf Creamery Co.,* 449 U.S. 456, 464, 101 S.Ct. 715, 724, 66

L.Ed.2d 659 (1981), and the relationship of the classification to its goal is not so attenuated as to render the distinction arbitrary or irrational, see *Cleburne v. Cleburne Living Center, Inc.,* 473 U.S., at 446, 105 S.Ct., at 3257. This standard is especially deferential in the context of classifications made by complex tax laws. "[I]n structuring internal taxation schemes the States have large leeway in making classifications and drawing lines which in their judgment produce reasonable systems of taxation." *Williams v. Vermont,* 472 U.S. 14, 22, 105 S.Ct. 2465, 2471, 86 L.Ed.2d 11 (1985), quoting *Lehnhausen v. Lake Shore Auto Parts Co.,* 410 U.S. 356, 359, 93 S.Ct. 1001, 1003, 35 L.Ed.2d 351 (1973). See also *Regan v. Taxation with Representation of Washington,* 461 U.S. 540, 547, 103 S.Ct. 1997, 2002, 76 L.Ed.2d 129 (1983) ("Legislatures have especially broad latitude in creating classifications and distinctions in tax statutes").

As between newer and older owners, Article XIIIA does not discriminate with respect to either the tax rate or the annual rate of adjustment in assessments. Newer and older owners alike benefit in both the short and long run from the protections of a 1% tax rate ceiling and no more than a 2% increase in assessment value per year. New owners and old owners are treated differently with respect to one factor only—the basis on which their property is initially assessed. Petitioner's true complaint is that the State has denied her—a new owner—the benefit of the same assessment value that her neighbors—older owners—enjoy.

We have no difficulty in ascertaining at least two rational or reasonable considerations of difference or policy that justify denying petitioner the benefits of her neighbors' lower assessments. First, the State has a legitimate interest in local neighborhood preservation, continuity, and stability. *Euclid v. Ambler Realty Co.,* 272 U.S. 365, 47 S.Ct. 114, 71 L.Ed. 303 (1926). The State therefore legitimately can decide to structure its tax system to discourage rapid turnover in ownership of homes and businesses, for example, in order to inhibit displacement of lower income families by the forces of gentrification or of established, "mom-and-pop" businesses by newer chain operations. By permitting older owners to pay progressively less in taxes than new owners of comparable property, the Article XIIIA assessment scheme rationally furthers this interest.

Second, the State legitimately can conclude that a new owner at the time of acquiring his property does not have the same reliance interest warranting protection against higher taxes as does an existing owner. The State may deny a new owner at the point of purchase the right to "lock in" to the same assessed value as is enjoyed by an existing owner of comparable property, because an existing owner rationally may be thought to have vested expectations in his property or home that are more deserving of protection than the anticipatory expectations of a new owner at the point of purchase. A new owner has full information about the scope of future tax liability before acquiring the property, and if he thinks the future tax burden is too demanding, he can decide not to complete the purchase at all. By contrast, the existing owner, already saddled with his purchase, does not have the option of deciding not to buy his home if taxes become prohibitively high. To meet his tax obligations, he might be forced to sell his home or to divert his income away from the purchase of food, clothing, and other necessities. In short, the State may decide that it is worse to have owned and lost, than never to have owned at all.

This Court previously has acknowledged that classifications serving to protect legitimate expectation and reliance interests do not deny equal protection of the laws. "The protection of reasonable reliance interests is not only a legitimate governmental objective: it provides an exceedingly persuasive justification * * *." (internal quotations omitted). *Heckler v. Mathews,* 465 U.S. 728, 746, 104 S.Ct. 1387, 1399, 79 L.Ed.2d 646 (1984). For example, in *Kadrmas v. Dickinson Public Schools,* 487 U.S. 450, 108 S.Ct. 2481, 101 L.Ed.2d 399 (1988), the Court determined that a prohibition on user fees for bus service in "reorganized" school districts but not in "nonreorganized" school districts does not violate the Equal Protection Clause, because "the legislature could conceivably have believed that such a policy would serve the legitimate purpose of fulfilling the reasonable expectations of those residing in districts with free busing arrangements imposed by reorganization plans." *Id.,* at 465, 108 S.Ct., at 2491. Similarly, in *United States Railroad Retirement Bd. v. Fritz, supra,* the Court determined that a denial of dual "windfall" retirement benefits to some railroad workers but not others did not violate the Equal Protection Clause, because "Congress could properly conclude that persons who had actually acquired statutory entitlement to windfall benefits while still employed in the railroad industry had a greater equitable claim to those benefits than the members of appellee's class who were no longer in railroad employment when they became eligible for dual benefits." 449 U.S., at 178, 101 S.Ct., at 461. Finally, in *New Orleans v. Dukes, supra,* the Court determined that an ordinance banning certain street-vendor operations, but grandfathering existing vendors who had been in operation for more than eight years, did not violate the Equal Protection Clause because the "city could reasonably decide that newer businesses were less likely to have built up substantial reliance interests in continued operation." 427 U.S., at 305, 96 S.Ct., at 2518.[5]

Petitioner argues that Article XIIIA cannot be distinguished from the tax assessment practice found to violate the Equal Protection Clause in *Allegheny Pittsburgh.* Like Article XIIIA, the practice at issue in *Allegheny Pittsburgh* resulted in dramatic disparities in taxation of properties of comparable value. But an obvious and critical factual difference between this case and *Allegheny Pittsburgh* is the absence of any indication in *Allegheny Pittsburgh* that the policies underlying an

5. Because we conclude that Article XIIIA rationally furthers the State's interests in neighborhood stability and the protection of property owners' reliance interests, we need not consider whether it permissibly serves other interests discussed by the parties, including whether it taxes real property according to the taxpayers' ability to pay or whether it taxes real property in such a way as to promote stability of local tax revenues.

acquisition-value taxation scheme could conceivably have been the purpose for the Webster County tax assessor's unequal assessment scheme. In the first place, Webster County argued that "its assessment scheme is rationally related to its purpose of assessing properties *at true current value*" (emphasis added). *Id.,* at 488 U.S., at 343, 109 S.Ct., at 637.[6] Moreover, the West Virginia "Constitution and laws provide that all property of the kind held by petitioners shall be taxed at a rate uniform throughout the State according to its estimated market value," and the Court found "no suggestion" that "the State may have adopted a different system in practice from that specified by statute." *Id.,* at 345, 109 S.Ct., at 638.

To be sure, the Equal Protection Clause does not demand for purposes of rational-basis review that a legislature or governing decisionmaker actually articulate at any time the purpose or rationale supporting its classification. *United States Railroad Retirement Bd. v. Fritz,* 449 U.S., at 179, 101 S.Ct., at 461. See also *McDonald v. Board of Election Comm'rs of Chicago,* 394 U.S. 802, 809, 89 S.Ct. 1404, 1408, 22 L.Ed.2d 739 (1969) (legitimate state purpose may be ascertained even when the legislative or administrative history is silent). Nevertheless, this Court's review does require that a purpose may conceivably or "may reasonably have been the purpose and policy" of the relevant governmental decisionmaker. *Allied Stores of Ohio, Inc. v. Bowers,* 358 U.S. 522, 528–529, 79 S.Ct. 437, 442, 3 L.Ed.2d 480 (1959). See also *Schweiker v. Wilson,* 450 U.S. 221, 235, 101 S.Ct. 1074, 1083, 67 L.Ed.2d 186 (1981) (classificatory scheme must "rationally advanc[e] a reasonable and *identifiable* governmental objective" (emphasis added)). *Allegheny Pittsburgh* was the rare case where the facts precluded any plausible inference that the reason for the unequal assessment practice was to achieve the benefits of an acquisition-value tax scheme. By contrast, Article XIIIA was enacted precisely to achieve the benefits of an acquisition-value system. *Allegheny Pittsburgh* is not controlling here.[8]

6. Webster County argued that the outdated assessments it used were consistent with current-value taxation, because periodic upward adjustments were made for inflation and it was not feasible to reassess individually each piece of property every year. Although the county obliquely referred in a footnote to the advantages of historical cost accounting, Brief for Respondent in *Allegheny Pittsburgh Coal Co. v. Webster County,* O.T.1988, No. 87-1303, p. 30, n. 23, this was not an assertion of the general policies supporting acquisition-value taxation. Even if acquisition-value policies had been asserted, the assertion would have been nonsensical given its inherent inconsistency with the county's principal argument that it was in fact trying to promote current-value taxation.

8. In finding *Allegheny Pittsburgh* distinguishable, we do not suggest that the protections of the Equal Protection Clause are any less when the classification is drawn by legislative mandate, as in this case, than by administrative action as in *Allegheny Pittsburgh.* See *Sunday Lake Iron Co. v. Wakefield,* 247 U.S. 350, 352, 38 S.Ct. 495, 495, 62 L.Ed. 1154 (1918). Nor do we suggest that the Equal Protection Clause constrains administrators, as in *Allegheny Pittsburgh,* from violating state law requiring uniformity of taxation of property. See *Nashville, C. & St. L.R. Co. v. Browning,* 310 U.S. 362, 368–370, 60 S.Ct. 968, 971–972, 84 L.Ed. 1254 (1940); *Puget Sound Power & Light Co. v. King County,* 264 U.S. 22, 27–28, 44 S.Ct. 261, 263, 68 L.Ed. 541 (1924). See generally *Snowden*

Finally, petitioner contends that the unfairness of Article XIIIA is made worse by its exemptions from reassessment for two special classes of new owners: persons aged 55 and older, who exchange principal residences, and children who acquire property from their parents. This Court previously has declined to hold that narrow exemptions from a general scheme of taxation necessarily render the overall scheme invidiously discriminatory. See, *e.g., Regan v. Taxation with Representation of Washington,* 461 U.S., at 550–551, 103 S.Ct., at 2003 (denial of tax exemption to nonprofit lobbying organizations, but with an exception for veterans' groups, does not violate equal protection). For purposes of rational-basis review, the "latitude of discretion is notably wide in * * * the granting of partial or total exemptions upon grounds of policy." *F.S. Royster Guano Co. v. Virginia,* 253 U.S., at 415, 40 S.Ct., at 562.

The two exemptions at issue here rationally further legitimate purposes. The people of California reasonably could have concluded that older persons in general should not be discouraged from moving to a residence more suitable to their changing family size or income. Similarly, the people of California reasonably could have concluded that the interests of family and neighborhood continuity and stability are furthered by and warrant an exemption for transfers between parents and children. Petitioner has not demonstrated that no rational bases lie for either of these exemptions.

III

Petitioner and *amici* argue with some appeal that Article XIIIA frustrates the "American dream" of home ownership for many younger and poorer California families. They argue that Article XIIIA places start-up businesses that depend on ownership of property at a severe disadvantage in competing with established businesses. They argue that Article XIIIA dampens demand for and construction of new housing and buildings. And they argue that Article XIIIA constricts local tax revenues at the expense of public education and vital services.

Time and again, however, this Court has made clear in the rational-basis context that the "Constitution presumes that, absent some reason to infer antipathy, even improvident decisions will eventually be rectified by the democratic process and that judicial intervention is generally unwarranted no matter how unwisely we may think a political branch has acted" (footnote omitted). *Vance v. Bradley,* 440 U.S. 93, 97, 99 S.Ct. 939, 942–943, 59 L.Ed.2d 171 (1979). Certainly, California's grand experiment appears to vest benefits in a broad, powerful, and entrenched segment of society, and, as the Court of Appeal surmised, ordinary democratic processes may be unlikely to prompt its reconsideration or repeal. See 225 Cal.App.3d, at 1282, n. 11, 275 Cal.Rptr., at 698, n. 11. Yet many wise and well-intentioned laws suffer from the same malady. Article XIIIA is not palpably arbitrary, and we must decline petitioner's request to upset the will of the people of California.

v. Hughes, 321 U.S. 1, 8–11, 64 S.Ct. 397, 401–403, 88 L.Ed. 497 (1944).

The judgment of the Court of Appeal is affirmed.

It is so ordered.

* * *

p. 718: Add to Note 2

Lee Hospital v. Cambria County Board of Assessment Appeals, 162 Pa. Cmwlth. 38, 638 A.2d 344 (1994) (non-profit hospital was treated identically and fairly compared to similarly situated hospitals and its rights to federal equal protection and state uniformity were not violated when it was placed on the tax roll). Uniformity requirements in the state constitutions reflect equal-protection principles. The uniformity concept may combine a direction that no assessment be higher than fair market value and a prescription that the ratio of taxation to value among comparable properties not be disproportionate. The proportionality language may appear in the uniformity clause or in a separate clause, and, as a practical matter, may result in a procedure whereby the property's market value is multiplied by an equalization ratio to assure proportional assessments. Appeal of City of Nashua, 138 N.H. 261, 638 A.2d 779 (1994).

p. 719: Add Note 6

6. **Local Taxes and the Commerce Clause.** Throughout these materials, it will be obvious that state and local taxes potentially discriminate in violation of the dormant Commerce Clause. Illustratively, in Diamond Shamrock Refining & Marketing Co. v. Nueces County Appraisal Dist., 876 S.W.2d 298 (Tex.1994), cert. denied, ___ U.S. ___, 115 S.Ct. 500, 130 L.Ed.2d 409 (1994), the court was presented with a challenge under the Import–Export and Commerce Clauses to a county property tax on oil temporarily stored in the county. The oil had entered the state from a foreign country and was destined for use within Texas. Although the oil might have been "in transit" through the county for Import–Export Clause purposes, it was not "in transit" through the state to another state. From a Commerce–Clause perspective, there was always a quantity of oil stored in the county and the permanent presence of a quantity of oil provided a sufficient nexus to government services to justify the imposition of ad valorem taxation by the county.

p. 724: Add to Note 7

As has been noted earlier in this Supplement, the Supreme Court has held that unless they are remanded for the purpose of deciding applicability, decisions of the Court in civil matters are to be given retroactive application, Harper v. Virginia Dept. of Taxation, ___ U.S. ___, 113 S.Ct. 2510, 125 L.Ed.2d 74 (1993), and has rejected tactical efforts to avoid the necessity of such post-payment remedies as refunds where taxes have been declared unconstitutional, Reich v. Collins, ___ U.S. ___, 115 S.Ct. 547, 130 L.Ed.2d 454 (1994), reported, supra, this Supplement.

c. *Tax Exemptions*

p. 724: Add to second paragraph of text

The Pennsylvania courts are increasingly scrutinizing traditionally exempt entities (hospitals, colleges) to verify if they fulfill the charitable and government-substitute grounds for tax exemptions. See, e.g., Pamela J. Leland, Responding To a Property Tax Challenge: Lessons Learned in Pennsylvania, 7 State Tax Notes 927 (Oct. 3, 1994).

p. 725: Add to first full paragraph

Congressional acts to assure non-discriminatory taxation of instruments of interstate commerce raise questions as to which particular aspects of a state or local tax are in fact discriminatory. With respect to taxation of congressionally protected railroads, for example, the Supreme Court held that a state may validly exempt non-railroad property from general property taxes without exempting railroad property. Department of Revenue of Oregon v. ACF Industries, Inc., ___ U.S. ___, 114 S.Ct. 843, 127 L.Ed.2d 165 (1994).

2. EXCISE TAXES

a. Income Taxes

p. 731: Add to first paragraph of Note 3

See Leonard Sloane, "State Laws On Where You Live and Earn," The New York Times, February 27, 1994, at F26.

Add to end of Note 3

Taxation of employment-related retirement benefits presents additional dimensions to tax problems. With regard to the intergovernmental tax immunity doctrine, please recall the discussion of intergovernmental immunity in Chapter V, in the *South Carolina v. Baker* case on page 325 of the principal text, the *Davis* case noted on page 336, and Harper v. Virginia Department of Taxation, ___ U.S. ___, 113 S.Ct. 2510, 125 L.Ed.2d 74 (1993). With regard to taxation of retirement benefits derived from employment in the taxing jurisdiction by retirees who now reside in other states, see, e.g., Walter Hellerstein and James Charles Smith, State Taxation of Nonresidents' Pension Income, State Tax Notes, July 13, 1992, at 221.

b. Business Excise Taxes

(1) Local Taxes on Interstate Business

p. 734–35: Add to text's citations

Northwest Airlines, Inc. v. County of Kent, ___ U.S. ___, 114 S.Ct. 855, 127 L.Ed.2d 183 (1994) (airport's user fee scheme did not violate either the federal anti-head-tax law or the dormant commerce clause); Sprint Communications v. Kelly, 642 A.2d 106 (D.C.App.1994), cert. denied, ___ U.S. ___, 115 S.Ct. 294, 130 L.Ed.2d 208 (1994) (tax on gross receipts from sale of toll services originating from or terminating on telecommunications equipment in the District of Columbia and billed to D.C. phones impermissibly discriminated against interstate commerce).

p. 737: Add after *Amerada Hess*

Note

The Supreme Court continues to exhibit strong aversion to discrimination against interstate commerce, see West Lynn Creamery v. Healy, ___

U.S. ___, 114 S.Ct. 2205, 129 L.Ed.2d 157 (1994) (voiding state milk pricing order that benefited local producers over those from out of state). For an analysis of *West Lynn Creamery* and the potential vulnerability of many state systems designed to provide incentives for local business, see Walter Hellerstein, West Lynn Creamery *v.* Healy *and the Constitutionality of State Tax Incentives: A Preliminary Analysis,* 7 State Tax Notes 1182 (1994).

The task of reconciling the competing needs and interests of state and local taxing governments and unitary, international businesses, and the proper role of the federal government in regulating interstate and foreign commerce has continued to demand Supreme Court attention. In Barclays Bank, PLC v. Franchise Tax Board of California, ___ U.S. ___, 114 S.Ct. 2268, 129 L.Ed.2d 244 (1994), the Court reaffirmed its earlier rulings upholding state taxation of unitary businesses using formulas that included worldwide income, and turned to the applicability of its foreign-commerce test, namely that the taxing scheme must not result in asymetry of tax systems risking multiplicity of taxation and must not interfere with the federal need to "speak with one voice." In elaborating upon the meaning of this factor, the Court said:

> In both *Wardair* and *Container Corp.,* the Court considered the "one voice" argument only after determining that the challenged state action was otherwise constitutional. An important premise underlying both decisions [21] is this: Congress may more passively indicate that certain state practices do *not* "impair federal uniformity in an area where federal uniformity is essential," *Japan Line,* 441 U.S., at 448, 99 S.Ct., at 1821; it need not convey its intent with the unmistakable clarity required to permit state regulation that discriminates against interstate commerce or otherwise falls short under *Complete Auto* inspection.
>
> * * *
>
> As in *Container Corp.* and *Wardair,* we discern no "specific indications of congressional intent" to bar the state action here challenged. Our decision upholding California's franchise tax in *Container Corp.* left the ball in Congress' court; had Congress, the branch responsible for the regulation of foreign commerce, see U.S. Const., Art. I, § 8, cl. 3, considered nationally uniform use of separate accounting "essential," *Japan Line, supra,* 441 U.S., at 448, 99 S.Ct., at 1821, it could have enacted legislation prohibiting the States from taxing corporate income based on the worldwide combined reporting method. In the 11 years that have elapsed since our decision in *Container Corp.,* Congress has failed to enact such legislation.

21. See also *Itel Containers Int'l Corp. v. Huddleston,* 507 U.S. ___, ___, 113 S.Ct. 1095, ___, 122 L.Ed.2d 421 (1993) (upholding Tennessee's tax on lease of cargo containers used exclusively in international shipping; because tax in question was not among those proscribed by "various conventions, statutes and regulations[,] * * * the most rational inference to be drawn is that th[e] tax, one quite distinct from the general class of import duties, is permitted").

In the past three decades—both before and after *Container Corp.*—Congress, aware that foreign governments were displeased with States' worldwide combined reporting requirements, has on many occasions studied state taxation of multinational enterprises. The numerous bills introduced have varied, but all would have prohibited the California reporting requirement here challenged. One group of bills would have prohibited States using combined reporting from compelling inclusion, in the combined reporting group, of corporate affiliates whose income was derived substantially from sources outside the United States. Another set would have barred the States from requiring taxpayers to report any income that was not subject to *federal* income tax; thus, "foreign source income" of foreign corporations ordinarily would not be reported. See *supra,* at 2273, n. 5. None of these bills, however, was enacted.

The history of Senate action on a United States/United Kingdom tax treaty, to which we referred in *Container Corp.,* see 463 U.S., at 196, 103 S.Ct., at 2956–2957, reinforces our conclusion that Congress implicitly has *permitted* the States to use the worldwide combined reporting method. As originally negotiated by the President, this treaty—known as the Convention for Avoidance of Double Taxation and the Prevention of Fiscal Evasion with Respect to Taxes on Income and Capital Gains—would have precluded States from requiring that United Kingdom-controlled corporate taxpayers use combined reporting to compute their state income. See Art. 9(4), 31 U.S.T. 5670, 5677, T.I.A.S. No. 9682. The Senate rejected this version of the treaty, 124 Cong.Rec. 18670 (1978), and ultimately ratified the agreement, *id.,* at 19076, "subject to the reservation that the provisions of [Article 9(4)] * * * shall not apply to any political subdivision or local authority of the United States." *Id.,* at 18416. The final version of the treaty prohibited state tax discrimination against British nationals, Art. 2(4), 31 U.S.T. 5671; Art. 24, *id.,* at 5687–5688, but did not require States to use separate accounting or water's edge apportionment of income. *Id.,* at 5709.

Given these indicia of Congress' willingness to tolerate States' worldwide combined reporting mandates, even when those mandates are applied to foreign corporations and domestic corporations with foreign parents, we cannot conclude that "the foreign policy of the United States—whose nuances * * * are much more the province of the Executive Branch and Congress than of this Court—is [so] seriously threatened," *Container Corp., supra,* 463 U.S., at 196, 103 S.Ct., at 2956, by California's practice as to warrant our intervention. This Court has no constitutional authority to make the policy judgments essential to regulating foreign commerce and conducting foreign affairs. Matters relating "to the conduct of foreign relations * * * are so exclusively entrusted to the political branches of government as to be largely immune from judicial inquiry or interference." *Harisiades v. Shaughnessy,* 342 U.S. 580, 589, 72 S.Ct. 512, 519, 96 L.Ed. 586 (1952). For this reason, Barclays' and its *amici*'s argument that California's worldwide combined reporting requirement is unconstitutional because it is likely to provoke retaliatory action by foreign governments is directed to the wrong forum. The judiciary is not vested with power to decide "how to balance a particular risk of retaliation against the sovereign right of the United States as a whole to let the States tax as they please." *Container Corp.,* 463 U.S., at 194, 103 S.Ct., at 2955.

* * *

The *Executive* statements to which Colgate refers, however, cannot perform the service for which Colgate would enlist them. The Constitution expressly grants Congress, not the President, the power to "regulate Commerce with foreign Nations." U.S. Const., Art. I., § 8, cl. 3. As we have detailed, *supra,* at 2283–2284, and nn. 23–27, Congress has focused its attention on this issue, but has refrained from exercising its authority to prohibit state-mandated world-wide combined reporting. That the Executive Branch proposed legislation to outlaw a state taxation practice, but encountered an unreceptive Congress, is not evidence that the practice interfered with the Nation's ability to speak with one voice, but is rather evidence that the preeminent speaker decided to yield the floor to others. Cf. *Itel Containers Int'l Corp. v. Huddleston,* 507 U.S. ___, ___, 113 S.Ct. 1095, 1108, 122 L.Ed.2d 421 (1993) (SCALIA, J., concurring in part and concurring in judgment) ("[The President] is better able to decide than we are which state regulatory interests should currently be subordinated to our national interest in foreign commerce. Under the Constitution, however, neither he nor we were to make that decision, but only the Congress.").

Congress may "delegate very large grants of its power over foreign commerce to the President," who "also possesses in his own right certain powers conferred by the Constitution on him as Commander-in-Chief and as the Nation's organ in foreign affairs." *Chicago & Southern Air Lines, Inc. v. Waterman S.S. Corp.,* 333 U.S. 103, 109, 68 S.Ct. 431, 435, 92 L.Ed. 568 (1948). We need not here consider the scope of the President's power to preempt state law pursuant to authority delegated by a statute or a ratified treaty; nor do we address whether the President may displace state law pursuant to legally binding executive agreements with foreign nations made "in the absence of either a congressional grant or denial of authority, [where] he can only rely upon his own independent powers." *Youngstown Sheet & Tube Co. v. Sawyer,* 343 U.S. 579, 637, 72 S.Ct. 863, 871, 96 L.Ed. 1153 (1952) (JACKSON, J., concurring). The Executive Branch actions—press releases, letters, and *amicus* briefs—on which Colgate here relies are merely precatory. Executive Branch communications that express federal policy but lack the force of law cannot render unconstitutional California's otherwise valid, congressionally condoned, use of worldwide combined reporting.

The Constitution does " 'not make the judiciary the overseer of our government.' " *Dames & Moore v. Regan,* 453 U.S. 654, 660, 101 S.Ct. 2972, 2976, 69 L.Ed.2d 918 (1981), quoting *Youngstown Sheet & Tube Co. v. Sawyer, supra,* 343 U.S., at 594, 72 S.Ct., at 889 (Frankfurter, J., concurring). Having determined that the taxpayers before us had an adequate nexus with the State, that worldwide combined reporting led to taxation which was fairly apportioned, nondiscriminatory, fairly related to the services provided by the State, and that its imposition did not result inevitably in multiple taxation, we leave it to Congress—whose voice, in this area, is the Nation's—to evaluate whether the national interest is best served by tax uniformity, or state autonomy. Accordingly, the judgments of the California Court of Appeal are

Affirmed.

c. *Sales Taxes*

p. 741: Renumber existing paragraph 3 of *Notes* as 4, and insert

3. In Oklahoma Tax Commission v. Sac and Fox Nation, ___ U.S. ___, 113 S.Ct. 1985, 124 L.Ed.2d 30 (1993), the Oklahoma Tax Commission argued that, because the Sac and Fox Nation lived on trust land and not a formal reservation, tribal members were not immune from state taxes. Citing the principal case, the Court held that, absent explicit Congressional direction, the presumption against state jurisdiction applies to all "Indian Country" (Congress' statutory term), not just formal reservations. The Court further held that the prohibition on state taxes also extended to excise and registration fees on motor vehicles.

In Anderson v. Wisconsin Department of Revenue, 169 Wis.2d 255, 484 N.W.2d 914 (1992), cert. denied, ___ U.S. ___, 113 S.Ct. 2418, 124 L.Ed.2d 640 (1993), the Wisconsin Supreme Court held that Wisconsin may levy an income tax on all citizens domiciled within the state. Specifically, a tribal member could be taxed for work performed at a school on an Indian reservation when he lived off the reservation. The state's taxing ability was not preempted by federal law as the imposition of the tax did not obstruct federal policies or fall on the tribe as such.

The principal case's suggestion of "assessing wholesalers" returned to the U.S. Supreme Court for consideration in Department of Taxation and Finance of New York v. Milhelm Attea & Bros., Inc., ___ U.S. ___, 114 S.Ct. 2028, 129 L.Ed.2d 52 (1994). There the Court reviewed New York cigarette-tax regulations designed to prevent tax avoidance by non-Indian purchasers of cigarettes from Indian retailers. The regulations, which imposed record-keeping requirements and quantity limitations on wholesalers that sell untaxed cigarettes to reservation Indians, were attacked as violations of the federal Indian Trader Statutes, 25 U.S.C.A. §§ 261–264. The Court rejected the facial challenge; federal law did not preempt taxation of sales to non-Indians or wholly exempt Indian traders from regulations that are reasonably necessary to collect lawful state taxes, and that has imposed burdens on the traders no greater than those that may be lawfully imposed on the reservation retailers.

Add to newly numbered paragraph 4

The Commerce and Due Process Clauses' impact on state and local efforts to collect use taxes on mail-order sales was addressed by the Supreme Court in the *Quill Corporation* case below. The Due Process Clause nexus was satisfied, but the Commerce Clause nexus was not. The remedy lies with Congress, which has been considering legislation. For commentary on the case, see Timothy J. Choppin, *Post–*Quill *Due Process Analysis of Interstate Commerce Taxation,* 5 State Tax Notes 1367 (1993).

QUILL CORPORATION v. NORTH DAKOTA

Supreme Court of the United States, 1992.
___ U.S. ___, 112 S.Ct. 1904, 119 L.Ed.2d 91.

JUSTICE STEVENS delivered the opinion of the Court.

This case, like *National Bellas Hess, Inc. v. Department of Revenue of Ill.,* 386 U.S. 753, 87 S.Ct. 1389, 18 L.Ed.2d 505 (1967), involves a State's attempt to require an out-of-state mail-order house that has neither outlets nor sales representatives in the State to collect and pay a use tax on goods purchased for use within the State. In *Bellas Hess* we held that a similar Illinois statute violated the Due Process Clause of the Fourteenth Amendment and created an unconstitutional burden on interstate commerce. In particular, we ruled that a "seller whose only connection with customers in the State is by common carrier or the United States mail" lacked the requisite minimum contacts with the State. *Id.,* at 758, 87 S.Ct., at 1392.

In this case the Supreme Court of North Dakota declined to follow *Bellas Hess* because "the tremendous social, economic, commercial, and legal innovations" of the past quarter-century have rendered its holding "obsole[te]." 470 N.W.2d 203, 208 (1991). Having granted certiorari, 502 U.S. ___, 112 S.Ct. 49, 116 L.Ed.2d 27, we must either reverse the State Supreme Court or overrule *Bellas Hess.* While we agree with much of the State Court's reasoning, we take the former course.

I

Quill is a Delaware corporation with offices and warehouses in Illinois, California, and Georgia. None of its employees work or reside in North Dakota and its ownership of tangible property in that State is either insignificant or nonexistent. Quill sells office equipment and supplies; it solicits business through catalogs and flyers, advertisements in national periodicals, and telephone calls. Its annual national sales exceed $200,000,000, of which almost $1,000,000 are made to about 3,000 customers in North Dakota. It is the sixth largest vendor of office supplies in the State. It delivers all of its merchandise to its North Dakota customers by mail or common carrier from out-of-state locations.

As a corollary to its sales tax, North Dakota imposes a use tax upon property purchased for storage, use or consumption within the State. North Dakota requires every "retailer maintaining a place of business in" the State to collect the tax from the consumer and remit it to the

State. N.D.Cent.Code § 57–40.2–07 (Supp.1991). In 1987 North Dakota amended the statutory definition of the term "retailer" to include "every person who engages in regular or systematic solicitation of a consumer market in th[e] state." § 57–40.2–01(6). State regulations in turn define "regular or systematic solicitation" to mean three or more advertisements within a 12–month period. N.D.Admin.Code § 81–04.1–01–03.1 (1988). Thus, since 1987, mail-order companies that engage in such solicitation have been subject to the tax even if they maintain no property or personnel in North Dakota.

Quill has taken the position that North Dakota does not have the power to compel it to collect a use tax from its North Dakota customers. Consequently, the State, through its Tax Commissioner, filed this action to require Quill to pay taxes (as well as interest and penalties) on all such sales made after July 1, 1987. The trial court ruled in Quill's favor, finding the case indistinguishable from *Bellas Hess;* specifically, it found that because the State had not shown that it had spent tax revenues for the benefit of the mail-order business, there was no "nexus to allow the state to define retailer in the manner it chose." App. to Pet. for Cert. A41.

The North Dakota Supreme Court reversed, concluding that "wholesale changes" in both the economy and the law made it inappropriate to follow *Bellas Hess* today. 470 N.W.2d, at 213. The principal economic change noted by the court was the remarkable growth of the mail-order business "from a relatively inconsequential market niche" in 1967 to a "goliath" with annual sales that reached "the staggering figure of $183.3 billion in 1989." *Id.*, at 208, 209. Moreover, the court observed, advances in computer technology greatly eased the burden of compliance with a " 'welter of complicated obligations' " imposed by state and local taxing authorities. *Id.*, at 215 (quoting *Bellas Hess*, 386 U.S., at 759–760, 87 S.Ct., at 1393).

Equally important, in the court's view, were the changes in the "legal landscape." With respect to the Commerce Clause, the court emphasized that *Complete Auto Transit, Inc. v. Brady*, 430 U.S. 274, 97 S.Ct. 1076, 51 L.Ed.2d 326 (1977), rejected the line of cases holding that the direct taxation of interstate commerce was impermissible and adopted instead a "consistent and rational method of inquiry [that focused on] the practical effect of [the] challenged tax." *Mobil Oil Corp. v. Commissioner of Taxes of Vt.*, 445 U.S. 425, 443, 100 S.Ct. 1223, 1234, 63 L.Ed.2d 510 (1980). This and subsequent rulings, the court maintained, indicated that the Commerce Clause no longer mandated the sort of physical-presence nexus suggested in *Bellas Hess.*

Similarly, with respect to the Due Process Clause, the North Dakota court observed that cases following *Bellas Hess* had not construed "minimum contacts" to require physical presence within a State as a prerequisite to the legitimate exercise of state power. The State Court then concluded that "the Due Process requirement of a 'minimal connection' to establish nexus is encompassed within the *Complete Auto* test" and that the relevant inquiry under the latter test was whether "the state has provided some protection, opportunities, or benefit for which it can expect a return." 470 N.W.2d, at 216.

Turning to the case at hand, the State Court emphasized that North Dakota had created "an economic climate that fosters demand for" Quill's products, maintained a legal infrastructure that protected that market, and disposed of 24 tons of catalogs and flyers mailed by Quill into the State every year. *Id.,* at 218–219. Based on these facts, the court concluded that Quill's "economic presence" in North Dakota depended on services and benefits provided by the State and therefore generated "a constitutionally sufficient nexus to justify imposition of the purely administrative duty of collecting and remitting the use tax." *Id.,* at 219.

II

As in a number of other cases involving the application of state taxing statutes to out-of-state sellers, our holding in *Bellas Hess* relied on both the Due Process Clause and the Commerce Clause. Although the "two claims are closely related," *Bellas Hess,* 386 U.S., at 756, 87 S.Ct., at 1391, the clauses pose distinct limits on the taxing powers of the States. Accordingly, while a State may, consistent with the Due Process Clause, have the authority to tax a particular taxpayer, imposition of the tax may nonetheless violate the Commerce Clause. See, *e.g., Tyler Pipe Industries, Inc. v. Washington State Dept. of Revenue,* 483 U.S. 232, 107 S.Ct. 2810, 97 L.Ed.2d 199 (1987).

The two constitutional requirements differ fundamentally, in several ways. As discussed at greater length below, see *infra,* at Part IV, the Due Process Clause and the Commerce Clause reflect different constitutional concerns. Moreover, while Congress has plenary power to regulate commerce among the States and thus may authorize state actions that burden interstate commerce, see *International Shoe Co. v. Washington,* 326 U.S. 310, 315, 66 S.Ct. 154, 157, 90 L.Ed. 95 (1945), it does not similarly have the power to authorize violations of the Due Process Clause.

Thus, although we have not always been precise in distinguishing between the two, the Due Process Clause and the Commerce Clause are analytically distinct.

> " 'Due process' and 'commerce clause' conceptions are not always sharply separable in dealing with these problems * * *. To some extent they overlap. If there is a want of due process to sustain the tax, by that fact alone any burden the tax imposes on the commerce among the states becomes 'undue.' But, though overlapping, the two conceptions are not identical. There may be more than sufficient factual connections, with economic and legal effects, between the transaction and the taxing state to sustain the tax as against due process objections. Yet it may fall because of its burdening effect upon the commerce. And, although the two notions cannot always be separated, clarity of consideration and of

decision would be promoted if the two issues are approached, where they are presented, at least tentatively as if they were separate and distinct, not intermingled ones." *International Harvester Co. v. Department of Treasury,* 322 U.S. 340, 353, 64 S.Ct. 1019, 1032–1033, 88 L.Ed. 1313 (1944) (RUTLEDGE, J., concurring in part and dissenting in part).

Heeding Justice Rutledge's counsel, we consider each constitutional limit in turn.

III

The Due Process Clause "requires some definite link, some minimum connection, between a state and the person, property or transaction it seeks to tax," *Miller Bros. Co. v. Maryland,* 347 U.S. 340, 344–345, 74 S.Ct. 535, 539, 98 L.Ed. 744 (1954), and that the "income attributed to the State for tax purposes must be rationally related to 'values connected with the taxing State.'" *Moorman Mfg. Co. v. Bair,* 437 U.S. 267, 273, 98 S.Ct. 2340, 2344, 57 L.Ed.2d 197 (1978) (citation omitted). Here, we are concerned primarily with the first of these requirements. Prior to *Bellas Hess,* we had held that that requirement was satisfied in a variety of circumstances involving use taxes. For example, the presence of sales personnel in the State, or the maintenance of local retail stores in the State, justified the exercise of that power because the seller's local activities were "plainly accorded the protection and services of the taxing State." *Bellas Hess,* 386 U.S., at 757, 87 S.Ct., at 1391. The furthest extension of that power was recognized in *Scripto, Inc. v. Carson,* 362 U.S. 207, 80 S.Ct. 619, 4 L.Ed.2d 660 (1960), in which the Court upheld a use tax despite the fact that all of the seller's in-state solicitation was performed by independent contractors. These cases all involved some sort of physical presence within the State, and in *Bellas Hess* the Court suggested that such presence was not only sufficient for jurisdiction under the Due Process Clause, but also necessary. We expressly declined to obliterate the "sharp distinction * * * between mail order sellers with retail outlets, solicitors, or property within a State, and those who do no more than communicate with customers in the State by mail or common carrier as a part of a general interstate business." 386 U.S., at 758, 87 S.Ct., at 1392.

Our due process jurisprudence has evolved substantially in the 25 years since *Bellas Hess,* particularly in the area of judicial jurisdiction. Building on the seminal case of *International Shoe Co. v. Washington,* 326 U.S. 310, 66 S.Ct. 154, 90 L.Ed. 95 (1945), we have framed the relevant inquiry as whether a defendant had minimum contacts with the jurisdiction "such that the maintenance of the suit does not offend 'traditional notions of fair play and substantial justice.'" *Id.,* at 316, 66 S.Ct., at 158 (quoting *Milliken v. Meyer,* 311 U.S. 457, 463, 61 S.Ct. 339, 343, 85 L.Ed. 278 (1940)). In that spirit, we have abandoned more formalistic tests that focused on a defendant's "presence" within a State in favor of a more flexible inquiry into whether a defendant's contacts with the forum made it reasonable, in the context of our federal system of government, to require it to defend the suit in that State. In *Shaffer v. Heitner,* 433 U.S. 186, 212, 97 S.Ct. 2569, 2584, 53 L.Ed.2d 683 (1977), the Court extended the flexible approach that *International Shoe* had prescribed for purposes of *in personam* jurisdiction to *in rem* jurisdiction, concluding that "all assertions of state-court jurisdiction must be evaluated according to the standards set forth in *International Shoe* and its progeny."

Applying these principles, we have held that if a foreign corporation purposefully avails itself of the benefits of an economic market in the forum State, it may subject itself to the State's *in personam* jurisdiction even if it has no physical presence in the State. As we explained in *Burger King Corp. v. Rudzewicz,* 471 U.S. 462, 105 S.Ct. 2174, 85 L.Ed.2d 528 (1985):

> "Jurisdiction in these circumstances may not be avoided merely because the defendant did not *physically* enter the forum State. Although territorial presence frequently will enhance a potential defendant's affiliation with a State and reinforce the reasonable foreseeability of suit there, it is an inescapable fact of modern commercial life that a substantial amount of business is transacted solely by mail and wire communications across state lines, thus obviating the need for physical presence within a State in which business is conducted. So long as a commercial actor's efforts are 'purposefully directed' toward residents of another State, we have consistently rejected the notion that an absence of physical contacts can defeat personal jurisdiction there." *Id.,* at 476, 105 S.Ct. at 2184 (emphasis in original).

Comparable reasoning justifies the imposition of the collection duty on a mail-order house that is engaged in continuous and widespread solicitation of business within a State. Such a corporation clearly has "fair warning that [its] activity may subject [it] to the jurisdiction of a foreign sovereign." *Shaffer v. Heitner,* 433 U.S., at 218, 97 S.Ct., at 2587 (STEVENS, J., concurring in judgment). In "modern commercial life" it matters little that such solicitation is accomplished by a deluge of catalogs rather than a phalanx of drummers: the requirements of due process are met irrespective of a corporation's lack of physical presence in the taxing State. Thus, to the extent that our decisions have indicated that the Due Process Clause requires physical presence in a State for the imposition of duty to collect a use tax, we overrule those holdings as superseded by developments in the law of due process.

In this case, there is no question that Quill has purposefully directed its activities at North Dakota residents, that the magnitude of those contacts are more than sufficient for due process purposes, and that the use tax is related to the benefits Quill receives from access to the State. We therefore agree with the North Dakota Supreme Court's conclusion that the Due Process Clause does not bar enforcement of that State's use tax against Quill.

IV

Article I, § 8, cl. 3 of the Constitution expressly authorizes Congress to "regulate Commerce with foreign Nations, and among the several States." It says nothing about the protection of interstate commerce in the absence of any action by Congress. Nevertheless, as Justice Johnson suggested in his concurring opinion in *Gibbons v. Ogden,* 9 Wheat. 1, 231–232, 239, 6 L.Ed. 23 (1824), the Commerce Clause is more than an affirmative grant of power; it has a negative sweep as well. The clause, in Justice Stone's phrasing, "by its own force" prohibits certain state actions that interfere with interstate commerce. *South Carolina State Highway Dept. v. Barnwell Bros., Inc.,* 303 U.S. 177, 185, 58 S.Ct. 510, 514, 82 L.Ed. 734 (1938).

Our interpretation of the "negative" or "dormant" Commerce Clause has evolved substantially over the years, particularly as that clause concerns limitations on state taxation powers. * * *

Bellas Hess was decided in 1967, in the middle of this latest rally between formalism and pragmatism. Contrary to the suggestion of the North Dakota Supreme Court, this timing does not mean that *Complete Auto* rendered *Bellas Hess* "obsolete." *Complete Auto* rejected *Freeman* and *Spector's* formal distinction between "direct" and "indirect" taxes on interstate commerce because that formalism allowed the validity of statutes to hinge on "legal terminology," "draftsmanship and phraseology." 430 U.S., at 281, 97 S.Ct., at 1080. *Bellas Hess* did not rely on any such labeling of taxes and therefore did not automatically fall with *Freeman* and its progeny.

While contemporary Commerce Clause jurisprudence might not dictate the same result were the issue to arise for the first time today, *Bellas Hess* is not inconsistent with *Complete Auto* and our recent cases. Under *Complete Auto's* four-part test, we will sustain a tax against a Commerce Clause challenge so long as the "tax [1] is applied to an activity with a substantial nexus with the taxing State, [2] is fairly apportioned, [3] does not discriminate against interstate commerce, and [4] is fairly related to the services provided by the State." 430 U.S., at 279, 97 S.Ct., at 1079. *Bellas Hess* concerns the first of these tests and stands for the proposition that a vendor whose only contacts with the taxing State are by mail or common carrier lacks the "substantial nexus" required by the Commerce Clause.

Thus, three weeks after *Complete Auto* was handed down, we cited *Bellas Hess* for this proposition and discussed the case at some length. In *National Geographic Society v. California Bd. of Equalization,* 430 U.S. 551, 559, 97 S.Ct. 1386, 1392, 51 L.Ed.2d 631 (1977), we affirmed the continuing vitality of *Bellas Hess'* "sharp distinction * * * between mail-order sellers with [a physical presence in the taxing] State and those * * * who do no more than communicate with customers in the State by mail or common carrier as part of a general interstate business." We have continued to cite *Bellas Hess* with approval ever since. For example, in *Goldberg v. Sweet,* 488 U.S. 252, 263, 109 S.Ct. 582, 589,

102 L.Ed.2d 607 (1989), we expressed "doubt that termination of an interstate telephone call, by itself, provides a substantial enough nexus for a State to tax a call. See *National Bellas Hess* * * * (receipt of mail provides insufficient nexus)." See also *D.H. Holmes Co. v. McNamara,* 486 U.S. 24, 33, 108 S.Ct. 1619, 1624, 100 L.Ed.2d 21 (1988); *Commonwealth Edison Co. v. Montana,* 453 U.S. 609, 626, 101 S.Ct. 2946, 2958, 69 L.Ed.2d 884 (1981); *Mobil Oil Corp. v. Commissioner of Taxes,* 445 U.S., at 437, 100 S.Ct., at 1231; *National Geographic Society,* 430 U.S., at 559, 97 S.Ct., at 1391. For these reasons, we disagree with the State Supreme Court's conclusion that our decision in *Complete Auto* undercut the *Bellas Hess* rule.

The State of North Dakota relies less on *Complete Auto* and more on the evolution of our due process jurisprudence. The State contends that the nexus requirements imposed by the Due Process and Commerce Clauses are equivalent and that if, as we concluded above, a mail-order house that lacks a physical presence in the taxing State nonetheless satisfies the due process "minimum contacts" test, then that corporation also meets the Commerce Clause "substantial nexus" test. We disagree. Despite the similarity in phrasing, the nexus requirements of the Due Process and Commerce Clauses are not identical. The two standards are animated by different constitutional concerns and policies.

Due process centrally concerns the fundamental fairness of governmental activity. Thus, at the most general level, the due process nexus analysis requires that we ask whether an individual's connections with a State are substantial enough to legitimate the State's exercise of power over him. We have, therefore, often identified "notice" or "fair warning" as the analytic touchstone of due process nexus analysis. In contrast, the Commerce Clause, and its nexus requirement, are informed not so much by concerns about fairness for the individual defendant as by structural concerns about the effects of state regulation on the national economy. Under the Articles of Confederation, State taxes and duties hindered and suppressed interstate commerce; the Framers intended the Commerce Clause as a cure for these structural ills. See generally The Federalist Nos. 7, 11 (A. Hamilton). It is in this light that we have interpreted the negative implication of the Commerce Clause. Accordingly, we have ruled that that Clause prohibits discrimination against interstate commerce, see, *e.g., Philadelphia v. New Jersey,* 437 U.S. 617, 98 S.Ct. 2531, 57 L.Ed.2d 475 (1978), and bars state regulations that unduly burden interstate commerce, see, *e.g., Kassel v. Consolidated Freightways Corp. of Del.,* 450 U.S. 662, 101 S.Ct. 1309, 67 L.Ed.2d 580 (1981).

The *Complete Auto* analysis reflects these concerns about the national economy. The second and third parts of that analysis, which require fair apportionment and non-discrimination, prohibit taxes that pass an unfair share of the tax burden onto interstate commerce. The first and fourth prongs, which require a substantial nexus and a relationship between the tax and State-provided services, limit the reach of State taxing authority so as to ensure that State taxation does not unduly burden interstate commerce.[6] Thus, the "substantial-nexus" requirement is not, like due process' "minimum-contacts" requirement, a proxy for notice, but rather a means for limiting state burdens on interstate commerce. Accordingly, contrary to the State's suggestion, a corporation may have the "minimum contacts" with a taxing State as required by the Due Process Clause, and yet lack the "substantial nexus" with that State as required by the Commerce Clause.[7]

* * *

Complete Auto, it is true, renounced *Freeman* and its progeny as "formalistic." But not all formalism is alike. *Spector*'s formal distinction between taxes on the "privilege of doing business" and all other taxes served no purpose within our Commerce Clause jurisprudence, but stood "only as a trap for the unwary draftsman." *Complete Auto,* 430 U.S., at 279, 97 S.Ct. at 1079. In contrast, the bright-line rule of *Bellas Hess* furthers the ends of the dormant Commerce Clause. Undue burdens on interstate commerce may be avoided not only by a case-by-case evaluation of the actual burdens imposed by particular regulations or taxes, but also, in some situations, by the demarcation of a discrete realm of commercial activity that is free from interstate taxation. *Bellas Hess* followed the latter approach and created a safe harbor for vendors "whose only connection with customers in the [taxing] State is by common carrier or the United States mail." Under *Bellas Hess,* such vendors are free from state-imposed duties to collect sales and use taxes.[8]

6. North Dakota's use tax illustrates well how a state tax might unduly burden interstate commerce. On its face, North Dakota law imposes a collection duty on every vendor who advertises in the State three times in a single year. Thus, absent the *Bellas Hess* rule, a publisher who included a subscription card in three issues of its magazine, a vendor whose radio advertisements were heard in North Dakota on three occasions, and a corporation whose telephone sales force made three calls into the State, all would be subject to the collection duty. What is more significant, similar obligations might be imposed by the Nation's 6,000–plus taxing jurisdictions. See *National Bellas Hess, Inc. v. Department of Revenue of Ill.,* 386 U.S. 753, 759–760, 87 S.Ct. 1389, 1393, 18 L.Ed.2d 505 (1967) (noting that the "many variations in rates of tax, in allowable exemptions, and in administrative and record-keeping requirements could entangle [a mail-order house] in a virtual welter of complicated obligations") (footnotes omitted); see also Shaviro, An Economic and Political Look at Federalism in Taxation, 90 Mich.L.Rev. 895, 925–926 (1992).

7. We have sometimes stated that the "*Complete Auto* test, while responsive to Commerce Clause dictates, encompasses as well * * * Due Process requirement[s]." *Trinova Corp. v. Michigan Dept. of Treasury,* 498 U.S. ___, ___, 111 S.Ct. 818, 828, 112 L.Ed.2d 884 (1991). Although such comments might suggest that every tax that passes contemporary Commerce Clause analysis is also valid under the Due Process Clause, it does not follow that the converse is as well true: a tax may be consistent with Due Process and yet unduly burden interstate commerce. See, *e.g., Tyler Pipe Industries, Inc. v. Washington State Dept. of Revenue,* 483 U.S. 232, 107 S.Ct. 2810, 97 L.Ed.2d 199 (1987).

8. In addition to its common-carrier contacts with the State, Quill also licensed software to some of its North Dakota clients. See *supra* n. 1. The State "concedes that the existence in North Dakota of a few floppy diskettes to which Quill holds title seems a slender thread upon which to base nexus." Brief for Respondent 46. We agree. Although title to "a few floppy diskettes" present in a State might constitute some minimal nexus, in *National Geographic Society v. California Bd. of Equalization,* 430 U.S. 551, 556, 97 S.Ct. 1386, 1390, 51 L.Ed.2d 631 (1977), we expressly rejected a " 'slightest presence' standard of constitutional nexus." We therefore conclude that Quill's licensing of software in this case does not meet the "substantial nexus" requirement of the Commerce Clause.

Like other bright-line tests, the *Bellas Hess* rule appears artificial at its edges: whether or not a State may compel a vendor to collect a sales or use tax may turn on the presence in the taxing State of a small sales force, plant, or office. Cf. *National Geographic Society v. California Bd. of Equalization,* 430 U.S. 551, 97 S.Ct. 1386, 51 L.Ed.2d 631 (1977); *Scripto, Inc. v. Carson,* 362 U.S. 207, 80 S.Ct. 619, 4 L.Ed.2d 660 (1960). This artificiality, however, is more than offset by the benefits of a clear rule. Such a rule firmly establishes the boundaries of legitimate state authority to impose a duty to collect sales and use taxes and reduces litigation concerning those taxes. This benefit is important, for as we have so frequently noted, our law in this area is something of a "quagmire" and the "application of constitutional principles to specific state statutes leaves much room for controversy and confusion and little in the way of precise guides to the States in the exercise of their indispensable power of taxation." *Northwestern States Portland Cement Co. v. Minnesota,* 358 U.S. 450, 457–458, 79 S.Ct. 357, 362, 3 L.Ed.2d 421 (1959).

Moreover, a bright-line rule in the area of sales and use taxes also encourages settled expectations and, in doing so, fosters investment by businesses and individuals.[9] Indeed, it is not unlikely that the mail-order industry's dramatic growth over the last quarter-century is due in part to the bright-line exemption from state taxation created in *Bellas Hess.*

Notwithstanding the benefits of bright-line tests, we have, in some situations, decided to replace such tests with more contextual balancing inquiries. * * * None of those factors obtains in this case. First, the *Attleboro* rule was "anachronistic" because it relied on formal distinctions between "direct" and "indirect" regulation (and on the regulatory counterparts of our *Freeman* line of cases); as discussed above, *Bellas Hess* turned on a different logic and thus remained sound after the Court repudiated an analogous distinction in *Complete Auto.* Second, unlike the *Attleboro* rule, we have, in our decisions, frequently relied on the *Bellas Hess* rule in the last 25 years, see *supra,* at 1912, and we have never intimated in our review of sales or use taxes that *Bellas Hess* was unsound. Finally, again unlike the *Attleboro* rule, the *Bellas Hess* rule has engendered substantial reliance and has become part of the basic

9. It is worth noting that Congress has, at least on one occasion, followed a similar approach in its regulation of state taxation. In response to this Court's indication in *Northwestern States Portland Cement Co. v. Minnesota,* 358 U.S. 450, 452, 79 S.Ct. 357, 359, 3 L.Ed.2d 421 (1959), that, so long as the taxpayer has an adequate nexus with the taxing State, "net income from the interstate operations of a foreign corporation may be subjected to state taxation," Congress enacted Pub.L. 86–272, codified at 15 U.S.C. § 381. That statute provides that a State may not impose a net income tax on any person if that person's "only business activities within such State [involve] the solicitation of orders [approved] outside the State [and] filled * * * outside the State." 15 U.S.C. § 381. As we noted in *Heublein, Inc. v. South Carolina Tax Comm'n,* 409 U.S. 275, 280, 93 S.Ct. 483, 487, 34 L.Ed.2d 472 (1972), in enacting § 381, "Congress attempted to allay the apprehension of businessmen that 'mere solicitation' would subject them to state taxation * * *. Section 381 was designed to define clearly a lower limit for the exercise of [the State's power to tax]. *Clarity that would remove uncertainty was Congress' primary goal.*" (Emphasis supplied.)

framework of a sizeable industry. The "interest in stability and orderly development of the law" that undergirds the doctrine of *stare decisis,* see *Runyon v. McCrary,* 427 U.S. 160, 190–191, 96 S.Ct. 2586, 2604–2605, 49 L.Ed.2d 415 (1976) (STEVENS, J., concurring), therefore counsels adherence to settled precedent.

In sum, although in our cases subsequent to *Bellas Hess* and concerning other types of taxes we have not adopted a similar bright-line, physical-presence requirement, our reasoning in those cases does not compel that we now reject the rule that *Bellas Hess* established in the area of sales and use taxes. To the contrary, the continuing value of a bright-line rule in this area and the doctrine and principles of *stare decisis* indicate that the *Bellas Hess* rule remains good law. For these reasons, we disagree with the North Dakota Supreme Court's conclusion that the time has come to renounce the bright-line test of *Bellas Hess.*

This aspect of our decision is made easier by the fact that the underlying issue is not only one that Congress may be better qualified to resolve, but also one that Congress has the ultimate power to resolve. No matter how we evaluate the burdens that use taxes impose on interstate commerce, Congress remains free to disagree with our conclusions. See *Prudential Insurance Co. v. Benjamin,* 328 U.S. 408, 66 S.Ct. 1142, 90 L.Ed. 1342 (1946). Indeed, in recent years Congress has considered legislation that would "overrule" the *Bellas Hess* rule. Its decision not to take action in this direction may, of course, have been dictated by respect for our holding in *Bellas Hess* that the Due Process Clause prohibits States from imposing such taxes, but today we have put that problem to rest. Accordingly, Congress is now free to decide whether, when, and to what extent the States may burden interstate mail-order concerns with a duty to collect use taxes.

Indeed, even if we were convinced that *Bellas Hess* was inconsistent with our Commerce Clause jurisprudence, "this very fact [might] giv[e us] pause and counse[l] withholding our hand, at least for now. Congress has the power to protect interstate commerce from intolerable or even undesirable burdens." *Commonwealth Edison Co. v. Montana,* 453 U.S. 609, 637, 101 S.Ct. 2946, 2964, 69 L.Ed.2d 884 (1981) (WHITE, J., concurring). In this situation, it may be that "the better part of both wisdom and valor is to respect the judgment of the other branches of the Government." *Id.,* at 638, 101 S.Ct., at 2964.

The judgment of the Supreme Court of North Dakota is reversed and the case is remanded for further proceedings not inconsistent with this opinion.

It is so ordered.

* * *

Note

Of course, even without the complications of mail-order sales, state and local use taxes that treat interstate commerce differently from intrastate will be invalidated as discriminatory. Consider, for example, statewide use taxes that may in part of the state be higher than the local sales taxes for which they are intended to be compensatory.

ASSOCIATED INDUSTRIES OF MISSOURI v. LOHMAN

Supreme Court of the United States, 1994.
___ U.S. ___, 114 S.Ct. 1815, 128 L.Ed.2d 639.

JUSTICE THOMAS delivered the opinion of the Court.

The State of Missouri imposes a uniform, statewide use tax on all goods purchased outside the State and stored, used, or consumed within the State. Although the tax is purportedly designed to "compensate" for sales taxes imposed by local jurisdictions on sales of goods in the State, local sales tax rates vary widely, and in many jurisdictions the use tax exceeds the sales tax. Petitioners contend that this system discriminates against interstate commerce in violation of the Commerce Clause, even though the local sales taxes across the State may, in the aggregate, place a greater burden on intrastate trade than the uniform use tax places on interstate trade. We agree that, in localities where the use tax exceeds the sales tax, the system is impermissibly discriminatory, and we therefore reverse the judgment of the Supreme Court of Missouri.

I

Missouri has a multitiered system of sales and use taxes. The State imposes by statute a tax of 4% on all sales of personal property in the State, Mo.Rev.Stat. § 144.020 (1986), and, through provisions in the State Constitution, provides for additional sales taxes of one-eighth of one percent and one-tenth of one percent on the same transactions. Mo. Const., Art. IV, §§ 43(a), 47(a). These levies are exactly paralleled by statutory and state constitutional provisions providing for use taxes of 4%, one-eighth of one percent, and one-tenth of one percent, respectively, on the "privilege of storing, using or consuming" within the State any article of personal property purchased outside the State. Mo.Rev. Stat. § 144.610(1); Mo. Const., Art. IV, §§ 43(a), 47(a). Thus, under these various provisions, the State imposes a statewide sales tax of 4.225% on sales of goods within the State and a statewide use tax of 4.225% on goods brought into the State after being purchased elsewhere. These taxes are not challenged here.

The State also imposes an "additional use tax" of 1.5% on the privilege of storing, using, or consuming within the State any article of personal property purchased outside the State. Mo.Rev.Stat. § 144.748 (Supp.1993). This use tax is not paired with any sales tax at the state level. The State, however, authorizes political subdivisions, including counties and incorporated municipalities, to impose a local sales tax. Over 1,000 localities have used that authority to enact sales taxes ranging from 0.5% to 3.5%, while at least one county has no local sales tax at all.

Petitioner Associated Industries of Missouri is a trade association representing businesses that operate in Missouri and businesses that sell to customers in Missouri. Out-of-state members of the organization must collect the additional use tax on sales made into the State. Petitioner Alumax Foils, Inc., is a manufacturing firm in Missouri that pays the additional use tax on goods purchased from outside the State. Petitioners brought this action in state court contending that the use tax impermissibly discriminates against interstate commerce in violation of the Commerce Clause. The State Circuit Court rejected petitioners' claims and granted respondents' motion for summary judgment.

The Supreme Court of Missouri affirmed. 857 S.W.2d 182 (1993). The court noted that the 1.5% use tax had been imposed to equalize taxes on in-state and out-of-state goods. Previously, political subdivisions of the State had imposed local sales tax burdens that were not paralleled by any use tax. Because the tax was designed to even exactions on intrastate and interstate trade, the court reasoned that the scheme should be analyzed under the "compensatory tax" doctrine, which the court summarized as permitting States to "impose * * * equivalent burden[s]"

* * *

II

Although the Commerce Clause is phrased merely as a grant of authority to Congress to "regulate Commerce ... among the several States," Art. I, § 8, cl. 3, it is well established that the Clause also embodies a negative command forbidding the States to discriminate against interstate trade. *See, e.g., Oregon Waste Systems, Inc. v. Department of Environmental Quality of Oregon,* 511 U.S. ___, ___, 114 S.Ct. 1345, 1349 (1994); *New Energy Co. of Indiana v. Limbach,* 486 U.S. 269, 273, 108 S.Ct. 1803, 1807, 100 L.Ed.2d 302 (1988). The Clause prohibits economic protectionism—that is, "regulatory measures designed to benefit in-state economic interests by burdening out-of-state competitors." *Id.,* at 273–274, 108 S.Ct. at 273. Thus, we have characterized the fundamental command of the Clause as being that "a State may not tax a transaction or incident more heavily when it crosses state lines than when it occurs entirely within the State," *Armco Inc. v. Hardesty,* 467 U.S. 638, 642, 104 S.Ct. 2620, 2622, 81 L.Ed.2d 540 (1984), and have applied a "virtually *per se* rule of invalidity" to provisions that patently discriminate against interstate trade. *Philadelphia v. New Jersey,* 437 U.S. 617, 624, 98 S.Ct. 2531, 2535, 57 L.Ed.2d 475 (1978).

A

By its terms, the additional use tax at issue in this case appears to violate the Commerce Clause's cardinal rule of nondiscrimination, for it exempts from its scope all sales of goods occurring within the State. See n. 2, *supra.* Nevertheless, our cases establish that such a levy may be saved from constitutional infirmity if it is a valid "compensatory tax" designed simply to make interstate commerce bear a burden already borne by intrastate commerce. Under the compensatory tax doctrine, a facially discriminatory tax that imposes on interstate commerce the equivalent of an "identifiable and substantially similar tax on intrastate commerce does not offend the negative Commerce Clause." *Oregon Waste, supra,* 511 U.S., at ___, 114 S.Ct., at 1352 (internal quotation marks omitted). To ensure that the State is indeed merely imposing countervailing burdens on comparable transactions, we have required that the taxes on interstate and intrastate commerce be imposed on "substantially equivalent event[s]." *Maryland v. Louisiana,* 451 U.S. 725, 759, 101 S.Ct. 2114, 2135, 68 L.Ed.2d 576 (1981). See also *Armco, supra,* 467 U.S., at 643, 104 S.Ct., at 2623. The end result under the theory of the compensatory tax is that, "[w]hen the account is made up, the stranger from afar is subject to no greater burdens * * * than the dweller within the gates. The one pays upon one activity or incident, and the other upon another, but the sum is the same when the reckoning is closed." *Henneford v. Silas Mason Co.,* 300 U.S. 577, 584, 57 S.Ct. 524, 527, 81 L.Ed. 814 (1937).

To justify any levy as a compensatory tax, "a State must, as a threshold matter, 'identif[y] * * * the [intrastate tax] burden for which the State is attempting to compensate.'" *Oregon Waste, supra,* 511 U.S., at ___, 114 S.Ct., at 1352 (quoting *Maryland, supra,* 451 U.S., at 758, 101 S.Ct., at 2135). Respondents urge that the local sales taxes imposed by over a thousand political subdivisions within the State provide the burden on intrastate commerce that Missouri seeks to counterbalance through the use tax in this case. There is no dispute that sales taxes and use taxes such as those at issue here are imposed on "substantially equivalent event[s]." *Maryland, supra,* 451 U.S., at 759, 101 S.Ct., at 1353. *Silas Mason* itself approved a system of sales and use taxes, and we have recognized that "[a] use tax is generally perceived as a necessary complement to [a] sales tax." *Williams v. Vermont,* 472 U.S. 14, 24, 105 S.Ct. 2465, 2472, 86 L.Ed.2d 11 (1985). Cf. *Halliburton Oil Well Cementing Co. v. Reily,* 373 U.S. 64, 66, 83 S.Ct. 1201, 1202, 10 L.Ed.2d 202 (1963) ("[T]he purpose of such a sales-use tax scheme is to make all tangible property used or consumed in the State subject to a uniform tax burden irrespective of whether it is acquired within the State * * * or from without the State").

Missouri's use tax scheme, however, runs afoul of the basic requirement that, for a tax system to be "compensatory," the burdens imposed on interstate and intrastate commerce must be equal. As we observed in *Maryland v. Louisiana,* the "common thread running through the cases upholding compensatory taxes is the equality of treatment between local and interstate commerce." 451 U.S., at 759, 101 S.Ct., at 2135. *See also Halliburton, supra,* 373 U.S., at 70, 83 S.Ct., at 1204 ("[E]qual treatment for in-state and out-of-state taxpayers similarly situated is the condition precedent for a valid use tax on goods imported from out-of-state"). Where a State imposes equivalent sales and use taxes, we have upheld the system under the Commerce Clause. *See Silas Mason, supra,* 300 U.S., at 584–587, 57 S.Ct., at 527–529. But in Missouri, whether the 1.5% use tax is equal to (or lower than) the local sales tax is a matter of fortuity, depending entirely upon the locality in which the Missouri purchaser happens to reside. Where the use tax exceeds the sales tax, the discrepancy imposes a discriminatory burden on interstate commerce. Out-of-state goods brought into such a jurisdiction are subjected to a higher levy than are goods sold locally. The resulting disparity is incompatible with what we have termed the "strict rule of equality adopted in *Silas Mason.*" *Halliburton, supra,* 373 U.S., at 73, 83 S.Ct., at 1206.

Respondents contend that the foregoing analysis is too myopic—that in reckoning the balance of accounts alluded to in *Silas Mason* we should focus, not on each political subdivision in which a disparity between the two taxes may result in discrimination against interstate commerce, but rather on the overall impact of the use tax and the various sales taxes on interstate commerce across the State as a whole. Respondents' theory assumes that discrimination in some parts of a state tax system may be permissible under the Commerce Clause as long as it is of a sufficiently limited magnitude to be offset by preferential treatment for interstate trade in other portions of the tax scheme. There is no question that, within a locality where the use tax exceeds the sales tax, the tax structure discriminates against interstate trade. Respondents merely argue that the local jurisdiction provides too narrow a framework for proper constitutional analysis.

We have never suggested, however, that patent discrimination in part of the operation of a tax scheme, not directly justified under any theory such as the compensatory tax doctrine, can be rendered inconsequential for Commerce Clause purposes by advantages given to interstate commerce in other facets of a tax plan or in other regions of a State. On the contrary, as a general matter we have rejected reliance on any calculus that requires a quantification of discrimination as a preliminary step to determining whether the discrimination is valid. Under our cases, unless one of several narrow bases of justification is shown, *see Oregon Waste,* 511 U.S., at ___–___, 114 S.Ct. at ___–___, actual discrimination, wherever it is found, is impermissible, and the magnitude and scope of the discrimination have no bearing on the determinative question whether discrimination has occurred. *See Wyoming v. Oklahoma,* 502 U.S. ___, ___, 112 S.Ct. 789, 801, 117 L.Ed.2d 1 (1992); *New Energy Co.,* 486 U.S., at 276, 108 S.Ct., at 1809; *Maryland, supra,* 451 U.S., at 760, 101 S.Ct., at 2136.

Moreover, two Terms ago we implicitly rejected any theory that would require aggregating the burdens on commerce across an entire State to determine the constitutionality of a burden on interstate trade imposed by a particular political subdivision of the State. We concluded that proper analysis of the practice of one county that discriminated against interstate trade was "unaffected by the fact that some other counties [in the State] ha[d] adopted a different policy." *Fort Gratiot Sanitary Landfill, Inc. v. Michigan Dept. of Natural Resources,* 504 U.S. ___, ___, 112 S.Ct. 2019, 2025, 119 L.Ed.2d 139 (1992). Contrary to respondents' suggestions, our reasoning indicates that discrimination is appropriately assessed with reference to the specific subdivision in which applicable laws reveal differential treatment.

Any other approach would frustrate the Commerce Clause's central objective of securing a national " 'area of free trade among the several States.' " *Boston Stock Exchange v. State Tax Comm'n,* 429 U.S. 318, 328, 97 S.Ct. 599, 606, 50 L.Ed.2d 514 (1977) (quoting *McLeod v. J.E. Dilworth Co.,* 322 U.S. 327, 330, 64 S.Ct. 1023, 1026, 88 L.Ed. 1304 (1944)). Under respondents' view, the Commerce Clause would interpose no bar to the systematic subdivision of the national market through discriminatory taxes as long as the taxes were imposed by counties, rather than by States—and provided, of course, that on balance each *State* as a whole did not discriminate against interstate trade. Such a rule "would invite a multiplication of preferential trade areas destructive of the very purpose of the Commerce Clause." *Dean Milk Co. v. Madison,* 340 U.S. 349, 356, 71 S.Ct. 295, 299, 95 L.Ed. 329 (1951). We have never suggested that the Commerce Clause will tolerate such discrimination. Rather, "our prior cases teach that a State (or one of its political subdivisions) may not avoid the strictures of the Commerce Clause by curtailing the movement of articles of commerce through subdivisions of the State, rather than through the State itself." *Fort Gratiot, supra,* at ___, 112 S.Ct., at 2024.

* * *

* * * To the extent that *General American*'s Equal Protection Clause discussion ever could have been read as suggesting appropriate Commerce Clause analysis, it has been bypassed by later decisions, and particularly by the "strict rule of equality adopted in *Silas Mason,*" *Halliburton,* 373 U.S., at 73, 83 S.Ct., at 1206, a rule that has controlled compensatory tax cases for over half a century. In *Silas Mason,* Justice Cardozo was explicit in explaining for the Court that the compensatory tax doctrine requires precision to ensure that, upon the "reckoning" of "account[s]," the "sum" on the interstate side of the ledger is "the same" as that on the intrastate side. 300 U.S., at 584, 57 S.Ct., at 527. More recently, we have reiterated that strict parity is demanded by the compensatory tax doctrine as we have explained that a compensatory tax leaves a consumer free to make choices "without regard to the tax consequences"; if he purchases within the State he may pay a tax, but if he purchases from outside the State he will pay a "tax of the *same amount.*" *Boston Stock Exchange, supra,* 419 U.S., at 332, 95 S.Ct., at 480 (emphasis added).

Respondents' final defense of the use tax is an appeal to Missouri's pure motives: that is, its lack of any intent to discriminate. As the product of a decentralized decisionmaking process that relies on the independent judgment of hundreds of local jurisdictions, the use tax scheme, in respondents' view, cannot reveal any overall design on the part of the State or any other governmental entity to disfavor interstate trade. In fact, respondents urge that holding this scheme unconstitutional would effectively eliminate the State's ability to delegate taxing authority to local jurisdictions. But a court need not inquire into the purpose or motivation behind a law to determine that in actuality it impermissibly discriminates against interstate commerce. *See, e.g., Philadelphia,* 437 U.S., at 626, 98 S.Ct., at 2536 (describing "legislative purpose" as "not * * * relevant to the constitutional issue to be decided"); *Hunt v. Washington State Apple Advertising Comm'n,* 432 U.S. 333, 352–353, 97 S.Ct. 2434, 2446–2447, 53 L.Ed.2d 383 (1977). *See also Chemical Waste Management, Inc. v. Hunt,* 504 U.S. ___, ___, 112 S.Ct. 2009, 2014–2015, 119 L.Ed.2d 121 (1992) (slip op., at 8–9).

It should be apparent that in holding this scheme unconstitutional we impose no new restrictions on the State's power to delegate its taxing authority as it sees fit. What a State may not do is appeal to decentralized decisionmaking to augment its powers: it may not grant its political subdivisions a power to discriminate against interstate commerce that State lacked in the first instance.

The State remains free to authorize political subdivisions to impose sales or use taxes, as long as discriminatory treatment of interstate commerce does not result. Other States apparently have had little difficulty in combining some local autonomy with the commands of the Commerce Clause. As the parties stipulated, App. 35, 28 States that provide political subdivisions some authority to impose use taxes have devised systems to ensure that use taxes are not higher than sales taxes within the same taxing jurisdiction. *See, e.g.,* Ga.Code Ann. § 48–8–110 (Supp.1993) (requiring the enactment of a local use tax to be coupled with the adoption of an equivalent sales tax).

B

As our discussion above makes clear, Missouri's use tax scheme impermissibly discriminates against interstate commerce only in those localities where the local sales tax is less than 1.5%. Apparently hoping to obtain a refund for all monies paid under the use tax, however, petitioners seek to have the tax struck down in its entirety. They urge us to hold that the tax is facially invalid in every jurisdiction because there is no countervailing statewide sales tax and no legislation ensuring that local sales taxes will always equal or exceed the use tax. The evil of the system, under this view, is not merely the actual discrimination that results in some localities, but the potential for discrimination in every locality. Indeed, the logic of petitioners' theory suggests that the potential for abuse would make Missouri's use tax scheme impermissibly discriminatory even if every political subdivision had chosen to impose a sales tax of greater than 1.5%.

But we have never deemed a hypothetical possibility of favoritism to constitute discrimination that transgresses constitutional commands. On the contrary, we repeatedly have focused our Commerce Clause analysis on whether a challenged scheme is discriminatory in "effect," *see, e.g., Bacchus Imports, Ltd. v. Dias,* 468 U.S. 263, 270, 104 S.Ct. 3049, 3054, 82 L.Ed.2d 200 (1984), and we have emphasized that "equality for the purposes of * * * the flow of commerce is measured in dollars and cents, not legal abstractions." *Halliburton,* 373 U.S., at 70, 83 S.Ct., at 1204. *See also Gregg Dyeing Co. v. Query,* 286 U.S. 472, 481, 52 S.Ct. 631, 635, 76 L.Ed. 1232 (1932) ("Discrimination, like interstate commerce itself, is a practical conception. We must deal in this matter, as in others, with substantial distinctions and real injuries"). A purely nominal distinction in a State's statutes between the methods of regulating intrastate and interstate commerce, as long as it is not translated into any difference in the substance of regulations imposed, cannot be said to provide "benefit[s]" to intrastate commerce or to impose discriminatory "burden[s]" on interstate trade. *New Energy,* 486 U.S., at 273, 108 S.Ct., at 1807. Thus, it would not violate the Commerce Clause.

For similar reasons, the mere fact that determining the compensatory character of the use tax in this case requires consideration of the sales taxes levied by hundreds of local jurisdictions does not mean that the use tax should be rejected *in toto* as facially discriminatory. A compensatory tax and the tax for which it compensates need not be promulgated in the same provision of state law, or even through the same governmental entity, to survive Commerce Clause scrutiny. Such matters of form do not determine in substance whether the tax merely requires interstate commerce to "pay its way," *Complete Auto Transit, Inc. v. Brady,* 430 U.S. 274, 281, 97 S.Ct. 1076, 1080, 51 L.Ed.2d 326 (1977) (internal quotation marks omitted), or discriminates against interstate trade. "The question of constitutional validity is not to be determined by artificial standards. What is required is that state action, whether through one agency or another, or through one enactment or more than one, shall be consistent with the restrictions of the Federal Constitution. There is no demand in that Constitution that the State shall put its requirements in any one statute. It may distribute them as it sees fit, if the result, taken in its totality, is within the State's constitutional power." *Gregg Dyeing, supra,* 286 U.S., at 480, 52 S.Ct., at 634. See also *Maryland,* 451 U.S., at 756, 101 S.Ct., at 2134; *Halliburton,* 373 U.S., at 69, 83 S.Ct., at 1203.[5] If a State may place the provisions perfecting a compensatory tax scheme in two or more statutes passed by the state legislature, there is no logical reason to think that a State's decision to implement its sales/use tax scheme through provisions promulgated at different levels of government within the State makes the system invalid.

5. Of course, this is not to suggest that courts should "plunge * * * into the morass of weighing comparative tax burdens," *American Trucking Assns., Inc. v. Scheiner,* 483 U.S. 266, 289, 107 S.Ct. 2829, 2843, 97 L.Ed.2d 226 (1987) (internal quotation marks omitted). But as far as the compensatory tax doctrine is concerned, a court that is confined to examining the rates specified in statutes, ordinances, or regulations for taxes assessed on "substantially equivalent event[s]," *Maryland v. Louisiana,* 451 U.S. 725, 759, 101 S.Ct. 2114, 2135, 68 L.Ed.2d 576 (1981)—even if the inquiry requires examination of hundreds of provisions for political units within the State—avoids being drawn into an amorphous inquiry that involves balancing incommensurate burdens imposed on disparate activities throughout the complex structure of a State's tax system.

C

That we have declared the tax scheme impermissibly discriminatory in some localities does not in itself dictate the relief that the State must provide. As we noted in *McKesson Corp. v. Division of Alcoholic Beverages and Tobacco,* 496 U.S. 18, 39–40, 110 S.Ct. 2238, 2552, 110 L.Ed.2d 17 (1990), a "State found to have imposed an impermissibly discriminatory tax retains flexibility in responding to this determination." We have suggested that the provision of a "meaningful opportunity for taxpayers to withhold contested tax assessments and to challenge their validity in a predeprivation hearing" is itself sufficient to satisfy constitutional concerns. *Id.,* at 38, n. 21, 110 S.Ct., at 2251, n. 21. Because the parties have not addressed the procedures that were available in Missouri to contest the tax, any effect Missouri's procedures might have on the appropriate remedy in this case is best left for consideration on remand. Even if no such predeprivation procedure existed, the Due Process Clause would demand only that, "to cure the illegality of the tax as originally imposed, the State must ultimately collect a tax for the contested tax period that in no respect impermissibly discriminates against interstate commerce." *Id.,* at 44, n. 27, 110 S.Ct., at 2254, n. 27. The methods best adapted to achieving equal treatment in this case, whether partial or complete refunds or other measures, are similarly matters properly left for determination on remand.

* * *

4. SPECIAL ASSESSMENTS

pp. 751–52: Add to Note 2(b)

Bennett v. Board of Equalization, 245 Neb. 838, 515 N.W.2d 776 (1994) (burdens of paving and improvements held to outweigh any benefit to assessed properties which, as a result, received no benefit exceeding that of the general public).

p. 761: Add a new section

b. Special Tax Benefit Districts

The benefit-cost-absorbing premise of special assessments has also provided one of the theories supporting development impact fees (see Chapter VII). It has also induced certain resident groups (notably in central Philadelphia, northern Virginia, New Jersey, New York City and Washington, D.C.) voluntarily to promote and accept additional taxes, specifically confined to them, in exchange for increased services (sanitation, public-safety, and transportation) that particularly enhance the value and use of their properties. See generally, Thomas J. Lueck, "Business Districts Grow At Price of Accountability," The New York Times, November 20, 1994, at 1.

The concept of special tax benefit district, with or without additional powers, folds the rationale of a special-benefit assessment district into the more familiar structure of a special-district form of government. It may also serve to preserve and empower roles of *private* organizations. The enormous special tax district approved by the Florida Legislature for a multi-jurisdiction project dramatically highlights these developments, although the development has subsequently been cancelled for economic reasons. See Digest, The Washington Post, December 12, 1994, at F1. The following case illustrates.

WILLIAMS v. ANNE ARUNDEL COUNTY

Supreme Court of Maryland, 1994.
334 Md. 109, 638 A.2d 74.

RODOWSKY, JUDGE.

This case involves the long-standing practice in Anne Arundel County of creating special community benefit tax districts in residential subdivisions in order to finance certain local improvements and services. Specifically, this case concerns Anne Arundel County Code (1985, 1993 Supp.) (A.A.Code), Art. 6, § 2–104(f–3) which creates the Cape St. Claire Community Benefit District (the District). Petitioners own real property in the District. They seek a judgment declaring invalid the ordinance creating the District, and they seek to enjoin collection of any tax levied under the authority of that ordinance by the Anne Arundel County Council on property in the District. Their principal contention is that the tax is not for a public purpose. The requested relief was denied by the Circuit Court for Anne Arundel County and, in an unreported opinion, by the Court of Special Appeals. For reasons hereinafter stated, we shall affirm.

The legal and historical background of the tax district concept, particularly as practiced in Anne Arundel County, will assist in understanding the issues presented here.

I

It appears that the earliest special community benefit tax district in Anne Arundel County (the County) was Herald Harbor on the Severn, created by Chapter 261 of the Acts of 1929 for the purpose of constructing and maintaining roads within that community, as defined. Under the format there employed the Board of County Commissioners of Anne Arundel County (the Commissioners) appointed a five person board from among the area's residents, and that board annually recommended to the Commissioners the amount to be raised by special tax in the district to carry out the statutory purpose.

By Chapter 366 of the Acts of 1939 the General Assembly authorized the Commissioners

> "to establish from time to time special zones * * * and to furnish and provide special privileges or benefits to persons or property in such zones, and to levy special taxes or assessments upon property in such zones receiving special benefit to pay the costs of furnishing * * * such special privileges or benefits."

Exercise by the Commissioners of the power conferred by Chapter 366 was conditioned on a petition, seeking creation of the zone, by a majority of the taxpayers therein and on publication.

The County has been a home rule county under Maryland Constitution Art. XI–A since November 1964. Article XI–A is implemented by the Express Powers Act, Md.Code (1957, 1990 Repl.Vol., 1993 Cum. Supp.), Art. 25A. One of the powers of chartered counties is to levy on land, improvements and personal property. Art. 25A, § 5(O). That provision was amended by Chapter 646 of the Acts of 1949 to confer power "to establish * * * special taxing areas for any of the purposes enumerated in Article 25A * * *."

At this time there are forty-two special community benefit districts located throughout the County. Each was originally created by a public local law of the General Assembly, by a resolution of the Commissioners, or by an ordinance of the County Council. These enactments are codified in A.A.Code, § 2–104(b) through (bb).

Cape St. Claire is a residential community of some 2200 homes on the south shore of the Magothy River, near its entrance into the Chesapeake Bay. Development of Cape St. Claire was begun in the 1940s by the River Bay Company which recorded subdivision plats and imposed covenants running with the land. The development plan included certain community property, consisting primarily of several beaches and parks. Recorded covenants require lot owners to pay a fee, apparently fixed at ten dollars per year, to the River Bay Company or its successor for the maintenance of community property. Title to the community property has been transferred to the Cape St. Claire Improvement Association, Inc. (the Association), a private membership corporation. Currently all persons owning property on the platted areas comprising Cape St. Claire are eligible for membership in the Association, but membership in the Association is limited to such persons.

In February 1989 a majority of the owners of the lots in Cape St. Claire petitioned the County Council, pursuant to A.A.Code § 2–103, for the establishment of a special community benefit district in Cape St. Claire. The District was created by Bill No. 19–89, enacted April 24, 1989, and codified as A.A.Code, § 2–104(f–3). Its purposes are:

> "(i) maintenance of community property, including lawn care, trash removal, repair, lighting, paving, and erosion prevention;
>
> "(ii) special security for community property;
>
> "(iii) acquisition, improvement, and construction of real and personal community property; and
>
> "(iv) funding administrative expenses incidental to carrying out these purposes, including mailing, secretarial, auditing, insurance, and legal costs."

§ 2–104(f–3)(2). The special community benefit tax in the District is "a uniform assessment for each real property tax account." A.A.Code § 2–

106(d)(3).[4]

"Unless otherwise provided by law, special taxing district budget requests [are] prepared by the board of directors of the civic or community association administering the district and submitted to the property owners for their comments * * *." A.A.Code § 8–106(a). Final budget requests must be submitted to the Anne Arundel County Budget Office on or before January 31 of each year. § 8–106(b)(1). These budget requests must include "[a] detailed listing of the purposes to which the special taxing district funds are to be applied." § 8–106(c)(1). The budget request must also state "the rate of special taxing district tax." § 8–106(c)(4).

The County charter embodies an executive budget system. A special taxing district must satisfy the County Executive that the requested appropriations be included in the County's annual budget and appropriation ordinance. *See* County Charter § 706 and, *e.g.,* Bill No. 54–93 (the County Budget and Appropriation Ordinance for the fiscal year ending June 30, 1994). The County Council, with certain exceptions not here relevant, may decrease or delete any item from the budget as proposed, but the County Council may not "increase any expenditure recommended by the County Executive." Charter § 709. A special community tax district's annual tax must also be included in the ordinance of levy for special tax districts. *See, e.g.,* Bill No. 55–93 for the fiscal year ending June 30, 1994.

Special benefit taxes are collected and enforced in the same manner as County real property taxes. A.A.Code § 2–107. The County Controller deposits a special tax district's tax collections into a special account. A.A.Code § 2–108(a). The Controller releases these collections to "[t]he Treasurer or other fiscal officer of each special community benefit district." § 2–108(b). Those recipients must be bonded. *Id.* Disbursements are made monthly after deduction of a fee paid to the general fund of the County of five percent of the collections, subject to an annual ceiling of $1,000 per tax district. § 2–108(c). Under pain of fine or imprisonment for violation of the restriction, "[f]unds disbursed to a special community benefit district shall be expended only for the purposes for which appropriations have been made in the budget as enacted by the County Council." § 2–108(d) and (e).

It is clear from the foregoing that the legal theory underlying the forty-two special community benefit districts in Anne Arundel County is that they are special benefit assessment areas. Thus, the special taxes levied in those areas are special benefit assessments. "The use of such 'special assessments' has a long history in the United States." O.

4. The uniformity requirement of Art. 15 of the Maryland Declaration of Rights, relating to ad valorem property taxes, does not apply to special or local benefit assessments. The latter may be, but are not required to be, based upon ad valorem assessments. *Leonardo v. County Comm'rs of St. Mary's County,* 214 Md. 287, 306–09, 134 A.2d 284, 293–94, *cert. denied,* 355 U.S. 906, 78 S.Ct. 332, 2 L.Ed.2d 260 (1957); *Leser v. Philip Wagner, Inc.,* 120 Md. 671, 680, 87 A. 1040, 1042, *aff'd,* 239 U.S. 207, 36 S.Ct. 66, 60 L.Ed. 230 (1913); 63 Op. Att'y Gen. 16 (1978).

Reynolds, Jr., *Local Government Law* § 99, at 300 (1982) (footnote omitted). In *Gould v. Mayor & City Council of Baltimore,* 59 Md. 378 (1883), this Court contrasted special assessments with the general property tax, saying:

> "The right to make such assessments is undoubtedly an exercise of the taxing power, but an assessment thus made differs from a general tax levied for State and city purposes. The latter is a tax imposed on all persons within the territorial limits according to the value of their property, in consideration of the protection, which the government affords alike to all. A local assessment, on the other hand, is a tax levied occasionally as may be required upon a limited class of persons interested in local improvement, and who are presumed to be benefited by the improvement over and above the ordinary benefit which the community in general derive from the expenditure of the money. In the payment of the assessment thus made, the adjacent owner is supposed to be compensated by the enhanced value of his property, arising from the improvement."

Id. at 380.

"In order to justify a special assessment for a local improvement * * * there must be both a public purpose and a special benefit to the properties to be assessed over and above that accruing to the public." *Montgomery County v. Schultze,* 302 Md. 481, 489, 489 A.2d 16, 20 (1985). *See also Silver Spring Memorial Post No. 2562, Veterans of Foreign Wars v. Montgomery County,* 207 Md. 442, 448, 115 A.2d 249, 251 (1955). One treatise expands on the concept, as follows:

> "In order to justify a local assessment the improvement must be a public one; that is, it must be one which confers a general benefit upon the public at large, and which, therefore, the public acting through its government may construct without the consent of the particular individuals affected thereby. Local assessment for benefits is a form of taxation and the very nature of taxation implies that it is for a public interest. An improvement which lacks this element is essentially a private improvement, and no matter how useful or advantageous it may be, the public cannot compel its construction, nor can it pay therefor by funds raised by general taxation."

1 W. Page & P. Jones, *Taxation by Local and Special Assessments* § 283, at 439 (1909) (footnotes omitted).

Although special benefit assessments were first utilized to finance certain capital improvements, typically elements of the infrastructure of local government, special benefit assessments may also be used to finance the operating expenses of local government for services beneficial to property in an area. *See Pumphrey v. County Comm'rs of Anne Arundel County,* 212 Md. 536, 130 A.2d 297 (1957) (rejecting landowner's challenge to a benefit assessment for garbage collection imposed against realty occupied by tenant); *City of Seattle v. Rogers Clothing for Men, Inc.,* 114 Wash.2d 213, 787 P.2d 39 (1990) (sustaining special assessment for promotional activities, cleaning, decorating, and security in the central business district of Seattle). *See generally* O. Reynolds, Jr., *supra,* § 15, at 38.

II

In the instant matter the County and the Association are the defendants. Following creation of the District, the Association annually has submitted to the County a requested budget and tax for the District. For the fiscal year ending June 30, 1990, the District tax was $29.09 per tax account, for fiscal 1991, $29.45, and for fiscal 1992, $30.01.

An affidavit submitted by the Association president reflects that the tax monies through June 30, 1992 were used for:

- Property maintenance, including grass cutting, tree trimming, trash bags and providing for dumpsters and their periodic emptying;
- Construction of a recreation pier;
- Outdoor lighting at beach facilities;
- Security patrolling (shared with others);
- Providing sanitary facilities at community properties;
- Constructing a storage facility for maintenance equipment;
- Removal of debris from community property;
- Installation and maintenance of outdoor pay telephones;
- Professional costs, including insurance, accounting, and legal, associated with the foregoing;
- Governmental fees and taxes;
- Administrative costs, including postage and shared secretarial and office expenses.

The circuit court decided this action by granting the County's second motion for summary judgment which was filed on the third court day (the fifth calendar day) prior to the trial date and was argued on the trial date without any written response to the motion by the petitioners. The trial court considered the facts stated in argument by petitioners' counsel as a proffer of what the petitioners could demonstrate in opposition to summary judgment. On that basis the circuit judge in essence concluded that there was no dispute of material fact.

III

Petitioners primarily contend that the acquisition and maintenance of the Association's community property cannot, as a matter of law, satisfy the public benefit requirement for a special benefit assessment because the use of the private property is limited to members of the Association, and presumably, their invitees. Petitioners say that this is a private use and that the services funded by the special assessment are not available to the general public. Relying on the 1909 treatise, *Taxation by Local and Special Assessments, supra,* §§ 283, 390, and 393, petitioners assert that there are three requirements in order for a local improvement to be regarded as public, namely, it must confer a general benefit on the public at large, it must be of a type that would justify the expenditure of general tax revenues, and it must be owned by or subject to an easement by the unit of local government assessing for the benefit. We disagree. Maryland law on the subject is far more flexible than petitioners' proposed criteria.

"What is a public purpose for which public funds may be expended is not a matter of exact definition; it is almost entirely a matter of general acceptation." *Finan v. Mayor & City Council of Cumberland,* 154 Md. 563, 565, 141 A. 269, 270 (1928). "[T]he line of demarcation" between a permissible public purpose and an impermissible private purpose "is not immutable or incapable of adjustment to changing social and economic conditions that are properly of public and governmental concern." *City of Frostburg v. Jenkins,* 215 Md. 9, 16, 136 A.2d 852, 855 (1957). Illustrating a private purpose, in violation of Art. 15 of the Declaration of Rights, was the tax levied "upon the property of the citizens of Talbot County, to pay to certain residents of that county the claims due to them by an insolvent railroad company." *Baltimore & E. Shore R.R. v. Spring,* 80 Md. 510, 517, 31 A. 208, 210 (1895).

This Court has said flatly that "the constitutional term 'public use' is not synonymous with physical use or access by the general public." *Prince George's County v. Collington Crossroads, Inc.,* 275 Md. 171, 187, 339 A.2d 278, 286 (1975). Similarly, "the public character of a condemnation is not necessarily changed because a private entity will own the property." *Id.* The decisions of this Court furnish multiple illustrations of expenditures of public funds for public purposes despite the fact that there was also a benefit to privately owned property from which the public at large could rightfully be excluded by the private owner.

Decisions involving public assistance to private business in order to stimulate or sustain economic activity and employment have approved those objectives as public purposes. * * *

Similarly, a public purpose is served when private property is condemned for resale to private business in the form of sites in an industrial park, *Collington Crossroads,* 275 Md. at 190, 339 A.2d at 288, and when, as part of a comprehensive plan for port redevelopment, land is condemned to construct wharves, docks, piers, and warehouses to be leased to private businesses. *Marchant v. Mayor & City Council of Baltimore,* 146 Md. 513, 522, 126 A. 884, 887 (1924). * * * And when private residences along a street are specially benefited by, and specially assessed for, the installation of public water and sewer in the street, the general public in the local governmental unit imposing the special assessment is also benefited, even though individual members of the general public are not free to enter the homes in order to make use of the sewer and water service. *Cf. Dinneen v. Rider,* 152 Md. 343, 366, 136 A. 754, 763 (1927) (where water and sewer installations were to be financed by connection charges and by benefit assessments on abutting owners, with any ultimate deficiency to be raised by the countywide ad valorem property tax, the benefit to the members of the class last referred to was "the remoter local or political interest of all the taxpayers in the general public welfare of the county as enhanced by public improvements in any of its parts * * * ").

Here, the benefit to the general public is the same as that arising from any special benefit assessment. The 2200 properties in the District are presumed to enjoy an increase in value as a result of the special benefits conferred. *See Leser v. Philip Wagner, Inc.,* 120 Md. 671, 677, 87 A. 1040, 1042 (1913); *Burns v. Mayor & City Council of Baltimore,* 48 Md. 198, 204 (1878). The increase in value of the properties in the District from the special benefits conferred also benefits the taxpayers of the County at large, just as the availability of employment in the industrial development cases benefits the community at large. That general benefit is reinforced in the County by the total scheme of special community benefit districts. The County Council could, within its discretion, view that total scheme as enhancing the assessable basis and the quality of life countywide, and thereby promoting the County as an attractive place in which to live and work.

The legislative judgment in levying benefit assessments on the District for the purposes described in A.A.Code § 2–104(f–3)(2) is entitled to the highest deference. "[I]n the absence of a showing of arbitrary action and plain abuse of power," the legislative body's decision is final. *Pumphrey,* 212 Md. at 542, 130 A.2d at 300. "And an assessment, if imposed according to a definite and just plan, will not be disturbed where neither fraud nor mistake appears." *Schultze,* 302 Md. at 490, 489 A.2d at 20.

* * *

IV

Next, the petitioners fall back to a position from which they aim their fire at the administrative expenses of the Association. One of their volleys is a legal argument, while the other is ostensibly factual.

A

The legal argument's premise is that the special community benefit tax districts in the County have no express powers and, petitioners assert, can have no implied powers. We agree that the District is simply an assessment area. From this, the petitioners conclude "that, as a matter of law, administrative expenses may not be paid from a special benefit tax," and that "the overhead expenses of the [Association], a private corporation, are not and can not be, incidental to the *County's* exercise of its express or implied powers." Appellants' Brief at 20–21. That conclusion does not follow from the legal distinction that petitioners emphasize, because here the distinction is irrelevant.

The Association is the vehicle or instrumentality that the County Council has recognized to administer and expend the special benefit assessments imposed and collected by the County. The County Council ordains the purposes for which those assessments may be expended. In the District those purposes expressly include "funding administrative expenses incidental to carrying out [the previously stated] purposes, including mailing, secretarial, auditing, insurance, and legal costs." A.A.Code § 2–104(f–3)(2)(iv). There is no need here to consider the extent to which the Association may imply authorization to expend tax funds for administrative expenses incidental to the other purposes for which the District is created. The authorization is express.

* * *

In any event, if we assume, *arguendo,* an affidavit in proper form presenting an admissible opinion, the opinion expressed is legally insufficient to generate an issue of fact concerning value that would defeat summary judgment. The opinion in essence presents a valuation theory under which the direct labor costs applicable to, and the costs of personalty consumed in, the maintenance of the community property contribute to the value of the community property and thereby to the dominant land, but that indirect costs of maintenance do not.

Supporting the motion for summary judgment is the County Council's appropriation for the District's special benefits and the levy of the special benefit assessment. Those actions include a legislative determination that the 2200 assessment accounts in the District were respectively benefited by the special services, including the indirect costs thereof, by approximately $30. That legislative determination is presumed to be correct. That rate will not be judicially disturbed "where neither fraud nor mistake appears." *Schultze,* 302 Md. at 490, 489 A.2d at 20. *See also Murphy v. Montgomery County,* 267 Md. 224, 236–37, 297 A.2d 249, 256 (1972).

The opinion of the property owner-affiant that the indirect costs associated with the special services in the District do not contribute to the value of homeowners' properties in the District is legally insufficient to defeat that presumption of validity. Even if we assume that the most qualified real estate expert could calibrate the valuation of residences in the District, with and without the services, within a tolerance of $30, that would not support a finding that the assessment was fraudulently or mistakenly levied. As a matter of law it was within the reasonable discretion of the County Council to conclude that a $30 assessment per lot equalled, or was exceeded by the value of the benefit to a property in the District of the direct services and indirect costs to be rendered and paid during the forthcoming tax year. No reasonable fact finder could conclude to the contrary.

The basis on which the circuit court granted the County's motion for summary judgment in this case was essentially that last set forth above. The circuit judge said that "there has to be a cost related to the * * * doing these services. And that requires salaries, insurance, and other administrative necessities."

* * *

The contention is that, in order to administer the tax funds, the Association must affirmatively show, apparently annually, that it is authorized by a majority of the property owners in the District to represent them.

The undisputed facts are that the District was formed after a majority of the property owners in Cape St. Claire petitioned to have the special community benefit district created. In order to comply with A.A.Code § 2–102(e)(2) the Association amended its bylaws "so that, if [the District were legislatively created], then everybody in the district becomes automatically a member of the improvement association." (Statement of counsel for petitioners in opposition to motion for summary judgment.) Members may vote by mail ballot or in person at an annual meeting for the officers of the Association.

Based on those undisputed facts, and on the absence of any evidence of an interim attrition in the membership below the originally petitioning majority, the circuit court concluded that the Association *represents* 100% of the property owners in the District. The Court of Special Appeals pointed out that there is no evidence of any rival to the Association as administrator of the District, or, in the words of that court, there was "no pretender to that throne." We agree.

The logical interpretation of § 2–102(e)(3) is that the community association-administrator must be organized on representative democratic principles. The statute in essence requires that the organizational structure of an association must "provide[ ]" for all property owners in the district to be members. Further, a majority of the property owners must retain the power, if exercised, to determine who the officers will be and, at least in the case of contested elections for office, what the association's policies will be. An administering association, however, need not affirmatively show that the then current officers actually have been elected by a majority of the entire membership. That would be a most unlikely interpretation to apply to membership corporations. *See* Md.Code (1975, 1993 Repl.Vol.), Corporations and Associations Article, § 5–202(b)(5) (permitting special quorum provisions in charter or bylaws); § 5–202(b)(8) (permitting provision for voting by mail in charter or bylaws); and § 5–206 (providing that, after an insufficient number of members is present at a meeting, an additional meeting may be called at which "the members present in person or by proxy constitute a quorum"). The philosophy of a required absolute majority which petitioners espouse, if applied at the national level, would leave the United States of America without a President.

For all the foregoing reasons, the Circuit Court for Anne Arundel County was correct in granting judgment in favor of the defendants, and the Court of Special Appeals was correct in affirming.

5. BORROWING

p. 766: Add after the citations in fourth full paragraph

The increasing sophistication of municipal financing schemes has presented enormous opportunities for cities to achieve politically important goals. There is much pressure on municipal officials to be expert in the ways and means, however. The risk to government funds has increased exponentially. The tale may be gleaned from the following sources. See, e.g., Allen D. Manvell, "Fiscal Facts & Figures: Trends in State–Local Indebtedness," Tax Notes, December 23, 1991, at 1435; Penelope Lemov, "The Brave New World Of Public Finance," Governing, February 1992, at 27 (interest swaps; certificates of participation); Gary Enos, "FGIC Opens Door To Variable–Rate Debt For N.Y.," City & State, March 23, 1992, at 2; Leonard Sloane, "Munis: Popular, Tax Free and Tricky," The New York Times, January 23, 1993, at 35; Jonathan Fuerbringer, "Yen Bonds To Be Offered By New York," The New York Times, March 9, 1993, at D1; James E. Lebherz, "Muni Bond Yields May Rise As Supply Falls in '94," The Washington Post, February 20, 1994, at H9; Penelope Lemov, "Muni Bonds After the Boom," Governing, February 1994, at 12; Penelope Lemov, "Tough Times For TIF," Governing, February 1994, at 18 (the popular method of redeveloping cities to borrow funds repaid from increased tax returns of enhanced-value, redeveloped areas faces dramatic slowing of real estate appreciation); Leslie Wayne, "Local Governments Lose Millions In Complex and Risky Securities," The New York Times, September 25, 1994, at A1 (using interest swaps, currency swaps, and mortgage derivatives to make money rather than hedge against market fluctuations).

b. Long–Term Debt

(1) Debt Limitations

p. 774: Add new Note 4

4. **Debt Limits and Moral Obligation Bonds.** The New York Court of Appeals has rejected the argument that the so-called moral obligation of the state to avoid ruinous credit consequences and to back the bonds of authorities constitutes the legally binding debt that is within the meaning of the constitutional debt-limitation provisions. Schulz v. New York, 84 N.Y.2d 231, 616 N.Y.S.2d 343, 639 N.E.2d 1140 (1994), cert. denied, ___ U.S. ___, 115 S.Ct. 936, ___ L.Ed.2d ___ (1995).

(2) Bonded Debt—General or Special Obligations?

p. 786: Add to Note 5, Special Taxing Districts

See note on the applications of the theory of special assessments, pp. 178–179, supra.

p. 787: Add to Note 7 before discussion of the SEC

Leslie Wayne, "The Fuss Over Nonrated Bonds," The New York Times, January 24, 1993, at F15.

Add to Note 7 after mention of the SEC

The SEC is seeking to impose more stringent disclosure requirements. (See amended Rule 15c–12, 59 FR 59590.) It, together with the Municipal Securities Regulatory Board, is also seeking to prohibit campaign contributions to municipal officials by parties that do or seek to do business with the municipality as underwriters or financial consultants in municipal borrowings. The U.S. Civil Rights Commission, however, has been asked to determine whether these prohibitions unfairly hurt women and minority political candidates. See, e.g., Joanne Kelley, "SEC To Target Municipal Securities: Rules Would Upgrade Disclosure Standards, Require Financial Data," The Washington Post, March 6, 1994, at H5; Jerry Knight, "Probe Urged of Campaign Bond Rules," The Washington Post, September 17, 1994, at B1; Jerry Knight, "Tackling the Murky World of Muni Bonds, SEC Pushes For Reforms to Give Small Investors a Clearer Picture of a $1.3 Trillion Market," The Washington Post, October 16, 1994, at H1.

c. *Protection of Bond Investors*

(1) Retrospective Validation

p. 795: Add to Note

Massachusetts Municipal Wholesale Electric Co. v. State of Vermont, ___ Vt. ___, 639 A.2d 995 (1994) (enactment of curative legislation re municipal contract authority).

(3) Constitutional Protection Against Impairment of Contracts

p. 802: Add to end of Note 1

Re the impact of the Contract Clause on retroactive legislation, see General Motors v. Romein, 503 U.S. 181, 112 S.Ct. 1105, 117 L.Ed.2d 328 (1992).

(4) Bona Fide Purchasers

p. 808: Add new Note

Note

Given the highly publicized travails of Orange County, California, St. Mary's County, Maryland, and other local governments that have sought to use such "cutting edge" investment devices as derivatives to enhance pooled fund earnings, the treatment of creditors would not be complete without reference to municipal bankruptcy. See Steven D. Conlon and Vincent M. Aquilino, Tax-Exempt Derivatives, Section of Urban, State and Local Government Law, American Bar Association 1994: Dorothy A. Brown, *Fiscal Distress and Politics: The Bankruptcy Filing of Bridgeport As a Case Study In Reclaiming Local Sovereignty,* 11 Emory Bankr.Dev.J. ___ (1995).

BANKRUPTCY CODE
CHAPTER 9—ADJUSTMENT OF DEBTS OF A MUNICIPALITY

(excerpts).

CHAPTER 9—ADJUSTMENT OF DEBTS OF A MUNICIPALITY EXCERPTS

* * *

§ 902. Definitions for this chapter

In this chapter—

(1) "property of the estate", when used in a section that is made applicable in a case under this chapter by section 103(e) or 901 of this title, means property of the debtor;

(2) "special revenues" means—

(A) receipts derived from the ownership, operation, or disposition of projects or systems of the debtor that are primarily used or intended to be used primarily to provide transportation, utility, or other services, including the proceeds of borrowings to finance the projects or systems;

(B) special excise taxes imposed on particular activities or transactions;

(C) incremental tax receipts from the benefited area in the case of tax-increment financing;

(D) other revenues or receipts derived from particular functions of the debtor, whether or not the debtor has other functions; or

(E) taxes specifically levied to finance one or more projects or systems, excluding receipts from general property, sales, or income taxes (other than tax-increment financing) levied to finance the general purposes of the debtor;

(3) "special tax payer" means record owner or holder of legal or equitable title to real property against which a special assessment or special tax has been levied the proceeds of which are the sole source of payment of an obligation issued by the debtor to defray the cost of an improvement relating to such real property;

(4) "special tax payer affected by the plan" means special tax payer with respect to whose real property the plan proposes to increase the proportion of special assessments or special taxes referred to in paragraph (2) of this section assessed against such real property; and

(5) "trustee", when used in a section that is made applicable in a case under this chapter by section 103(e) or 901 of this title, means debtor, except as provided in section 926 of this title.

§ 903. Reservation of State power to control municipalities

This chapter does not limit or impair the power of a State to control, by legislation or otherwise, a municipality of or in such State in the exercise of the political or governmental powers of such municipality, including expenditures for such exercise, but—

(1) a State law prescribing a method of composition of indebtedness of such municipality may not bind any creditor that does not consent to such composition; and

(2) a judgment entered under such a law may not bind a creditor that does not consent to such composition.

§ 904. Limitation on jurisdiction and powers of court

Notwithstanding any power of the court, unless the debtor consents or the plan so provides, the court may not, by any stay, order, or decree, in the case or otherwise, interfere with—

(1) any of the political or governmental powers of the debtor;

(2) any of the property or revenues of the debtor; or

(3) the debtor's use or enjoyment of any income-producing property.

* * *

§ 922. Automatic stay of enforcement of claims against the debtor

(a) A petition filed under this chapter operates as a stay, in addition to the stay provided by section 362 of this title, applicable to all entities, of—

(1) the commencement or continuation, including the issuance or employment of process, of a judicial, administrative, or other action or proceeding against an officer or inhabitant of the debtor that seeks to enforce a claim against the debtor; and

(2) the enforcement of a lien on or arising out of taxes or assessments owed to the debtor.

(b) Subsections (c), (d), (e), (f), and (g) of section 362 of this title apply to a stay under subsection (a) of this section the same as such subsections apply to a stay under section 362(a) of this title.

(c) If the debtor provides, under section 362, 364, or 922 of this title, adequate protection of the interest of the holder of a claim secured by a lien on property of the debtor and if, notwithstanding such protection such creditor has a claim arising from the stay of action against such property under section 362 or 922 of this title or from the granting of a lien under section 364(d) of this title, then such claim shall be allowable as an administrative expense under section 503(b) of this title.

(d) Notwithstanding section 362 of this title and subsection (a) of this section, a petition filed under this chapter does not operate as a stay of application of pledged special revenues in a manner consistent with section 927 of this title to payment of indebtedness secured by such revenues.

* * *

§ 926. Avoiding powers

(a) If the debtor refuses to pursue a cause of action under section 544, 545, 547, 548, 549(a), or 550 of this title, then on request of a creditor, the court may appoint a trustee to pursue such cause of action.

(b) A transfer of property of the debtor to or for the benefit of any holder of a bond or note, on account of such bond or note, may not be avoided under section 547 of this title.

* * *

§ 928. Post petition effect of security interest

(a) Notwithstanding section 552(a) of this title and subject to subsection (b) of this section, special revenues acquired by the debtor after the commencement of the case shall remain subject to any lien resulting from any security agreement entered into by the debtor before the commencement of the case.

(b) Any such lien on special revenues, other than municipal betterment assessments, derived from a project or system shall be subject to the necessary operating expenses of such project or system, as the case may be.

* * *

§ 930. Dismissal

(a) After notice and a hearing, the court may dismiss a case under this chapter for cause, including—

(1) want of prosecution;

(2) unreasonable delay by the debtor that is prejudicial to creditors;

(3) failure to propose a plan within the time fixed under section 941 of this title;

(4) if a plan is not accepted within any time fixed by the court;

(5) denial of confirmation of a plan under section 943(b) of this title and denial of additional time for filing another plan or a modification of a plan; or

(6) if the court has retained jurisdiction after confirmation of a plan—

(A) material default by the debtor with respect to a term of such plan; or

(B) termination of such plan by reason of the occurrence of a condition specified in such plan.

(b) The court shall dismiss a case under this chapter if confirmation of a plan under this chapter is refused.

* * *

SUBCHAPTER III—THE PLAN

§ 941. Filing of plan

The debtor shall file a plan for the adjustment of the debtor's debts. If such a plan is not filed with the petition, the debtor shall file such a plan at such later time as the court fixes.

* * *

§ 943. Confirmation

(a) A special tax payer may object to confirmation of a plan.

(b) The court shall confirm the plan if—

(1) the plan complies with the provisions of this title made applicable by sections 103(e) and 901 of this title;

(2) the plan complies with the provisions of this chapter;

(3) all amounts to be paid by the debtor or by any person for services or expenses in the case or incident to the plan have been fully disclosed and are reasonable;

(4) the debtor is not prohibited by law from taking any action necessary to carry out the plan;

(5) except to the extent that the holder of a particular claim has agreed to a different treatment of such claim, the plan provides that on the effective date of the plan each holder of a claim of a kind specified in section 507(a)(1) of this title will receive on account of such claim cash equal to the allowed amount of such claim;

(6) any regulatory or electoral approval necessary under applicable nonbankruptcy law in order to carry out any provision of the plan has been obtained, or such provision is expressly conditioned on such approval; and

(7) the plan is in the best interests of creditors and is feasible.

§ 944. Effect of confirmation

(a) The provisions of a confirmed plan bind the debtor and any creditor, whether or not—

(1) a proof of such creditor's claim is filed or deemed filed under section 501 of this title;

(2) such claim is allowed under section 502 of this title; or

(3) such creditor has accepted the plan.

(b) Except as provided in subsection (c) of this section, the debtor is discharged from all debts as of the time when—

(1) the plan is confirmed;

(2) the debtor deposits any consideration to be distributed under the plan with a disbursing agent appointed by the court; and

(3) the court has determined—

(A) that any security so deposited will constitute, after distribution, a valid legal obligation of the debtor; and

(B) that any provision made to pay or secure payment of such obligation is valid.

(c) The debtor is not discharged under subsection (b) of this section from any debt—

(1) excepted from discharge by the plan or order confirming the plan; or

(2) owed to an entity that, before confirmation of the plan, had neither notice nor actual knowledge of the case.

§ 945. Continuing jurisdiction and closing of the case

(a) The court may retain jurisdiction over the case for such period of time as is necessary for the successful implementation of the plan.

(b) Except as provided in subsection (a) of this section, the court shall close the case when administration of the case has been completed.

C. EXPENDITURE CONTROLS

1. PUBLIC PURPOSE LIMITATIONS

p. 818: Add to Note 2

One of the most extensive efforts meeting the public-purpose requirement involves direct expenditures and tax expenditures designed to achieve successful economic development, thereby increasing jobs and ancillary tax revenues. In the absence of a national policy, competition among states and localities to become sites for domestic and international business persists, especially during periods of economic downturn. Although there are varied opinions on what works, the techniques range from tax expenditures to sharing employee-paid tax revenues with employers. For a thoughtful and comprehensive analysis of techniques and issues, see the commentary by Dr. Harold Hovey in State Policy Reports, Issue 8, April 1994, at 1–24. See also City of Ypsilanti v. General Motors Corp., 201 Mich.App. 128, 506 N.W.2d 556 (1993), appeal denied and remanded, 443 Mich. 882, 509 N.W.2d 152 (1993) (unsuccessful assertion of promissory estoppel to prevent closing of plant that had been aided by government economic incentives); Note, *Can State and Local Tax Incentives and Other Contributions Stimulate Economic Development,* 44 Tax Lawyer 285 (1990). Cf. Armando Gomez, *Limited Liability Companies: Passthrough Entity of the Future,* 12 J.State Tax. 1 (1994); Christopher Schwarz, "Zone Defense," State Government News, April 1994, at 18 (enterprise zones); Revenue Reconciliation Act of 1993, § 13301, 26 U.S.C.A. §§ 1391 ff. (empowerment zones).

2. CONTROLS ON THE PROCESSES OF CONTRACTING

a. Required Authorization and Procedure

p. 820: Add new Note 4

4. **Apparent Authority of City Attorney.** In a disagreement between the city and its franchisee over the meaning of the franchise agreement, the city was held bound by the written interpretation of the City Attorney. The parties had acted thereon. The state-law requirement of formal contract approval by the City Commission meant that the City Attorney could not enact, amend or nullify a contract ordinance without the commission's formal approval. But contract interpretation did not involve contract amendment, and the City Attorney had at least the apparent

authority to bind the city to the interpretation in question. City of Wichita v. Southwestern Bell Telephone Co., 24 F.3d 1282 (10th Cir.1994).

p. 827: Add to Note 1

A site-plan agreement between the city and a developer whereby the latter would pay for traffic-signal installation materials while the cost of street widening would be borne by other parties was deemed to have restricted the powers of successor councils impermissibly. Marco Development Corp. v. City of Cedar Falls, 473 N.W.2d 41 (Iowa 1991).

c. *Conflicts of Interest in Public Contracts*

p. 835: Add to Note 1

Compare Appeal of Philip Morris U.S.A., 335 N.C. 227, 436 S.E.2d 828 (1993), cert. denied, ___ U.S. ___, 114 S.Ct. 2726, 129 L.Ed.2d 850 (1994) (contingent fee contract between county and private tax auditor which guaranteed auditor a percentage of personal-property tax revenues which the auditor "discovers" did not violate North Carolina public policy since Legislature could forbid such contracts if it so desired).

d. *Bidding Requirements*

(1) Administrative Requirements

p. 853–55: Add to Note 3

A statutory 7% price preference for state and local vendors and products in the award of state contracts was upheld as serving legitimate interests of the state as a market participant, and not violating the Equal Protection or Commerce Clauses. Smith Setzer & Sons, Inc. v. South Carolina Procurement Review Panel, 20 F.3d 1311 (4th Cir.1994). For other examples of the application of market-participant theory, see, Associated Builders and Contractors, Inc. v. City of Seward, 966 F.2d 492 (9th Cir.1992), cert. denied, 113 S.Ct. 1577 (1993); Big Country Foods, Inc. v. Board of Education of Anchorage Sch. Dist., 952 F.2d 1173 (9th Cir.1992).

Add to Note 3 after the *K.S.B. Technical Sales Corp.* citation

"Buy American" and local-product preferences may be treated differently under the recently completed Uruguay Round of G.A.T.T. than they were under the earlier agreement.

Add to Note 3 after the *United Building Trades–Camden* citation

The Third Circuit considered *Camden* to apply only to private employment, ruling that public employment was not a fundamental right protected by the Privileges and Immunities Clause, and upholding a residency requirement. Salem Blue Collar Workers Ass'n v. City of Salem, 33 F.3d 265 (3d Cir.1994).

Add to Note 4

The Supreme Court reversed *Associated Builders and Contractors of Massachusetts/Rhode Island, Inc.* and held that the NLRA does not preempt the authority of a state agency, acting as the owner of a construction project, to enforce an otherwise lawful, pre-hire, collective-bargaining agreement negotiated by private parties. Building and Construction Trades Council of the Metropolitan Dist. v. Associated Builders and Contractors of Massachusetts/Rhode Island, Inc., ___ U.S. ___, 113 S.Ct. 1190, 122 L.Ed.2d 565 (1993).

(2) Lowest "Responsible" Bidder

p. 866–67: Add to Note 2

To the *Austin* citation: *semble,* Shook Heavy and Environmental Construction Group v. City of Kokomo, 632 N.E.2d 355 (Ind.1994) (statute covering awarding of bids only permits challenges by citizens or taxpayers of the municipality).

To the end of Note 2: Where state procurement law creates a property interest for a low bidder in the award of a public contract, the bidder has standing to protect that interest under the Due Process Clause of the fourteenth amendment in a federal civil rights suit (42 U.S.C.A. § 1983). Pataula Electric Membership Corporation v. Whitworth, 951 F.2d 1238 (11th Cir.1992), cert. denied, ___ U.S. ___, 113 S.Ct. 302, 121 L.Ed.2d 225 (1993). The fifth Circuit has held that the owner of a wrecking service could sue under the first amendment and 42 U.S.C.A. § 1983, charging that the city excluded him from the accident-removal rotation list because he criticized the city's bidding procedures for wrecking services. Blackburn v. City of Marshall, 42 F.3d 925 (5th Cir.1995).

(4) Affirmative Action in Public Contract Awards

p. 874–75: Add to Note 1

O'Donnell Construction Co. v. District of Columbia, 963 F.2d 420 (D.C.Cir. 1992) (D.C.'s 35% dollar-amount set aside for MBEs not supported by *Croson* factors); Associated General Contractors of Connecticut v. City of New Haven, 791 F.Supp. 941 (D.Conn.1992) (reenactment of minority set-aside ordinance originally soundly based on appropriate evidence of discrimination now violates equal protection without present evidence that current reasonable level of contract awards would abate without it). Cf. Associated General Contractors of California v. Coalition for Economic Equity, 950 F.2d 1401 (9th Cir.1991), cert. denied, ___ U.S. ___, 112 S.Ct. 1670, 118 L.Ed.2d 390 (1992) (detailed findings distinguish this valid ordinance from *Croson*); Cone Corp. v. Hillsborough County, 908 F.2d 908 (11th Cir.1990), cert. denied, 498 U.S. 493, 111 S.Ct. 516, 112 L.Ed.2d 528 (1990) (statistical demonstration of underrepresentation clearly distinguished the challenged plan from *Croson*). Reliance upon the policy of federal transportation statutes to avoid the *Croson* restraints has also produced mixed results. Compare Harrison & Burrowes Bridge Constructors, Inc. v. Cuomo, 981 F.2d 50 (2d Cir.1992) (New York set aside is within tolerances of the goal of the 1987 Surface Transportation and Uniform Relocation Assistance Act and need not be supported by the detailed evidence required in *Croson*), with H.K. Porter Co. v. Metropolitan Dade County, 975 F.2d 762 (11th Cir.1992) (opinion vacated 998 F.2d 892 (1993)) (1978 Surface Transportation Assistance Act, which requires Secretary to "take affirmative action," does not authorize local government set-aside program absent specific findings indicated by *Croson*).

Add to Note 2

The Supreme Court has agreed to review a case which held that *Fullilove,* not *Croson,* provided the proper standard on which to evaluate a federal program set up pursuant to the federal Small Business Act, § 502. Adarand Constructors, Inc. v. Pena, 16 F.3d 1537 (10th Cir.1994), cert. granted, ___ U.S. ___, 115 S.Ct. 41, 129 L.Ed.2d 936 (1994).

Add to Note 4

The Civil Rights Act of 1991 (summarized at p. 200, infra) overruled *Martin v. Wilks.* The standing issue, however, continues to be raised. Illustratively, in Northeastern Florida Chapter of the Associated General Contractors of America v. City of Jacksonville, ___ U.S. ___, 113 S.Ct. 2297, 124 L.Ed.2d 586 (1993), the Court held that, when government-created barriers make it more difficult for members of one group to obtain a benefit than for members of another group, the disadvantaged group members have standing to challenge the barrier without alleging that, but for the barrier, they would have in fact received the benefit. To establish standing, they need to demonstrate that the members are ready and able to bid on contracts and that a discriminatory policy prevented them from doing so on an equal basis. Compare that ruling with the Eleventh Circuit decision that non-minority contractors lacked standing to challenge a county set-aside program for minority subcontracts (as causing them lost profits) because their factual allegations were not sufficient to show that they suffered a discrimination injury in fact. Cone Corp. v. Hillsborough County, 908 F.2d 908 (11th Cir.1990), cert. denied, 498 U.S. 983, 111 S.Ct. 516, 112 L.Ed.2d 528 (1991).

Chapter IX

STAFFING LOCAL GOVERNMENT

A. OFFICERS

2. QUALIFICATION AND ELIGIBILITY FOR PUBLIC OFFICE AND EMPLOYMENT

p. 897: Add to *Residency Requirements*

Salem Blue Collar Workers Assn. v. City of Salem, 33 F.3d 265 (3d Cir.1994) (residency requirement for municipal employees does not violate the Privileges and Immunities Clause).

p. 899: Add to text before *Professional Licensure*

Term Limits—Whether term limits are viewed as ballot-access limitations or as qualification to run again for elective office, officeholders at local, state, and, perhaps, federal levels face an eruption of efforts to limit the number of terms they may serve, a new reform trend that has not run its course. See, e.g., Miyazawa v. City of Cincinnati, 825 F.Supp. 816 (S.D.Ohio 1993) affirmed 45 F.3d 126 (6th Cir.1995) (upholding term limits for city council members); California v. Eu, 54 Cal.3d 492, 286 Cal.Rptr. 283, 816 P.2d 1309 (1991), cert. denied, ___ U.S. ___, 112 S.Ct. 1292, 117 L.Ed.2d 516 (1992) (upholding term limits for state legislators and constitutional officers); U.S. Term Limits, Inc. v. Hill, 316 Ark. 251, 872 S.W.2d 349 (1994) (upholding term limits for state officers, but not for federal officers); Thorsted v. Gregoire, 841 F.Supp. 1068 (W.D.Wash.1994) (rejecting term limits re Congress). The Supreme Court has granted certiorari in the Arkansas case. U.S. Term Limits, Inc. v. Thornton, ___ U.S. ___, 114 S.Ct. 2703, 129 L.Ed.2d 832 (1994). The U.S. House of Representatives, in early 1995, failed to pass a term-limits constitutional amendment.

Ethics Laws—Newly adopted codes of ethics are having increased practical impact, particularly with reference to official appointments, relations with lobbyists and others while in office, and employment after leaving office. See, e.g., DiPrete v. Morsilli, 635 A.2d 1155 (R.I.1994) (Governor improperly recommended a business associate's law firm in violation of code); In re Advisory from Governor, 633 A.2d 664 (R.I. 1993) ("revolving door" legislation regulating post-tenure employment);

Joyce Bullock, "In Search of the Toughest State Ethics Law," State Government News, May 1994, at 34.

3. PLURAL OFFICE HOLDING

p. 908: Add to Note 4 after *Fox v. Swing* case

The Pennsylvania courts continue to view incompatibility as an exclusively legislative issue. Commonwealth v. Lucas, 534 Pa. 293, 632 A.2d 868 (1993) ("appointive township office or position," within meaning of township code provision prohibiting supervisor from holding another elected or appointed position, does not include membership on municipal authority board; if Legislature finds these offices incompatible, it should so state as court will not supply what the Legislature did not include).

4. SELF-APPOINTMENT AND NEPOTISM

p. Add to note on Nepotism

The Iowa Supreme Court upheld an anti-nepotism ordinance that forbade employment of spouses in the same municipal department as supported by legitimate considerations of avoiding the conflicts that nepotism presents, and it rejected claims that the ordinance was overbroad and unconstitutionally burdened rights to marry (privacy) and to freedom of association. Sioux City Police Officers' Assoc. v. City of Sioux City, 495 N.W.2d 687 (Iowa 1993).

B. PUBLIC EMPLOYEES

1. QUALIFICATIONS AND ELIGIBILITY FOR EMPLOYMENT

p. 935: Add to Note 3

Newman v. Voinovich, 986 F.2d 159 (6th Cir.1993), cert. denied, ___ U.S. ___, 113 S.Ct. 3041, 125 L.Ed.2d 727 (1993) (Ohio judges are policy makers whose appointment by the Governor though based on political affiliation does not violate the first amendment); Akers v. Caperton, 998 F.2d 220 (4th Cir.1993) (statute specifying party affiliation as requirement for various state jobs, including county road supervisor, is unsupported by evidence of a vital government interest furthered by employee's political-patronage transfer; transfer is impermissible infringement on employee's first-amendment rights). However, state officials responsible for the transfer in 1989, before unconstitutionality became firmly established, enjoy qualified immunity from damage liability for effecting the transfer under the voided law. Id.

b. Employment Discrimination and Affirmative Action

p. 940: Add to second full paragraph

Tranello v. Frey, 962 F.2d 244 (2d Cir.1992), cert. denied, ___ U.S. ___, 113 S.Ct. 813, 121 L.Ed.2d 686 (1992) (deputy county attorney appointed by county attorney, who was in turn appointed by elected county executive, is not an appointee of an elected official excepted thereby from coverage of the ADEA).

Add to the fourth full paragraph

Hazen Paper Co. v. Biggins, ___ U.S. ___, 113 S.Ct. 1701, 123 L.Ed.2d 338 (1993) (violation of the ADEA is willful if alleged violator either knew or showed reckless disregard for whether conduct was prohibited by the statute; without more, discharge of employee to prevent pension benefits from vesting did not violate ADEA).

pp. 948–952: Replace Notes 4 through 7 and the *Martin v. Wilks* case with the following (confirming the predicted changes from the Civil Rights Act of 1991)

4. **Summary of Provisions of the Civil Rights Act of 1991, Pub. l. No. 102–166, 105 Stat. 1071 (1991).**

Civil Rights Act of 1991, Pub.L. No. 102–166, 105 Stat. 1071 (1991).

The purposes of the Act, stated in § 3, were to remedy intentional discrimination in the workplace, to codify Supreme Court decisions prior to the 1989 term (Wards Cove Packing Co. v. Atonio, 490 U.S. 642 (1989)), to confirm authority for adjudicating disparate impact suits under Title VII of the Civil Rights Act of 1964 (42 U.S.C. 2000e et seq.), and to expand the scope of civil rights statutes in response to decisions of the Supreme Court in the 1989 and 1990 terms.

§ 101 adds to the Civil Rights Act of 1964 (42 USC § 1981) that its term "make and enforce contracts" includes the "making, performance, modification, and termination of contracts, and the enjoyment of all benefits, privileges, terms, and conditions of the contractual relationship. This section also adds that the rights protected by § 1981 are "protected against impairment by nongovernmental discrimination and impairment under color of State law."

§ 102 adds to § 1981 a section providing damages in cases of intentional discrimination in employment.

(a)(1) Civil Rights—In jury-trial cases for intentional discrimination, including non-racial claims where the plaintiff cannot recover under § 1981, compensatory and punitive damages are allowed, in addition to relief authorized by Title VII.

(a)(2) Disability—In cases of unlawful intentional discrimination under the Americans with Disabilities Act of 1990 or the Rehabilitation Act of 1973, compensatory and punitive damages are allowed.

(a)(3) Good Faith—Damages may not be awarded under the previous section where the defendant demonstrates good faith efforts to make reasonable accommodations for the plaintiff.

(b)(1) Punitive damages are allowed where the plaintiff shows that the defendant acted with "malice or reckless indifference" to the defendant's rights.

(b)(2) Compensatory damages do not include backpay or interest thereon.

(b)(3) Compensatory damages, including future pecuniary losses, emotional pain, suffering, inconvenience, mental anguish, loss of enjoyment of life, and other nonpecuniary losses, and punitive damages are capped, depending on the number of people the defendant employs, between $50,000 and $300,000.

(c) Any party may demand a jury trial. The court does not inform the jury of the damages limitations.

(d) Defines "complaining party" and "discriminatory practice."

§ 103 applies the provisions regarding attorney fees in § 1988 to the sections added to § 1981 above.

§ 104 defines "complaining party", "demonstrates" (meets burden of production and persuasion), and "respondent."

§ 105 Disparate Impact Cases—If the plaintiff demonstrates that a particular employment practice or practices (or the entire decision-making process if its elements are not capable of being separated for analysis) causes a disparate impact on the basis of race, color, religion, sex, or national origin, and the defendant fails to demonstrate that the practice(s) is required by business necessity or does not cause the disparate impact, or if the plaintiff responds to a practice shown to be required by business necessity by offering a different available employment practice which will have less disparate impact and would serve the defendant's legitimate interests as well and the defendant refuses to adopt such practice, the plaintiff carries the burden of proof.

Business necessity is not a defense against a claim of intentional discrimination.

Barring employment for drug use is unlawful only if it is intended to discriminate on the basis of race, color, religion, sex, or national origin.

§ 106 Adjusting the scores of, using different cutoff scores for, or otherwise altering the results of employment related tests on the basis of race, color, religion, sex, or national origin in connection with hiring or referring candidates for hiring or promotion is an unlawful employment practice.

§ 107 adds to Title VII a subsection providing that an unlawful employment practice is established when the plaintiff demonstrates that race, color, religion, sex, or national origin was a motivating factor for any employment practice, even if there were other motivating factors. Where the defendant shows it would have taken the action in the absence of the impermissible motivating factor, the court may grant declaratory and injunctive relief and attorney's fees and costs directly attributable to the claim under this subsection and shall not award damages or issue an order requiring any admission, reinstatement, hiring, promotion, or payment.

§ 108 Facilitating prompt and orderly resolution of challenges—practices within a consent decree or court order may not be challenged by a person who prior to the entry of judgment had notice and reasonable opportunity to object or by a person whose interests were adequately represented by another person who previously challenged the order or decree.

§ 109 applies the Act's protections to U.S. citizens employed in foreign countries by domestic corporations and delineates a test for whether a foreign entity is controlled by a U.S. corporation.

§ 110 establishes a Technical Assistance and Training Institute.

§ 111 requires the Commission to carry out education and outreach activities.

§ 112 provides that a seniority system adopted for an intentionally discriminatory purpose is an unlawful employment practice when an individual becomes subject to the seniority system or when a person is injured by its application.

§ 113 allows the court to award expert fees under Title VII.

§ 114 extends the statute of limitations under Title VII from 30 to 90 days and allows collection of interest for delay in payment from government entities.

§ 115 provides that a person may bring a claim under the Age Discrimination in Employment Act of 1967 within 90 days of the Commission dismissing the complaint.

§ 116 states that nothing in the Act is intended to affect court-ordered remedies, affirmative action, or conciliation agreements that are in accordance with the law.

§ 117 outlines the coverage of House of Representatives and legislative agencies.

§ 118 encourages alternative dispute resolution.

5. **Post-enactment developments.** Since the new law effectively displaced the cases previously reported in the principal text, but spoke to its retroactivity only in some provisions, courts were immediately faced with questions concerning the Act's applicability to cases then pending trial and decision. The Supreme Court held that the compensatory and punitive damages provisions and the jury trial provision of the Act do not apply to a case pending on appeal at the time of the enactment. Landgraf v. USI Film Products, ___ U.S. ___, 114 S.Ct. 1483, 128 L.Ed.2d 229 (1994). The Court also held that the Act's section defining "make and enforce contract" to include the termination of contracts did not apply retroactively. Rivers v. Roadway Express, Inc., ___ U.S. ___, 114 S.Ct. 1510, 128 L.Ed.2d 274 (1994). See also Chenault v. U.S. Postal Service, 37 F.3d 535 (9th Cir.1994) (Act's section extending time for federal-employee filing of discrimination suits may not be applied retroactively to revive claim time-barred under prior limits); Maitland v. University of Minnesota, 43 F.3d 357 (8th Cir.1994) (Provision of Civil Rights Act of 1991 that bars challenges to employment practices resulting from consent decrees by parties who had notice and opportunity to object does not apply retroactively). See generally, Symposium, *The Civil Rights Act of 1991: Theory and Practice,* 68 Notre Dame L.Rev. 911 (1993).

2. LABOR MANAGEMENT RELATIONS IN THE PUBLIC SECTOR

b. Public Employee Labor Relations Patterns

(2) The Right to Bargain Collectively

p. 960: Add to Note 3

See also Moreau v. Klevenhagen, ___ U.S. ___, 113 S.Ct. 1905, 123 L.Ed.2d 584 (1993) (Fair Labor Standards Act construed to permit state and local governments to enter into agreements with individual employees giving compensatory time instead of overtime notwithstanding their designation of a union bargaining representative); Hill–Murray Federation of Teachers v. Hill–Murray High School, 487 N.W.2d 857 (Minn.1992) (application of Minnesota's Labor Relations Act to allow lay employees of religious school to negotiate terms and conditions of employment does not violate the first amendment's religion clauses or the state constitution's freedom of conscience clause). Cf. Collins v. City of Harker Heights, 503 U.S. 115, 112 S.Ct. 1061, 117 L.Ed.2d 261 (1992), reported, infra, this supplement (Due Process Clause does not impose independent federal obligation upon municipalities to provide certain minimal levels of safety and security in the workplace).

(3) Bargainable Subjects

p. 972: Add to Note 2

See also State v. State Troopers Fraternal Assn., 134 N.J. 393, 634 A.2d 478 (1993) (amendment to statute, covering public employees, providing that discipline was a subject of negotiation, held not to apply to the state police); Drivers, Chauffers and Helpers Local Union No. 639 v. District of Columbia, 631 A.2d 1205 (D.C.App.1993) (public employees board was justified in concluding that union proposals concerning several categories of employees intruded upon management prerogatives and were non-negotiable or were not mandatory subjects of negotiation).

Add to Note 3

Judicial efforts to reconcile converging statutes on labor relations and related subjects continue apace. Newark Valley Central School Dist. v. Public Employment Relations Bd., 83 N.Y.2d 315, 610 N.Y.S.2d 134, 632 N.E.2d 443 (1994), held that neither the state's education laws nor its public health laws (a smoke-free environment statute) authorize a school district to impose a non-negotiated bus-driver smoking ban in empty buses, and that a state labor law required bargaining on that topic. See also, Local 1186 of Council No. 4, AFSCME, AFL–CIO v. State Bd. of Labor Rel., 224 Conn. 666, 620 A.2d 766 (1993) (board must negotiate secondary impact of managerial decision to institute smoke-free workplace policy, as permitted by state law, if implementation has substantial secondary impact on working conditions).

(4) Exclusive Representation

p. 979: Add to Note 2

The National Labor Relations Act does not preempt enforcement by a state agency, acting in its proprietary capacity, of bidding specifications requiring all contractors working on the Boston harbor's large, publicly funded construction job to abide by a lawful, pre-hire, collective bargaining contract negotiated by private parties. Building and Construction Trades Council of the Metropolitan Dist. v. Associated Builders and Contractors of Massachusetts/Rhode Island, Inc., ___ U.S. ___, 113 S.Ct. 1190, 122 L.Ed.2d 565 (1993).

The Virginia Supreme Court ruled that private employees working at Washington National Airport did not have to join unions under the state's

Right–To–Work Law because, under applicable federal law, the state law takes precedence over federal labor law. Singleton v. International Assoc. of Machinists, 240 Va. 403, 397 S.E.2d 856 (1990).

(a) Union Security

p. 987: Add to Note 3

See also Mitchell v. Los Angeles Unified School Dist., 963 F.2d 258 (9th Cir.1992), cert. denied, ___ U.S. ___, 113 S.Ct. 375, 121 L.Ed.2d 287 (1993) (union which provides for non-members in bargaining unit an opportunity to object to portion of agency-shop dues spent on non-representational activities prior to deduction from paycheck does not also have to seek affirmative consent to deduction in order to satisfy first-amendment obligations).

(5) Dispute Resolution

(a) Arbitration

p. 988: Add to text citations

Rhode Island Brotherhood of Correctional Officers v. State, 643 A.2d 817 (R.I.1994) (reinstatement of officer was arbitrable *grievance* even though action taken pursuant to merit system); Municipality of Metropolitan Seattle v. Amalgamated Transit Union, 118 Wash.2d 639, 826 P.2d 167 (1992) (municipality has authority to enter into contract for *interest arbitration* of terms in collective bargaining agreement); City of Portsmouth v. Association of Portsmouth Teachers, NEA—New Hampshire, 134 N.H. 642, 597 A.2d 1063 (1991) (state statute did not preempt city's authority to prohibit *binding interest arbitration*). *Compare* Washington County Educational Classified Employees Assn. v. Board of Educ. of Washington County, 97 Md.App. 397, 629 A.2d 1330 (1993), cert. denied, 333 Md. 201, 634 A.2d 62 (1993) (board's unilateral modification of employees' salary step placement was integral part of reclassification process and beyond scope of lawful negotiation and arbitration), *with* Mayor v. Baltimore Fire Fighters, Local 734, 93 Md.App. 604, 613 A.2d 1023 (1992), cert. denied, 329 Md. 337, 619 A.2d 547 (1993) (fire commissioners' decisions to reduce staffing levels on engines and to limit employee use of accrued vacation leave prior to retirement were grievable and not so intimately involved with management prerogatives as to render them not subject to compulsory arbitration), *and* City of Danbury v. International Assn. of Firefighters, I.A.F.F., Local 801, 221 Conn. 244, 603 A.2d 393 (1992) (arbitration is mandatory and binding only on matters affecting wages, hours, and other conditions of employment; establishment of paramedic unit not a "condition of employment" and agreement to negotiate did not constitute agreement to mandatory, binding arbitration).

(b) Strikes—Their Use, Abuse and Control

p. 1004: Add to Note 3

Reichley by Wall v. North Penn School Dist., 533 Pa. 519, 626 A.2d 123 (1993), upheld the constitutionality of Public Employee Relations Act allowing strikes by public educators which may be enjoined on a showing that the strike "creates a clear and present danger or threat to the health, safety or welfare of the public."

d. Unionization and Municipal Finance

p. 1007: Add to first full paragraph of text

See generally, O. James Lighthizer, *The Pros and Cons of Privatization,* State Government News, February 1994, at 27.

C. PUBLIC EMPLOYEE CIVIL RIGHTS

1. EMPLOYEE FREEDOM OF ASSOCIATION AND EXPRESSION

p. 1009: Add to freedom of speech decisions

Waters v. Churchill, ___ U.S. ___, 114 S.Ct. 1878, 128 L.Ed.2d 686 (1994) (government must have reasonable and good faith belief as to substance of employee's speech before disciplining employee); Brown v. Polk County, Iowa, 37 F.3d 404 (8th Cir.1994) (public employer's requirements that employee refrain from using government resources to promote religious organization and that he remove religious articles, including a bible, from his office, do not violate employee's freedom of speech or religion); Kinsey v. Salado Indep. School Dist., 950 F.2d 988 (5th Cir.1992), cert. denied, ___ U.S. ___, 112 S.Ct. 2275, 119 L.Ed.2d 201 (1992) (removal of superintendent by board members whose election he opposed did not violate his freedom of speech and political association).

2. EMPLOYEE "PRIVACY" ISSUES

p. 1010–11: Add to *Informational Privacy*

Kurtz v. City of North Miami, 625 So.2d 899 (Fla.App.1993), review granted, 640 So.2d 1106 (Fla.1994) (city regulation requiring city job applicants to sign affidavit stating that they have not used tobacco or tobacco products for at least one year prior to application violates state constitutional right to privacy despite city's argument that it has compelling interest in saving taxpayer money by employing only healthy applicants); Eisenbud v. Suffolk County, 841 F.2d 42 (2d Cir.1988) (county's financial-disclosure ordinance that made demonstrable efforts to "narrowly target and focus the obligations of financial disclosure upon individuals who are most vulnerable to financial conflicts and pressures" upheld under heightened scrutiny as justified by strong government purpose which subordinated recognized privacy interest in avoiding disclosure of personal matters).

p. 1011–12: Add to *Testing For Drugs and Disease,* fourth paragraph

Even as to armed personnel involved in health and safety occupations, both the federal circuits and the state courts have continued to struggle with random-testing programs, and the need for individualized suspicion under the federal constitution. Provisions of state constitutions, possibly more strictly interpreted, must also be considered. See, e.g., Jackson v. Gates, 975 F.2d 648 (9th Cir.1992), cert. denied, ___ U.S. ___, 113 S.Ct. 2996, 125 L.Ed.2d 690 (1993) (discharge of police officer for failure to obey order directing him to submit to urinalysis drug testing following arrest of fellow officer with whom he had been seen in area known for drug sales was actionable under 42 U.S.C.A. § 1983, since the order was not based on articulable, individualized suspicion of drug use as required by fourth amendment); Ford v. Dowd, 931 F.2d 1286 (8th Cir.1991) (government drug testing of police officers, in absence of uniform or systematic random selection of subjects, is reasonable only if selection is based on specific, objective facts that support reasonable inferences and suspicion of drug use); Bolden v. Southeastern Pennsylvania Transportation Authority, 953 F.2d 807 (3d Cir. en banc 1991), cert. denied, ___ U.S. ___, 112 S.Ct. 2281, 119 L.Ed.2d 206 (1992) (public employee union may consent on behalf of an employee it represents to drug testing which implicates that employee's federal fourth-amendment rights); Guiney v. Police Comm'r of Boston, 411 Mass. 328, 582 N.E.2d 523 (1991) (random urinalysis of municipal police officers constituted unreasonable search under state constitution absent evidence of problems involving police officers' illicit use of drugs, and the likelihood that information from random testing will help to identify those whose on-duty performance will be harmed thereby).

The AIDs epidemic adds special complications to drug testing and privacy issues. In Anonymous Fireman v. City of Willoughby, 779 F.Supp. 402 (N.D.Ohio 1991), the court upheld the city's mandatory AIDS testing of firefighters and paramedics against fourth-amendment and privacy challenges, and found that, for employees at high risk of contracting and transmitting the disease, the city had a compelling interest in protecting the served public and other employees.

p. 1012: Add new paragraph

Other Constitutional Provisions. Federal and state constitutional provisions other than those above discussed may provide grounds to preserve public-employee interests. Opinion of the Justices (Furlough), 135 N.H. 625, 609 A.2d 1204 (1992), held that a requirement that state employees take unpaid leave violates the collective bargaining agreement, constitutes substantial contract impairment, and is neither reasonable nor necessary to important governmental interests. But the Contracts Clause and its state counterparts have not proven to be a strong barrier to contract alterations. See, e.g., Spiller v. State, 627 A.2d 513 (Me.1993) (statute establishing pension benefits for state employees did not create contractual rights so that modifications did not unconstitutionally impair contracts under either federal or state constitutions); Baltimore Teachers Union v. Mayor and City Council of Baltimore, 6 F.3d 1012 (4th Cir.1993), cert. denied, ___ U.S. ___, 114 S.Ct. 1127, 127 L.Ed.2d 435 (1994) (furlough of city employees to offset reductions in state aid not violative of Contract Clause); Opinion of the Justices (Furlough), 135 N.H. 625, 609 A.2d 1204 (N.H.1992).

Chapter X

LOCAL GOVERNMENT TORTS—STATE LAW

A. GOVERNMENTAL TORT LIABILITY AND IMMUNITY

p. 1017: Add to Note 3

North Dakota has joined the list of state jurisdictions where governmental immunity was judicially abrogated. Bulman v. Hulstrand Const. Co. and State of North Dakota, 521 N.W.2d 632 (N.D.1994).

1. EXCEPTIONS TO IMMUNITY DEFENSES

c. *Ministerial Actions*

p. 1032: Add new Note 4

4. **Policy-operational.** The difficulties of determining what acts are discretionary have moved some courts to venture a policy-oriented test for immunity. On the question whether the planning-operational test avoids those difficulties, consider the following opinion. See also Mullin v. Municipal City of South Bend, 639 N.E.2d 278 (Ind.1994).

DOE v. COFFEE COUNTY BOARD OF EDUCATION

Court of Appeal of Tennessee, 1993.
852 S.W.2d 899.

KOCH, JUDGE.

This appeal concerns a basketball coach who engaged in improper sexual activities with students at the high school where he worked. Four students and their parents filed suit in the Circuit Court for Coffee County against the coach, the school board, and four school employees. The trial court granted a summary judgment dismissing the claims against the school board and its employees based on the discretionary function exception to the Tennessee Governmental Tort Liability Act. It also dismissed two of the students' claims based on the statute of limitations. The students and their parents take issue on this appeal with the trial court's interpretation of the discretionary function exception and the statute of limitations. While we affirm the dismissal of the claims based on the statute of limitations, we find that the trial court erred by dismissing three of the remaining claims based on the discretionary function exception.

* * *

III.

We turn first to the statute of limitations defense. All the defendants assert that Jane Doe B's and Jane Doe D's claims and their father's derivative claim were not timely filed. The affected plaintiffs respond that the "discovery rule" tolled the running of the statute of limitations until Jane Doe B and Jane Doe D discovered that they had been "emotionally harmed."

Mr. Peercy's conduct is an invidious breach of the teacher-student relationship, and it warrants the severest possible condemnation by all right thinking persons of compassion. However, our decision with regard to the timeliness of these claims must be based on the statutes and precedents. Notwithstanding our revulsion for Mr. Peercy's conduct, we find no legal or equitable basis for preserving Jane Doe B's, Jane Doe D's, or their father's claims.

A.

Jane Doe B was a minor when Mr. Peercy committed sexual acts with her from November 1985 through November 1986. She had her eighteenth birthday on March 11, 1987, and she graduated from Central High School and enrolled in college later that year. Since she was a minor when the sexual conduct occurred, Tenn.Code Ann. § 28–1–106 (1980) postponed the running of the applicable statutes of limitation with regard to her claims until March 11, 1988. She did not file suit until November 17, 1989.

Jane Doe D was also a minor in late 1987 when she had her encounter with Mr. Peercy. She graduated from high school in 1988 and had her eighteenth birthday on August 17, 1988. Accordingly, as with Jane Doe B, Tenn.Code Ann. § 28–1–106 postponed the running of the statute of limitations with regard to her claim until August 17, 1989. Like her older sister, Jane Doe D did not file suit until November 17, 1989.

B.

We need not use this case as an occasion to incorporate the discovery rule into our statute of limitations jurisprudence since the Tennessee Supreme Court has already done so. The court first applied the discovery rule in 1974 in a surgical malpractice case. * * *

Under our formulation of the discovery rule, the statute of limitations begins to run when the injury occurs or when the plaintiff discovers or should have discovered that he or she has a right of action. * * * cause of action is deemed to be discovered when the plaintiff knows that he or she has been injured and who caused the injury. * * * Discovery is not postponed until the plaintiff becomes fully aware of all the injurious effects of the defendant's conduct. * * *

It tolls the running of the statute of limitations only during the period when the plaintiff has no knowledge at all that a wrong has occurred. * * *

C.

Both Jane Doe B and Jane Doe D concede that they knew that they had been victims of Mr. Peercy's wrongdoing even while the acts were occurring. * * *

IV.

Jane Doe B and Jane Doe D also urge this court to follow the lead of several other states that have used the post-traumatic stress syndrome to circumvent the statute of limitations in child sexual abuse cases. Since the General Assembly has already addressed this matter in Tenn. Code Ann. § 28–1–106, any further liberalization of statute is properly a legislative prerogative. Based on the undisputed facts, neither Jane Doe B nor Jane Doe D is entitled to take advantage of Tenn.Code Ann. § 28–1–106.

* * *

Jane Doe B and Jane Doe D have never totally repressed their memories of Mr. Peercy's conduct and have never been rendered incapable of attending to their business. Jane Doe B stated that the experience was "something I have tried so hard to forget" and that she "didn't want any one else to ever find out that anything had happened * * *" Her psychologist also stated that she remained "consciously aware that she had intercourse with the man" but that she "had tried to avoid dealing with the facts and the feelings."

Jane Doe D did not repress her memory of the incident because she discussed it with her boyfriend soon after it occurred. Even though she was angry, she "didn't want anybody to know it" and decided that she would not humiliate herself by talking about what happened to her until she found out "that other people were involved to a great extent." Thus, she did not tell her father about Mr. Peercy until her sister, Jane Doe C, told him that she too had been accosted by Mr. Peercy.

Neither Jane Doe B nor Jane Doe D may take advantage of Tenn. Code Ann. § 28–1–106 under these facts. By the time they filed suit, three years had elapsed since Jane Doe B's last sexual encounter with Mr. Peercy, and two years since Jane Doe D's. They did not repress the memory of the incidents and remained aware of their injuries and the wrongfulness of Mr. Peercy's conduct. Rather than being incapable of protecting their rights, they consciously chose not to pursue the matter to avoid embarrassment. Their reluctance to come forward cannot postpone the commencement of the running of either Tenn.Code Ann. § 28–3–104(a)(1) or Tenn.Code Ann. § 29–20–305(b).

V.

The remaining issue involves the school board's and its employees' Tenn.Code Ann. § 29–20–205(1) defense. The trial court summarily dismissed all claims against these defendants because it determined that the challenged acts involved "discretionary decisions." However, after the trial court granted the summary judgment, the Tennessee Supreme Court decided *Bowers v. City of Chattanooga,* 826 S.W.2d 427 (Tenn. 1992) which clarified and redefined the scope of the Tenn.Code Ann. § 29–20–205(1) defense. In light of the *Bowers* decision, we find that the school board and its employees have not demonstrated that they are entitled to a judgment as a matter of law under Tenn.Code Ann. § 29–20–205(1) with regard to all the plaintiffs' claims.

A.

Local governmental entities are immune from suit except when the General Assembly has, by statute, explicitly permitted them to be sued. *Fretwell v. Chaffin,* 652 S.W.2d 755, 756 (Tenn.1983); Tenn.Code Ann. § 29–20–201(a) (Supp.1992). In 1973 the General Assembly explicitly removed local governments' immunity from suit "for injury proximately caused by a negligent act or omission of any employee within the scope of his employment." Tenn.Code Ann. § 29–20–205. However, the General Assembly also carved out eight exceptions to this waiver of immunity, and it is the scope of one of these exceptions that is at issue in this case.

Tenn.Code Ann. § 29–20–205(1) embodies what is commonly referred to as the discretionary function exception. It provides that local governmental entities cannot be held liable for any negligent conduct that "[a]rises out of the exercise or performance or the failure to exercise or perform a discretionary function, whether or not this discretion is abused." The Tennessee Governmental Tort Liability Act does not define "discretionary function", and thus the defense has proved to be somewhat of an enigma to the courts. *Bowers v. City of Chattanooga,* 826 S.W.2d at 430; 5 Kenneth C. Davis, *Administrative Law Treatise* § 27:11 (2d ed. 1984) ("Davis").

Traditionally our courts, like most of their counterparts in other jurisdictions, developed and used literal, rather rigid, tests based on the distinction between discretionary and ministerial functions. *Hale v. Johnston,* 140 Tenn. 182, 197, 203 S.W. 949, 953 (1918). Earlier this year, the Tennessee Supreme Court abandoned the discretionary-ministerial test in favor of the planning-operational test. Under the new test,

> decisions that rise to the level of planning or policy-making are considered discretionary acts which do not give rise to tort liability, while decisions that are merely operational are not considered discretionary acts and, therefore, do not give rise to immunity.

Bowers v. City of Chattanooga, 826 S.W.2d at 430.

The planning-operational test did not spring full-grown from the Supreme Court's judicial ingenuity. It is the culmination of jurisprudential efforts that have been taking place in the federal courts and other state courts for many years. Thus, looking to other jurisdictions' precedents concerning the planning-operational test can provide us with helpful guidance concerning the proper interpretation of the *Bowers* decision.

The *Bowers* decision wrought a "fundamental, sound, and durable" change in the scope of the discretionary function exception. *See* Kenneth C. Davis, *Administrative Law of the Eighties* § 27:11, at 446 (Supp.1989). Now, "discretionary function immunity attaches to all conduct properly involving the balancing of policy considerations" or to "operational act[s] * * * where * * * the operational actor is properly charged with balancing policy considerations." *Bowers v. City of Chattanooga,* 826 S.W.2d at 431. Thus, the focus has shifted from the decision-maker to the decision itself. *See United States v. Gaubert,* 499 U.S. ___, ___, ___, 111 S.Ct. 1267, 1273, 113 L.Ed.2d 335 (1991).

Our Supreme Court has equated "planning" with governmental actions and decisions involving public policy considerations. Thus, following the United States Supreme Court's interpretation of the principle,

> the discretionary function exception insulates the Government from liability if the action challenged in the case involves the permissible exercise of policy judgment.

Berkovitz v. United States, 486 U.S. 531, 537, 108 S.Ct. 1954, 1959, 100 L.Ed.2d 531 (1988). In the words of Professor Davis, " 'discretion' is no longer the key to the discretionary function exception. 'Policy' is." Kenneth C. Davis, *Administrative Law of the Eighties* § 27:12, at 448 (Supp.1989).

Identifying the governmental decisions and actions that involve policy judgment requires a consideration of the original purpose of the discretionary function exemption. The purpose of the Tennessee Governmental Tort Liability Act is to define the circumstances when local governmental entities may be sued for negligence as if they were a private person. Tenn.Code Ann. § 29–20–206 (1980). In recognition of the constitutional principle of separation of powers, the discretionary function exception was intended to prevent the use of tort actions to second-guess what are essentially executive or legislative decisions involving social, political, economic, scientific, or professional policies or some mixture of these policies. *United States v. Gaubert,* 499 U.S. at ___–___, 111 S.Ct. at 1273–74; *Bowers v. City of Chattanooga,* 826 S.W.2d at 431; Davis § 27:13, at 73; W. Page Keeton, *Prosser and Keeton on the Law of Torts* § 131, at 1039 (5th ed. 1984).

In light of *Bowers,* we construe Tenn.Code Ann. § 29–20–205(1) to prevent the use of tort actions to challenge policy but not necessarily to prevent challenging the government's conduct in implementing policy. *Aslakson v. United States,* 790 F.2d 688, 693 (8th Cir.1986). Conduct specifically required by pre-existing statutes, regulations, policies, or standards cannot give rise to liability because the conduct is not the product of judgment or choice. *Berkovitz v. United States,* 486 U.S. at 536, 108 S.Ct. at 1958–59; *Nusbaum v. Blue Earth County,* 422 N.W.2d 713, 723 (Minn.1988). However, conduct that fails to comply with legal requirements may give rise to liability. *Aslakson v. United States,* 790 F.2d at 692; *Bowers v. City of Chattanooga,* 826 S.W.2d at 431.

B.

Applying the discretionary function exception requires a thorough examination of the challenged conduct, the decision-making process producing the conduct, and the propriety of permitting the courts to review the decision. *Bowers v. City of Chattanooga,* 826 S.W.2d at 431. Thus, we must now turn our attention to the specific conduct on which the complaint is based.

* * *

The trial court found that each of these acts were covered by the discretionary function exception in Tenn.Code Ann. § 29–20–205(1). While we agree that the adoption and enforcement of an effective sexual abuse policy is a discretionary function, we do not agree that Tenn.Code Ann. § 29–20–205(1) shields the school board and its employees from liability for the other challenged conduct.

The Negligent Hiring Claim

We turn first to the negligent hiring claim. The plaintiffs assert that the school board and its staff were negligent because their pre-employment investigation into Mr. Peercy's background did not uncover earlier sexual misconduct. The record, however, contains no reliable proof that Mr. Peercy had ever engaged in sexual misconduct with students prior to being employed at Central High School and is silent concerning the additional steps that the school board should have taken in the hiring process.

The courts that have been called upon to determine whether hiring a governmental employee is a discretionary act are not in agreement. Those applying the planning-operational test hold that hiring is an operational decision and, therefore, that hiring does not fit within the discretionary function exception. *Brantly v. Dade County Sch. Bd.,* 493 So.2d 471, 472 (Fla.Dist.Ct.App.1986); *Willis v. Dade County Sch. Bd.,* 411 So.2d 245, 246 (Fla.Dist.Ct.App.1982); *Pacifico v. Froggatt,* 249 N.J.Super. 153, 591 A.2d 1387, 1389 (Ct.Law Div.1991). Those applying the traditional discretionary-ministerial test hold to the contrary. *Foster v. Pearcy,* 387 N.E.2d 446, 449–50 (Ind.1979); *Rosacrans v. Kingon,* 154 Mich.App. 381, 397 N.W.2d 317, 319 (1986); *Mon v. City of New York,* 78 N.Y.2d 309, 574 N.Y.S.2d 529, 533, 579 N.E.2d 689, 693 (1991).

We find that the Supreme Court narrowed the scope of the discretionary function exception when it adopted the planning-operational test in *Bowers v. City of Chattanooga.* Accordingly, like the courts in Florida and New Jersey, we find that the hiring of governmental employees is not a discretionary act in every instance.

Adopting policies and procedures governing the hiring of employees is clearly a planning function that will not give rise to liability under Tenn.Code Ann. § 29–20–205. Likewise, hiring decisions made in conformance with applicable statutes, ordinances, policies and procedures are not amenable to suit. However, hiring decisions that fail to comply with applicable legal requirements may give rise to liability if the failure to follow the requirements is the proximate cause of injury.

The record before us contains little evidence concerning the policies and procedures governing the hiring of teachers and coaches in Coffee County. While state law contains several general requirements for all persons employed as teachers, it does not prescribe the procedures to be used for screening job applicants. It simply requires that teachers must submit written employment applications. Tenn.Code Ann. § 49–5–406(a) (Supp.1992). The record contains no evidence concerning the personnel requirements, policies, or procedures that the local school board may have adopted.

With the record in its present condition, we cannot determine with any reliability whether the manner in which the school board hired Mr. Peercy complied with the applicable requirements for hiring teachers and coaches in Coffee County. Accordingly, since hiring teachers is not presumptively a discretionary function, we find that the school board and its employees have not demonstrated that they are entitled to a judgment as a matter of law on this claim.

Our holding that Tenn.Code Ann. § 29–20–205(1) is inapplicable to the negligent hiring claim under the facts so far developed does not imply that the plaintiffs will or even should prevail on this claim. In order to recover, the plaintiffs must prove that the defendants did not comply with the policies and procedures governing the employment of teachers and that their acts were negligent and proximately caused the plaintiffs' injuries.

The Implementation of a Sexual Abuse Policy

The plaintiffs have not pointed to, and our research has failed to find, any legal requirement that local school boards adopt and enforce an effective sexual abuse policy. Adopting such a policy is precisely the type of conduct that Tenn.Code Ann. § 29–20–205(1) is intended to insulate from suit under the Tennessee Governmental Tort Liability Act. The courts should not second-guess governmental entities in policy matters, and accordingly, we hold that the school board's failure to adopt or enforce a sexual abuse policy falls within the discretionary function exception.

The Installation of Locks Claim

The record contains little proof concerning the school board's or Central High School's policies concerning security of the school building or its contents, placing locks on doors, or employees' access to keys. Thus, we cannot determine whether permitting Mr. Peercy to change the lock on his office door was consistent or contrary to existing policy. If it was consistent, then permitting Mr. Peercy to change his locks will not give rise to liability. If the acts were contrary to policy, the defendants will be liable only if the plaintiffs prove that permitting Mr. Peercy to change the locks on his office door was negligent and was the proximate cause of Jane Doe A's and Jane Doe C's injuries.

The Failure to Report Claim

Teachers and other school officials and personnel have a legal obligation to report suspected child sexual abuse to the Department of Human Services. Tenn.Code Ann. §§ 37–1–403(a)(4), 37–1–605(a)(4) (1991). Thus, teachers like Marion Brandon have a non-discretionary duty to report students' complaints of child sexual abuse. Their failure to do so can give rise to liability under Tenn.Code Ann. § 29–20–205 and does not fall within the discretionary act exception in Tenn.Code Ann. § 29–20–205(1).

As with any other negligence claim, civil damage liability for failing to report complaints of child sexual abuse will only arise when it proximately causes injury to another. Under the facts in this record, it is unlikely that Jane Doe A or Jane Doe C will be able to establish a causal connection between their injuries and Mrs. Brandon's alleged failure to report their complaints concerning Mr. Peercy to the Department of Human Services. Taking the plaintiffs' allegations as true even though they are contested by Mrs. Brandon, Mrs. Brandon did not receive the complaints about Mr. Peercy's conduct until after the incidents involving Jane Doe A and Jane Doe C had already occurred.

VI.

In summary, we affirm the summary judgment dismissing the claims of Jane Doe B and Jane Doe D against all defendants because they are barred by the statute of limitations. We also affirm the summary judgment dismissing the claims based on the failure to adopt and enforce an effective sexual abuse policy. We vacate the remaining portions of the summary judgment because the school board and its employees have not demonstrated as a matter of law that the challenged conduct is protected by Tenn.Code Ann. § 29–20–205(1). We remand the case for further proceedings consistent with this opinion and tax the costs of the appeal to the Coffee County Board of Education.

LEWIS and CANTRELL, JJ., concur.

p. 1033: Add to Note 1

The classification of a relationship as that of master and servant, pointing to respondeat superior, or independent contractor has renewed importance with increasing privatization of government services. See, e.g., Smith v. Porter Township, Clinton County, 141 Pa.Cmwlth. 244, 595 A.2d 693 (1991).

d. "Special Duty" Doctrines

p. 1040: Add to Note 1

Peck v. Siau, 65 Wash.App. 285, 827 P.2d 1108 (1992), review denied, 120 Wash.2d 1005, 838 P.2d 1142 (1992) (in absence of actual or imputable knowledge of teacher's actions, school district held not liable for failing to maintain safe premises); Allison Gas Turbine Div. of Gen'l Motors Corp. v. District of Columbia, 642 A.2d 841 (D.C.App.1994) (police officers' conduct of rescue operations and interference with private rescue efforts at helicopter crash site were integral to their general duty to the public and do not involve special relationship that would render city liable).

The courts of Massachusetts and New Hampshire have rejected the public duty/special relationship analysis as serving to revive old immunity doctrines. Acknowledging that failing to protect the government in the exercise of a "public duty" might increase its exposure to liability, those courts note that the plaintiff still must prove the case and that damages have been capped at reasonable ceilings. Jean W. v. Commonwealth, 414 Mass. 496, 610 N.E.2d 305 (1993); Doucette v. Town of Bristol, 138 N.H. 205, 635 A.2d 1387 (1993).

p. 1043–44: Add to (e) *Police Protection*

In Doe v. Calumet City, 161 Ill.2d 374, 204 Ill.Dec. 274, 641 N.E.2d 498 (1994), the court found no special relationship to impose a duty on a police officer to rescue children from their mother's rapist who locked himself and her children in her apartment, since the officer had not initiated the circumstances that caused the harm. But the court found that liability might arise independently of a special relationship, on allegations of willful and wanton conduct and intentional infliction of emotional distress, grounds which are exceptions to the public duty doctrine.

p. 1045: Add to "Public Educational Institutions"

Cf. Eisel v. Board of Educ. of Montgomery County, 324 Md. 376, 597 A.2d 447 (1991) (common law duty of school counselors to prevent student's threatened suicide may include warning the parents when information concerning that student's suicidal intentions is received).

2. PUBLIC TORT CLAIMS STATUTES

a. Legislated Restoration or Modification of Common Law Immunity

p. 1051: Add at end of first sentence in last paragraph

Crowell v. City of Philadelphia, 531 Pa. 400, 613 A.2d 1178 (1992) (city can be subjected to liability despite presence of an additional tortfeasor, where facts fall squarely within statutory exception to immunity and city's actions would be sufficient to preclude it from obtaining indemnity from another for injuries rendered to third person).

p. 1052: Add to *Waiver by Insurance,* second paragraph

Khawaja v. City of Rockville, 89 Md.App. 314, 598 A.2d 489 (1991), cert. granted, 325 Md. 551, 601 A.2d 1114 (1992) (municipal waiver of immunity to extent of insurance). Cf. Googe v. Florida Int'l Indemnity Co., 262 Ga. 546, 422 S.E.2d 552 (1992) (member of the public does not qualify as third party beneficiary of municipal liability insurance absent legislatively mandated insurance coverage, and thus lacked standing to seek reformation of insurance policy issued to protect government agency).

3. STATUTORY RESTRICTIONS ON TORT REMEDIES

a. Time Bars—Claim Notices and Suit

p. 1054: Add to Note 1, second paragraph

Johnson v. Maryland State Police, 331 Md. 285, 628 A.2d 162 (1993) (notice requirement not tolled during plaintiff's minority and lack of prejudicial delay does not an excuse default of notice; requirement is constitutional).

c. Dollar Limits On Recoveries

p. 1057: Add after second *Smith* case in first paragraph of text

Colorado v. DeFoor, 824 P.2d 783 (Colo.1992), cert. denied, ___ U.S. ___, 113 S.Ct. 483, 121 L.Ed.2d 387 (1992) (statute fixing damage ceilings on state tort liability does not violate federal or state equal protection provisions or state constitutional right of access to courts); cf. Peters v. Saft, 597 A.2d 50 (Me.1991) (statutory recovery cap of $250,000 on non-medical damages from server of liquor held constitutional under federal and state constitutions).

p. 1058: Add to *Punitive Damages*

Following *Haslip,* the Supreme Court examined other due-process objections to punitive damages. The due process prohibition of grossly excessive awards did not require rejection of a ten million dollar punitive damage award in TXO Production Corp. v. Alliance Resources Corp., ___ U.S. ___, 113 S.Ct. 2711, 125 L.Ed.2d 366 (1993). But due process barriers to arbitrary imposition of such damages required invalidation of an Oregon system which was seen as a denial of judicial review of punitive-damage awards in Honda Motor Co. v. Oberg, ___ U.S. ___, 114 S.Ct. 2331, 129 L.Ed.2d 336 (1994). The lower federal and the state courts have added their views of due process limitations. See, e.g., Dunn v. HOVIC, 13 F.3d 58 (3d Cir. en banc, 1993), cert. denied, ___ U.S. ___, 114 S.Ct. 650, 126 L.Ed.2d 608 (1994) (imposition of successive punitive damage awards against single defendant in mass torts cases arising from same series of events does not violate Due Process Clause); Hodges v. S.C. Toof & Co., 833 S.W.2d 896 (Tenn.1992) (announcing a new procedure designed to guide the jury in awarding punitives, including requirement that plaintiff establish defendant's actions as intentional, fraudulent, malicious, or reckless in order to receive punitive damages). An attempt to treat punitive damages as a species of fines, by requiring recipients to pay one third of punitive recoveries to the state treasury, was invalidated as an unconstitutional taking without just compensation. Kirk v. Denver Publishing Co., 818 P.2d 262 (Colo. en banc 1991).

B. LIABILITY OF INDIVIDUAL OFFICERS AND EMPLOYEES

p. 1064: Add to Note

The quandary of ascertaining which levels of employee action qualify as discretionary and as entitled to the shield of tort immunity continues to vex the courts, particularly with regard to police activity. The varying rationales for immunizing municipalities and against immunizing individuals for discretionary acts complicates that process. For example, in a police-pursuit case, if the city is potentially liable while the officer is potentially immune, the ensuing investigation into the officer's exercise of judgment in order to reach a conclusion against the city would undo all the protection for the officer intended by official immunity. One solution is to award vicarious immunity to the city. See, e.g., Pletan v. Gaines, 494 N.W.2d 38 (Minn. 1992) (immunity of police officer extended to employer in suit by parents of student killed by fleeing suspects' automobile). An alternative solution would be specific legislation to govern the nettlesome problem of police pursuits. See, e.g., Colvin v. City of Gardena, 11 Cal.App.4th 1270, 15 Cal.Rptr.2d 234 (1992); cf. Tice v. Cramer, 133 N.J. 347, 627 A.2d 1090 (1993) (police in pursuit granted absolute immunity by state tort claims act).

Where police officers are not involved, even though there is some "discretion" in interacting with members of the public, the confinement of immunity to its appropriate policy objectives may not be as difficult. See, e.g., Hudson v. Town of East Montpelier, 161 Vt. 168, 638 A.2d 561 (1993) (employee who had discretion in deciding how best to cover a ledge and place warnings there was not entitled to immunity for alleged negligence in covering the ledge with gravel; the decisions in question did not involve weighing of type of public policy considerations that would warrant shielding).

Courts may refine the discretionary-act immunity of individuals by adding nuances to the general doctrine that in reality revise it. For example, the Connecticut Supreme Court has said that its cases recognize three exceptions to a municipal employee's qualified immunity for discretionary acts, namely: where action or inaction would likely subject an identifiable person to immediate harm; where a statute specifically provides a cause of action for failure to enforce certain laws; and where the employee acted with malice, wantonness, or intent to injure. Burns v. Board of Educ., 228 Conn. 640, 645, 638 A.2d 1, 3 (1994). Compare the *McCorkle* case on p. 1066 of the principal text.

Another refinement, often called the "Fireman's Rule," bars claims by a police officer or firefighter against the city for a fellow officer's or firefighter's negligence as long as the injury arose from the special risks normally associated with the duties of the actor. See, e.g., Cooper v. City of New York, 81 N.Y.2d 584, 601 N.Y.S.2d 432, 619 N.E.2d 369 (1993).

Chapter XI

LOCAL GOVERNMENT TORTS—FEDERAL LAW

B. LOCAL GOVERNMENT LIABILITY UNDER § 1983

p. 1072: Add to Note 2, first paragraph

Hafer v. Melo, 502 U.S. 21, 112 S.Ct. 358, 116 L.Ed.2d 301 (1991) (holding that the *Will* case does not preclude individual liability of state officers, as persons under § 1983, for actions taken in their official capacities and that the eleventh amendment does not bar the suit in federal court for their conduct); cf. Jackson v. Georgia Dept. of Transportation, 16 F.3d 1573 (11th Cir.1994), cert. denied, ___ U.S. ___, 115 S.Ct. 320, 130 L.Ed.2d 281 (1994) (state liability fund to indemnify employees for personal liability for damages does not render state the real party in interest for eleventh-amendment purposes when employees are sued in their individual capacities).

p. 1073: Add to fourth paragraph of Note 2

See Hess v. Port Authority Trans–Hudson Corp., ___ U.S. ___, 115 S.Ct. 394, 130 L.Ed.2d 245 (1994), reported, supra at p. 24, where the Court held that the Port Authority Trans–Hudson Corporation, a wholly owned subsidiary of a bistate agency created by interstate compact, was not an arm of the state, entitled to sovereign immunity from suit in federal court under the eleventh amendment. See generally, Alex E. Rogers, *Clothing State Governmental Entities With Sovereign Immunity: Disarray in the Eleventh Amendment Arm-of-the-State Doctrine,* 92 Colum.L.Rev. 1243 (1992) (in deciding whether to shield a political subdivision under the eleventh amendment, courts look at: the entity's functions, characteristics, and powers; the state-law classification; the degree of state control and supervision, the entity's "jural independence"; the likelihood that judgment will be satisfied against the state treasury; and the classification of the entity's functions as governmental or proprietary).

1. THE RANGE OF FEDERAL RIGHTS PROTECTED BY 42 U.S.C. § 1983

a. *Rights Founded in Federal Statutes*

p. 1076: Add to Note 2

Annis v. County of Westchester, New York, 36 F.3d 251 (2d Cir.1994) (Title VII is not exclusive remedy for employment discrimination so as to preclude police officer from bringing claim of sexual harassment under § 1983 as a violation of equal protection); Beardsley v. Webb, 30 F.3d 524 (4th Cir.1994) (damages and jury trial provisions of the 1991 Civil Rights Act were not intended to make Title VII exclusive remedy; hence employee may seek recovery for employment discrimination under § 1983); Lampkin v. District of Columbia, 27 F.3d 605 (D.C.Cir.1994), cert. denied, ___ U.S. ___, 115 S.Ct. 578, 130 L.Ed.2d 493 (1994) (McKinney Act provisions that describe actions states must take with respect to education of homeless children are sufficiently specific to create substantive rights which parents of homeless children may enforce in a private action under § 1983).

b. *Rights Founded in the Constitution*

p. 1085: Add to Note 2

Questions regarding the appropriate characterization of constitutional grievances and rights are well illustrated by the various opinions in Albright v. Oliver, ___ U.S. ___, 114 S.Ct. 807, 127 L.Ed.2d 114 (1994). The Court upheld dismissal of a suit based upon a substantive due process claim (liberty interest) to be free from criminal prosecution without probable cause. (The plaintiff's prosecution had been dismissed pre-trial because the conduct and charge did not constitute an offense under the state's law.) But the justices parted in their views of possible constitutional claims that the facts might have supported. Four (the Chief Justice and Justices O'Connor, Scalia, and Ginsburg) mentioned the fourth amendment but declined to express a view on its applicability because petitioner had not raised it. Justice Kennedy, with Justice Thomas concurring, viewed the case as one of malicious initiation of a baseless prosecution for which no due process standard was available. Justice Souter found no support for the claim in due process.

The confusion between substantive due process rights and specifically protected constitutional rights has arisen most frequently in arrests and certain pretrial matters where the lines of demarcation among due process, the fourth amendment, and the eighth amendment remain blurred. Compare the *relative* ease of finding the correct constitutional standard in first amendment cases. McDonald v. City of Freeport, 834 F.Supp. 921 (S.D.Tex. 1993) (dismissal of police officers for speaking out as "whistleblowers").

Add to Note 3, second paragraph

Recent cases of interest on the scope of protected "liberty interests" include: Valmonte v. Bane, 18 F.3d 992 (2d Cir.1994) (plaintiff's showing of the high risk of error in statutory scheme keeping plaintiff's name on register of child abusers sufficient to prove due process violation, not just state law defamation, notwithstanding administrative hearing that produced "some credible evidence"; Crumpton v. Gates, 947 F.2d 1418 (9th Cir.1991) (even though father was killed when child was fetus, child's allegation that he was deprived at birth of liberty interest in familial paternal companionship as a result of city police "death squad's" killing is actionable under § 1983).

Add to end of second paragraph, Note 3

Cf. United States v. James Daniel Good Real Property, ___ U.S. ___, 114 S.Ct. 492, 126 L.Ed.2d 490 (1993) (real property used in drug transactions may not be forfeited without pre-seizure notice and opportunity for hearing; principle that as to persons the fourth amendment alone contains sufficient procedural protections without augmentation by the fifth amendment is distinguishable).

Add new paragraph to Note 3

As noted elsewhere, alleged constitutional violations must be complete before a § 1983 action will be entertained. Thus, in an alleged taking without compensation, efforts to avoid the taking and to seek compensation must have failed before the matter is ripe for decision. In allegations of denial of procedural due process, the denial must have occurred in fact. The assertion of a procedural due process violation based, not upon a state-designed pattern of conduct, but rather upon a random, unauthorized occurrence, is complete only if the state does not provide appropriate remedial process. If the matter is redressable under appropriate state process, the complainant is relegated to that process. *Compare* Parratt v. Taylor, 451 U.S. 527, 101 S.Ct. 1908, 68 L.Ed. 420 (1981), partially overruled on other grounds, Daniels v. Williams, 447 U.S. 327, 330, and Charbonnet v. Lee, 951 F.2d 638 (5th Cir.1992), cert. denied, ___ U.S. ___, 112 S.Ct. 2994, 120 L.Ed.2d 871 (1992), *with* Zinermon v. Burch, 494 U.S. 113, 110 S.Ct. 975, 108 L.Ed.2d 100 (1990).

c. *Rights Founded in "Special Duties"*

p. 1090: Add to *Students in Public School Custody*

DeShaney did not serve to diminish the number of relevant questions regarding possible fourteenth-amendment duties to protect students, the nature of compulsory education, and the possible special relationships created by that context. Courts with some discomfort find that compulsory attendance laws do not create special relationships even during school hours or after-school events. See, e.g., D.R. v. Middle Bucks Area Vocational Tech. School, 1991 WL 276292 (3d Cir.1991), on rehearing 972 F.2d 1364 (3d Cir.1992), cert. denied, ___ U.S. ___, 113 S.Ct. 1045, 122 L.Ed.2d 354 (1993); Maldonado v. Josey, 975 F.2d 727 (10th Cir.1992), cert. denied, ___ U.S. ___, 113 S.Ct. 1266, 122 L.Ed.2d 662 (1993); Leffall v. Dallas Indep. School Dist., 28 F.3d 521 (5th Cir.1994). Compare Doe v. Taylor Indep. School Dist., 975 F.2d 137 (5th Cir.1992), cert. denied, ___ U.S. ___, 113 S.Ct. 1066, 122 L.Ed.2d 371 (1993). When compelled attendance is coupled with residential custody, however, the special relationship may be easier to establish. Walton v. Alexander, 20 F.3d 1350 (5th Cir.1994) (residential, special-educational program). See William D. Valente, *Liability For Teacher Sexual Misconduct With Students,* 74 Ed.Law Rep. 1021 (1992).

Add to Note 3

Gregory v. Rogers, cited in Note 3, was reversed by the court en banc. 974 F.2d 1006 (8th Cir.1992), cert. denied, ___ U.S. ___, 113 S.Ct. 1265, 122 L.Ed. 661 (1993) (trier of fact could not reasonably find that officers knew or should have known that passengers were intoxicated, and even had they such knowledge, they could not foresee the designated-driver's abdication of responsibilities by leaving the keys in the car).

d. Rights Founded Upon an Official "Policy" of Deliberate Indifference

p. 1095: Insert before Note 1 the following case

COLLINS v. CITY OF HARKER HEIGHTS

Supreme Court of the United States, 1992.
503 U.S. 115, 112 S.Ct. 1061, 117 L.Ed.2d 261.

JUSTICE STEVENS delivered the opinion of the Court.

The question presented is whether § 1 of the Civil Rights Act of 1871, 42 U.S.C. § 1983, provides a remedy for a municipal employee who is fatally injured in the course of his employment because the city customarily failed to train or warn its employees about known hazards in the workplace. Even though the city's conduct may be actionable under state law, we hold that § 1983 does not apply because such conduct does not violate the Due Process Clause.

On October 21, 1988, Larry Michael Collins, an employee in the sanitation department of the city of Harker Heights, Texas, died of asphyxia after entering a manhole to unstop a sewer line. Petitioner, his widow, brought this action alleging that Collins "had a constitutional right to be free from unreasonable risks of harm to his body, mind and emotions and a constitutional right to be protected from the city of Harker Heights' custom and policy of deliberate indifference toward the safety of its employees." App. 7. Her complaint alleged that the city violated that right by following a custom and policy of not training its employees about the dangers of working in sewer lines and manholes, not providing safety equipment at job sites, and not providing safety warnings. The complaint also alleged that a prior incident had given the city notice of the risks of entering the sewer lines and that the city had systematically and intentionally failed to provide the equipment and training required by a Texas statute. *Ibid.* The District Court dismissed the complaint on the ground that a constitutional violation had not been alleged. No. W–89–CA–168 (W.D.Tex., Oct. 30, 1988), App. 20. The Court of Appeals for the Fifth Circuit affirmed on a different theory. 916 F.2d 284 (CA5 1990). It did not reach the question whether the city had violated Collins' constitutional rights because it denied recovery on the ground that there had been no "abuse of governmental power," which the Fifth Circuit had found to be a necessary element of a § 1983 action.[2] *Id.*, at 287–288, and n. 3.

The contrary decision in *Ruge v. City of Bellevue,* 892 F.2d 738 (CA8 1989), together with our concern about the Court of Appeals' interpretation of the statute, prompted our grant of certiorari, 499 U.S. ___, 111 S.Ct. 1579, 113 L.Ed.2d 644 (1991).

I

Our cases do not support the Court of Appeals' reading of § 1983 as requiring proof of an abuse of governmental power separate and apart from the proof of a constitutional violation. Although the statute provides the citizen with an effective remedy against those abuses of state power that violate federal law, it does not provide a remedy for abuses that do not violate federal law, see, *e.g., Martinez v. California,* 444 U.S. 277, 100 S.Ct. 553, 62 L.Ed.2d 481 (1980), *DeShaney v. Winnebago County Department of Social Services,* 489 U.S. 189, 109 S.Ct. 998, 103 L.Ed.2d 249 (1989). More importantly, the statute does not draw any distinction between abusive and nonabusive federal violations.

The Court of Appeals' analysis rests largely on the fact that the city had, through allegedly tortious conduct, harmed one of its employees rather than an ordinary citizen over whom it exercised governmental power. The employment relationship, however, is not of controlling significance. On the one hand, if the city had pursued a policy of equally deliberate indifference to the safety of pedestrians that resulted in a fatal injury to one who inadvertently stepped into an open manhole, the Court of Appeals' holding would not speak to this situation at all, although it would seem that a claim by such a pedestrian should be analyzed in a similar manner as the claim by this petitioner. On the other hand, a logical application of the holding might also bar potentially meritorious claims by employees if, for example, the city had given an employee a particularly dangerous assignment in retaliation for a political speech, cf. *St. Louis v. Praprotnik,* 485 U.S. 112, 108 S.Ct. 915, 99 L.Ed.2d 107 (1988), or because of his or her gender, cf. *Monell v. New York City Dept. of Social Services,* 436 U.S. 658, 98 S.Ct. 2018, 56 L.Ed.2d 611 (1978). The First Amendment, the Equal Protection and Due Process Clauses of

2. The Court of Appeals explained:

"The question presented in this case is whether a plaintiff seeking recovery under § 1983 for injury to a governmental employee must demonstrate, *inter alia,* that the conduct in issue was an abuse of *governmental* power. More particularly, does alleged wrongful conduct by government—in its capacity as employer rather than as a governing authority—that deprives its employee of an alleged constitutional right give rise to a § 1983 action? We base our holding on the abuse of government power standard, separate from the constitutional deprivation element or standard. The district court appears to have merged those two standards, which are among those necessary for bringing § 1983 into play here. In reviewing this Rule 12(b)(6) dismissal, we will keep them separate.

* * *

"In this Circuit, there is a separate standard that must also be satisfied—an abuse of government power. While this element is in many ways similar to, and often blends with, other necessary elements for a § 1983 action, such as deprivation of a constitutional right, and springs from the same sources as the deprivation element, it is separate nonetheless." 916 F.2d 284, 286–287 (CA5 1990).

the Fourteenth Amendment, and other provisions of the Federal Constitution afford protection to employees who serve the government as well as to those who are served by them, and § 1983 provides a cause of action for all citizens injured by an abridgement of those protections. Neither the fact that petitioner's decedent was a government employee nor the characterization of the city's deliberate indifference to his safety as something other than an "abuse of governmental power" is a sufficient reason for refusing to entertain petitioner's federal claim under § 1983.

Nevertheless, proper analysis requires us to separate two different issues when a § 1983 claim is asserted against a municipality: (1) whether plaintiff's harm was caused by a constitutional violation, and (2) if so, whether the city is responsible for that violation. See *Oklahoma City v. Tuttle,* 471 U.S. 808, 817, 105 S.Ct. 2427, 2433, 85 L.Ed.2d 791 (1985) (opinion of REHNQUIST, J.); *id.,* at 828–829, 105 S.Ct., at 2438–2439 (opinion of BRENNAN, J., concurring in part and concurring in judgment). Because most of our opinions discussing municipal policy have involved the latter issue, it is appropriate to discuss it before considering the question whether petitioner's complaint has alleged a constitutional violation.

* * *

Our purpose in citing these cases is to emphasize the separate character of the inquiry into the question of municipal responsibility and the question whether a constitutional violation occurred. It was necessary to analyze whether execution of a municipal policy inflicted the injury in these cases because, unlike ordinary tort litigation, the doctrine of *respondeat superior* was inapplicable. The city is not vicariously liable under § 1983 for the constitutional torts of its agents: It is only liable when it can be fairly said that the city itself is the wrongdoer. Because petitioner in this case relies so heavily on our reasoning in *Canton v. Harris,* 489 U.S. 378, 109 S.Ct. 1197, 103 L.Ed.2d 412 (1989)—and in doing so, seems to assume that the case dealt with the constitutional issue—it is appropriate to comment specifically on that case. * * * We did not suggest that all harm-causing municipal policies are actionable under § 1983 or that all such policies are unconstitutional. Moreover, we rejected the city's argument that only unconstitutional policies can create municipal liability under the statute. *Id.,* at 387, 109 S.Ct., at 1204. Instead, we concluded that if a city employee violates another's constitutional rights, the city may be liable if it had a policy or custom of failing to train its employees and that failure to train caused the constitutional violation. In particular, we held that the inadequate training of police officers could be characterized as the cause of the constitutional tort if—and only if—the failure to train amounted to "deliberate indifference" to the rights of persons with whom the police come into contact. *Id.,* at 388, 109 S.Ct., at 1204.

Although the term "deliberate indifference" has been used in other contexts to define the threshold for finding a violation of the Eighth

Amendment, see *Estelle v. Gamble,* 429 U.S. 97, 104, 97 S.Ct. 285, 291, 50 L.Ed.2d 251 (1976), as we have explained, that term was used in the *Canton* case for the quite different purpose of identifying the threshold for holding a city responsible for the constitutional torts committed by its inadequately trained agents. In this case, petitioner has used that term to characterize the city's failure to train the employees in its sanitation department. We assume for the purpose of decision that the allegations in the complaint are sufficient to provide a substitute for the doctrine of *respondeat superior* as a basis for imposing liability on the city for the tortious conduct of its agents, but that assumption does not confront the question whether the complaint has alleged a constitutional violation. To that question we now turn.

III

Petitioner's constitutional claim rests entirely on the Due Process Clause of the Fourteenth Amendment. The most familiar office of that Clause is to provide a guarantee of fair procedure in connection with any deprivation of life, liberty, or property by a State. Petitioner, however, does not advance a procedural due process claim in this case. Instead, she relies on the substantive component of the Clause that protects individual liberty against "certain government actions regardless of the fairness of the procedures used to implement them." *Daniels v. Williams,* 474 U.S. 327, 331, 106 S.Ct. 662, 665, 88 L.Ed.2d 662 (1986).

As a general matter, the Court has always been reluctant to expand the concept of substantive due process because guideposts for responsible decisionmaking in this unchartered area are scarce and open-ended. *Regents of University of Michigan v. Ewing,* 474 U.S. 214, 225–226, 106 S.Ct. 507, 513–514, 88 L.Ed.2d 523 (1985). The doctrine of judicial self-restraint requires us to exercise the utmost care whenever we are asked to break new ground in this field. It is important, therefore, to focus on the allegations in the complaint to determine how petitioner describes the constitutional right at stake and what the city allegedly did to deprive her husband of that right.

A fair reading of petitioner's complaint does not charge the city with a wilful violation of Collins' rights. Petitioner does not claim that the city or any of its agents deliberately harmed her husband. In fact, she does not even allege that his supervisor instructed him to go into the sewer when the supervisor knew or should have known that there was a significant risk that he would be injured. Instead, she makes the more general allegation that the city deprived him of life and liberty by failing to provide a reasonably safe work environment.[9] Fairly analyzed, her claim advances two theories: that the Federal Constitution imposes a duty on the city to provide its employees with minimal levels of safety

9. Petitioner alleges that her husband had "a constitutional right to be free from unreasonable risks of harm to his body, mind and emotions and a constitutional right to be protected from the City of Harker Heights' custom and policy of deliberate indifference toward the safety of its employees." App. 7. The city's policy and custom of not training its employees and not warning them of the danger allegedly caused Collins' death and thus deprived him of those rights. *Id.,* at 8.

and security in the workplace, or that the city's "deliberate indifference" to Collins' safety was arbitrary Government action that must "shock the conscience" of federal judges. Cf. *Rochin v. California,* 342 U.S. 165, 172, 72 S.Ct. 205, 209, 96 L.Ed. 183 (1952).

Neither the text nor the history of the Due Process Clause supports petitioner's claim that the governmental employer's duty to provide its employees with a safe working environment is a substantive component of the Due Process Clause. "[T]he Due Process Clause of the Fourteenth Amendment was intended to prevent government 'from abusing [its] power, or employing it as an instrument of oppression.'" *DeShaney v. Winnebago County Department of Social Services,* 489 U.S., at 196, 109 S.Ct., at 1003 (quoting *Davidson v. Cannon,* 474 U.S. 344, 348, 106 S.Ct. 668, 670, 88 L.Ed.2d 677 (1986)). As we recognized in *DeShaney,*

> "The Clause is phrased as a limitation on the State's power to act, not as a guarantee of certain minimal levels of safety and security. It forbids the State itself to deprive individuals of life, liberty, or property without 'due process of law,' but its language cannot fairly be extended to impose an affirmative obligation on the State to ensure that those interests do not come to harm through other means. Nor does history support such an expansive reading of the constitutional text." 489 U.S., at 195, 109 S.Ct., at 1003.[10]

Petitioner's submission that the city violated a federal constitutional obligation to provide its employees with certain minimal levels of safety and security is unprecedented. It is quite different from the constitutional claim advanced by plaintiffs in several of our prior cases who argued that the State owes a duty to take care of those who have already been deprived of their liberty. We have held, for example, that apart from the protection against cruel and unusual punishment provided by the Eighth Amendment, cf. *Hutto v. Finney,* 437 U.S. 678, 98 S.Ct. 2565, 57 L.Ed.2d 522 (1978), the Due Process Clause of its own force requires that conditions of confinement satisfy certain minimal standards for pretrial detainees, see *Bell v. Wolfish,* 441 U.S. 520, 535, n. 16, 545, 99 S.Ct. 1861, 1872, n. 16, 1877, 60 L.Ed.2d 447 (1979), for persons in mental institutions, *Youngberg v. Romeo,* 457 U.S. 307, 315–316, 102

10. "Historically, this guarantee of due process has been applied to *deliberate* decisions of government officials to deprive a person of life, liberty, or property. *E.g., Davidson v. New Orleans,* 96 U.S. 97 [24 L.Ed. 616] (1878) (assessment of real estate); *Rochin v. California,* 342 U.S. 165 [72 S.Ct. 205, 96 L.Ed. 183] (1952) (stomach pumping); *Bell v. Burson,* 402 U.S. 535 [91 S.Ct. 1586, 29 L.Ed.2d 90] (1971) (suspension of driver's license); *Ingraham v. Wright,* 430 U.S. 651 [97 S.Ct. 1401, 51 L.Ed.2d 711] (1977) (paddling student); *Hudson v. Palmer,* 468 U.S. 517 [104 S.Ct. 3194, 82 L.Ed.2d 393] (1984) (intentional destruction of inmate's property). No decision of this Court before *Parratt* [*v. Taylor,* 451 U.S. 527, 101 S.Ct. 1908, 68 L.Ed.2d 420 (1981)] supported the view that negligent conduct by a state official, even though causing injury, constitutes a deprivation under the Due Process Clause. This history reflects the traditional and common-sense notion that the Due Process Clause, like its forebear in the Magna Carta, see Corwin, The Doctrine of Due Process of Law Before the Civil War, 24 Harv.L.Rev. 366, 368 (1911), was 'intended to secure the individual from the arbitrary exercise of the powers of government,' *Hurtado v. California,* 110 U.S. 516, 527 [4 S.Ct. 111, 117, 28 L.Ed. 232] (1884)." *Daniels v. Williams,* 474 U.S. 327, 331, 106 S.Ct. 662, 665, 88 L.Ed.2d 662 (1986).

S.Ct. 2452, 2457–2458, 73 L.Ed.2d 28 (1982), for convicted felons, *Turner v. Safley,* 482 U.S. 78, 94–99, 107 S.Ct. 2254, 2265–2267, 96 L.Ed.2d 64 (1987), and for persons under arrest, see *Revere v. Massachusetts General Hospital,* 463 U.S. 239, 244–245, 103 S.Ct. 2979, 2983–2984, 77 L.Ed.2d 605 (1983). The "process" that the Constitution guarantees in connection with any deprivation of liberty thus includes a continuing obligation to satisfy certain minimal custodial standards. See *DeShaney,* 489 U.S., at 200, 109 S.Ct., at 1005. Petitioner cannot maintain, however, that the city deprived Collins of his liberty when it made, and he voluntarily accepted, an offer of employment.

We also are not persuaded that the city's alleged failure to train its employees, or to warn them about known risks of harm, was an omission that can properly be characterized as arbitrary, or conscience-shocking, in a constitutional sense. Petitioner's claim is analogous to a fairly typical state law tort claim: The city breached its duty of care to her husband by failing to provide a safe work environment. Because the Due Process Clause "does not purport to supplant traditional tort law in laying down rules of conduct to regulate liability for injuries that attend living together in society," *Daniels v. Williams,* 474 U.S., at 332, 106 S.Ct., at 665, we have previously rejected claims that the Due Process Clause should be interpreted to impose federal duties that are analogous to those traditionally imposed by state tort law, see, *e.g., id.,* at 332–333, 106 S.Ct., at 665–666; *Baker v. McCollan,* 443 U.S. 137, 146, 99 S.Ct. 2689, 2695, 61 L.Ed.2d 433 (1979); *Paul v. Davis,* 424 U.S. 693, 701, 96 S.Ct. 1155, 1160, 47 L.Ed.2d 405 (1976). The reasoning in those cases applies with special force to claims asserted against public employers because state law, rather than the Federal Constitution, generally governs the substance of the employment relationship. See, *e.g., Bishop v. Wood,* 426 U.S. 341, 350, 96 S.Ct. 2074, 2080, 48 L.Ed.2d 684 (1976); *Board of Regents of State Colleges v. Roth,* 408 U.S. 564, 577–578, 92 S.Ct. 2701, 2709–2710, 33 L.Ed.2d 548 (1972).

Our refusal to characterize the city's alleged omission in this case as arbitrary in a constitutional sense rests on the presumption that the administration of Government programs is based on a rational decision-making process that takes account of competing social, political, and economic forces. Cf. *Walker v. Rowe,* 791 F.2d 507, 510 (CA7 1986). Decisions concerning the allocation of resources to individual programs, such as sewer maintenance, and to particular aspects of those programs, such as the training and compensation of employees, involve a host of policy choices that must be made by locally elected representatives, rather than by federal judges interpreting the basic charter of Government for the entire country. The Due Process Clause "is not a guarantee against incorrect or ill-advised personnel decisions." *Bishop v. Wood,* 426 U.S., at 350, 96 S.Ct., at 2080. Nor does it guarantee municipal employees a workplace that is free of unreasonable risks of harm.

Finally, we reject petitioner's suggestion that the Texas Hazard Communication Act supports her substantive due process claim. We assume that the Act imposed a duty on the city to warn its sanitation employees about the dangers of noxious gases in the sewers and to provide safety training and protective equipment to minimize those dangers. We also assume, as petitioner argues, that the Act created an entitlement that qualifies as a "liberty interest" protected by the Due Process Clause. But even with these assumptions, petitioner's claim must fail for she has not alleged that the deprivation of this liberty interest was arbitrary in the constitutional sense. Cf. *Harrah Independent School Dist. v. Martin,* 440 U.S. 194, 198–199, 99 S.Ct. 1062, 1064–1065, 59 L.Ed.2d 248 (1979). The reasons why the city's alleged failure to train and warn did not constitute a constitutionally arbitrary deprivation of Collins' life, see *supra,* at 1070, apply *a fortiori* to the less significant liberty interest created by the Texas statute.

In sum, we conclude that the Due Process Clause does not impose an independent federal obligation upon municipalities to provide certain minimal levels of safety and security in the workplace and the city's alleged failure to train or to warn its sanitation department employees was not arbitrary in a constitutional sense. The judgment of the Court of Appeals is therefore affirmed.

It is so ordered.

p. 1095: Replace Note 1 with the following

1. **Definition of "deliberate indifference."** Following the *Collins* case, the Third Circuit, over a strong dissent, rejected the "reckless indifference" test of a violation of due process rights and adopted the stricter "shocks the conscience" standard. Fagan v. City of Vineland, 22 F.3d 1296 (3d Cir.1994). The U.S. Supreme Court, in a cognate *Bivens* challenge, meanwhile, was required to define the term "deliberate indifference" in an eighth amendment challenge. It there stated:

> [w]ith deliberate indifference lying somewhere between the poles of negligence at one end and purpose or knowledge at the other, the Courts of Appeals have routinely equated deliberate indifference with recklessness * * * It is, indeed, fair to say that acting or failing to act with deliberate indifference to a substantial risk of serious harm to a prisoner is the equivalent of recklessly disregarding that risk * * *. That does not, however, fully answer the pending question about the level of culpability deliberate indifference entails, for the term recklessness is not self-defining. * * * We reject petitioner's invitation to adopt an objective test for deliberate indifference. We hold instead that a prison official cannot be found liable under the Eighth Amendment for denying an inmate humane conditions of confinement unless the official knows of and disregards an excessive risk to inmate health or safety; the official must be both aware of facts from which the inference could be drawn that a substantial risk of serious harm exists, and he must also draw the inference * * *. But an official's failure to alleviate a significant risk that he should have perceived but did not, while no cause for commendation, cannot under our cases be condemned as the infliction of punishment * * *. *Canton's* objective standard, however, is not an appropriate test for determining the liability of prison officials under the

> Eighth Amendment * * * the "term was used in the *Canton* case for the quite different purpose of identifying the threshold for holding a city responsible for the constitutional torts committed by its inadequately trained agents," *Collins* * * *.

Farmer v. Brennan, ___ U.S. ___, ___, ___, 114 S.Ct. 1970, 1978–79, 1981, 128 L.Ed.2d 811 (1994).

3. THE POLICY OR CUSTOM BASIS OF LIABILITY

p. 1115: Add to Note 1

The Seventh Circuit ruled that only those officers with legislative authority can make policy, and that the police superintendent accused of racially discriminatory employment practices was not a policy maker. Its opinion carefully attempted to address the question, "Who is a policy maker"?

> Unless an entirely executive decision establishes municipal policy because it is final, the plaintiffs must lose.
>
> To state the issue in this way is to imply the answer. For what can it mean to say "no vicarious liability" unless there is a distinction between creation and implementation of rules? * * * That a particular agent is the apex of a bureaucracy makes the decision "final" but does not forge a link between "finality" and "policy" * * *.
>
> "Policy" has a normative as well as a positive dimension. That an agent of the municipality did something tells us the positive side, the "is" of public action; to discern the city's policy we also need to know the "ought" of its action. * * * Unless today's decision ought to govern tomorrow's case under a law or a custom with the force of law, it cannot be said to carry out the municipality's policy * * *.
>
> * * * For the reasons we have given, *Monell's* effort to limit municipal liability under § 1983 to acts that carry out local policy entails distinguishing legislative from executive functions—a distinction always present in principle even though blurry in practice. "Responsibility for making law or setting policy"—the objective under *Praprotnik* of our search through local law—is authority to adopt rules for the conduct of government. Authority to make a final decision need not imply authority to establish rules. In Chicago it does not.

Auriemma v. Rice, 957 F.2d 397, 400–01 (7th Cir.1992).

C. INDIVIDUAL AND OFFICIAL LIABILITY UNDER § 1983

3. OFFICIAL AND INDIVIDUAL IMMUNITY

a. Scope of Immunized Functions

p. 1122–23: Add to Note 1(a)

Zamsky v. Hansell, 933 F.2d 677 (9th Cir.1991) (members of Oregon Land Use Planning Commission, in requiring county to rezone in order for its land-use plan to meet state requirements, were acting in an executive rather than a legislative capacity, and, consequently, were not entitled to absolute immunity but were required to prove that they were entitled to qualified immunity).

Add to Note 1(b)

Wagshal v. Foster, 1993 WL 86499 (D.D.C.1993), affirmed 28 F.3d 1249 (1994), cert. denied, ___ U.S. ___, 115 S.Ct. 1314, ___ L.Ed.2d ___ (court appointees who are directly involved in court-authorized, alternative-dispute-resolution programs have the absolute immunity accorded to the judicial function while acting in these roles).

Add to Note 1(c)

Buckley v. Fitzsimmons, ___ U.S. ___, 113 S.Ct. 2606, 125 L.Ed.2d 209 (1993) (prosecutor charged with fabrication of evidence was acting in investigatory, not prosecutorial, function when trying to determine whether boot-print at scene-of-crime was that of a suspect, and hence was entitled only to qualified, not absolute, immunity).

b. Qualified Immunity—The Applicable Standard

p. 1131: Add to Note 1

See, e.g., Umbehr v. McClure, 44 F.3d 876 (10th Cir.1995) (while an independent contractor's allegation that the county terminated their contract to retaliate for his speech on a variety of public matters raised an actionable first-amendment issue, county officials enjoyed qualified immunity from suit for damages, given the uncertainty of the amendment's application to independent contractors); Heleba v. Allbee, 160 Vt. 283, 628 A.2d 1237 (1992), cert. denied, ___ U.S. ___, 114 S.Ct. 388, 126 L.Ed.2d 336 (1993) (state officials in individual capacity entitled to qualified immunity); Mulligan v. Rioux, 229 Conn. 716, 643 A.2d 1226 (1994) (standard of qualified immunity shielding public officials from § 1983 liability arising from exercise of their discretionary functions, is distinct from that established under common law); Estate of Sinthasomphone v. City of Milwaukee, 838 F.Supp. 1320 (E.D.Wis.1993) (police officers who released naked, injured young man back to care of serial killer who murdered him were entitled to qualified immunity in substantive due process action by the victim's family); Davis v. DiPino, 99 Md.App. 282, 637 A.2d 475 (1994), cert. granted, 335 Md. 455, 664 A.2d 488 (1994) (law enforcement officers' judicially created qualified immunity from suit in § 1983 actions would not apply to suit for violation of rights under the state constitution unless they were granted such immunity by state law); Robinson v. City of Seattle, 119 Wash.2d 34, 830 P.2d 318 (1992); Sintra, Inc. v. City of Seattle, 119 Wash.2d 1, 829 P.2d 765 (1992), both cert. denied, ___ U.S. ___, 113 S.Ct. 676, 121 L.Ed.2d 598 (1992) (continued enforcement of ordinance on advice of counsel after trial court declared it invalid probably did not entitle official to qualified immunity); Schnabel v. Tyler, 230 Conn. 735, 646 A.2d 152 (1994) (officer's clearly established right at time of chief's allegedly harassing, retaliatory treatment to be free from retaliation for exercise of free speech rights is relevant to the issue of the chief's claim of qualified immunity).

Add to Note 4

Elder v. Holloway, ___ U.S. ___, 114 S.Ct. 1019, 127 L.Ed.2d 344 (1994) (in reviewing determination whether qualified immunity exists and whether a federal constitutional right was clearly established at the time of alleged injury, appellate court must consider de novo all relevant precedents, not just those that were made part of the record below).

D. OTHER DEFENSES

pp. 1133–35: Add to the text under *Statutes of Limitations*

See Lufkin v. McCallum, 956 F.2d 1104 (11th Cir.1992), cert. denied, ___ U.S. ___, 113 S.Ct. 326, 121 L.Ed.2d 246 (1992) (rule of *Owens v. Okure* must be applied retroactively to bar suits that may have been timely filed under pre-*Owens* law).

Add to end of text

The Supreme Court has rejected a heightened pleading standard in civil rights cases alleging municipal liability under § 1983. Leatherman v. Tarrant County Narcotics Intelligence and Coordination Unit, ___ U.S. ___, 113 S.Ct. 1160, 122 L.Ed.2d 517 (1993). See also, Pineville Real Estate Operation Corp. v. Michael, 32 F.3d 88 (4th Cir.1994) (*Leatherman* obviates requirement that plaintiffs plead multiple incidents of misconduct in support of allegation of municipal § 1983 liability); but cf. Branch v. Tunnell, 14 F.3d 449 (9th Cir.1994), cert. denied, ___ U.S. ___, 114 S.Ct. 2704, 129 L.Ed.2d 832 (1994) (*Bivens* action requirement that complaints must state non-conclusory allegations of official's unlawful subjective intent is unaffected by *Leatherman*).

E. ALLOWABLE REMEDIES

2. LEGAL RELIEF

p. 1138: Add to Note 1

Heck v. Humphrey, ___ U.S. ___, 114 S.Ct. 2364, 129 L.Ed.2d 383 (1994) (in order to recover damages for unconstitutional conviction or imprisonment, or for unlawful actions that render a conviction or sentence invalid, a § 1983 plaintiff must prove that the conviction or sentence has been reversed on appeal, expunged by executive order, declared invalid by authorized state tribunal, or called into question by a federal writ of habeas corpus, a conclusion derived from recognition that common-law tort provides the appropriate starting point for a § 1983 inquiry).

3. ATTORNEY'S FEE AWARDS—AN OVERVIEW

pp. 1139–40: Add to text under *The Prevailing Party Requirement*

Judicial creation of an expanded standard and class of "prevailing" parties may be seen in the following cases: Farrar v. Hobby, ___ U.S. ___, 113 S.Ct. 566, 121 L.Ed.2d 494 (1992) (plaintiff who obtains relief on the merits which materially alters the parties' legal relationship and modifies defendant's behavior in a way that directly benefits the plaintiff is a prevailing party, even though plaintiff only recovered nominal damages); S–1 and S–2 v. State Bd. of Educ., 6 F.3d 160 (4th Cir.1993), on rehearing 21 F.3d 49 (4th Cir.1994), cert. denied, ___ U.S. ___, 115 S.Ct. 205, 130 L.Ed.2d 135 (1994) (plaintiff, whose suit was dismissed as moot but served as catalyst for amendment of regulations, not barred by *Farrar* from seeking attorney's fees, though suit was dismissed as moot); Paris v. U.S. Department of Housing and Urban Dev., 988 F.2d 236 (1st Cir.1993) (party who lost the litigated claim but whose suit was catalyst for intervening legislation that provided the relief sought is a prevailing party). Cf. Domegan v. Ponte, 972 F.2d 401 (1st Cir.1992) (where case established significant procedural due process deprivation, claimant was prevailing party though only nominal damages were awarded), cert. granted, judgment vacated and remanded for consideration in light of Ponte v. Domegan, ___ U.S. ___, 113 S.Ct. 1378, 122 L.Ed.2d 754 (1993); semble, Romberg v. Nichols, 953 F.2d 1152 (9th Cir.1992), cert. granted, judgment vacated and remanded for consideration in light of Nichols v. Romberg, ___ U.S. ___, 113 S.Ct. 1038, 122 L.Ed.2d 348 (1993), on remand, 993 F.2d 1453 (9th Cir.1993).

p. 1141: Add to *Size of Fee Awards*

The attorneys for the prevailing parties in *Farrar v. Hobby,* supra, a nominal-damages case, were awarded fees of $280,000 by the court. The award of substantial fees for establishing principles whose violation did not require compensation is a result the efficacy and reasonableness of which may only be immediately apparent to, and appreciated by, lawyers, not a burdened taxpayer. Not all circuits readily embrace opportunities to be generous with public funds. Contingency enhancements of reasonable lodestar fees under federal fee-shifting statutes may not be made in the District of Columbia. King v. Palmer, 950 F.2d 771 (D.C.Cir. en banc 1991), cert. denied, ___ U.S. ___, 112 S.Ct. 3054, 120 L.Ed.2d 920 (1992).

Add to end of text

Notes of Interest. Under state civil rights acts that also provide for fee awards, state courts will join the federal courts in resolving the complexities of fee shifting. See, e.g., Robb v. Ridgewood Bd. of Educ., 269 N.J.Super. 394, 635 A.2d 586 (1993).

State-federal complexities have another dimension. State courts are far from one mind on the disposition of attorneys fees requests made in 42 U.S.C.A. § 1983 actions in state court. When the *Quill* case, reported at p. 161 of this Supplement, was remanded, the state court denied a request for attorneys fees, reasoning as follows: in effect, a state court hearing § 1983 actions was like a federal court doing the same; but since a federal court could not hear a challenge to state and local taxes if there were adequate state remedies, the state court likewise need not hear the tax challenge under § 1983, but would do so under state processes, despite § 1983 allegations in the complaint. The state court thus denied attorneys fees under § 1988. State By and Through Hanson v. Quill Corp., 500 N.W.2d 196 (N.D.1993), cert. denied, ___ U.S. ___, 114 S.Ct. 173, 126 L.Ed.2d 132 (1993). Compare Dennis v. Higgins, 498 U.S. 439, 111 S.Ct. 865, 112 L.Ed.2d 969 (1991) (wherein a suit challenging state taxes under the Commerce Clause was brought in state court under § 1983). The Supreme Court has granted review of the second ruling by the Oklahoma Supreme Court (the first was vacated and remanded under *Dennis v. Higgins*) in Private Truck Council, Inc. v. Oklahoma Tax Commission, 879 P.2d 137 (Okl.1994), cert. granted, ___ U.S. ___, 115 S.Ct. 714, ___ L.Ed.2d ___ (1995). The Oklahoma court declined to decide a state and local tax Commerce–Clause challenge under § 1983, with attorneys fees under § 1988, because federal courts would have been prohibited from doing so by the Tax Injunction Act. See generally, Note, "Clarifying Comity: State Court Jurisdiction and Section 1983 State Tax Challenges," 103 Harv.L.Rev. 1888 (1990).

†